teach®
yourself

new testament
greek
gavin betts

For over 60 years, more than
40 million people have learnt over
750 subjects the **teach yourself**
way, with impressive results.

be where you want to be
with **teach yourself**

The author wishes to acknowledge the help of
Alan Henry, Peggy Molloy and John Burke.

For UK order enquiries: please contact Bookpoint Ltd, 130 Milton Park, Abingdon, Oxon OX14 4SB. Telephone: +44 (0) 1235 827720, Fax: +44 (0) 1235 400454. Lines are open 9.00–18.00, Monday to Saturday, with a 24-hour message answering service. Details about our titles and how to order are available at www.teachyourself.co.uk

For USA order enquiries: please contact McGraw-Hill Customer Services, P.O. Box 545, Blacklick, OH 43004-0545, USA. Telephone: 1-800-722-4726. Fax: 1-614-755-5645.

For Canada order enquiries: please contact McGraw-Hill Ryerson Ltd, 300 Water St, Whitby, Ontario L1N 9B6, Canada. Telephone: 905 430 5000. Fax: 905 430 5020.

Long renowned as the authoritative source for self-guided learning – with more than 30 million copies sold worldwide – the *Teach Yourself* series includes over 300 titles in the fields of languages, crafts, hobbies, business, computing and education.

British Library Cataloguing in Publication Data: a catalogue entry for this title is available from The British Library.

Library of Congress Catalog Card Number: on file.

First published in UK 2004 by Hodder Headline, 338 Euston Road, London, NW1 3BH.

First published in US 2004 by Contemporary Books, a division of The McGraw-Hill Companies, 1 Prudential Plaza, 130 East Randolph Street, Chicago, Illinois 60601 USA.

This edition published 2004.

The 'Teach Yourself' name is a registered trade mark of Hodder & Stoughton Ltd.

Typeset by Transet Limited, Coventry, England.
Printed in Great Britain for Hodder & Stoughton Educational, a division of Hodder Headline, 338 Euston Road, London NW1 3BH by Cox & Wyman Ltd, Reading, Berkshire.

Papers used in this book are natural, renewable and recyclable products. They are made from wood grown in sustainable forests. The logging and manufacturing processes conform to the environmental regulations of the country of origin.

Impression number 10 9 8 7 6 5 4 3 2 1
Year   2010 2009 2008 2007 2006 2005 2004

contents

How to use this book

When Saint Jerome decided to translate the Old Testament into Latin from the original text he was obliged to learn Hebrew, and to do this he is said to have retired into the desert for a number of years. It is the author's hope that the student who wants to read the New Testament in its original form will not find a similar retreat necessary. However, learning a language on one's own requires a special approach. Apart from the key, you will have few checks on your progress, and you must follow up any doubt, however small, about meanings of words and points of grammar. To be able to do this you must make yourself completely familiar with the arrangement of the book's contents.

A knowledge of the basics of traditional English grammar is essential, as this is the framework used to explain the structure of Greek. You should be conversant with the **parts of speech** (*adjective, adverb, article, conjunction, interjection, noun, preposition, pronoun, verb*) and with the meaning of such terms as *finite, transitive/intransitive, clause, phrase, subject, object,* etc. If these are new to you, consult the **Glossary of grammatical and other terms**, which follows this section of the introduction. There you will find much information on the salient points of Greek grammar, which has much in common with that of English. Start with the entries suggested above, and consult others as the need arises. Do not try to digest the whole glossary before starting on the first unit.

The main part of the book consists of twenty-one units. Each contains either two or three sections. The first section is taken up with grammar, the second contains sentences and passages of Greek for reading, while the third section deals with some background aspects of NT Greek studies.

The grammatical sections, which are headed .1, are carefully graded over the course of the book and set out the basic features of Greek grammar. Each should be mastered before tackling the next. Very often a particular section cannot be understood without mastering what has gone before.

Grammar as a whole can be divided into two parts; one involves the forms which a word can take (e.g. those of a second declension masculine noun, 2.1/2), the other deals with the ways in which these forms are used to make up phrases and sentences (e.g. the uses of the dative case, 2.1/3(e)). The former we must learn by heart. The latter we can only fully understand when, after learning a general rule, we see, and are able to understand, examples of it in use. Because of the importance of this, almost all sentences given in grammatical explanations (as well as the sentences and passages in the reading exercises) are taken from the NT itself. For all these extracts from the NT a reference is given, and if any change has been made the reference is preceded by an asterisk. You will be familiar with many of these in translation. Sometimes you may feel inclined to look up the passage from which a sentence has been taken; sometimes you may be moved to learn the Greek by heart. Both practices will help your progress.

The reading exercises should not be attempted with one finger in the corresponding page of the key, although you should make full use of any help provided by the notes which follow each exercise. It is only by analysing the forms of words and patiently working out the construction of clauses and sentences that you will make progress. Write out a full translation of an exercise and then compare it with the key. When you discover you have made a mistake, you must meticulously hunt out the point of grammar concerned and see how you came to be wrong. To help you do this many cross references have been supplied in all parts of the book (a reference of the form 18.1/2 is for the **grammatical** section (.1) of a unit, but one such as 18.2.2 is to the **reading** section (.2)). Your final step should be to read through the Greek aloud until you are able to translate it without reference to your own version or the key. This will familiarize you with the construction employed and any new vocabulary. Some rote learning of new words is, of course, inevitable. If, however, you go to the trouble of memorizing some of the many famous verses contained in the reading you will find your grasp on the language extending itself in an enjoyable and rewarding fashion.

Appendices 1–6 give grammatical tables and other information to supplement particular units. **Appendix 7** is on accentuation and can be consulted regularly and mastered over the course of the whole book. The section **Principal parts of verbs** complements the vocabulary with full information about more difficult verbs. For ease of reference to grammatical points an index is provided.

The book is oriented completely towards the form of Greek found in the New Testament. Less emphasis is placed on features of the language, such as the optative, which are in the process of disappearing. In the case of that perennial scourge of beginners, the -μι verbs, forms that actually occur in the New Testament are clearly distinguished from those that do not. If you are not interested in other early Christian literature, you need not worry yourself with the latter.

It is not necessary to acquire a text of the Greek New Testament until you have finished the book and wish to pursue your studies further. The recommended edition is that published by the United Bible Societies; details will be found in **Suggestions for further study**.

glossary of grammatical and other terms

The following list contains the grammatical terms which we shall use in approaching Greek; most are part of traditional English grammar. If you are not familiar with this terminology you should study the following list carefully. Start with the **parts of speech**, viz **adjective, adverb, article, conjunction, interjection, noun, preposition, pronoun, verb.** These are the categories into which words are classified for grammatical purposes and are the same for Greek as for English.

active See **voice.**

adjective An adjective is a word which qualifies (i.e. tells us of some quality of) a noun or pronoun: *a **high** pyramid; a **short** Egyptian; the high priest was **intelligent**; he is **thin.***

adverb Adverbs qualify verbs, adjectives, or other adverbs: *she talks **quickly**; an **extremely** fat man; the ship was going **very slowly.*** Certain adverbs can qualify nouns and pronouns: *even a child can see that.* They may even qualify a whole clause: *we went to Jerusalem last year; we **also** saw Bethlehem.*

apposition A noun (or noun phrase) is in apposition to another noun or pronoun when it follows by way of explanation and is exactly parallel in its relation to the rest of the sentence: *he, **a just man**, was wrongly convicted; I, **the undersigned**, will inform my solicitor.*

article English has two articles *the* and *a/an.* *The* is called the definite article because a noun preceded by it refers to someone or something definite: ***the** cat belonging to the neighbours kept me awake last night.* *A/an* is called the indefinite article because a noun preceded by it refers to someone or something indefinite: *No, I do not want **a** dog.*

aspect This is the term applied to the use of verbal forms to express an action in respect not of the time when it occurs but of its inception, duration, or completion. It is most commonly employed in Greek in connection with the moods (other than the indicative) of the present and aorist tenses; e.g. the present imperative is used for continual actions (*keep hitting that Philistine!*), but for single actions (*hit that Philistine!*) we have another form of the verb (the aorist imperative).

Attic Greek This was the dialect used in Athens of the fifth and fourth centuries BC. In it are written most of the literary masterpieces of the period and it came to be recognized as the normal idiom for prose. From it developed the Koine, the form of Greek used in the NT (see also 1.3).

attributive *Attributive* and *predicative* are the terms applied to the two ways in which adjectives can be used. An adjective used attributively forms a phrase with the noun it qualifies, and in English always comes immediately before it: ***ancient** Jerusalem, a **tall** mountain, the **true** prophet*. An adjective used predicatively tells us what is predicated of, or asserted about, a person or thing. A verb is always involved in this use, and in English a predicative adjective always, in prose, follows the noun or pronoun it qualifies, generally with the verb coming between them: *men are **mortal**, the centurion was **bald***. This use frequently involves the verb *to be*, but there are other possibilities: *the priest was considered **pious**, we thought the tax collector **avaricious***. All adjectives can be used in either way, with the exception of some possessive adjectives in English such as *my, mine* (the first can be only attributive, the second only predicative).

auxiliary verb Many tenses in English are formed with the present or past participle of a verb together with some part of *have* or *be* (or both); when so used the latter are called auxiliary verbs: *he **was** running when I saw him; I **have** read this glossary five times; we **have been** working for the past week at Greek*. These combinations (*was running, have read*, etc.) are called composite tenses. Other auxiliary verbs in English are *shall, will, should, would*. Greek has a much smaller number of composite tenses.

case In any type of expression where it occurs, a noun (or pronoun) stands in a certain relationship to the other words, and this relationship is determined by the meaning we want to convey. The two sentences *my brothers bite dogs* and *dogs bite* *my brothers* contain exactly the same words but have opposite meanings, which are shown by the relationship in each sentence of the nouns *brothers* and *dogs* to the verb *bite*; here (as is normal in English) this relationship is indicated by word order. In Greek, where word order is used somewhat differently, it is indicated by particular case endings applied to nouns. If a noun is the subject of a verb (i.e. precedes it in a simple English sentence such as the above), it must, in Greek, be put into the nominative case with the appropriate ending; if it is the object of a verb (i.e. follows it in English) Greek puts it into the accusative case. In English we still have this system with pronouns; we say *I saw her today,* we cannot say *me saw her* because *I* is the nominative case, required here to show the subject of the verb, whereas *me* is the accusative case. With nouns in English we only have one case which can be indicated by an ending and this is the genitive; *girl's, boy's.* In Greek we have five cases, **nominative, vocative, accusative, genitive, dative.**

clause A clause is a group of words forming a sense unit and containing one finite verb, e.g. *the peasant **feared** the centurion; I **am** not happy today* (the finite verb is in bold type). We can have either **main clauses**, which can stand on their own, or **subordinate clauses**, which cannot. In the sentence *Herod owned a palace which had cost much money,* the first four words constitute the main clause and this forms a complete sense unit; if, however, you were to say to a friend *which had cost much money* and nothing else, you would risk being thought odd because these words form a subordinate clause. Subordinate clauses are divided into **adverbial** which function as adverbs, **adjectival**, which function as adjectives, and **noun** clauses, which function as nouns.

comparison (of adjectives and adverbs)   See **inflexion.**

conjugation   See **inflexion.**

conjunction Conjunctions are **joining words** and do not vary in form. Some conjunctions can join clauses, phrases or individual words (e.g. *and, or*) but most have a more restricted use. Those that are used to join clauses are divided into **co-ordinating** conjunctions (*and, or, but*), which join a main clause to a preceding one (*I went to the temple, **but** you were not there*), and **subordinating** conjunctions, which subordinate one clause to another (*the doctor came **because** I was ill*).

declension   See **inflexion.**

dental This term is used to describe those consonants which are pronounced with the tongue touching the teeth, in English **t**, **d**; in Greek τ, δ, θ.

deponent A deponent verb is one which is middle or passive in form (see **voice**) but active in meaning. Deponent verbs do not exist in English but are common in Greek.

enclitics These are Greek words of one or two syllables whose accentuation, or lack of it, is determined by the previous word; because of this they normally cannot stand at the beginning of a clause; see also **Appendix 7, (d)**.

finite This term is applied to those forms of verbs which can function by themselves as the verbal element of a clause. The only non-finite forms of a verb in English and Greek are participles and infinitives. We can say *the Israelites defeated their enemies* because *defeated* is a finite form of the verb *to defeat*. We cannot say *the Israelites to have defeated their enemies* because *to have defeated* is an infinitive and therefore non-finite, nor can we say (as a full sentence) *the Israelites having defeated their enemies* because *having defeated* is a participle.

gender In English we only observe natural gender (apart from such eccentricities as supposing ships feminine). If we are talking about a man we refer to him by the masculine pronoun *he*, but we refer to a woman by the feminine pronoun *she*, and we refer to a thing, such as a table or chair, by the neuter pronoun *it*. Greek, however, observes natural gender with living beings (generally), but other nouns, which may denote things, qualities and so on, are not necessarily neuter. For example τράπεζα *table* is feminine, λόγος *speech* is masculine. This has important grammatical consequences, but the gender of individual nouns is not difficult to learn as, in most cases, it is shown by the ending. In vocabularies and dictionaries a noun is always accompanied by the appropriate form of the definite article, and this also indicates its gender.

imperative See **mood**.

indeclinable This term is applied to nouns which have only one form and whose case is determined by the surrounding words. Most indeclinable nouns are names of Hebrew or Aramaic origin which have not been assimilated to the Greek system of declensions. Examples are Ἀβραάμ *Abraham,* Ἰσραήλ *Israel,* Βηθλέεμ *Bethlehem*.

indicative   See **mood.**

infinitive   Infinitives are those parts of a verb which in English are normally preceded by *to*, e.g. *to see, to be seen, to have seen, to have been seen*. These are, respectively, the present active, present passive, past active, and past passive infinitives of the verb *see*. As in English, a Greek verb has active and passive infinitives, and infinitives exist in different tenses. A Greek infinitive is not preceded by anything corresponding to the English *to*.

inflexion   The form of adjectives, adverbs, nouns, pronouns, and verbs changes in English and in Greek (but much more so) according to the requirements of meaning and grammar. **Inflexion** is the overall term for such changes and covers **conjugation**, which applies only to verbs, **declension**, which applies to nouns, pronouns, and adjectives (which include participles), and **comparison**, which applies to adjectives and adverbs. The term **conjugation** is also used for the categories into which verbs are classified, and the term **declension** is similarly used for those of nouns and adjectives.

interjection   Interjections are words used to express one's emotions. They do not form part of sentences and have only one form (i.e. are not subject to inflexion). An example is οὐαί *alas!*

intransitive   This is a term applied to verbs which cannot, because of their meaning, take a normal object, e.g. *come, die, go*. The opposite term is **transitive**; transitive verbs (e.g. *make, hit, repair*) can take an object. *He hit the man* is a perfectly possible sentence, but *he dies the man* is nonsense. Sometimes in English we have pairs of verbs, one transitive and the other intransitive, which are obviously connected in sense and etymology, as *to fall* and *to fell*. We can say *John is falling from the tree* but *John is falling the tree* is without sense. If we mean *John is causing the tree to fall*, we can say *John is felling the tree*; hence *to fall* is intransitive, *to fell* is transitive. Some verbs are transitive in English but intransitive in Greek, and vice-versa. There are also a number of verbs in English, such as *move*, which can be either transitive or intransitive, while their Greek equivalents are exclusively one or the other: *I moved the lamp from its place* (transitive); *the previous year he moved from Damascus to Egypt* (intransitive). The Greek κινέω *move*, however, can, in the active, only be used transitively.

koine   This is the name given to the dialect of Greek which developed in the third century BC in the wake of the conquest of

Alexander the Great. It is the language in which the NT is written. For details see 1.3.

labial This term is used to describe those consonants which are pronounced by bringing the lips together, in English **p**, **b**; in Greek π, β, φ.

middle See **voice**.

mood This term is applied to verbs. Every finite form of a Greek verb is in one of four moods, which are:

indicative, to express a fact: *the doctor operated on me yesterday.*
subjunctive, which originally expressed what the speaker willed or expected (*let us go* is expressed in Greek by a single subjunctive form of the verb *go*; cf. *be that as it may*, i.e. *let that be as it may*). In Greek it is used in a number of idiomatic ways which cannot be given a single meaning. A few relics of the subjunctive survive in English (*if I were you*; *be* in the above example). A Greek subjunctive is often to be translated with an English auxiliary verb such as *let, may, would,* etc.
optative, which originally expressed what the speaker desired or considered possible. Like the subjunctive it cannot be given a single meaning. In one of its uses it expresses a wish of the type *May that not happen!* Its use in the New Testament is very restricted and it later disappeared from Greek completely.
imperative, to give an order: *do this immediately!*

There is also a fifth mood, the infinitive mood, which is solely taken up by infinitives; these by definition are non-finite. The other part of the Greek verb, participles, is not considered to be in any mood.

noun A noun is a naming word: **book, river, truth, Paul, Nazareth**. Proper nouns are those we write with a capital letter, all others are common nouns.

number A noun, or pronoun, or verb is normally either **singular** or **plural** in Greek just as in English.

object A noun or pronoun which is the object of an active verb suffers or receives the action of that verb: *Matthew wrote a gospel*; *the devil tempted many gentiles*; *the Romans destroyed the temple.* By definition we cannot have an object of this sort after intransitive verbs or (normally) after verbs in the passive voice. It is sometimes called a **direct object** to distinguish it from an **indirect object** which we get after verbs of saying and giving: *he told a story to **the child**.* In English we can express this slightly differently: *he told **the child** a story;* but *child* is still the indirect object because the direct object is *story*. In Greek an indirect object is put into the dative case.

oblique cases The overall term applied to the accusative, genitive, and dative cases.

optative See **mood.**

palatal This term is used to describe those consonants which are pronounced by bringing the tongue into contact with the upper palate, in English **k, g**; in Greek κ, γ, χ.

parse To parse a word is to define it grammatically. For nouns it is necessary to give case and number (*men's* is the genitive plural of *man*), for finite verbs the person, number, tense, mood and voice.

participle Participles are those forms of a verb which function as adjectives: *the **running** horse, a **fallen** tree.*

particle Under the term **particle** are included adverbs which give a particular nuance to individual words, phrases or sentences, as well as certain shorter conjunctions (see 4.1/4).

passive see **voice.**

person There are three persons, **first, second,** and **third. First person** is the person(s) speaking, i.e. *I* or *we;* **second person** is the person(s) spoken to, i.e. *you;* and **third person** is the person(s) or thing(s) spoken about, i.e. *he, she, it, they.* The term **person** has reference to pronouns and also to verbs because finite verbs must agree with their subject in **number** and **person.** Naturally, when we have a noun as subject of a verb, e.g. *the dog is running across the road,* the verb is in the third person.

phrase A phrase is an intelligible group of words which does not have a finite verb: *into the woods, the Syrian's five tired donkeys.* A phrase can only be used by itself in certain circumstances, as in answer to a question.

postpositive This term is used of words (mainly particles) which, if qualifying a word, must be placed after it, or, if qualifying a clause, cannot stand as its first word.

predicate The predicate is what is said about the subject of a clause. In *John wrote the fourth Gospel* the subject is *John* and what is said about him (*wrote the fourth Gospel*) is the predicate. In *the high priest was furious* the adjective *furious* is used predicatively because it is part of the predicate (*was furious*).

predicative   See **attributive**.

preposition   Prepositions are invariable words which govern a noun or pronoun and show the relationship of the noun or pronoun to the rest of the sentence: *Joseph went **to** Nazareth*; *we live **in** Samaria*; *I saw John **with** him*.

pronoun   Pronouns stand in place of nouns. The English personal pronouns are: *I, you, he, she, it, we, they* (in the accusative case *me, you, him, her, it, us, them*). Other words such as *this, that* can function as pronouns (*I do not like **that**!*) or as adjectives (*I do not like **that** habit!*); for convenience we shall call them demonstrative pronouns. We also have reflexive pronouns (*he loves **himself***) and relative pronouns (*I do not like the woman **who** was here*).

sentence   A sentence is a unit of speech which normally contains at least one main clause. It may be either a statement, question or command. For the Greek marks of punctuation used with each see Unit 1.

stem   The stem is the form of a word before endings are applied. In Greek, nouns normally have only one stem, which sometimes cannot be deduced from the nominative singular. With verbs in Greek we have different stems for some, but not all, tenses. English verbs such as *to break* are comparable; *break-* is the present stem and to it the ending of the third person singular is added (giving *breaks*); *brok-* is the past stem, giving us *brok-en* for the past participle.

subject   A noun or pronoun which is the subject of a verb performs the action of that verb: ***Paul** went on a journey to Rome*; *the **tax-collector** amassed a large amount of money*; *on the third day the **soldier** died*. It is normal to speak of the subject as governing its verb. In English and Greek a finite verb's person and number are determined by the subject. We cannot say *I is* because *I* is the first person singular pronoun and *is* is the third person singular of the verb *to be* (present tense); we must here use the first person (singular) form *am*. Likewise we must say *we are* and not *we am* because *we* is plural. An easy way to find the subject in English is to put *who* or *what* in front of the verb; with the sentence *the ship was hit by a submerged rock*, we ask the question *what was hit by a submerged rock?* and the answer, *the ship*, is the subject of the clause.

subjunctive   See **mood**.

tense   Tense is a term applied to verbs. Every finite form of a verb, as well as participles and infinitives, indicates that the action or state expressed takes place in a particular time; for a complication in Greek see **aspect**. The verb in *I am sick* refers to the present, in *I will be sick* to the future. These temporal states are called tenses, and in Greek we have six: **present, future, imperfect, aorist, perfect, pluperfect.**

transitive   See **intransitive**.

verb   A verb, when finite, is the **doing** or **being** word of its clause. It must agree with the subject in **person** and **number**. For non-finite forms of verbs see **finite**. A finite verb varies according to **person, number, tense, mood,** and **voice**.

voice   This term is applied to verbs, whether finite or non-finite. In English there are two voices, **active** and **passive**. The subject of an active verb is the doer of the action; *the soldier lifted his shield*. With a passive verb the subject suffers or receives the action: *the shield was lifted by the soldier*. Greek has another voice, the **middle**, which originally meant to do something to or for oneself; its use in New Testament Greek will be explained at 8.1/1.

abbreviations

a. *or* acc.	accusative	ind.	indicative
absol.	absolute	indecl.	indeclinable
Ac	Acts	indef.	indefinite
act.	active	indir.	indirect
adj.	adjective	inf.	infinitive
adv.	adverb	interrog.	interrogative
aor.	aorist	intr.	intransitive
AV	King James	1 J	1 John
	translation of the	2 J	2 John
	New Testament	3 J	3 John
c.	about,	Jd	Jude
	approximately	Jn	John
cap.	capital	Js	James
cf.	compare	*l.*	line
Col	Colossians	lit.	literally
compar.	comparative	Lk	Luke
conj.	conjunction	*ll.*	lines
1 Cor	1 Corinthians	m. *or* m	masculine
2 Cor	2 Corinthians	mid.	middle
dat.	dative	Mk	Mark
Eph	Ephesians	Mt	Matthew
ex.	example	n. *or* n	neuter
f. or f	feminine	n. *or* nom.	nominative
f.	following	NT	New Testament
fut.	future	opt.	optative
Gal	Galatians	pass.	passive
gen.	genitive	perf.	perfect
Hb	Hebrews	pers.	person
imp.	imperative	Phil	Philippians
impers.	impersonal	Phlm	Philemon
impf.	imperfect	pl.	plural

plpf.	pluperfect	s.	singular
poet.	poetical	*sc.*	namely
poss.	possessive	subj.	subjunctive
pple.	participle	supl.	superlative
prep.	preposition	1 Th	1 Thessalonians
pres.	present	2 Th	2 Thessalonians
pron.	pronoun	1 Ti	1 Timothy
1 Pt	1 Peter	2 Ti	2 Timothy
2 Pt	2 Peter	Tit	Titus
refl.	reflexive	tr.	transitive
rel.	relative	trans.	translate
Ro	Romans	v. *or* voc.	vocative
Rv	Revelation	viz	that is to say

Round brackets ( ) contain explanatory material or a literal translation; in the vocabulary round brackets are also used to indicate alternative forms.

Square brackets [ ] are used in two ways:

(a) With English words they enclose something required by English idiom but which has no equivalent in the Greek original; not all such words are marked in this way.

(b) With Greek words they indicate that a form does not occur in the NT but is included, usually in a table, to give a clearer overall picture.

+ means *in conjunction with, compounded with,* or *followed by.*

< means *is derived from.*

> means *produce(s).*

marks a word which cannot stand first in a clause or phrase.

* precedes a reference and indicates that the verse quoted has been altered in some way (most often a word is omitted).

† is explained in the introductory note to the vocabulary.

1.1 Grammar

1.1/1 The Greek alphabet and its pronunciation

The names of the twenty-four letters of the Greek alphabet are traditional. Today the alphabet is used in upper and lower case, although in antiquity it was written only in capitals. The value assigned below to each letter does not always reflect what is known of the ancient pronunciation, which in any case developed over time and varied from one locality to another. However, as we learn Greek in order to read what has been written in the language, not to speak it, the need for absolute accuracy in pronunciation does not arise

	Name	Pronunciation
A α	alpha (ἄλφα)	*a* (as in *father*, never as in *cat*)
B β	bêta (βῆτα)	*b*
Γ γ	gamma (γάμμα)	*g* (as in *gain*, never as in *gesture*, but as *n* in *king* before κ, ξ, χ or another γ; see below)
Δ δ	delta (δέλτα)	*d*
E ε	epsilon (ἒ ψιλόν)	short *e* (as in *set*)
Z ζ	zêta (ζῆτα)	*z* (as in *squeeze*)
H η	êta (ἦτα)	long *e* (like *ê* in *fête* or *ai* in *fairy*)
Θ θ	thêta (θῆτα)	*th* (as in *thought*; see below)
I ι	iôta (ἰῶτα)	*i* as in *sit*
K κ	kappa (κάππα)	*k* (but represented in English as *c*)
Λ λ	lambda (λάμβδα)	*l*
M μ	mû (μῦ)	*m*
N ν	nû (νῦ)	*n*
Ξ ξ	xei (ξεῖ)	*cs* (as *x* in *tax*; see below)

O o	omicron (ὂ μικρόν)	short o (as in *cot*)
Π π	pei (πεῖ)	*p*
Ρ ρ	rhô (ῥῶ)	*r*
Σ σ, ς	sigma (σίγμα)	*s* (as in *same*)
Τ τ	tau (ταῦ)	*t*
Υ υ	upsilon (ὒ ψιλόν)	*u* (represented in English as *y*)
Φ φ	phei (φεῖ)	*ph* (see below)
Χ χ	chei (χεῖ)	*ch* (see below)
Ψ ψ	psei (ψεῖ)	*ps* (as in *caps*)
Ω ω	ômega (ὦ μέγα)	long o (like *oa* in *broad*)

A circumflex (ˆ) above a vowel in the English transliterations indicates a longer pronunciation (compare êta with epsilon).

When taking Greek words directly into English we normally use the phonetic equivalent of Greek letters except where indicated above, e.g. cosmos (κόσμος), pathos (πάθος). For proper nouns and derivatives see note 1.

(a) Consonants
Where no example is given above, consonants are pronounced as their English equivalent. Chei (χ) should be pronounced as the *ch* in the Scottish pronunciation of *loch* in order to distinguish it from kappa (κ). The double consonants ξ and ψ are the equivalents of κσ, πσ respectively, and must always be used when word formation brings κ or π immediately before σ: e.g. when σ is added to the stem Αἰθιοπ- we must write Αἰθίοψ *Ethiopian*, never Αἰθίοπς (5.l/l(a)).[1] Note that zêta (ζ) was not pronounced as a double consonant in NT times, as is sometimes stated.

Examples of the second pronunciation of γ are: σπόγγος (spóngos) *sponge*, σάλπιγξ (sálpinx) *trumpet*, ἔλεγχος (élenchos) *proof* (on accents see below).

There are two forms of lower case sigma: σ which is used for an initial and medial sigma, ς which is used for a final sigma, e.g σύστασις *gathering*. In upper case sigma has only one form, e.g. ΣΥΣΤΑΣΙΣ (accents are not indicated with upper case).

(b) Vowels
In the fifth and fourth centuries BC all Greek vowels had a long and short pronunciation, although only in the case of ε/η and o/ω were these values given separate letters. By the first century

---

[1] This does not apply to compounds of ἐκ, e.g. ἔκστασις (from ἐκ + στάσις).

AD this distinction between long and short vowels had
disappeared but this was not reflected in writing, where ε/η and
o/ω were retained. The pronunciation given above is convenient
for us today, even though it is not historical. The New
Testament was written in a conventional spelling which
reflected the pronouncing of Greek several centuries earlier
and not that current at the time of its authors.

(c) Diphthongs

Here too modern pronunciation does not aim at strict historical
accuracy and the pronunciation given below is that of the earlier
language.

Greek had two types of diphthongs:

(i) where both vowels are written normally and pronounced as
  follows:

> αι as *ai* in *aisle*   οι as *oi* in *soil*
> αυ as *ow* in *now*   ου as *oo* in *pool*
> ει as *ei* in *rein*   υι as *we*
> ευ/ηυ as *eu* in *feud*

  When one of these combinations is not to be pronounced as
  a diphthong, the second is marked with a diaeresis (¨):
  Ἑβραϊστί (Hebra-istí) *in Hebrew*.

(ii) where η, ω or an original long α, is combined with an ι. Here
  the iota is placed **below** the vowel (**iota subscript**), not after
  it: ᾳ, ῃ, ῳ. In the first century AD these were pronounced as
  simple α, η, ω, and the same practice is followed today.

(d) Breathings

When a word begins with a vowel or diphthong it must have
either a rough (ʽ) or smooth (ʼ) breathing. The first denotes an
initial *h*, the second its absence: ἡμέρα (hêméra) *day*, ἀγαθός
(agathós) *good*. A breathing is placed over the second vowel of
a type (i) diphthong: αἴνιγμα (aínigma) *riddle*; Αἴγυπτος
(Aíguptos) *Egypt*; but when an initial vowel which does not
form part of a diphthong is in upper case, the breathing is
placed in front: Ἀνδρέας (Andréas) *Andrew*. All words
beginning with υ have a rough breathing ὕδωρ (húdor) *water*;
ὕψος (húpsos) *height*. Initial ρ is always given a rough breathing
because it was pronounced *rh*: ῥῆμα (rhêma) *word*. Breathings
are written before an acute or grave accent (see below), but
under a circumflex accent, e.g. ἄγγελος *angel*, αἷμα *blood*.

Notes

1 Greek proper names (and also many Greek derivatives) are spelled and pronounced in English according to the Roman system of transliteration: Λιβύα (Libúa) *Libya*; Κρίσπος (Kríspos) *Crispus* (cf. καταστροφή [katastrophé] *catastrophe*). However, the English form of Hebrew proper names usually reflects the Hebrew original and cannot always be predicted from the Greek version. This is particularly the case when the Hebrew name has been given a Greek ending e.g. Ἰερεμίας *Jeremiah* (for further details see 4.1/3).

2 Greek has four marks of punctuation. The full stop and comma are used as in English but our colon and semicolon are represented by a single sign, which is a dot at the top of the line (·). A question mark in Greek is the same as our semicolon (;). The exclamation mark is not used and direct speech is not indicated by inverted commas. A capital letter is used at the beginning of a paragraph but not with each new sentence (see also 7.1/3).

I.I/2 Accents

Accents are often supposed to strike terror into the hearts of beginners, and some elementary books either wholly dispense with them or retain them for a very limited number of words. However, as the Greek New Testament is always printed with accents, a beginner completely unfamiliar with them will be somewhat disoriented on progressing to the stage of reading in a normal modern edition. In any case, they are vital for distinguishing certain homographs.

This aversion to accents arises from the fact that they are often not used today for their original purpose, viz to assist pronunciation. They should be taken to indicate where a word should be stressed. The three marks used (´ **acute**, ` **grave**, ˆ **circumflex**) indicate where the pitch accent of earlier Greek fell (and what type of pitch it was), but by the first centuries of the Christian era the three varieties of pitch had changed into a single stress accent of the same sort as we use in English. This should be our practice when reading NT Greek aloud. The few words without an accent, which all have only one or two syllables, should be lightly pronounced; words with a single accent (the vast majority) should be given a stress accent as in English; and the occasional word bearing two accents should be stressed on the first with the second ignored.

The theory of accentuation and its rules are given in **Appendix 7** and can be consulted and mastered when desired. However, for the purposes of learning the language, readers should follow the practice recommended above.

1.2 Exercise

1 Read aloud and transliterate the following names and then find the normal form used in English:

Ἀσία, Βηθλέεμ, Βεελζεβούλ, Ἰερουσαλήμ, Ἰωάννης, Ἰώβ, Ἰωνᾶς, Ἰωσήφ, Καῖσαρ, Λουκᾶς, Μαθθαῖος, Μαρία, Μάρκος, Παῦλος, Πέτρος, Πιλᾶτος, Ῥώμη, Σίμων.

2 Read aloud and transliterate the following words and then look up their meaning in the vocabulary (all have been taken into English, though in different ways):

ἄγγελος, ἀνάθεμα, ἀνάλυσις, ἀντίθεσις, ἄρωμα, ἄσβεστος, αὐτόματον, βάθος, γένεσις, διάγνωσις, δόγμα, δρᾶμα, ζώνη, ἦθος, ἠχώ, θέατρον, θερμός, ἰδέα, κάμηλος, κίνησις, κλῖμαξ, κόσμος, κρίσις, κριτήριον, κῶλον, μανία, μέτρον, μητρόπολις, μίασμα, ὀρφανός, πάθος, παραλυτικός, σκηνή, στίγμα, τραῦμα, ὕβρις, φαντασία, χαρακτήρ, χάσμα, ψυχή.

1.3 Excursus

The nature of New Testament Greek and its history

In the first century AD the Roman empire extended over all countries bordering on the Mediterranean as well as most of what we now call western Europe. However, it was only in the western half of the empire that Latin was the official language. In the east the language used for administration and many, if not most, forms of communication was Greek, which had been imposed on the area several centuries before. Languages such as Aramaic (spoken in Syria, Palestine and other regions to the east) and Coptic (the descendant of the language represented in Egyptian hieroglyphs) survived in the countries to which they were native, but the official use of Greek, combined with the prestige accorded to Greek culture, gave it an authority which the local vernaculars could not rival. The history of the Greek language and how it came to be the dominant language in half the Roman empire is important for the study of the form it had developed when the New Testament was written.

The original speakers of Greek entered Greece in several waves over the course of the second millennium BC, each wave speaking its own particular dialect. When Greeks first appear in recorded history we find them organized into hundreds of separate independent communities, which we call city states. These varied in size and were not confined to what we now think of as Greece. As a result of colonization, which started in the eighth century BC, settlements were established from the western coast of Asia Minor to southern Italy and Sicily, and even beyond. Many developed into flourishing cities but, whether in the Greek homeland or abroad, the independence they claimed always led to interminable squabbles and wars, to which no external threat or attempted internal union could bring a lasting conclusion. The linguistic consequence of this political discord was that the dialects of Greek, which had multiplied greatly over the centuries, remained.

By the beginning of the fourth century BC the cultural pre-eminence of Athens had established its dialect, Attic Greek, as the language of most forms of literature, including prose. This is the form of Greek used by the tragedians, Aeschylus, Sophocles and Euripides, and by Aristophanes, Thucydides, Plato and Demosthenes. When ancient Greek was still an important part of the school curriculum in countries where the humanistic traditions of the Renaissance persisted, pupils always began with the Attic dialect. Because it has always been used as a standard with which other forms of the language are compared, it is often referred to by the term classical Greek, in contrast to Homeric Greek (the language of the Iliad and Odyssey), New Testament Greek, Byzantine Greek and so on.

However, despite its primacy in matters of culture Athens came to be eclipsed politically, a fate shared by the rest of mainland Greece. The middle of the fourth century BC saw the appearance of a new power in the Greek world. Under Philip II (382–336 BC) Macedonia, a kingdom to the north of Greece, developed to such an extent that it began to threaten the old city states of the south. Philip`s territorial ambitions were achieved and far surpassed by his son, Alexander the Great (356–323 BC). After establishing dominion over Greece itself, Alexander successfully overran the vast empire of the Persians, which encompassed all of what we now call the Middle East, as well as Egypt. On his death this area was divided into different kingdoms, all of which were ruled by Greeks. Greek was the official language and the form this took was a modified Attic. Three centuries later when the Romans finally gained complete control of the countries bordering on the eastern Mediterranean, they made no attempt to supplant Greek as the dominant language of the area. Hence it was that Greek was spoken in the Roman province of Judaea at the time of Christ, although it had not supplanted the native Aramaic.

The principal form of Greek of this period is called the *koine* (from ἡ κοινὴ διάλεκτος *the common dialect*). It was basically Attic but without many of the latter`s subtleties and grammatical complexities. Some of its vocabulary came from other dialects of Greek or from the native languages of the countries where it was used. Its most important feature was that it was the language of the street, akin to the form of English spoken today by the relatively uneducated, and not to the standard English we use today for communication in quality newspapers and the like; and although the koine was spoken over most of the eastern Mediterranean, the form it took in a particular area reflected the local culture.

What we call New Testament Greek is the koine as used in Judaea of the first century AD. Most of the differences between it and the koine of other parts of the eastern Roman empire came from its Jewish environment. When we compare New Testament Greek with the classical language (i.e. Attic of the fifth and fourth centuries BC) we find that it contains Semitic elements of Hebrew or Aramaic origin. These are of three kinds:

Points of style
An example is Hebrew practice of joining clauses by *and* rather than by subordinating one to another, as was normal in Greek. Mark gives the time of the crucifixion with the words ἦν δὲ ὥρα τρίτη καὶ ἐσταύρωσαν αὐτόν (Mk 15.25), lit. *and it was [the] third hour and they crucified him* whereas in English (and classical Greek) we would subordinate one clause to the other and say either *and when it was the third hour they crucified him* or *and it was the third hour when they crucified him*.

Semitic idioms
Many expressions occur in the NT which are a literal translation of a Semitic expression but quite unidiomatic by the standards of classical Greek. Examples are:

The future indicative is used to express an order where classical Greek used an imperative (17.1.1). The most notable instances are the ten commandments as given in the Septuagint (the koine Greek version of the Old Testament; see 12.3), which are quoted in the NT, e.g. Κύριον τὸν θεόν σου προσκυνήσεις καὶ αὐτῷ μόνῳ λατρεύσεις (Lk 4.8) *you shall worship the Lord your God and serve him alone.*

The word υἱός *son* is used metaphorically in the sense of *person associated with* and followed by a genitive; classical Greek (and English) would require a completely different expression, e.g. υἱὸς εἰρήνης (Lk 10.6) lit. *son of peace*, i.e *a peaceful person*; οἱ υἱοὶ τοῦ νυμφῶνος (Mk 2.19) lit. *sons of the bridal chamber*, i.e. *the wedding party.*

For expressions to be translated as *it happened* or *it came to pass*, which have a Semitic origin, see 8.1/2.

Transliterations
Semitic names of people and places were put into the Greek alphabet. Sometimes they were given a Greek ending and declined, e.g., Ἰωάννης *John*, but sometimes they were simply transliterated and treated as indeclinable, with one fixed form, e.g. Βηθλέεμ *Bethlehem*. See 4.1/3.

2.1 Grammar

2.1/1 Nouns in Greek

In Greek, as in English, we consider that a noun has gender, but in English this depends upon its meaning; *man* is masculine, *woman* is feminine, *house* is neuter, and *he, she, it* are the pronouns we use when referring to these. The gender of a Greek noun is often arbitrary and does not necessarily indicate anything about what the noun denotes. For example, ἀνήρ *man* is masculine and γυνή *woman* is feminine, but λόγος *word* is masculine, γλῶσσα *tongue* is feminine, though ἔργον *work* is, understandably, neuter. In most cases we cannot see any reason for the gender of a particular noun but it is often possible to identify a noun's gender by its ending in the nominative and genitive singular, and these endings also determine to which of the three classes or **declensions** it belongs. Each declension has a distinctive set of endings which indicate both **case** and **number** (see **Glossary of grammatical and other terms**), just as in English we have *child* (nominative or accusative singular), *child's* (genitive singular), *children* (nominative or accusative plural), *children's* (genitive plural), but Greek distinguishes more cases. To list all possible forms of a noun is to **decline** it.

Because the second declension presents the fewest complications we shall take it first.

2.1/2 Second declension and the masculine and neuter definite article

The second declension is divided into two groups:

(i) Nouns whose nominative singular ends in -ος, which, with a few exceptions, are masculine.

(ii) Nouns whose nominative singular ends in -ov, which are all neuter.

ὁ ἄνθρωπος *the human being*

	SINGULAR		PLURAL	
Nominative	ὁ	ἄνθρωπ-ος	οἱ	ἄνθρωπ-οι
Vocative	—	ἄνθρωπ-ε	—	ἄνθρωπ-οι
Accusative	τὸν	ἄνθρωπ-ον	τοὺς	ἀνθρώπ-ους
Genitive	τοῦ	ἀνθρώπ-ου	τῶν	ἀνθρώπ-ων
Dative	τῷ	ἀνθρώπ-ῳ	τοῖς	ἀνθρώπ-οις

τὸ ἔργον *the work*

	SINGULAR		PLURAL	
Nominative	τὸ	ἔργ-ον	τὰ	ἔργ-α
Vocative	—	ἔργ-ον	—	ἔργ-α
Accusative	τὸ	ἔργ-ον	τὰ	ἔργ-α
Genitive	τοῦ	ἔργ-ου	τῶν	ἔργ-ων
Dative	τῷ	ἔργ-ῳ	τοῖς	ἔργ-οις

It should be noted that:

(a) Except for ὁ and τό, the endings of the definite article are the same as those of the nouns in each group.

(b) The endings for the genitive and dative (both singular and plural) of the first group are the same as those of the second.

(c) The genitive plural of all nouns, regardless of declension, has the ending -ων.

(d) The nominative plural, vocative plural and accusative plural of all neuter nouns, regardless of declension, have the ending -α (for an apparent exception see 6.1/1(c)).

Notes

1 The definite article must agree with the noun it qualifies in number, gender, and case: τῶν ἔργων *of the works* (genitive plural), τοὺς ἀνθρώπους *the human beings* (accusative plural). This does **not** necessarily mean that the ending of the article will be the same as that of the noun with which it agrees (see 3.1/1 note 2).

Contexts where the definite article is used in Greek but not in English are:

(i) with proper nouns and with abstract nouns, where it is optional (there is no difference in sense; in English we do not use the definite article with either); examples are: ὁ Παῦλος or simply Παῦλος *Paul*; ὁ θάνατος or θάνατος *death*. When referring to the Judeo-Christian God the definite article is also optional: ὁ θεός or θεός *God*, ὁ κύριος or κύριος *the Lord* (in English we use the article with the latter but not the former; note that θεός and κύριος are not given an initial capital).

(ii) with nouns (usually plural) when they indicate a general class: οἱ ἄνθρωποι *human beings* (as a class); οἱ ἄνθρωποι can also mean *the* (particular) *human beings* where the context requires. An example of this use with a singular noun is τὸ ἀκάθαρτον πνεῦμα (Mt 12.43); as the context here shows us that we have an account of the behaviour of unclean spirits in general, English idiom requires the translation *an unclean spirit*.

In translating a common noun in the singular without the definite article, *a* should be supplied in English:, ἵππος *a horse* but ὁ ἵππος *the horse*. However, NT use is inconsistent and we often must supply the definite article in English where it does not occur in Greek, e.g. γῆ Σοδόμων (Mt 10.15) which is to be translated as *the land of Sodom*, not *land of Sodom*.

2 Neuter nouns do not necessarily denote inanimate objects. Examples are παιδίον, τέκνον both *child*, δαιμόνιον *evil spirit*.

3 It is a rule in Attic Greek (the language of Athens in the fifth and fourth centuries BC) that a finite verb which has a plural **neuter** noun as its subject is always *singular*. This curious idiom, which has not been satisfactorily explained, is observed sometimes, but not always, in the New Testament; we see it in Jn 10.3 τὰ πρόβατα τῆς φωνῆς αὐτοῦ ἀκούει *the sheep* (τὰ πρόβατα) *hear his voice* (τῆς φωνῆς αὐτοῦ; ἀκούει is 3rd s. pres. ind. act. of ἀκούω – see below 2.1/5; it is followed by the genitive), but not in *Jn 10.27 τὰ πρόβατα τῆς φωνῆς μου ἀκούουσιν *the sheep hear my voice* (τῆς φωνῆς μου; ἀκούουσιν is 3rd pl. pres. ind. act. of ἀκούω – see below 2.1/5).

4 The proper name Ἰησοῦς *Jesus* belongs to the second declension but is irregular: nom. Ἰησοῦς, voc. Ἰησοῦ, acc. Ἰησοῦν, gen. Ἰησοῦ, dat. Ἰησοῦ (note that the genitive and dative are the same).

5 For the few feminine nouns of the second declension, which are declined in exactly the same way as masculines, see 3.1/1 note 2.

6 In the second declension (and in the first declension) when the final syllable bears an acute in the nominative, as in ποταμός *river*, the accent becomes a circumflex in the genitive and dative, e.g. nom. s ποταμός, gen. s. ποταμοῦ, dat. s. ποταμῷ, gen. pl. ποταμῶν, dat. pl. ποταμοῖς (for further information on accents see **Appendix 7**).

2.1/3 Basic uses of cases

The only case ending for nouns in English is that of the genitive (as in *girl's, men's,* etc.). Elsewhere, a noun's function is shown by its position in relation to the other words in its clause (the difference in meaning between *the peasant hit the tax collector* and *the tax collector hit the peasant* depends solely on the word order) or by a preposition, e.g. *the tax collector was hit by a stone* (here the part played by the stone is indicated by the preposition *by*). In Greek, however, the function of a noun is indicated by its **case**:

(a) The subject of a clause must be put in the **nominative**.
(b) When we address a person the **vocative** is used; this is sometimes preceded by ὦ O and followed by a mark of punctuation. The vocative is given for ἔργον because, although ἔργον itself does not occur in this case, we do find the vocative of other nouns of the same class, e.g. τέκνον *child*.
(c) The direct object of a verb must be put in the **accusative**.
(d) The **genitive** can express possession: *the Samaritan's donkey* (in English we can also say *the donkey of the Samaritan*). The genitive in Greek has other uses (e.g. to express separation 20.1/3(g)).
(e) With nouns denoting living things the **dative** expresses the indirect object after verbs of saying, giving and promising (21.1/1(a)(i)). In *the Samaritan gave a donkey to the teacher* the direct object is *donkey* (answering the question *gave what?*), which in Greek would be put into the accusative ὄνον; the indirect object is *the teacher* (*gave to whom?*), which would be put in the dative τῷ διδασκάλῳ with no preposition (we may also say in English *the Samaritan gave the teacher a donkey* but there is no alternative of this sort in Greek). With nouns denoting living things the dative has

other uses which can nearly always be translated by *to* or *for*. With inanimate nouns (e.g. *Tyre, arrow, boat*) different uses are possible.

The term **oblique cases** is used for referring to the accusative, genitive, and dative as a group. In addition to the uses given above, these cases are also used after **prepositions**, which perform the same function in Greek as in English, i.e. they define the relation between the word they govern and the rest of the clause in which they are used. In Greek the word governed is normally a noun or pronoun. The rules for prepositions indicating **motion** and **rest** are:

(f) Prepositions indicating **motion towards** govern (i.e. are followed by) the accusative, e.g. εἰς τὸν οἶκον *into the house,* πρὸς τὸν ἀγρόν *towards the field.*

(g) Prepositions indicating **motion away from** govern the genitive, e.g. ἀπὸ τοῦ θρόνου *from the throne,* ἐκ τοῦ ἀγροῦ *out of the field.*

(h) Prepositions indicating **rest** or **fixed position** govern the dative, e.g. ἐν τῷ ἀγρῷ *in the field.*

All the above prepositions, except πρός (3.1/5), take only the case given above.

2.1/4 Verbs in Greek

A finite form of a verb is one that can function as the verb of a clause (see **Glossary of grammatical and other terms**). In Greek a finite verb is defined in terms of person, number, tense, mood, and voice. **Person** and **number** are determined by its subject: a finite verb must agree with its subject in both (just as in English we cannot say *we is*). First person is the person(s) speaking, i.e. *I* or *we*; second person is the person(s) spoken to, i.e. *you*; third person is the person(s) or thing(s) spoken about, which can be a pronoun (*he, she, it, they*) or a noun (e.g. *the donkeys are in the field*). The concept of number is the same as with nouns; we have either singular (e.g. *is, are*) or plural (e.g. *are, were*). **Tense** indicates the time in which the action of the verb takes place. **Mood** tells us something about the nature of the verb's action in a particular context, but we are now only concerned with the **indicative** mood, which is used to express facts (e.g. *John baptized by the Jordan*). **Voice** shows the relation of the subject to the verb. We shall first deal with the **active**, which is the voice used when the subject is the doer of the action (e.g. *The Romans captured Jerusalem*).

With a finite Greek verb the person, number, tense, mood and voice are shown by the stem and ending. For example, we can tell by the stem and ending that λύσουσι is third person plural future indicative active of the verb λύω *I loosen*, and therefore means *they will loosen*. It is superfluous to add the Greek word for *they* (unless for emphasis), as this is part of the information conveyed by the ending. Auxiliary verbs (*shall/will, have, be* etc.) are used to form most tenses of an English verb (*I shall teach, he has taught, we shall be taught*); Greek has similar composite verbal forms, but they are much less common than in English and need not concern us at this point.

Verbs in Greek belong to one of two groups (called **conjugations**). These are distinguished from each other by the ending of the first person singular present indicative active, the form in which Greek verbs are customarily cited in works of reference (contrast the convention in English of referring to a verb by its present infinitive active):

-ω verbs, e.g. λύω *I loosen* (this is by far the larger class);
-μι verbs, e.g. εἰμί *I am* (3.1/6), δίδωμι *I give* (18.1/2).

The meaning given in the vocabulary for these verbs is simply *loosen, be, give.*

2.1/5 Present and future indicative active of -ω verbs

		Present		Future	
SINGULAR	1	λύ-ω	*I loosen*	λύσ-ω	*I shall loosen*
	2	λύ-εις	*you (s.) loosen*	λύσ-εις	*you (s.) will loosen*
	3	λύ-ει	*he, she, it loosens*	λύσ-ει	*he, she, it will loosen*
PLURAL	1	λύ-ομεν	*we loosen*	λύσ-ομεν	*we shall loosen*
	2	λύ-ετε	*you (pl.) loosen*	λύσ-ετε	*you (pl.) will loosen*
	3	λύ-ουσι(ν)	*they loosen*	λύσ-ουσι(ν)	*they will loosen*
Infinitive		λύ-ειν	*to loosen*		

The present indicative active (and the present infinitive active) is formed by taking the present stem (λυ- i.e. λύω minus ω) and adding the endings given above. For the future indicative active we make up the future stem by adding sigma to that of the present (i.e. λυ + σ > λυσ-) and we then apply the same endings.

Notes

1 In English the present tense has different forms, *I loosen, I am loosening, I do loosen* and so on, and there are distinctions in usage between these. Greek has only one present tense and we must decide from the context which English form we should use to translate a Greek verb in this tense. In one context λύουσι might mean *they loosen*, in another *they are loosening* or *do they loosen*. Likewise, λύσω can also mean *I shall be loosening*.

2 In a narrative about the past, Greek often uses the present tense for vividness (vivid present); we have the same idiom in English but it is by no means as common.

3 The Greek second person singular is always used when addressing one person, the plural when addressing more than one person. There are no familiar or polite forms of the second person, as in French, German and other modern languages.

4 The forms λύει and λύσει are given the meanings *he, she, it loosens/will loosen*. Which pronoun is required in English will be obvious in a particular context, but if there is any possibility of confusion a pronoun in the nominative will be given in the Greek (9.1/1). Where a noun is the subject these forms simply mean *loosens/will loosen*, e.g. ὁ ἀδελφὸς λύει τὸν ὄνον *the brother loosens the donkey*.

5 In each form of the above table the stem is followed by an o- or e- sound. This is called the **thematic vowel**, and it is most clearly seen in the first and second persons plural. The same pattern, which marks these tenses as **thematic**, is repeated in the imperfect (4.1/1). The thematic vowel occurs in the endings of some tenses (present, future, imperfect), but not in others (aorist, perfect, pluperfect). It is a useful aid in remembering the differences between sets of endings.

6 The final ν shown in brackets in the ending of the third person plural is called the movable ν. Ancient grammarians state that it should be used (without brackets) only when a word with this ending is followed by a word beginning with a vowel or diphthong or stands at the end of a clause; however, this rule is very often broken in the New Testament. Movable ν occurs here and in a few other endings.

7 To form the future of πέμπω *send,* the final π of the present stem is combined with σ to give πέμψ-ω *I will send.* Other final consonants in present stems will be treated at 6.1/4 and 11.1/3.

8 A future infinitive occurs in the verb *to be* (8.1/1 note 3) but elsewhere is rare and its authenticity open to question.

2.1/6 Word order and elision

(a) The arrangement of words within a Greek sentence is often similar to that of English, but Greek word order is generally much less predictable than in English. In English there is a close link between the order in which words occur and their function (see above 2.1/3). In Greek, however, where the grammatical function of a word is indicated by its form, not by its position, word order can be varied much more than in English. This is mainly done to emphasize a particular word or phrase. If in the English sentence *the brother is good* we wished to emphasize *good* we would, in speech, articulate it with greater weight (in writing we could underline it or put it in italics). In Greek the emphasis would be conveyed by a change in the word order; ὁ ἀδελφός ἐστιν (*is*) ἀγαθός (*good*) would become ἀγαθός ἐστιν ὁ ἀδελφός. Emphasis apart, two further points regarding word order should be noted here:

(i) The negative οὐ(κ) *not* precedes the word it negates: οὐκ ἔχω ... *I do not have* ... (οὐκ is the form used before vowels and diphthongs with a smooth breathing; it becomes οὐχ if the following vowel or diphthong has a rough breathing, e.g. οὐχ εὑρίσκω *I do not find.* Before consonants it is simply οὐ).

(ii) Just as in English we can say *the field of the Cyrenian* or *the Cyrenian's field,* so in Greek we have ὁ ἀγρὸς τοῦ Κυρηναίου and ὁ τοῦ Κυρηναίου ἀγρός (note that the article of ἀγρός must be retained in the latter). As a third possibility we have ὁ ἀγρὸς ὁ τοῦ Κυρηναίου with no difference in meaning.

(b) Prepositions and conjunctions ending in α, ε, ο lose this vowel when standing before a word beginning with a vowel or diphthong, e.g. ἀπ' ἀγροῦ (= ἀπὸ ἀγροῦ) *from a field;* δι' ἐσόπτρου (= διὰ ἐσόπτρου) *through a mirror;* this loss is called elision and is marked with an apostrophe as shown. If the vowel or diphthong of the second word has a rough breathing and the letter before the lost α, ε, ο is π or τ, this letter becomes φ or θ respectively, e.g. ἀφ' ἁμαρτωλοῦ (= ἀπὸ ἁμαρτωλοῦ) *from a sinner*, μεθ' ἁμαρτωλοῦ (= μετὰ ἁμαρτωλοῦ) *with a sinner*. Elision is not consistently found with prepositions; it sometimes occurs with other parts of speech.

2.2 Greek reading

In reading Greek the following steps should be followed:

(a) Look up each word in the vocabulary at 2.2/1 and parse it (i.e. define it grammatically; this is particularly necessary with words which vary in form).

(b) Mark all finite verbs as this will indicate the number of clauses.

(c) By observing punctuation and conjunctions used to join clauses, work out where each clause begins and ends.

(d) Take each clause separately and see how each word relates to the finite verb of its clause (subject, object, part of an adverbial phrase, etc.).

(e) See from the conjunctions how the clauses are related to each other and work out the overall meaning of the sentence.

An analysis of sentences 4 and 11 will be found in the key.

1 ἐγγίζει ὁ καιρὸς τῶν καρπῶν. (*Mt 21.34)[1]
2 οὐκ ἐκβαλλει τὰ δαιμόνια. (Mt 12.24)
3 ἀποστέλλει πρὸς τοὺς γεωργοὺς δοῦλον. (*Mk 12.2)
4 διὰ τί μετὰ τῶν ἁμαρτωλῶν ἐσθίετε καὶ πίνετε; (*Lk 5.30)
5 βλέπεις τὸν ὄχλον. (Mk 5.31)
6 διδάσκαλε, ὀρθῶς λέγεις καὶ διδάσκεις καὶ οὐ λαμβάνεις πρόσωπον. (*Lk 20.21)
7 βλέπω τοὺς ἀνθρώπους. (Mk 8.24)
8 οὐδὲν κακὸν (*nothing wrong*) εὑρίσκομεν ἐν τῷ ἀνθρώπῳ. (Ac 23.9)
9 δῶρα πέμψουσιν. (Rv 11.10)
10 τότε νηστεύσουσιν. (Lk 5.35)
11 ὁ δοῦλος μισθὸν λαμβάνει καὶ συνάγει καρπόν. (*Jn 4.36)
12 πῶς κρίνει ὁ θεὸς τὸν κόσμον; (*Ro 3.6)
13 νεκροὺς ἐγείρετε, λεπροὺς καθαρίζετε, δαιμόνια ἐκβάλλετε. (*Mt 10.8)
14 τὸ πρόσωπον τοῦ οὐρανοῦ γινώσκετε διακρίνειν. (*Mt 16.3)

---

[1] An asterisk before a reference indicates that a slight change has been made in the text.

15 ἀκούετε καὶ βλέπετε. (Mt 11.4)
16 δαιμόνιον ἔχεις. (Jn 7.20)
17 οἱ νεκροὶ ἀκούσουσιν. (Jn 5.25)
18 ἤρξατο (*began*) ὁ Ἰησοῦς κηρύσσειν καὶ λέγειν. (Mt 4.17)
19 τότε οἱ δίκαιοι ἐκλάμψουσιν ὡς ὁ ἥλιος. (Mt 13.43)
20 κηρύσσομεν Ἰησοῦν Χριστὸν κύριον. (*2 Cor 4.5)

Notes

1 ὁ καιρὸς τῶν καρπῶν lit. *the time of the fruits*, i.e. the harvest;
καρπῶν has the definite article τῶν because fruits generally
are meant and so constitute a general class – 2.1/2 note 1(ii)
– trans. *the time of fruits*.

4 τῶν ἁμαρτωλῶν the article indicates that a general class is
meant – it can be omitted in English.

6 Take ὀρθῶς with both λέγεις and διδάσκεις. The expression
λαμβάνω πρόσωπον (lit. *take face*) is a Semitism meaning
show partiality.

7 τοὺς ἀνθρώπους the context of this clause indicates that a
general class is meant.

8 ἄνθρωπος in the singular means *human being* and in the
plural can be translated as *people* (as in 7). The singular
here is to be translated as *man* because it is preceded by the
masculine definite article (if a woman had been meant the
article would be feminine).

11 Supply *his* with μισθόν and *the* with καρπόν (here simply
harvest).

13 Take the verbs as indicative (in their original context they
are imperatives – 17.1/1)

19 οἱ δίκαιοι the general class is meant; ἐκλάμψουσιν fut. of
ἐκλάμπω.

2.2/1 Vocabulary

Individual vocabularies are provided for Units 2–9. The
meaning given to each word is that appropriate to its use in the
preceding reading; for a fuller range of meanings the main
vocabulary should be consulted. Words already given in a
grammatical table (or in an earlier vocabulary) are not repeated,
except where a different meaning is involved.

It is normal practice in Greek dictionaries and lists of Greek
words to give the nominative singular of a noun, its genitive
(usually in abbreviated form) and the appropriate nominative
singular form of the article; this information establishes both its
declension and gender, e.g. ἥλιος, -ου, ὁ (note that the accent in

the genitive – here ἡλίου – is not always on the same syllable as in the nominative; see **Appendix 7, a**). Verbs are cited in the first person singular present indicative, e.g. κρίνω.

ἄγω *lead, bring*
ἀκούω *hear*
ἁμαρτωλός, -οῦ, ὁ *sinner*
ἄνθρωπος, -ου, ὁ *human being, person*
ἀποστέλλω *send, dispatch*
ἀπόστολος, -ου, ὁ *apostle*
βλέπω *see*
γεωργός, -οῦ, ὁ *tenant farmer*
γινώσκω *know*
δαιμόνιον, -ου, τό *evil spirit*
διὰ τί; *on account of what? why?*
διακρίνω *judge correctly*
διδάσκαλος, -ου, ὁ *teacher, master*
διδάσκω *teach*
δίκαιος, -ου, ὁ *just person*
δοῦλος, -ου, ὁ *slave* (often translated *servant*)
δῶρον, -ου, τό *gift*
ἐγγίζω *approach* (intr.)
ἐγείρω *raise*
ἐκ (prep. + gen.) *out of, from*
ἐκβάλλω *cast out*
ἐκλάμπω *shine forth*
ἐν (prep. + dat.) *in*
ἐσθίω *eat*
εὑρίσκω *find*
ἔχω *have*
ἥλιος, -ου, ὁ *sun*

θεός, -οῦ, ὁ *God*
καθαρίζω *cleanse*
καί (conj.) *and*
καιρός, -οῦ, ὁ *time*
καρπός, -οῦ, ὁ *fruit, harvest*
κηρύσσω *make known, preach*
κόσμος, -ου, ὁ *world*
κρίνω *judge*
κύριος, -ου, ὁ *the Lord*
λαμβάνω *take*
λέγω *say, speak*
λεπρός, -οῦ, ὁ *leper*
μετά (prep. + gen.) *in the company of, with*
μισθός, -οῦ, ὁ *pay, salary*
νεκρός, -ου, ὁ *dead (person)*
νηστεύω *fast*
ὀρθῶς (adv.) *rightly*
οὐ, οὐκ *not*
οὐρανός, -οῦ, ὁ *sky, heavens*
ὄχλος, -ου, ὁ *crowd*
πέμπω *send*
πίνω *drink*
πρός (prep. + acc.) *towards, to*
πρόσωπον, -ου, τό *face*
πῶς (interrog.) *how?*
συνάγω *gather up*
τότε *then*
ὡς (conj.) *like*

3.1 Grammar

3.1/1 First declension (feminine nouns) and the feminine definite article

The majority of first declension nouns are feminine and end in -η or -α (for the few masculines see 3.1/2). Those in -α change alpha to eta in the genitive and dative singular unless the alpha is preceded by a vowel or ρ, but all first declension nouns have the same endings in the plural. The feminine form of the definite article is declined in the same way as the feminines in -η.

	ἡ	τιμή	ἡμέρα	θάλασσα
	the	*honour*	*day*	*sea*
SINGULAR				
Nominative	ἡ	τιμ-ή	ἡμέρ-α	θάλασσ-α
Accusative	τήν	τιμ-ήν	ἡμέρ-αν	θάλασσ-αν
Genitive	τῆς	τιμ-ῆς	ἡμέρ-ας	θαλάσσ-ης
Dative	τῇ	τιμ-ῇ	ἡμέρ-ᾳ	θαλάσσ-ῃ
PLURAL				
Nominative	αἱ	τιμ-αί	ἥμερ-αι	θάλασσ-αι
Accusative	τάς	τιμ-άς	ἡμέρ-ας	θαλάσσ-ας
Genitive	τῶν	τιμ-ῶν	ἡμερ-ῶν	θαλασσ-ῶν
Dative	ταῖς	τιμ-αῖς	ἡμέρ-αις	θαλάσσ-αις

Notes

1 The vocative is the same as the nominative, e.g. Μαρία.
2 There are a few feminine nouns in the second declension, which are declined in exactly the same way as masculine nouns. These require the feminine form of the definite article (and of adjectives; see 3.1/3): ἡ νῆσος *the island*, τῆς νήσου *of*

the island. Only rarely can they be recognized as feminine by their meaning, e.g. ἡ παρθένος *the girl.*

3 Some nouns in -ρα are irregular and follow τιμή in the genitive and dative singular, e.g. σπεῖρα *cohort,* gen. σπείρης. Conversely, some nouns whose final alpha is not preceded by a vowel or rho follow ἡμέρα, e.g. Μάρθα *Martha,* gen. Μάρθας.

4 In the genitive plural all first declension nouns have a circumflex on their final syllable.

3.1/2 First declension (masculine nouns)

Masculine nouns of the first declension end in -ας or -ης and have the same -ου ending for the genitive singular as the second declension, except those in -ας with a final circumflex (i.e. -ᾶς, as Σατανᾶς), which have a genitive singular in -ᾶ. Many common nouns in -ης involve males or male occupations (e.g. ναύτης *sailor,* στρατιώτης *soldier*); most ending in -ας are proper nouns.

	ὁ *the*	κριτής *judge*		Ἀνδρέας *Andrew*	Σατανᾶς *Satan*
		SINGULAR	PLURAL		
Nominative	ὁ	κριτ-ής	κριτ-αί	Ἀνδρέ-ας	Σαταν-ᾶς
Vocative	—	κριτ-ά	κριτ-αί	Ἀνδρέ-α	Σαταν-ᾶ
Accusative	τόν	κριτ-ήν	κριτ-άς	Ἀνδρέ-αν	Σαταν-ᾶν
Genitive	τοῦ	κριτ-οῦ	κριτ-ῶν	Ἀνδρέ-ου	Σαταν-ᾶ
Dative	τῷ	κριτ-ῇ	κριτ-αῖς	Ἀνδρέ-ᾳ	Σαταν-ᾷ

Notes

1 As shown above, the definite article (and adjectives) must be masculine when used with these nouns.

2 The very few common nouns in -ας are declined in the same way as Ἀνδρέας in the singular and follow κριτής in the plural.

3 The proper noun Μωϋσῆς *Moses* does not belong here (see 11.1/4), but its nominative form (Μωϋσῆς) will be found in the Greek reading.

3.1/3 First and second declension adjectives

With the exception of *this* (pl. *these*) and *that* (pl. *those*) adjectives in English have only one form (as *good, bad,* etc.). In Greek, adjectives must agree with the nouns they qualify (i.e. go with and describe) in case, number and gender.

Like nouns, adjectives in Greek are classified according to how they are declined. The first category of adjectives is called **first and second declension adjectives** because they are declined in the feminine like first declension feminine nouns and in the masculine and neuter like nouns of the second declension. First and second declension adjectives thus have a feminine in -η (or -α, when preceded by ε, ι or ρ) when used with feminine nouns, a masculine in -ος when used with masculine nouns, and a neuter in -ον when used with neuter nouns. For the other categories of adjectives see 10.1/3, 10.1/4.

καλός *beautiful, noble* is declined:

| | SINGULAR | | | PLURAL | | |
	M.	F.	N.	M.	F.	N.
Nom.	καλ-ός	καλ-ή	καλ-όν	καλ-οί	καλ-αί	καλ-ά
Voc.	καλ-έ	καλ-ή	καλ-όν	καλ-οί	καλ-αί	καλ-ά
Acc.	καλ-όν	καλ-ήν	καλ-όν	καλ-ούς	καλ-άς	καλ-ά
Gen.	καλ-οῦ	καλ-ῆς	καλ-οῦ	καλ-ῶν	καλ-ῶν	καλ-ῶν
Dat.	καλ-ῷ	καλ-ῇ	καλ-ῷ	καλ-οῖς	καλ-αῖς	καλ-οῖς

ἅγιος *holy* and αἰσχρός *ugly, shameful* are declined as follows in the singular:

	M.	F.	N.	M.	F.	N.
Nom.	ἅγι-ος	ἁγί-α	ἅγι-ον	αἰσχρ-ός	αἰσχρ-ά	αἰσχρ-όν
Voc.	ἅγι-ε	ἁγί-α	ἅγι-ον	αἰσχρ-έ	αἰσχρ-ά	αἰσχρ-όν
Acc.	ἅγι-ον	ἁγί-αν	ἅγι-ον	αἰσχρ-όν	αἰσχρ-άν	αἰσχρ-όν
Gen.	ἁγί-ου	ἁγί-ας	ἁγί-ου	αἰσχρ-οῦ	αἰσχρ-ᾶς	αἰσχρ-οῦ
Dat.	ἁγί-ῳ	ἁγί-ᾳ	ἁγί-ῳ	αἰσχρ-ῷ	αἰσχρ-ᾷ	αἰσχρ-ῷ

The plural is the same as for καλός.[1]

In the vocabulary (and in dictionaries) these adjectives are cited as καλός, -ή, -όν; ἅγιος, -α, -ον; αἰσχρός, -ά, -όν.

Some first and second declension adjectives have no separate feminine form (**two-termination** adjectives) and employ the -ος forms for masculine and feminine alike. These are mostly compounds, e.g. ἀνθρωποκτόνος *murderer* (ἄνθρωπος *person* + κτόνος *killing*); ἔντιμος *honoured* (ἐν + τιμή *honour*). Compounds with the negative ἀ- prefix (or ἀν- before a vowel; cf. English *in-, un-*) are common, e.g. ἄπιστος *unbelieving* (ἀ + πιστός *believing*); ἀνάξιος *unworthy* (ἀν + ἄξιος *worthy*). These adjectives are cited in the form ἄπιστος, -ον; ἔντιμος, -ον.

---

[1] The accent in the genitive plural feminine is ἁγίων, not ἁγιῶν which we would have expected on the analogy of first declension nouns (3.1/1 note 4).

Examples of them in agreement with feminine nouns are: ἡ ἄγαμος δούλη *the unmarried female slave*; αἱ ἔντιμοι παιδίσκαι *the respected slave girls*. Common two-termination adjectives which are not compounds are: αἰώνιος *eternal*; ἁμαρτωλός *sinful*; οὐράνιος *heavenly*.

Two common adjectives, πολύς *much* (pl. *many*), and μέγας *great, big,* are irregular in the masculine and neuter nominative and accusative singular. Elsewhere they are declined exactly as if their nominative singular masculine were πολλ-ός and μεγάλ-ος. In the singular they are declined:

	M.	F.	N.	M.	F.	N.
Nom.	**πολύς**	πολλ-ή	**πολύ**	**μέγας**	μεγάλ-η	**μέγα**
Acc.	**πολύν**	πολλ-ήν	**πολύ**	**μέγαν**	μεγάλ-ην	**μέγα**
Gen.	πολλ-οῦ	πολλ-ῆς	πολλ-οῦ	μεγάλ-ου	μεγάλ-ης	μεγάλ-ου
Dat.	πολλ-ῷ	πολλ-ῇ	πολλ-ῷ	μεγάλ-ῳ	μεγάλ-ῃ	μεγάλ-ῳ

The plural is regular and follows καλός.

Position of adjectives

(a) When the noun qualified has no definite article:

An adjective usually comes after its noun: ἄνθρωπος ἐχθρός *a hostile man*; however, an adjective may come first without any difference in meaning διὰ ἀνύδρων τόπων (Mt 12.43) *through waterless places.*

(b) When the noun qualified has the definite article:

There are several possibilities. An **attributive** adjective (see **Glossary of grammatical and other terms**) may occupy the same position as in English: τὸ αἰώνιον πῦρ *the eternal fire.* But this can also be expressed as τὸ πῦρ τὸ αἰώνιον with the article repeated (both these positions are regarded as attributive); we may even have πῦρ τὸ αἰώνιον with exactly the same meaning. However, where the adjective without an article appears outside the article-noun complex, as in ὁ ἄνθρωπος ἀγαθός or ἀγαθὸς ὁ ἄνθρωπος, it is considered as functioning **predicatively**, and so the meaning is *the man is good* (on the omission of ἐστί *is* see 3.1/6).

3.1/4 Adverbs

Many adverbs are formed from adjectives by adding -ως to the stem. In effect this means changing the final ν of the gen. pl. m. of the adjective to ς, e.g. δίκαιος (gen. pl. m. δικαίων) *just*, adv. δικαίως *justly*; κακός (gen. pl. m. κακῶν) *bad*, adv. κακῶς *badly*.

A few adverbs are the same as the neuter nom./acc. singular of the adjective: μικρόν *for a short while*, τρίτον *(for) the third time*. Others have no special ending: νῦν (or νυνί) *now*, τότε *then*, εὖ *well*.

3.1/5 Prepositions

We have already seen some prepositions (εἰς, ἐκ, ἐν) which indicate motion or rest (2.1/3(f), (g), (h)). While some prepositions only govern one case (as ἐν + dat. *in*), some govern both the accusative and genitive (as διά, see below), some the accusative, genitive and dative (as παρά). There are always differences of meaning involved, e.g. παρά + acc. = *to(wards)*; + gen. = *from*; + dat. = *at, beside*, e.g. παρὰ Κάρπῳ (2 Ti 4.13) lit. *at Carpus*, i.e. *at [the house of] Carpus* (Carpus is a man's name, cf. Fr. *chez moi*).

The following are particularly common:

(a) with accusative:	διά	*on account of*
	μετά	*after*
	περί	*around* (time, place or number)
	ὑπέρ	*above*
(b) with genitive:	ἀντί	*instead of, in place of*
	διά	*through, by means of*
	μετά	*(in company) with*
	ὑπέρ	*on behalf of*
	περί	*concerning*

3.1/6 Present indicative and infinitive of εἰμί *I am*

The verb εἰμί is irregular. Although classified as a -μι verb it has little in common with other verbs in this class (18.1/1).

SINGULAR	1	εἰμί	*I am*	PLURAL	ἐσμέν	*we are*
	2	εἶ	*you* (s.) *are*		ἐστέ	*you* (pl.) *are*
	3	ἐστί(ν)	*he, she, it is*		εἰσί(ν)	*they are*
INFINITIVE		εἶναι	*to be*			

On the accentuation of εἰμί see **Appendix 7**, (d).

As εἰμί does not express an action inflicted by the subject on the object it **never** governs an accusative. What is said about the subject in clauses involving this verb is put into the **nominative**: εἰμὶ πρεσβύτης (Lk 1.18) *I am an old man*; εἰμὶ ὁ ἄρτος τῆς ζωῆς (Jn 6.35) *I am the bread* of life; οἱ θερισταὶ ἄγγελοί εἰσιν (*Mt

13.39) *the reapers are* **angels**. In this type of clause the appropriate form of εἰμί is often omitted; this is most common with ἐστί or εἰσί (cf. above 3.1/3(b)): ἄξιος ὁ ἐργάτης τοῦ μισθοῦ αὐτοῦ (*Lk 10.7) *the labourer* [*is*] *worthy of his* (αὐτοῦ) *wage*; μακάριοι οἱ εἰρηνοποιοί (Mt 5.9) *blessed* [*are*] *the peacemakers*.

Sometimes we can translate ἐστί and εἰσί by *there is* and *there are* respectively; ἐν τῇ οἰκίᾳ τοῦ πατρός μου μοναὶ πολλαί εἰσιν (Jn 14.2) *in my father's* (τοῦ πατρός μου) *house there are many dwelling places* (we could also say in English *in my father's house are many dwelling places*).

3.2 Greek reading

An analysis of sentence 15 will be found in the key.

1 μετὰ πολὺν χρόνον. περὶ τῆς βασιλείας τοῦ θεοῦ. περὶ τρίτην ὥραν. ὀφθαλμὸς ἀντὶ ὀφθαλμοῦ. διὰ τῆς πύλης. ὑπὲρ πολλῶν. ἐν τῇ νήσῳ. εἰς τὰς συναγωγάς.

2 οὐ βάλλουσιν οἶνον νέον εἰς ἀσκοὺς παλαιούς. (*Mt 9.17)

3 Μωϋσῆς γράφει τὴν δικαιοσύνην τὴν ἐκ τοῦ νόμου. (*Ro 10.5)

4 ἤδη καθαροί ἐστε διὰ τὸν λόγον. (*Jn 15.3)

5 ὁ φίλος τοῦ νυμφίου χαρᾷ χαίρει διὰ τὴν φωνὴν τοῦ νυμφίου. (*Jn 3.29)

6 διὰ τί μετὰ τῶν τελωνῶν καὶ ἁμαρτωλῶν ἐσθίει ὁ διδάσκαλος; (*Mt 9,11)

7 οὐκ ἐσμὲν ὑπὸ νόμον. (Ro 6.15)

8 ἐλέγξει τὸν κόσμον περὶ ἁμαρτίας καὶ περὶ δικαιοσύνης. (Jn 16.8)

9 οὐκ ἔστιν μαθητὴς ὑπὲρ τὸν διδάσκαλον. (Lk 6.40)

10 εἶ ὁ Χριστὸς ὁ υἱὸς τοῦ θεοῦ. (Mt 16.16)

11 τί δειλοί ἐστε, ὀλιγόπιστοι; (Mt 8.26)

12 διδάσκαλε, ποία ἐντολὴ μεγάλη ἐν τῷ νόμῳ; (Mt 22.36)

13 μετὰ φωνῆς μεγάλης δοξάζει τὸν θεόν. (*Lk 17.15)

14 ἔστιν ἀληθῶς ὁ προφήτης. (Jn 7.40)

15 εἰ νόμον κρίνεις, οὐκ εἶ ποιητὴς νόμου ἀλλὰ κριτής. (*Js 4.11)

16 τὸ σάββατον διὰ τον ἄνθρωπον ἐγένετο (*was made*) καὶ οὐχ ὁ ἄνθρωπος διὰ τὸ σάββατον. (Mk 2.27)

17 ὁ πιστεύων (*the man believing*) εἰς τὸν υἱὸν ἔχει ζωὴν αἰώνιον. (Jn 3.36)

18 ὁ μισθὸς πολὺς ἐν τοῖς οὐρανοῖς. (*Mt 5.12)

19 πολλοὶ ἀπὸ ἀνατολῶν καὶ δυσμῶν ἥξουσιν. (Mt 8.11)

20 ἡ θάλασσα οὐκ ἔστιν ἔτι. (Rev 21.1)

Notes

1 On the meaning of the prepositions used in these phrases see above 3.1/5.

3 τὴν δικαιοσύνην τὴν ἐκ τοῦ νόμου lit. *the justice from the law* i.e. the just practices which a person would derive from the prescriptions of Moses.

4 The 'word' is Christ's message.

5 χαρᾷ χαίρει lit. *rejoices in joy* a Hebraism used to intensify the verb, trans. *rejoices greatly*.

8 ἐλέγξει (< ἐλέγχ-σει) fut. of ἐλέγχω.

11 ὀλιγόπιστοι is vocative; in English we must supply *you* and translate [*you*] *of little faith*.

12 Supply ἐστί; ποία *which* agrees with ἐντολή and introduces the question.

14 ὁ προφήτης is the predicate; the subject is [*he*].

17 εἰς here should be translated by *in* rather than *into*.

18 Supply ἐστί; τοῖς οὐρανοῖς translate by the singular *heaven*; the plural is often used of heaven when conceived as the abode of God.

19 ἀνατολῶν … δυσμῶν Greek uses the plural for the directions *east* and *west*; ἥξουσιν fut. of ἥκω.

3.2/1 Vocabulary

The prepositions given in 3.1/5 are not listed below.

αἰώνιος, -ον *eternal*
ἀληθῶς (adv.) *truly*
ἁμαρτία, -ας, ἡ *sin*
ἀνατολή, -ῆς, ἡ (in pl.) *east*
ἀσκός, -οῦ, ὁ *wine-skin*
βάλλω *put*
βασιλεία, -ας, ἡ *kingdom*
γράφω *write, write of*
δειλός, -ή, -όν *timid*
δικαιοσύνη, -ης, ἡ *justice*
δοξάζω *praise*
δυσμή, -ῆς, ἡ (in pl.) *west*
ἐλέγχω *convict*
ἐντολή, -ῆς, ἡ *commandment*
ἔτι (adv.) *still*
   οὐ … ἔτι *no longer*
ζωή, -ῆς, ἡ *life*
ἤδη (adv.) *already*

ἥκω *come*
καθαρός, -ά, -όν *pure*
λόγος, -ου, ὁ *word*
μαθητής, -οῦ, ὁ *pupil*
Μωϋσῆς, -έως, ὁ *Moses* (11.1/4)
νέος, -α, -ον *new, young*
νῆσος, -ου, ἡ *island*
νόμος, -ου, ὁ *law*
νυμφίος, -ου, ὁ *bridegroom*
οἶνος, -ου, ὁ *wine*
ὀλιγόπιστος, -ον *possessing little faith*
ὀφθαλμός, -οῦ, ὁ *eye*
παλαιός, -ά, -όν *old*
ποιητής, -οῦ, ὁ *doer, one who complies with*
ποῖος, -α, -ον *which?, what?*

προφήτης, -ου, ὁ *prophet*
πύλη, -ης, ἡ *door*
σάββατον, -ου, τό *sabbath*
συναγωγή, -ῆς, ἡ *synagogue*
τελώνης -ου, ὁ *tax-collector*
τί (interrog.) *why?*
τρίτος, -η, -ον *third*
υἱός, -οῦ, ὁ *son*

ὑπό (prep. + acc.) *under*
φίλος, -ου, ὁ *friend*
φωνή, -ῆς, ἡ *voice*
χαίρω *rejoice*
χαρά, -ᾶς, ἡ *joy*
Χριστός, -οῦ, ὁ *Anointed One*
χρόνος, -ου, ὁ *time*
ὥρα, -ας, ἡ *hour*

unit 04

4.1 Grammar

4.1/1 Imperfect indicative, weak aorist indicative and infinitive of -ω verbs (active)

Both English and Greek have an imperfect tense (*I was giving money to the poor*; normally called the past continuous in English; in Greek it would be better termed the *past* imperfect) and an aorist (*I gave money to the poor*; normally called the simple past or past indefinite in English). The Greek imperfect can also refer to habitual action in the past, which we translate as *I used to give money to the poor*, but the aorist (in the indicative) simply tells us that an action (or state) occurred in the past.

In λύω and other verbs beginning with a consonant, the stem of the imperfect consists of the present stem (λυ-) with a prefixed ἐ, giving us ἔλυ-. This prefix is called the **augment** because it increases the length of the stem.

The aorist stem is formed in one of two ways:

- The **weak** aorist, where σ is added to the present stem: λυ + σ > λυσ- (the stem is identical to that of the future).
- The **strong** aorist, where the present stem is modified in some other way, such as changing the vowel (cf. English *break > broke*). This form of the aorist is treated at 7.1/1.

It is necessary to learn whether the aorist of a particular verb is weak or strong, but most are weak. The augment must be used with both aorists in the indicative (e.g. the aorist indicative stem of λύω is ἐλυσ-) but not in the other moods.

There are similarities between the endings of the imperfect and the weak aorist but in the latter the vowel immediately following the stem is α in five of the six forms, while in the imperfect there is the same pattern of o- and e- sounds as in the present (cf. 2.1/5 note 5):

		IMPERFECT	WEAK AORIST
SINGULAR	1	ἔλυ-ον *I was loosening, used to loosen*	ἔλυσ-α *I loosened*
	2	ἔλυ-ες	ἔλυσ-ας
	3	ἔλυ-ε(ν)	ἔλυσ-ε(ν)
PLURAL	1	ἐλύ-ομεν	ἐλύσ-αμεν
	2	ἐλύ-ετε	ἐλύσ-ατε
	3	ἔλυ-ον	ἔλυσ-αν
INFINITIVE		——	λῦσ-αι

While the aorist indicative views something that happened in the past as a simple event, the imperfect indicative views it as a process, either continuous or habitual; the choice between *I was loosening* (continuous action) and *I used to loosen* (habitual action) depends on the context. The difference between the two tenses usually depends on how we perceive a past happening. In a particular context we may see this simply as something that occurred in the past (*we stayed in Spain last year*; the aorist would be used here in Greek), but in another context we may want to describe the same happening as something continuous (*we were staying in Spain last year when the hijacking occurred*) or repeated (*we used to stay in Spain every time we had sufficient money*; the imperfect would be used for both in Greek).There are, of course, many past actions and events which we do not normally describe in more than one way (*Queen Victoria died in 1902*). The term **aspect** is used for this distinction in perspective. Both these tenses of the indicative describe something that happened in the past, but the aorist indicative expresses a **momentary** aspect while the imperfect a **continuous** or **habitual** aspect.

The distinction between the imperfect and the aorist applies to the **infinitives** of the **present** and **aorist** (the imperfect does **not** have an infinitive); λύειν and λῦσαι can both be translated as *to loosen* with no specific time reference. Here Greek has a distinction we do not have in English: the present infinitive is used for an action or event which is seen as going on, in the process of happening or being repeated, while the aorist infinitive is used for an action or event which is seen simply as a single happening. Often both are to be translated in English simply by a present infinitive:

ἔπεμψεν αὐτὸν (*him*) εἰς τοὺς ἀγροὺς βόσκειν χοίρους. (*Lk 15.15) *He sent him into the fields to feed pigs.* (the prodigal son is not to feed pigs on one single occasion but whenever this is required).

τίς ἄξιος ἀνοῖξαι τὸ βιβλίον καὶ λῦσαι τὰς σφραγῖδας; (*Rev 5.2) *Who [is] worthy to open the book and loosen the seals?* (two single actions are mentioned; ἀνοῖξαι (ἀνοῖγ- + σαι from ἀνοίγω *open*) and λῦσαι are both aorist infinitives).

The imperfect exists only in the indicative but the aorist has other moods (13.1/1). The distinction of aspect, not time, between the present and aorist infinitives also exists between the present and aorist subjunctive and imperative (13.1/2, 17.1/1).

Notes

1 The indicative forms of the three **historic** tenses (the tenses whose indicative describes something in the past, viz imperfect, aorist, pluperfect (16.1/2)) must be prefixed with the augment, but the augment is not used with the three **primary** tenses (the tenses whose indicative describes something in the present or future, viz present, future, perfect (14.1/2)). An important difference in form exists between the two groups in the 3rd pl. ind. act. ending where the historic tenses have a final -ν (e.g. ἔλυον, ἔλυσαν), but the primary tenses end in -σι(ν) (e.g. λύουσι(ν), λύσουσι(ν)).

2 There are two types of augment:

   (i) the **syllabic** augment (see above), which is used with verbs beginning with a consonant. It is called syllabic because an extra syllable is added to the forms where it is used. In earlier Greek an initial ρ was doubled (e.g. ῥίπτω *throw*, impf. ἔρριπτον), but in NT Greek this rule is not always observed; hence we find ἐρρ- and ἐρ- .

   (ii) the **temporal** augment, which is used with verbs beginning with a vowel or diphthong. It is called temporal because it originally lengthened the time required to pronounce the initial syllable according to the following table:

α > η	ε > η	ο > ω
αυ > ηυ	ει > η	οι > ῳ (or οι)
αι > ῃ	ευ > ηυ (or ευ)	
ι, η, υ and ω remain unchanged		

Note that α is lengthened to η and that ι, when the second element of a diphthong, becomes subscript. Examples of the temporal augment are: ἀκούω *hear,* impf. ἤκουον, aor. ἤκουσα; ἐλπίζω *hope,* impf. ἤλπιζον, aor. ἤλπισα; οἰκοδομέω *build,* impf. ᾠκοδόμουν, aor. ᾠκοδόμησα (the forms ἤλπισα, ᾠκοδόμουν, ᾠκοδόμησα will be explained at 6.1/4(b) and 5.1/2 respectively). ευ and οι are often not changed, e.g. εὐκαιρέω *spend time,* impf. stem εὐκαιρε- or ηὐκαιρε-. ἔχω *have* forms its imperfect irregularly: εἶχον; ἐάω *allow* has the same temporal augment (ει) in both the imperfect and aorist.

3 The imperfect has two other meanings, which are less common: *began to (I began to teach* etc. **inceptive imperfect)** and *tried to (I tried to prevent* etc. **conative imperfect);** the context will show what meaning is intended.

4 As the endings of the lst s. and 3rd pl. of the imperfect indicative active are the same we must always use the context of a particular form to determine which person is meant.

5 The imperfect of εἰμί is irregular: ἤμην *I was,* ἦς or ἦσθα *you* (s.) *were,* ἦν *he/she/it was,* ἦμεν or ἤμεθα *we were,* ἦτε *you* (pl.) *were,* ἦσαν *they were.* This is the only past tense of εἰμί. For a table of the forms of εἰμί see **Appendix 3.**

4.1/2 Personal pronouns

The first and second person pronouns are declined in Greek as follows:

	First person		Second person	
	SINGULAR			
Nom.	ἐγώ	*I*	σύ (also voc.)	*you* (s.)
Acc.	ἐμέ, με	*me*	σέ, σε	*you*
Gen.	ἐμοῦ, μου	*of me*	σοῦ, σου	*of you*
Dat.	ἐμοί, μοι	*to/for me*	σοί, σοι	*to/for you*
	PLURAL			
Nom.	ἡμεῖς	*we*	ὑμεῖς (also voc.)	*you* (pl.)
Acc.	ἡμᾶς	*us*	ὑμᾶς	*you*
Gen.	ἡμῶν	*of us*	ὑμῶν	*of you*
Dat.	ἡμῖν	*to/for us*	ὑμῖν	*to/for you*

The forms without an accent (με, μου, μοι, σε, σου, σοι) are unemphatic and enclitic, i.e. their accent is thrown back on to the preceding word (see **Appendix 7,** (d)): διώκει με ὁ τελώνης *the tax-collector is pursuing me.* The other forms are emphatic: οὐ σέ, ἀλλὰ ἐμὲ διώκει ὁ τελώνης *it's me, not you, that the tax-collector is pursuing* (lit. *the tax-collector is pursuing not you* *but me*). With prepositions the emphatic forms are used, e.g. μετὰ σοῦ *with you,* except usually with πρός: πρός με *towards me.* The nominative forms, ἐγώ, σύ, ἡμεῖς, ὑμεῖς, are only used when emphasis is required because the endings of verbs indicate the person involved, e.g. διώκομεν τὸν τελώνην *we are pursuing the tax-collector* but if emphasis is needed we have ἡμεῖς διώκομεν τὸν τελώνην *we are pursuing the tax-collector* or *it's us who are pursuing the tax-collector.*

As an unemphatic third person pronoun Greek has αὐτός, -ή, -ό *he, she, it* (pl. *they*), which is declined exactly like the corresponding forms of καλός (3.1/3) except that the neuter nominative and accusative singular is αὐτό; the -o ending in these cases also occurs in the definite article (τό), the relative pronoun (ὅ, 9.1/2) the demonstratives τοῦτο, ἐκεῖνο (9.1/1) and ἄλλο *other.*

	SINGULAR			PLURAL		
	M.	F.	N.	M.	F.	N.
Nom.	αὐτ-ός	αὐτ-ή	αὐτ-ό	αὐτ-οί	αὐτ-αί	αὐτ-ά
Acc.	αὐτ-όν	αὐτ-ήν	αὐτ-ό	αὐτ-ούς	αὐτ-άς	αὐτ-ά
Gen.	αὐτ-οῦ	αὐτ-ῆς	αὐτ-οῦ	αὐτ-ῶν	αὐτ-ῶν	αὐτ-ῶν
Dat.	αὐτ-ῷ	αὐτ-ῇ	αὐτ-ῷ	αὐτ-οῖς	αὐτ-αῖς	αὐτ-οῖς

Examples of αὐτός are: οἱ ἑπτὰ ἔσχον αὐτὴν γυναῖκα (*Lk 20.33) *the seven had her* [*as*] *wife*; ἐδίδασκεν αὐτοὺς ἐν τῇ συναγωγῇ αὐτῶν (Mt 13.54) *he used to teach them in their synagogue.*

In earlier Greek αὐτός, -ή, -ό was employed in the nominative with the meaning *(he) himself, (she) herself, (it) itself* (although the oblique cases were used without any notion of emphasis in the sense *him, her, it,* as in NT Greek). Vestiges of this older use remain in the NT, but generally the nominative forms occur where no particular emphasis is involved, e.g. αὐτὸς δὲ ἐκάθευδεν (Mt 8.24) *but he was sleeping,* although a pronoun is unnecessary in such a context (cf. 2.1/4). Where emphasis is required in the nominative or the oblique cases Greek uses the demonstrative pronouns (9.1/1). For other uses of αὐτός see 9.1/3.

Notes

1 The possessive genitive of the **unemphatic** personal pronoun is usually placed after the noun which it qualifies, εἰς τὸν οἶκον μου *into my house* (lit. *into the house of me*); ἐκ τοῦ οἴκου αὐτῶν *from their house* (lit. *from the house of them*);

occasionally it occurs before the phrase containing the word it qualifies, μου ὑπὸ τὴν στέγην (Mt 8.8) *under my roof*. For the position of the genitive of the **emphatic** personal pronouns see 9.1/5.

2 In the plural of αὐτός Greek distinguishes between the genders, but as we cannot do this in English we must translate αὐτοί and αὐταί by *they* or by *the men, the women* if the reference is to people and greater precision is required, e.g. εἶχεν αὐτὰς τρόμος (*Mk 16.8) lit. *fear held them* but as αὐτάς is feminine (and we know from the context that the reference is to people) we could also render *fear held the women*. The translation of the neuter αὐτά depends on the context (*they/them/these things* is usually adequate).

3 Because all nouns in Greek have gender, αὐτός is used to refer to a masculine noun of any sort, αὐτή to a feminine and αὐτό to a neuter, and in some contexts each would be translated by *it*, e.g. in τοῦ κυρίου γὰρ ἡ γῆ καὶ τὸ πλήρωμα αὐτῆς (1 Cor 10.26) *for the earth is the Lord's and everything in it* (lit. *and the contents of it*) αὐτῆς is feminine because it refers to the feminine noun γῆ but we must translate by *of it* because in English we have natural gender and nouns such as *earth* are regarded as neuter.

4.1/3 Non-Greek proper nouns

The vast majority of proper nouns in the New Testament, whether the names of people or those of places, are Semitic. In the Greek form given to these we see a distinction between those which in their original Hebrew or Aramaic form end in a consonant and those which end in a vowel.

The former are represented by a simple transliteration into Greek characters and are not declined. Because of differences between the Hebrew and Greek alphabets, the Greek form is often not a completely accurate representation. For example, Hebrew has a consonant which we represent in English as *j,* but nothing similar exists in Greek. Where this occurs at the beginning of a Semitic proper noun the Greek transliteration has an iota, although this is a vowel, not a consonant: Ἰακώβ *Jacob*. The English version of names of this type is often somewhat different from the Greek because we have gone back to the original, e.g. Δαυίδ *David*, Βηθλέεμ *Bethlehem*.[1]

---

[1] Where the English version of these names differs, the form used in this book is that given in *A Greek–English Lexicon of the New Testament and Other Early Christian Literature* (see **Suggestions for further study**).

As these nouns are not declined, we must discover their case from the context. Very often they are preceded by the definite article, e.g. Σαλμὼν ἐγέννησεν τὸν Βόες ἐκ τῆς Ῥαχάβ (*Mt 1.5) *Salmon begat Boaz from Rahab*; here τόν and τῆς indicate the case of the noun which each precedes; Σαλμών, which has no article, can only be the subject (who else is there to do the begetting?).

Names which in their Hebrew or Aramaic original end in a vowel are adapted to the Greek system of declension, e.g. Ἰησοῦς *Jesus* (2.1/2 note 4), Μαθθαῖος (2nd decl.) *Matthew*, Ἄννα (1st decl.; note rough breathing!) *Anna*, Ἰωάννης (1st decl. m.; gen. Ἰωάννου) *John*.

Among the exceptions to this general pattern are a few proper nouns which have both an indeclinable and a declinable form: Μαριάμ (indeclinable) and Μαρία (1st decl.) *Mary*, Ἰεροσαλήμ (indeclinable, used with the feminine article) and Ἰεροσόλυμα (2nd declension neuter plural; gen. Ἰεροσολύμων) *Jerusalem* (note that the second form has a rough breathing as well as other differences).

4.1/4 Connecting particles

Two striking differences between Greek and English style are:

(a) The connection of a sentence or phrase with what precedes to an extent that we would consider quite unnecessary in English.

(b) The use of an additional word to express a particular nuance with a word, phrase or sentence where in spoken English we would use a variation in the tone or emphasis of the voice.

For both purposes Greek employs **particles**. These are short, indeclinable words some of which are **postpositive**, i.e. they cannot occur as first word in the phrase or sentence where they are used (here and in the vocabulary these are marked with #); others such as καί *and* and ἀλλά *but,* which are not postpositive, are also called conjunctions.

Here we will deal mainly with connectives. Other particles will be explained as they occur in the reading and at 15.1/2.

After the beginning in a passage of Greek, most main clauses, whether they make up a full sentence or not, are connected to what precedes by a connecting particle. The commonest of these is δέ# *and,* which is regularly used to connect a string of main clauses where in English we would avoid any connecting word at all, e.g. Ἀβραὰμ ἐγέννησεν τὸν Ἰσαάκ, Ἰσαὰκ δὲ ἐγέννησεν τὸν Ἰακώβ, Ἰακὼβ δὲ ἐγέννησεν τὸν Ἰούδαν καὶ τοὺς ἀδελφοὺς αὐτοῦ (Mt 1.2) lit. *Abraham begat Isaac, and Isaac begat Jacob, and Jacob begat Judas and his brothers* but in English we would normally say *Abraham begat Isaac, Isaac begat Jacob, Jacob begat Judas and his brothers.* δέ# can also denote a slight contrast and be translated by *but:* ὑμεῖς ἔνδοξοι, ἡμεῖς δὲ ἄτιμοι (1 Cor 4.10) *You [are] famous but* (or *while*) *we [are] without honour.* A strongly contrasting *but* is expressed by ἀλλά, e.g. οὐκέτι ἐστὲ ξένοι καὶ πάροικοι, ἀλλὰ ἐστὲ συμπολῖται τῶν ἁγίων (Eph 2.19) *you are no longer strangers and aliens but you are fellow-citizens of God's people.*

The particle γάρ# *for, as,* which introduces the **reason** for what goes before, τίμιος ὁ γάμος … πόρνους γὰρ καὶ μοιχοὺς κρίνει ὁ θεός. (*Hb 13.4) *marriage [is] honorable, for God judges fornicators and adulterers.*

Similarly οὖν# *therefore, so,* introduces the **result** of what goes before, οἱ ἀδελφοὶ αὐτοῦ οὐκ ἐπίστευον εἰς αὐτόν. λέγει οὖν αὐτοῖς ὁ Ἰησοῦς, Ὁ καιρὸς ὁ ἐμὸς οὔπω πάρεστιν (*Jn 7.5f.) *his brothers did not believe in* (εἰς) *him. Therefore Jesus said to them, 'My* (ὁ ἐμὸς 9.1/5) *time is not yet come.'*

καί *and* is most often used as a simple conjunction connecting words, clauses or sentences, Πέτρος καὶ Ἀνδρέας *Peter and Andrew.* καὶ … καί means *both … and* καὶ ὁ ἄνεμος καὶ ἡ θάλασσα *both the wind and the sea,* and the same sense can also be conveyed by τε# … καί, but since τε# is postpositive (and enclitic; see **Appendix 7**, (d)), the above phrase would become ὅ τε ἄνεμος καὶ ἡ θάλασσα. τε# most commonly means *and,* e.g. ἡ Μεσοποταμία Ἰουδαία τε καὶ Καππαδοκία *Mesopotamia and Judaea and Cappadocia.*

καί is used **adverbially** in the sense *also, even, actually,* καὶ σύ, τέκνον *even you* (or *you too*), *[my] child*; in this usage καί stands immediately before the word it modifies. The negative of adverbial καί is οὐδέ, *not even,* e.g. οὐδὲ Σολομών (Mt 6.29) *not even Solomon.* As a conjunction οὐδέ also means *nor* or *and … not:* ὅπου κλέπται οὐ διορύσσουσιν οὐδὲ κλέπτουσιν (Mt 6.20) *where thieves do not break in* [lit. *dig through*] *nor steal* (we could also translate *and do not steal*).

4.2 Greek reading

An analysis of sentence 9 will be found in the key.

1 ἐν ἀρχῇ ἦν ὁ λόγος, καὶ ὁ λόγος ἦν πρὸς τὸν θεόν, καὶ θεὸς ἦν ὁ λόγος. (Jn 1.1)

2 ποῦ σου, θάνατε, τὸ κέντρον; (1 Cor 15.55)

3 εἶπαν (they said) αὐτῷ, Τί οὖν βαπτίζεις εἰ σὺ οὐκ εἶ ὁ Χριστὸς οὐδὲ Ἠλίας οὐδὲ ὁ προφήτης; (Jn 1.25)

4 ὁμοίως καθὼς ἐγένετο (happened) ἐν ταῖς ἡμέραις Λώτ, ἤσθιον, ἔπινον. (Lk 17.28)

5 εὐθὺς λέγουσιν αὐτῷ περὶ αὐτῆς. (Mk 1.30)

6 ἄγγελος δὲ κυρίου ἤνοιξε τὰς θύρας τῆς φυλακῆς. (*Ac 5.19)

7 κύριε, καλόν ἐστιν ἡμᾶς ὧδε εἶναι. (Mt 17.4)

8 νῦν ὑμεῖς οἱ Φαρισαῖοι τὸ ἔξωθεν τοῦ ποτηρίου καθαρίζετε, τὸ δὲ ἔσωθεν ὑμῶν γέμει ἁρπαγῆς καὶ πονηρίας. (*Lk 11.39)

9 οὐκέτι εἶ δοῦλος ἀλλὰ υἱός· εἰ δὲ υἱός, καὶ κληρονόμος διὰ θεοῦ. (Gal 4.7)

10 διό, ἀδελφοί, οὐκ ἐσμὲν παιδίσκης τέκνα ἀλλὰ τῆς ἐλευθέρας. (Gal 4.31)

11 ἐγὼ ἤμην δυνατὸς κωλῦσαι τὸν θεόν; (*Ac 11.17)

12 οὕτως καὶ ἡμεῖς, ὅτε ἦμεν νήπιοι, ὑπὸ τὰ στοιχεῖα τοῦ κόσμου ἤμεθα δεδουλωμένοι (enslaved). (Gal 4.3)

13 ἐδίδασκεν γὰρ τοὺς μαθητὰς αὐτοῦ καὶ ἔλεγεν αὐτοῖς. (Mk 9.31)

14 ἦσαν δὲ ἐν Ἀντιοχείᾳ προφῆται καὶ διδάσκαλοι ὅ τε Βαρναβᾶς καὶ Συμεών. (*Ac 13.1)

15 ἐξουσίαν ἔχω ἀπολῦσαί σε. (Jn 19.10)

16 ἐγώ εἰμι ὁ θεὸς Ἀβραὰμ καὶ ὁ θεὸς Ἰσαὰκ καὶ ὁ θεὸς Ἰακώβ. (Mt 22.32)

17 ἔλεγεν γὰρ ὁ Ἰωάννης αὐτῷ, Οὐκ ἔξεστίν σοι ἔχειν αὐτήν. (Mt 14.4)

18 ἴδε νῦν ἠκούσατε τὴν βλασφημίαν. (Mt 26.65)

19 ἰδοὺ ἐγὼ ἀποστέλλω ὑμᾶς ὡς πρόβατα ἐν μέσῳ λύκων. (Mt 10.16)

20 καὶ οἱ ἄνεμοι καὶ ἡ θάλασσα αὐτῷ ὑπακούουσιν. (Mt 8.27)

Notes

1 πρός here with.

2 Supply ἐστί.

3 Τί note the capital letter; as Greek does not use inverted commas to mark off direct speech (7.1/2), modern editions of the New Testament indicate its beginning in this way.

6 ἤνοιξε aorist of ἀνοίγω.

7 καλόν ἐστιν in impersonal expressions of this type the neuter form of the adjective is used; trans. *it is good.*

8 οἱ Φαρισαῖοι is in apposition to ὑμεῖς (trans. *you, the Pharisees,* or *you Pharisees*); ἔξωθεν and ἔσωθεν are adverbs used as noun-substitutes and used in much the same way as their English equivalents *outside* and *inside.*

9 Supply εἶ twice in the second sentence; καί *also.*

12 καί *even*; both forms of the 1st pl. imperf. of εἰμί (ἦμεν, ἤμεθα) occur in this verse; στοιχεῖα the exact meaning is disputed – perhaps the *elemental spirits* of contemporary paganism.

13 ἐδίδασκεν and ἔλεγεν are inceptive imperfects (4.1/1 note 3) – translate *began to …*

16 Ἀβραάμ, Ἰσαάκ, Ἰακώβ are all indeclinable names and the context shows that they must be understood as genitives (*of Abraham* etc.).

18 ἴδε a common particle (originally an imperative 17.1/1) used as an exclamation to draw attention to something, *there (you are!).*

19 ἰδού another particle used as an exclamation, *behold!*

20 ὑπακούω (lit. *be obedient*) is followed by the dative (here αὐτῷ)

4.2/1 Vocabulary

Ἀβραάμ, ὁ (indecl.) *Abraham*
ἄγγελος, -ου, ὁ *angel*
ἀδελφός, -οῦ, ὁ *brother*
ἀλλά (conj.) *but*
ἄνεμος, -ου, ὁ *wind*
ἀνοίγω *open*
Ἀντιόχεια, -ας, ἡ *Antioch*
ἀπολύω *free*
ἁρπαγή, -ῆς, ἡ *greed*
ἀρχή, -ῆς, ἡ *beginning*
βαπτίζω *baptize*
Βαρναβᾶς, -ᾶ, ὁ *Barnabas*
βλασφημία, -ας, ἡ *blasphemy*
γέμω (+ gen.) *be full (of)*
διό (adv.) *therefore*
δυνατός, -ή, -όν *able*
εἰ (conj.) *if*

ἐλεύθερος, -α, -ον *free*
ἔξεστι(ν) (+ dat.) *it is permitted (to)*
ἐξουσία, -ας, ἡ *authority, power*
ἔξωθεν (adv.) *outside*
ἔσωθεν (adv.) *inside*
εὐθύς (adv.) *immediately*
Ἠλίας, -ου, ὁ *Elijah*
ἡμέρα, -ας, ἡ *day*
θάνατος, -ου, ὁ *death*
θύρα, -ας, ἡ *door*
Ἰακώβ, ὁ (indecl.) *Jacob*
ἴδε (exclamation) *there (you are!)*
ἰδού (exclamation) *behold!*
Ἰσαάκ, ὁ (indecl.) *Isaac*

Ἰωάννης, -ου, ὁ   *John*
καθώς (conj.)   *just as*
κέντρον, -ου, τό   *sting*
κληρονόμος, -ου, ὁ   *heir*
κωλύω   *hinder*
λύκος, -ου, ὁ   *wolf*
Λώτ, ὁ (indecl.)   *Lot*
μαθητής, -οῦ, ὁ   *disciple*
μέσῳ (+ gen.)   *in the midst
(of)*
νήπιος, -α, -ον   *very young*, (as
noun) *young child*
νῦν (adv.)   *now*
ὁμοίως (adv.)   *similarly*
ὅτε (conj.)   *when*
οὐκέτι (adv.)   *no longer*

οὕτως (adv.)   *thus, in this way*
παιδίσκη, -ης, ἡ   *slave girl*
πονηρία, -ας, ἡ   *wickedness*
ποτήριον, -ου, τό   *cup*
ποῦ (interrog.)   *where?*
πρόβατον, -ου, τό   *sheep*
στοιχεῖον, -ου, τό   *element* (see
note on 12)
Συμεών, ὁ (indecl.)   *Symeon*
τέκνον, -ου, τό   *child*
ὑπακούω (+ dat.)   *be obedient
(to), obey*
Φαρισαῖος, -ου, ὁ   *Pharisee*
φυλακή, -ῆς, ἡ   *prison*
ὧδε (adv.)   *here*

4.3 Excursus

Books in antiquity – the papyrus roll

In the first century AD, when the New Testament was written, the normal form of books and the manner of producing them were completely different from what we have today. Books throughout the whole of the Roman empire were the same as they had been four centuries earlier in the heyday of Greek civilization; the Greeks themselves had taken over techniques from Egypt, where both writing and papyrus, the ancient equivalent of paper, had been invented.

Printing was over a thousand years away, and every copy of a book had to be individually written out by hand. This did not make the cost of books high as the scribes who produced them were usually slaves. However, apart from the time and labour needed to transcribe each and every copy of a book, the method had a fatal flaw: unlike the results of printing, no two copies could ever be guaranteed to be exactly identical. Even today with computers it is difficult to avoid introducing errors when making a copy of a document – how much more so when the person doing the copy is using pen and ink. To ensure that a book would circulate in a reasonably accurate form, it would have been necessary to proofread every copy, and this required a person of some education. Even with this precaution it was inevitable that each copy of a book had its own peculiar variations and, as the process was repeated over centuries, more variations crept into the text. To know exactly what the author had originally written became progressively more difficult.

Equally surprising to a modern reader was the traditional form of a book. Ever since its invention by the Egyptians a book consisted of a roll of papyrus, a material resembling paper, with a length of 6–8 metres (20 to 26 feet) and a width of 250 mm (10 inches), though sizes varied considerably. The text was written on this in narrow columns which were at right angles to the roll's length. A roll consisted of up to twenty papyrus sheets, which were slightly overlapped to allow for gluing. To make up the sheets themselves, the stalks of the papyrus plant, which resembled a very large reed and grew in profusion by the Nile, were shredded into thin strips. A number of these were placed side by side to make up the dimension of the sheet required (usually about 250 x 200 mm. [10 x 8 inches]) and these were completely covered with another layer of strips placed at right-angles to the first. As this was done with the strips still moist, the sap acted as a glue when the sheet was placed in a press. After removal the sheet was smoothed with pumice, or some similar abrasive, and trimmed. Many examples of papyrus rolls have survived and show that as a material for writing it is comparable to paper, though it differs in being less flexible.

After a roll had been made up, a turned wooden rod, resembling a small rolling pin, was added to each end, and projecting handles of these allowed the long papyrus strip to be rolled up from either direction. A text could then be transcribed on to one side of the roll – the back was left blank – and the roll was then ready for use. The lower handle of the rod on the outer end was held in the left hand and the corresponding handle of the other rod in the right. As the beginning of the roll was unwound, the first columns were read. The reader's right and left hands kept unrolling and rolling up respectively until the end was reached, when the roll, like a modern video cassette, had to be rewound for the next user. The whole procedure was best performed if the roll was on the knees of the reader when seated (much the same as when we read a book by the fire), and it is in this position that ancient sculpture depict a person reading. Papyrus rolls were not suited to desks as we know them.

However, the reader's problems were not confined to manipulating the roll, as conventions of presenting a text were different from those today. Scribes wrote in capitals as an equivalent of our lower case had yet to develop. This in itself would not have created difficulty, but a line of capitals gave no indication of where one word ended and the next began; words were simply not separated. In addition, breathings and accents were omitted and punctuation was rarely given. The unfortunate reader was faced with a string of letters and was obliged to split these up, first into words, then into clauses and then into sentences. As an example we may take a sentence from 1 Cor 12.15, which would appear in a text of the early centuries of the Christian era as follows:

OTIOYKEIMIXEIPOYKEIMIEKTOYCΩMATOC i.e. ὅτι οὐκ εἰμὶ χείρ, οὐκ εἰμὶ ἐκ τοῦ σώματος *because I am not a hand I am not [part] of the body* (note that the form of the sigma used at this period was different).

It is little wonder that ancient readers always read aloud. The act of articulation would have helped them recognize the different divisions (words, clauses, sentences) which had to be made before a text could be understood.

The upper limit of what could be put on one roll was about 18,000 words (seventy pages of a modern book); a longer one would have been too cumbersome to use. Most works of Greek and Roman literature are of course much longer and so had to be accommodated on two or more rolls, and this led to longer poems and prose works being written (i.e. split up) in sections, each of which was contained within one roll. The Greek and Latin terms which we translate by *book* (βιβλίον, *liber*) refer to a single papyrus roll. Thus a longer literary work contained as many books as the rolls necessary to record it; the *Aeneid* of the Roman poet Vergil is in twelve books and so took up twelve rolls. For the New Testament this meant that the Gospels and Acts would have originally circulated and been preserved in five separate rolls. Shorter books could have been combined on to a single roll. No roll contained what we today would consider a book of normal size (i.e. 200–300 pages).

We do not have the original author's copy of any part of the New Testament. The earliest texts we possess are papyrus fragments dating from the third century AD. How many times their words had been re-copied since the author first put pen to papyrus we have no way of knowing.

5.1 Grammar

5.1/1 Third declension – consonant stem nouns (1)

The third declension contains nouns of all three genders and is divided into two classes, nouns with stems ending in a consonant and nouns with stems ending in a vowel or diphthong. Within the sub-groups of each class masculine and feminine nouns have the same case endings but neuters always follow the rule previously given (3.1/1) for the nominative, vocative and accusative (not every sub-group has each gender). The gender of a third declension noun is only sometimes predictable from its ending.

The stem of all consonant stem nouns is obtained by subtracting -ος from the genitive singular (e.g. φλόξ *flame*, gen. φλογός, stem φλογ-); the other case endings are added to this. As the stem is modified in the nominative singular, both nominative and genitive singular must be learnt. The vocative is only given in the following tables and elsewhere for nouns where a form different from the nominative occurs in the NT.

(a) *Stems in* κ, γ, χ *(palatals),* π, β, φ *(labials), and* τ, δ, θ *(dentals)*

Masculine and feminine nouns in these sub-groups have a nominative singular in ς, which combines with, or replaces, the final consonant of the stem as follows:

κ/γ/χ + ς > ξ; π/β/φ + ς > ψ; τ/δ/θ + ς > ς

Similar changes occur with the dative ending -σι(ν) (and with the σ of the weak aorist stem – see 6.1/4).

	φύλαξ (m) *guard*	σκόλοψ (m) *thorn*	ἐλπίς (f) *hope*	σῶμα (n) *body*
stem	φυλακ-	σκολοπ-	ἐλπιδ-	σωματ-

SINGULAR

Nom.	φύλαξ	σκόλοψ	ἐλπίς	σῶμα
Acc.	φύλακ-α	σκόλοπ-α	ἐλπίδ-α	σῶμα
Gen.	φύλακ-ος	σκόλοπ-ος	ἐλπίδ-ος	σώματ-ος
Dat.	φύλακ-ι	σκόλοπ-ι	ἐλπίδ-ι	σώματ-ι

PLURAL

Nom.	φύλακ-ες	σκόλοπ-ες	ἐλπίδ-ες	σώματ-α
Acc.	φύλακ-ας	σκόλοπ-ας	ἐλπίδ-ας	σώματ-α
Gen.	φυλάκ-ων	σκολόπ-ων	ἐλπίδ-ων	σωμάτ-ων
Dat.	φύλαξι(ν)	σκόλοψι(ν)	ἐλπί-σι(ν)	σώμα-σι

A number of abstract nouns (all feminine) have a stem in τητ and only occur in the singular, e.g. νεότης *youth*, ἁγιότης *holiness*, σεμνότης *dignity*. The first is declined: nom. νεότης, acc. νεότητα, gen. νεότητος, dat. νεότητι.

Neuters all have a τ stem. The vast majority of these have a nominative singular in -μα and are declined like σῶμα. A few have -ας in the nominative singular but are otherwise declined in the same way, e.g. κέρας, κέρατος *horn*.

(b) **Stems in ντ (all masculine)**

Nouns in -ντ have a nominative singular in -ας or -ων. In the dative plural ντ + σ becomes σ, with lengthening of the preceding α (as is shown by the accent) but in ἄρχων and similar words the o of the stem is lengthened to ου (not ω). This lengthening occurs to compensate for the reduction of three consonants to one.

	ἱμάς (m) *strap*		ἄρχων (m) *ruler*	
stem	ἱμαντ-		ἀρχοντ-	

	SINGULAR	PLURAL	SINGULAR	PLURAL
Nom.	ἱμάς	ἱμάντ-ες	ἄρχων	ἄρχοντ-ες
Acc.	ἱμάντ-α	ἱμάντ-ας	ἄρχοντ-α	ἄρχοντ-ας
Gen.	ἱμάντ-ος	ἱμάντ-ων	ἄρχοντ-ος	ἀρχόντ-ων
Dat.	ἱμάντ-ι	ἱμᾶ-σι(ν)	ἄρχοντ-ι	ἄρχου-σι(ν)

Notes

1 Some nouns with these stems are slightly irregular, mostly in the nominative singular. The most common are:

γόνυ, γόνατος (n)   *knee*   ὀδούς, ὀδόντος (m)   *tooth*
γυνή, γυναικός (f)   *woman*   οὖς, ὠτός (n)   *ear*
  (voc. s. γύναι)   παῖς, παιδός (m or f)   *child*;
θρίξ, τριχός (f)   *hair* (dat. pl.   *slave*
  θριξί(ν))   πούς, ποδός (m)   *foot*
νύξ, νυκτός (f)   *night* (dat.   ὕδωρ, ὕδατος (n)   *water*
  pl. νυξί(ν))   φῶς, φωτός (n)   *light*

2 ἔρις, ἔριδος (f) *strife,* has an irregular accusative singular ἔριν. χάρις, χάριτος (f) *favour, grace* has an accusative χάριν or χάριτα.

5.1/2 Contracted verbs

We have already met verbs with stems ending in ι and υ (ἐσθί-ω *eat*, λύ-ω *loosen*) where an ending is simply added to the stem. However, verbs whose stems end in α, ε or ο contract their stem vowel with the initial vowel of the endings in the present and imperfect; in other tenses, where the stem is formed by the addition of a consonant (e.g. σ in the future and aorist – see note 2), the possibility of contraction does not arise. Examples of contracted verbs are: τιμά-ω *honour,* ποιέ-ω *do, make,* δηλό-ω *make clear, show.* These verbs are always cited in dictionaries and vocabularies in their **uncontracted** form (τιμάω, ποιέω, δηλόω) to allow the user to identify the stem. Paradigms for the three types are given in **Appendix 2**. The endings are the same as for λύω.[1] The rules for contraction are as follows:

(a) *Stems in α (model τιμάω)*
  α + an e-sound (ε, η) > α: ἐτίμα (ἐτίμα-ε)
  α + an o-sound (ο, ου, ω) > ω: τιμῶσι (τιμά-ουσι); τιμῶμεν (τιμά-ομεν)
  α + an ι-diphthong (ει, ῃ, οι) obeys the above rules but retains the iota as a subscript in the contracted form: τιμᾷ (τιμά-ει)

The combinations of α + η/ῃ/οι occur in forms treated in future units.

---

[1] For the rules governing the accentuation of contracted verbs see **Appendix 7**, (b) (i).

(b) *Stems in ε* (*model* ποιέω)

  ε + ε > ει: ποιεῖτε (ποιέ-ετε)

  ε + ο > ου: ἐποίουν (ἐποίε-ον)

  ε disappears before a long vowel or diphthong: ποιῶ (ποιέ-ω); ποιοῦσι (ποιέ-ουσι).

(c) *Stems in* ο (*model* δηλόω)

  ο + ε/ο/ου > ου: ἐδήλου (ἐδήλο-ε); δηλοῦμεν (δηλό-ομεν); δηλοῦσι (δηλό-ουσι)

  ο + η/ω > ω: δηλῶ (δηλό-ω)

  ο + an ι-diphthong (ει, οι, η) > οι: δηλοῖ (δηλό-ει)

  The combinations ο + η/οι/η occur in forms treated in future units.

The above vowel contractions cover all forms of contracted verbs; they also occur in other parts of speech.

Future and weak aorist active of contracted verbs

The future and weak aorist active stems of contracted verbs are formed by lengthening the stem vowel before adding the usual σ (see 2.1/5, 4.1/1):

	PRESENT	FUTURE	AORIST	
α > η	τιμάω	τιμήσω	ἐτίμησα	*honour*
ε > η	ποιέω	ποιήσω	ἐποίησα	*do, make*
ο > ω	δηλόω	δηλώσω	ἐδήλωσα	*make clear, show*

A few verbs do not lengthen the final vowel of the stem:

γελάω	γελάσω	ἐγέλασα	*laugh*
πεινάω	πεινάσω	ἐπείνασα	*be hungry*
καλέω	καλέσω	ἐκάλεσα	*call*
τελέω	τελέσω	ἐτέλεσα	*complete*

Notes

1 In the present infinitive active α- and ο-stems contract to -αν and -ουν respectively (**not** -ᾳν and -οιν) giving τιμᾶν from τιμάω and δηλοῦν from δηλόω. The corresponding form of ποιέω is the expected ποιεῖν.

2 Contracted verbs in α where the alpha is preceded by ε, ι or ρ form their future and aorist stem in -ασ (not -ησ), e.g. κοπιάω *work hard*, aorist ἐκοπίασα.

3 A contracted future sometimes occurs in a few verbs in -ίζω (6.1/4(b)) and in all verbs with stems in λ, ν, ρ (11.1/3). These futures have a stem in ε (i.e. the contraction is -ῶ, -εῖς, -εῖ, etc., exactly as the present of ποιέω), e.g. ἐλπίζω *hope*, future ἐλπιῶ.

4 ζάω *be alive* contracts to η where other -άω verbs have α: pres.
ind. act. ζῶ, ζῇς, ζῇ, ζῶμεν, ζῆτε, ζῶσι(ν), inf. ζῆν; in the impf.
ind. act. the only forms that occur are ἔζων (1st s.), ἐζῆτε
(2nd pl.).

5 Disyllabic verbs in -εω (as πλέω *sail,* πνέω *breathe,* ῥέω *flow*)
contract only when ε is followed by ε. The pres. ind. act. of
πλέω is πλέω, πλεῖς, πλεῖ, πλέομεν, πλεῖτε, πλέουσι(ν); impf.
ἔπλεον, ἔπλεις, ἔπλει, ἐπλέομεν, ἐπλεῖτε, ἔπλεον. The 3rd s.
act. of an otherwise obsolete verb of this type δέω *need,* pres.
δεῖ, impf. ἔδει, is used impersonally in the sense of *it is/was
necessary.* It is construed with the **accusative** of the person
involved and an infinitive: τί με δεῖ ποιεῖν; (Ac 16.30) *What
is it necessary for me to do?*

5.1/3 Further uses of the definite article

In English the definite article can be used with an adjective to
form a noun-equivalent: *only the good die young; only the brave
deserve the fair.* This type of expression is more common in
Greek where the definite article can be prefixed to various parts
of speech (adjective, adverb, infinitive) or a prepositional phrase
to form a noun equivalent: ὁ πονηρός *the evil* [*one*], i.e. *the
Devil;* ἡ σοφή *the wise* [*woman*]; ὁ πλησίον *the nearby* [*man*] i.e.
the neighbour; οἱ παρὰ τὴν ὁδόν (Mk 4.15) *the* [*men*] *by the road*
(the last example can also mean *the* [*people*] *by the road,* as
Greek uses the masculine article to refer to mixed groups);
Πέτρος καὶ οἱ σὺν αὐτῷ (Lk 9.32) *Peter and those with him.* The
neuter singular article (τό) is used with adjectives to express
abstractions: τὸ ἀγαθόν σου (Phlm 14) *your goodness,* τὸ
χρηστὸν τοῦ θεοῦ (Ro 2.4) *the kindness of God.* Similarly, the
neuter plural article (τά) can be followed by a phrase and has the
literal meaning of *the* [*things*] ... : τὰ νῦν *the* [*things*] *now* i.e.
the present; τὰ ὧδε (Col 4.9) *the* [*things*] *here* i.e. *matters here;*
τὰ κατὰ τὸν Παῦλον (Ac 25.14) lit. *the* [*things*] *concerning Paul*
i.e. *Paul's circumstances;* τὰ περὶ τοῦ Ἰησοῦ (Ac 18.25) *the
[things, i.e. facts] about Jesus:* our translation must take the
context into account.

The article used with a prepositional phrase can follow a noun
and qualify it; such expressions must sometimes be translated by
an adjectival clause: Πάτερ ἡμῶν ὁ ἐν τοῖς οὐρανοῖς (Mt 6.9) lit.
Father (Πάτερ) *of us, the* [*one*] *in the heavens,* i.e. *our Father
who art in heaven.*

Each of these noun-equivalents functions exactly like any normal noun, and the case of the article (and of an accompanying adjective) varies according to a particular context: λέγει τοῖς ἐκεῖ ... (Mt 26.71) *he says to the men there...*; περὶ τοῦ κακοῦ (Jn 18.23) *concerning the evil [thing]* i.e. *crime.*

When put before an infinitive (the **articular infinitive**, i.e. the article + an infinitive) τό forms an equivalent of a verbal noun in English: τὸ γράφειν ὑμῖν (2 Cor 9.1) *the [act of] writing to you* or simply *writing to you*; τὸ φεύγειν *the [act of] fleeing, flight.* This construction is very common in the NT and it can occur after prepositions with the article put in the appropriate case: ἐν τῷ ἐλαύνειν (Mk 6.48) *in the [act of] rowing*; διὰ τὸ ἀκούειν περὶ αὐτοῦ (Lk 23.8) *on account of hearing about him.* Its use after the preposition ἐν is often the equivalent of an adverbial clause of time and must be so translated: ἐν τῷ σπείρειν αὐτὸν (Mt 13.4) *in the [act of] him sowing* i.e. *while he was sowing.* When the subject of the infinitive is expressed, as it is here, it is put in the accusative (here αὐτόν; cf. the accusative pronoun *him* in the English *for him to want more money is ridiculous*); an example of a noun so used is ἐν τῷ καθεύδειν τοὺς ἀνθρώπους (*Mt 13.25) *while the people were sleeping.*

The article can also be used as a third person pronoun when followed by δέ viz ὁ δὲ ... *and he ...*; ἡ δὲ ... *and she ...*; οἱ δὲ ... *and they...*: ὁ δὲ ἔφη αὐτοῖς (Mt 13.28) *and he said to them*; ἡ δὲ ἤνοιξεν τοὺς ὀφθαλμοὺς αὐτῆς (Ac 9.40) *and she opened her eyes* (lit. *the eyes of her*); οἱ δὲ λέγουσιν αὐτῷ (Mt 14.17) *and they say to him.*

Notes

1 Adjectives without the definite article can also be used as nouns but they then have an indefinite sense: προνοοῦμεν γὰρ καλά (2 Cor 8.21) *for we have regard for fair [actions].* When used indefinitely in the singular an adjective is normally accompanied by the indefinite pronoun τις (10.1/1).

2 In expressions such as Ἰάκωβος ὁ τοῦ Ζεβεδαίου (Mt 10.2) *James, the [son] of Zebedee* the article is followed by the genitive and the word for son or daughter is omitted. In societies which do not use surnames, the name of a person's father is often given to achieve greater precision.

5.2 Greek reading

1 The following are phrases; some of those containing an infinitive would be best translated by a subordinate clause. (i) εἰς τὸ πέραν. (Mt 8.18) (ii) ἐν δὲ τῷ ὑποστρέφειν τὸν Ἰησοῦν. (Lk 8.40) (iii) ἐν δὲ τῷ λαλῆσαι. (Lk 11.37) (iv) τὸ ἀγαπᾶν τὸν πλησίον. (Mk 12.33) (v) πρὸ τοῦ ὑμᾶς αἰτῆσαι αὐτόν. (Mt 6.8) (vi) τὰ Καίσαρος (Mt 22.21) (vii) τὰ παρ' ὑμῶν. (Phil 4.18) (viii) οἱ ἀπὸ τῆς ἐκκλησίας. (*Ac 12.1) (ix) τὰ μωρὰ τοῦ κόσμου. (1 Cor 1.27) (x) τὰ κρυπτὰ τῆς καρδίας. (1 Cor 14.25)

2 Ἰησοῦς ἐμαρτύρησεν ὅτι προφήτης ἐν τῇ ἰδίᾳ πατρίδι τιμὴν οὐκ ἔχει. (Jn 4.44)

3 καὶ διὰ τὸ ὁμότεχνον εἶναι ἔμενεν παρ' αὐτοῖς. (Ac 18.3)

4 ἠρώτησαν αὐτόν, Τί οὖν σύ; Ἡλίας εἶ; καὶ λέγει, Οὐκ εἰμί. (Jn 1.21)

5 ἐθαύμαζον ἐν τῷ χρονίζειν ἐν τῷ ναῷ αὐτόν. (Lk 1.21)

6 λέγει αὐτοῖς ὁ Πιλᾶτος, Τί οὖν ποιήσω Ἰησοῦν; (Mt 27.22)

7 ὁ λύχνος τοῦ σώματός ἐστιν ὁ ὀφθαλμός. (Lk 11.34)

8 εἰ γὰρ κατὰ σάρκα ζῆτε, μέλλετε ἀποθνήσκειν. (Ro 8.13)

9 εἶπεν (*he spoke*) παραβολὴν διὰ τὸ ἐγγὺς εἶναι Ἰερουσαλὴμ αὐτόν. (Lk 19.11)

10 ὅτε ἤμην νήπιος, ἐλάλουν ὡς νήπιος, ἐφρόνουν ὡς νήπιος. (1 Cor 13.11)

11 οἱ δὲ ἀρχιερεῖς (*high priests*) καὶ ὅλον τὸ συνέδριον ἐζήτουν κατὰ τοῦ Ἰησοῦ μαρτυρίαν εἰς τὸ θανατῶσαι αὐτόν, καὶ οὐχ ηὕρισκον. (Mk 14.55)

12 ὑμεῖς ἐκ τῶν κάτω ἐστέ, ἐγὼ ἐκ τῶν ἄνω εἰμί. (Jn 8.23)

13 λέγει αὐτῇ Ἰησοῦς, Γύναι, τί κλαίεις; (Jn 20.15)

14 Λοιπὸν οὖν, ἀδελφοί, ἐρωτῶμεν ὑμᾶς καὶ παρακαλοῦμεν ἐν κυρίῳ Ἰησοῦ. (1 Th 4.1)

15 δεῖ τοὺς δούλους ὑπακούειν τοῖς κατὰ σάρκα κυρίοις μετὰ φόβου καὶ τρόμου ἐν ἁπλότητι τῆς καρδίας ὡς τῷ Χριστῷ. (*Eph 6.5)

16 ἐδάκρυσεν ὁ Ἰησοῦς. ἔλεγον οὖν οἱ Ἰουδαῖοι, Ἴδε πῶς ἐφίλει αὐτόν. (Jn 11.35f.)

17 φύλακες πρὸ τῆς θύρας ἐτήρουν τὴν φυλακήν. (Ac 12.6)

18 σπουδάζετε τηρεῖν τὴν ἑνότητα τοῦ πνεύματος ἐν τῷ συνδέσμῳ τῆς εἰρήνης. (*Eph 4.3)

19 οἱ δὲ Φαρισαῖοι ἔλεγον, Ἐν τῷ ἄρχοντι τῶν δαιμονίων ἐκβάλλει τὰ δαιμόνια. (Mt 9.34)

20 ὁ δὲ ἔφη αὐτῷ, Ἀγαπήσεις κύριον τὸν θεόν σου ἐν ὅλῃ τῇ καρδίᾳ σου καὶ ἐν ὅλῃ τῇ ψυχῇ σου. (Mt 22.37)

Notes

1 (i) εἰς here *to*; πέραν is an adverb *on the other side* but τὸ πέραν simply means *the other side*. (iii) Supply αὐτόν as the subject of λαλῆσαι. (iv) Take τὸν πλησίον as the object of the infinitive. (v) The context shows that ὑμᾶς is the subject of αἰτῆσαι and αὐτόν the object. (vii) παρ' = παρά (2.1/6(b) also in 3 below).

2 ἰδίᾳ lit. *one's own* takes its meaning from its context; here it refers to the prophet's own country.

3 ἔμενεν is an inceptive imperfect (4.1/1 note 3), lit. *began to stay*, but trans. simply *stayed*.

4 τί here means *what* (10.1/1), but in 13 it means *why*; λέγει vivid pres. (2.1/5 note 2).

5 The first ἐν gives the reason for their amazement; trans. *at his staying*.

6 ποιέω here has two accusatives and the meaning is *do [something] to/with [somebody]*.

9 The context shows that we must take Ἰερουσαλήμ (the indecl. form of Jerusalem – 4.1/3) as dative with the adverb ἐγγύς *close [to]*.

10 What is the sense of the imperfects ἐλάλουν and ἐφρόνουν (and ἐζήτουν in 11)?

11 εἰς here means *for* and is used to express purpose.

15 δεῖ *it is necessary* takes the accusative (here τοὺς δούλους); ὑπακούειν *obey* takes the dative (here τοῖς κυρίοις and τῷ Χριστῷ, cf. 4.2.20); on such verbs see 15.1.1(b); κατὰ σάρκα *in the flesh*, i.e masters here on earth by contrast with Christ (the phrase has a different connotation in 8).

16 ἔλεγον lit. *were saying* the imperfect indicates that the words were uttered more than once, but English idiom requires *said* (the same applies in 19).

18 Take σπουδάζετε as indicative *you take pains* (in the orginal context it is imperative – 17.1/1)

19 Ἐν τῷ ἄρχοντι i.e. *in [the name of] the leader*.

20 ἀγαπήσεις the future is used here to express an emphatic command (17.1/1 note 5(i)); ἐν trans. *with* (cf. 11.1/2)

5.2/1 Vocabulary

ἀγαπάω *love*
αἰτέω *ask* [someone a request]
ἄνω (adv.) *above*
ἁπλότης, -ητος, ἡ *sincerity*

ἀπό (prep. + gen.) *from*
ἀποθνήσκω (note iota subscript) *die*
δακρύω *weep*
δεῖ (impers.) *it is necessary*

ἐγγύς (adv.)   *near, close*
εἰρήνη, -ης, ἡ   *peace*
ἐκκλησία, -ας, ἡ   *church*
ἑνότης, -ητος, ἡ   *unity*
ἐρωτάω   *ask* [someone a question]
ζάω   *live, be alive*
ζητέω   *seek, look for*
θανατόω   *kill*
θαυμάζω   *marvel, be surprised*
ἴδιος, -α, -ον   *one's own*
Ἰουδαῖος, -ου, ὁ   *Jew*
Καῖσαρ, -αρος, ὁ   *Caesar*
καρδία, -ας, ἡ   *heart*
κατά (+ acc.)   *according to;* (+ gen.) *against*
κάτω (adv.)   *below*
κλαίω   *weep*
κρυπτός, -ή, -όν   *hidden, secret*
λαλέω   *speak*
λοιπόν (adv.)   *furthermore*
λύχνος, -ου, ὁ   *lamp*
μαρτυρέω   *declare*
μαρτυρία, -ας, ἡ   *testimony*
μέλλω (+ inf.)   *be going to, be destined to*
μένω   *stay, dwell*
μωρός, -ά, -όν   *foolish*
ναός, -οῦ, ὁ   *temple*
ὅλος, -η, -ον   *whole, entire, all*

ὁμότεχνος, -ον   *of* [i.e. *belong to*] *the same trade* (τέχνη)
παρά (+ dat.)   *at the house of*
παραβολή, -ῆς, ἡ   *parable*
παρακαλέω   *entreat*
πατρίς, -ίδος, ἡ   *homeland,* [one's own] *country*
πέραν (adv.)   *on the other side*
Πιλᾶτος, -ου, ὁ   *Pilate*
πλησίον (adv.)   *near,* (as indecl. noun) *neighbour*
πνεῦμα, -ατος, τό   *spirit*
ποιέω   *do* (see note on 6)
πρό (prep. + gen.)   *before*
πῶς (exclamation)   *how …!*
σάρξ, σαρκός, ἡ   *flesh*
σπουδάζω   *be eager, take pains*
σύνδεσμος, -ου, ὁ   *bond*
συνέδριον, -ου, τό   *council*
τηρέω   *keep watch over, guard; preserve*
τιμή, -ῆς, ἡ   *honour, reverence*
τρόμος, -ου, ὁ   *trembling*
ὑποστρέφω   *return*
φιλέω   *love*
φόβος, -ου, ὁ   *fear*
φρονέω   *think, have an opinion*
χρονίζω   *linger*

6.1 Grammar

6.1/1 Third declension – consonant stem nouns (2)

(a) *Stems in ν (masculine with an occasional feminine)*

The nominative singular ends in -ην or -ων with a genitive -ενος/-ηνος or -ονος/-ωνος (there is no rule to determine whether a particular word has a long or short vowel in its stem). Those with a short vowel do not lengthen it in the dative plural because here we have ν + σ > σ, not ντ + σ > σ (cf. 5.1/1(b)).

Here, as elsewhere, the vocative is only given when a form different from the nominative occurs in the NT.

	ποιμήν (m) *shepherd*	μήν (m) *month*	ἡγεμών (m) *governor*	αἰών (m) *age*
stem	ποιμεν-	μην-	ἡγεμον-	αἰων-
SINGULAR				
Nom.	ποιμήν	μήν	ἡγεμών	αἰών
Acc.	ποιμέν-α	μῆν-α	ἡγεμόν-α	αἰῶν-α
Gen.	ποιμέν-ος	μην-ός	ἡγεμόν-ος	αἰῶν-ος
Dat.	ποιμέν-ι	μην-ί	ἡγεμόν-ι	αἰῶν-ι
PLURAL				
Nom.	ποιμέν-ες	μῆν-ες	ἡγεμόν-ες	αἰῶν-ες
Acc.	ποιμέν-ας	μῆν-ας	ἡγεμόν-ας	αἰῶν-ας
Gen.	ποιμέν-ων	μην-ῶν	ἡγεμόν-ων	αἰών-ων
Dat.	ποιμέ-σι(ν)	μη-σί(ν)	ἡγεμό-σι(ν)	αἰῶ-σι(ν)

Notes

1 ὠδίν, ὠδῖνος (f) *pain of childbirth* has a stem in -ιν and is declined in the same way as αἰών.

2 κύων, κυνός (m or f) *dog* has an irregular stem κυν-.

(b) *Stems in ρ (mainly masculine)*

A few nouns have a nom. s. -ηρ, gen. -ηρος or nom. s. -ωρ, gen. -ορος. Two other nouns belong here, μάρτυς *witness* and χείρ *hand* (the dat. pl. of both is irregular) as well as πῦρ πυρός (n) *fire* which only occurs in the singular and is regular.

	σωτήρ (m) *saviour*	ῥήτωρ (m) *speaker*	μάρτυς (m) *witness*	χείρ (f) *hand*
stem	σωτηρ-	ῥητορ-	μαρτυρ-	χειρ-
SINGULAR				
Nom.	σωτήρ	ῥήτωρ	μάρτυς	χείρ
Acc.	σωτήρ-α	ῥήτορ-α	μάρτυρ-α	χεῖρ-α
Gen.	σωτήρ-ος	ῥήτορ-ος	μάρτυρ-ος	χειρ-ός
Dat.	σωτῆρ-ι	ῥήτορ-ι	μάρτυρ-ι	χειρ-ί
PLURAL				
Nom.	σωτῆρ-ες	ῥήτορ-ες	μάρτυρ-ες	χεῖρ-ες
Acc.	σωτῆρ-ας	ῥήτορ-ας	μάρτυρ-ας	χεῖρ-ας
Gen.	σωτήρ-ων	ῥητόρ-ων	μαρτύρ-ων	χειρ-ῶν
Dat.	σωτῆρ-σι(ν)	ῥήτορ-σι(ν)	μάρτυ-σι(ν)	χερ-σί(ν)

Three relationship nouns with a nom. s. in -ηρ form a special sub-group and are declined alike: πατήρ *father*, μήτηρ *mother*, θυγάτηρ *daughter* (γαστήρ (f) *stomach* follows the same pattern). Also given below is the slightly irregular ἀνήρ *man, male, husband*.

	πατήρ (m) *father*	μήτηρ (f) *mother*	θυγάτηρ (f) *daughter*	ἀνήρ (m) *man*
stem	πατ(ε)ρ-	μητ(ε)ρ-	θυγατ(ε)ρ-	ἀνδρ-
SINGULAR				
Nom.	πατήρ	μήτηρ	θυγάτηρ	ἀνήρ
Voc.	πάτερ	μῆτερ	θύγατερ	ἄνερ
Acc.	πατέρ-α	μητέρ-α	θυγατέρ-α	ἄνδρ-α
Gen.	πατρ-ός	μητρ-ός	θυγατρ-ός	ἀνδρ-ός
Dat.	πατρ-ί	μητρ-ί	θυγατρ-ί	ἀνδρ-ί

PLURAL

N., V.	πατέρ-ες	μητέρ-ες	θυγατέρ-ες	ἄνδρ-ες
Acc.	πατέρ-ας	μητέρ-ας	θυγατέρ-ας	ἄνδρ-ας
Gen.	πατέρ-ων	μητέρ-ων	θυγατέρ-ων	ἀνδρ-ῶν
Dat.	πατρά-σι(ν)	μητρά-σι(ν)	θυγατρά-σι(ν)	ἀνδρά-σι(ν)

(c) *Neuters in -ος*

Neuters in -ος, as γένος, γένους *race, clan* (original stem γενεσ-), form a large class. They appear to be irregular because they were affected by a sound change at an earlier stage of Greek whereby intervocal sigma was lost and the two previously separated vowels were contracted in Attic Greek; these contracted forms passed over into the Koine. The original forms are given in brackets.

	SINGULAR		PLURAL	
Nom.	γένος		γένη	(<γένεσ-α)
Acc.	γένος		γένη	
Gen.	γένους	(<γένεσ-ος)	γενῶν	(<γενέσ-ων)
Dat.	γένει	(<γένεσ-ι)	γένεσι (ν)	(<γένεσ-σι)

6.1/2 οἶδα *know*

We shall meet the perfect tense at 14.1/2 but οἶδα, which is perfect in form, can be conveniently introduced here because it presents no special difficulty and occurs frequently throughout the entire NT.

Although οἶδα has the endings of the perfect tense, its meaning is present, viz *know*. It does not have any forms which can *grammatically* be classified as present, imperfect or aorist. Its perfect forms are

	SINGULAR		PLURAL
1	οἶδα *I know*		οἴδαμεν
2	οἶδας		οἴδατε
3	οἶδε(ν)		οἴδασι(ν) (ἴσασι in Ac 26.4)
	INFINITIVE	εἰδέναι	

The endings are the same as for the weak aorist except for the 3 pl. (on this see 4.1/1 note 1). For the other forms of οἶδα see 20.1/4(b). Examples of its use are: οὐκ οἶδα τί λέγεις (Mt 26.70) *I do not know what you are saying*; οἴδασιν τὴν φωνὴν αὐτοῦ (Jn 10.4) *they know his voice* (lit. *the voice of him*).

6.1/3 Compound verbs formed with prepositional prefixes

Greek has many compounds where a verb is prefixed with one (or sometimes more than one) preposition. An example which we have already seen is ἐκβάλλω *cast out* (2.2.2) from ἐκ *out of* and βάλλω *throw, cast*. In these compounds sound changes occur when certain vowels and consonants are juxtaposed:

(a) With the exception of περί, πρό and one instance of ἀμφί *around* (ἀμφιέννυμι), prepositions ending in a vowel drop this vowel (by elision) when compounded with a verb which begins with a vowel or diphthong: ἀπάγω (ἀπό + ἄγω) *lead away*, παρέχω (παρά + ἔχω) *provide*, but προάγω *lead forward*, περιάγω *lead round*.

(b) When, owing to the elision of the final vowel of the preposition, π and τ are brought into contact with an initial aspirated vowel or diphthong, these consonants must themselves adopt their aspirated forms, φ and θ respectively: ἀφαιρέω (ἀπό + αἱρέω) *take away*; καθαιρέω (κατά + αἱρέω) *take down, destroy*.

(c) When compounded with a verb beginning with a vowel or diphthong, ἐκ becomes ἐξ: ἐξάγω (ἐκ + ἄγω) *lead out*; ἐξαιρέω (ἐκ + αἱρέω) *take out*.

(d) When compounded with a verb beginning with a consonant, the ν of ἐν and σύν is assimilated as follows:

> ν before π, β, φ, ψ and μ becomes μ: συμβουλεύω (συν + βουλεύω) *advise*
> ν before γ, κ, χ, and ξ becomes nasal γ: ἐγγράφω (ἐν + γράφω) *write in, enrol*
> ν before λ becomes λ: συλλαμβάνω (συν + λαμβάνω) *seize*
> ν of σύν is dropped before σ: συστρέφω (συν + στρέφω) *gather together*.

(e) When a verb compounded with a preposition is used in a tense which requires the augment, the augment comes between the preposition and the verb, **not** in front of the preposition: προσεκύνησα (<προσκυνέω) *I worshipped*. If the insertion of the augment results in the clash of two vowels, e.g. κατά + ἐ-γίνωσκον the same process as in (a) above will apply: so κατεγίνωσκον (<καταγινώσκω) *I was condemning*; κατεγέλων (<καταγελάω) *I was ridiculing*; but προέκοπτον (<προκόπτω) *I was progressing*, περιεπάτησα (<περιπατέω) *I walked around* because πρό and περί are not elided (see (a) above).

(f) The assimilation of ἐν and σύν described in (d) is blocked by the syllabic augment in the augmented tenses; thus συμβουλεύω but συνεβούλευον.

Notes

1 The meaning of a compound verb cannot always be predicted from its constituent parts (e.g. παρέχω *provide*).

2 Some compound verbs have completely replaced the simple verbs from which they are formed, e.g. ἀποκτείνω is the normal word for *kill* and κτείνω is no longer used. Similarly, ἀνοίγω *open* replaced the earlier οἴγω but is usually treated as a simple verb with the augment applied to the initial vowel, viz ἤνοιξα (the highly irregular forms ἠνέῳξα and ἀνέῳξα also occur).

3 With compound verbs of this type the prefix is often repeated as a normal preposition, e.g. ἐνοικήσω ἐν αὐτοῖς (2 Cor 6.16) *I shall dwell in them.*

4 οἰκοδομέω originally meant *build a house* (οἶκος *house*) but came to mean simply *build*. Its augmented form is ᾠκοδόμησα because its first element is not a preposition.

5 The manuscripts of the New Testament (21.3) are inconsistent in the application of rule (d) and sometimes have forms where the ν of ἐν and σύν is not assimilated to a following consonant. This is reflected in some editions of the New Testament but not in that of the United Bible Societies, which is recommended.

6.1/4 -ω verbs with stems in palatals, labials, dentals

The sound changes shown by nouns with these stems (5.1/l(a)) also occur in the corresponding verbs when a sigma is added to form the future or weak aorist. Some have a simple present stem to which the sigma is added (as happens with λύω), but the majority have a suffix in their present stem which is not kept elsewhere.

(a) *Verbs of the above type with no suffix in the present stem*

πλέκω	*plait*	fut.	πλέξω	aor. ἔπλεξα
πέμπω	*send*	fut.	πέμψω	aor. ἔπεμψα
πείθω	*persuade*	fut.	πείσω	aor. ἔπεισα

(b) Verbs with a suffix in the present stem

A consonant pronounced as the y in the English yes originally existed in Greek but had disappeared before the introduction of the alphabet. This sound had been used as a suffix to form the present stem of many -ω verbs whose original stem ended in a consonant. In this context it combined with the preceding consonants and the combinations which concern us here are κ/γ/χ + y > σσ; π/β/φ + y > πτ; τ/δ/θ + y > ζ. As this suffix (and others – see below) was used to form only the present stem, the future and weak aorist are formed by applying σ to the original stem. Examples are (the original stem is given in brackets):

PALATALS

φυλάσσω	guard	(φυλακ-)	fut.	φυλάξω	aor.	ἐφύλαξα
ἀλλάσσω	change	(ἀλλαγ-)	fut.	ἀλλάξω	aor.	ἤλλαξα

LABIALS

κλέπτω	steal	(κλεπ-)	fut.	κλέψω	aor.	ἔκλεψα
βάπτω	dip	(βαφ-)	fut.	βάψω	aor.	ἔβαψα

DENTALS

φράζω	tell	(φραδ-)	fut.	φράσω	aor.	ἔφρασα

The original stem occurs in cognate words (e.g. φυλακή act of guarding, κλοπή damage). Note that a few verbs in -ζω are palatals, not dentals, as e.g. σφάζω slaughter (σφαγ-) fut. σφάξω, aor. ἔσφαξα (cf. σφαγή [act of] slaughtering).

Verbs in -ίζω form a large class as ιζ (stem ιδ), which began as an integral part of verbs such as ἐλπίζω hope, was in turn employed as a suffix and used to form verbs from nouns, e.g. γαμίζω give in marriage (from γάμος marriage), ἀποκεφαλίζω behead (from κεφαλή head). A few verbs in -ίζω have a contracted future in -ιῶ (<-ιέω), e.g. ἐλπίζω, fut. ἐλπιῶ, ἐλπιεῖς, ἐλπιεῖ etc. (cf. 5.1/2 note 3), but the majority follow φράζω, e.g. χωρίζω separate, fut. χωρίσω.

Another suffix used to form the present stem is σκ, e.g. διδάσκω (<διδαχ + σκ-ω) teach, fut. διδάξω (<διδαχ + σ-ω), aor. ἐδίδαξα (<ἐδίδαχ + σ-α). On the suffix αν see 7.1/1 note 4)

6.2 Greek reading

1 (i) τὸ σωτῆρα τοῦ ἔθνους οἴδαμεν. (ii) οἱ ποιμένες τὰ πρόβατα ἐφύλαξαν. (iii) οἱ ῥήτορες τοὺς ἡγεμόνας κατεθεμάτιζον. (iv) τὸν λόγον τοῦ θεοῦ ἀπαγγελῶ. (v) αἱ μητέρες τὰ τῶν

θυγατέρων ὀνόματα ἤλλαξαν. (vi) οἶδας τὸν ἄνδρα τε καὶ τὴν θυγατέρα; (vii) βασιλεύσει ἐπὶ τὸν οἶκον Ἰακὼβ εἰς τοὺς αἰῶνας. (Lk 1.33) (viii) πέμψω τὸν υἱόν μου τὸν ἀγαπητόν. (Lk 20.13) (ix) οἱ λόγοι τῶν μαρτύρων τὴν ἀπάτην ἀπεκάλυψαν. (x) ῥήματα ζωῆς αἰωνίου ἔχεις. (Jn 6.68)

2 βλέπουσι τὸ πρόσωπον τοῦ πατρός μου τοῦ ἐν οὐρανοῖς. (Mt 18.10)

3 κατήγγελλον τὸν λόγον τοῦ θεοῦ ἐν ταῖς συναγωγαῖς τῶν Ἰουδαίων. (Ac 13.5)

4 δαιμόνια πολλὰ ἐξέβαλλον, καὶ ἤλειφον ἐλαίῳ πολλοὺς ἀρρώστους καὶ ἐθεράπευον. (Mk 6.13)

5 ἐλαίῳ τὴν κεφαλήν μου οὐκ ἤλειψας· αὕτη (this woman) δὲ μύρῳ ἤλειψεν τοὺς πόδας μου. (Lk 7.46)

6 ἀνήρ ἐστιν κεφαλὴ τῆς γυναικὸς ὡς καὶ ὁ Χριστὸς κεφαλὴ τῆς ἐκκλησίας. (Eph 5.23)

7 θυγάτηρ ἦν αὐτῷ ὡς ἐτῶν δώδεκα. (*Lk 8.42)

8 ἡ μέριμνα τοῦ αἰῶνος καὶ ἡ ἀπάτη τοῦ πλούτου συμπνίγει τὸν λόγον. (Mt 13.22)

9 τί δὲ βλέπεις τὸ κάρφος τὸ ἐν τῷ ὀφθαλμῷ τοῦ ἀδελφοῦ σου, τὴν δὲ ἐν τῷ σῷ ὀφθαλμῷ δοκὸν οὐ κατανοεῖς; (Mt 7.3)

10 τότε ἤρξατο (he began) καταθεματίζειν καὶ ὀμνύειν, Οὐκ οἶδα τὸν ἄνθρωπον. καὶ εὐθέως ἀλέκτωρ ἐφώνησεν. (*Mt 26.74)

11 οὐκ ἐπίστευσαν οἱ Ἰουδαῖοι ὅτι ἦν τυφλὸς καὶ ἀνέβλεψεν. (*Jn 9.18)

12 μακάριος εἶ, Σίμων Βαριωνᾶ, ὅτι σὰρξ καὶ αἷμα οὐκ ἀπεκάλυψέν σοι ἀλλ' ὁ πατήρ μου ὁ ἐν τοῖς οὐρανοῖς. (Mt 16.17)

13 ἐκόπασεν ὁ ἄνεμος. οἱ δὲ ἐν τῷ πλοίῳ προσεκύνησαν αὐτῷ λέγοντες (saying), Ἀληθῶς θεοῦ υἱὸς εἶ. (Mt 14.32f.)

14 οὐ φονεύσεις, οὐ μοιχεύσεις, οὐ κλέψεις, οὐ ψευδομαρτυρήσεις. (Mt 19.18)

15 ὑποκριταί, τὸ πρόσωπον τῆς γῆς καὶ τοῦ οὐρανοῦ οἴδατε δοκιμάζειν. (Lk 12.56)

16 ἐγὼ πάντοτε ἐδίδαξα ἐν συναγωγῇ καὶ ἐν τῷ ἱερῷ. (Jn 18.20)

17 ἔρριψαν αὐτοὺς παρὰ τοὺς πόδας αὐτοῦ, καὶ ἐθεράπευσεν αὐτούς. (Mt 15.30)

18 καὶ ἰδοὺ ἄνδρες δύο συνελάλουν αὐτῷ. (Lk 9.30)

19 τῷ ὀνόματι αὐτοῦ ἔθνη ἐλπιοῦσιν. (Mt 12.21)

20 ἐγὼ ἐβάπτισα ὑμᾶς ὕδατι, αὐτὸς δὲ βαπτίσει ὑμᾶς ἐν πνεύματι ἁγίῳ. (Mk 1.8)

Notes

1 (ii) τὰ πρόβατα trans. [*their*] *sheep*; the shepherds were guarding their own sheep – if the sheep had belonged to someone else this would have been stated (cf. note on 6 below). (iv) ἀπαγγελῶ fut. of ἀπαγγέλλω – 5.1/2 note 3 and 11.1/3. (v) τῶν θυγατέρων trans. *of* [*their*] *daughters* (cf. note on (ii)). (vi) τὴν θυγατέρα [*his*] *daughter* (cf. note on (ii)). (vii) lit. *for the ages* [*to come*], i.e. *forever.*

2 τοῦ πατρός μου lit. *of the Father of me.*

3 The context shows that κατήγγελλον is 3 pl. not 1 s. (likewise ἐξέβαλλον, ἤλειφον and ἐθεράπευον in 4).

5 ἤλειψας < ἀλείφω; trans. δέ by *but* because the two clauses are contrasted (4.1/4).

6 ἀνήρ has no article because it is indefinite *a man*, but γυναικός has the definite article because the meaning is *his wife* (Greek often uses the article where English has the possessive adjective *my, your, his* etc.; see 9.1/5 and cf. 1(i, ii, vi) above); κεφαλή lit. *head*, i.e. *leader, master* (patriarchy was the social norm in the 1st century AD).

7 αὐτῷ *for him*; ὡς (here *about*) qualifies δώδεκα; ἐτῶν is a genitive qualifying θυγάτηρ (in English we would express this sentence in a different way).

8 The original meaning of αἰών is *lengthy period of time, an age* (cf. 1(vii) above), and this occurs in the NT; it is also used in a more restricted sense of *the present age*, as here in ἡ μέριμνα τοῦ αἰῶνος *the anxiety* (i.e *worries*) *of the present time*; the verb (συμπνίγει) is singular because it agrees only with the closer of the two nouns in the nominative (ἀπάτη) (in English we must use the pl. *choke* not *chokes* – this is a common Greek idiom and also occurs in 12 – σὰρξ καὶ αἷμα).

9 ἐν τῷ σῷ ὀφθαλμῷ lit. *in the your eye*, i.e. *in your eye* (on possessive adjectives see 9.1/5).

12 σὰρξ καὶ αἷμα is a poetical way of saying *any human being* (on the double subject with a singular verb see note on 8); in translating supply *this* as the object of ἀπεκάλυψεν (the reference is to the previous verse); ὁ ἐν τοῖς οὐρανοῖς lit. *the* [*one*] *in heaven* is best translated by an adjectival clause, *who is …*

13 προσεκύνησαν *did obeisance*, this was a regular way of showing extreme respect in the ancient East; it consisted of prostrating oneself in front of the other person.

14 As in English, the future tense can be used for strong commands, cf. 5.2.20 and 17.1/1.

15 οἴδατε ... *you know* [*how*] ...
16 ἱερόν has the article because the temple at Jerusalem is meant; συναγωγή does not because its basic meaning is *meeting place* of which there were many.
17 ἔρριψαν < ῥίπτω; translate the first αὐτούς by *themselves* (9.1/4).
18 συνελάλουν < συλλαλέω.
19 Translate the dative by *in the name* ...; ἐλπιοῦσιν fut. of ἐλπίζω (6.1/4(b)); the verb is plural although we have a neuter plural subject (ἔθνη) – this neglect of the rule given at 2.1/2 note 3 is common in the NT.
20 Translate the dative ὕδατι by *with* (ἐν here should be translated in the same way; see 11.1/2). πνεῦμα ἅγιον *Holy Ghost* (hence no article just as with θεός *God*), lit. *Holy Spirit*.

6.2/1 Vocabulary

ἀγαπητός, -ή, -όν *beloved*
ἅγιος, -α, -ον *holy*
αἷμα, -ατος, τό *blood*
ἀλείφω *anoint*
ἀλέκτωρ, -ορος, ὁ *cock*
ἀναβλέπω *gain one's sight*
ἀπαγγέλλω *proclaim*
ἀπάτη, -ης, ἡ *deception*
ἀποκαλύπτω *reveal*
ἄρρωστος, -ον *sick*
Βαριωνᾶς, -ᾶ, ὁ *son of Jonah*
βασιλεύω *rule*
γῆ, γῆς, ἡ *earth*
γυνή, γυναικός, ἡ *woman, wife*
δοκιμάζω *examine*
δοκός, -οῦ, ἡ *beam*
δώδεκα (indecl.) *twelve*
ἔθνος, -ους, τό *nation, people*
ἔλαιον, -ου, τό *(olive) oil*
ἐν (prep. + dat.) *with* (in 20)
ἐπί (prep. + acc.) *over*
ἔτος, -ους, τό *year*
εὐθέως (adv.) *immediately*
ἤ (conj.) *or*
θεραπεύω *heal*

ἱερόν, -οῦ, τό *temple*
κάρφος, -ους, τό *speck*
καταγγέλλω *proclaim*
καταθεματίζω *curse*
κατανοέω *notice*
κεφαλή, -ῆς, ἡ *head*
κλέπτω *steal*
κοπάζω *abate*
μακάριος, -α, -ον *fortunate*
μέριμνα, -ης, ἡ *anxiety, care*
μοιχεύω *commit adultery*
μύρον, -ου, τό *perfume*
ὀμνύω *swear*
ὄνομα, -ατος, τό *name*
ὅτι (conj.) *because*
πάντοτε (adv.) *always*
παρά (+ acc.) *to, towards*
Πέτρος, -ου, ὁ *Peter*
πιστεύω *believe*
πλοῖον, -ου, τό *boat*
πλοῦτος, -ου, ὁ *wealth*
πούς, ποδός, ὁ *foot*
προσκυνέω (+ dat.) *do obeisance to*
ῥῆμα, -ατος, τό *word*
ῥίπτω *throw*

Σίμων, -ωνος, ὁ *Simon*
σός, σή, σόν (poss. adj.) *your*
  (s.)
συλλαλέω (+ dat.) *talk (with)*
συμπνίγω *choke*
τυφλός, -ή, -όν *blind*
ὕδωρ, ὕδατος, τό *water*

ὑποκριτής, -οῦ, ὁ *hypocrite*
φονεύω *murder*
φωνέω *make a sound, crow*
ψευδομαρτυρέω *bear false witness*
ὡς (conj. in 6) *just as*; (adv. in 7) *about*

7.1 Grammar

7.1/1 Strong aorist indicative and infinitive active of -ω verbs

-ω verbs have either a weak or a strong aorist (4.1/1); the distinction between the two is solely one of form. The endings of the strong aorist indicative are the same as those of the **imperfect**; the strong aorist infinitive has the same ending as the **present** infinitive. The strong aorist needs no suffix because its stem always differs from that of the present; the present stem can have a special suffix (6.1/4(b)) and/or a different vowel, or be based on a completely different verb. Some strong aorist stems are simply irregular and must be learnt.

The following are the most common verbs with a strong aorist. Forms preceded by a hyphen occur only in compounds; those in square brackets are not found in the NT but are included to give a full presentation:

PRESENT INDICATIVE	PRESENT INFINITIVE	AORIST INDICATIVE	AORIST INFINITIVE
ἄγω *lead, bring*	ἄγειν	ἤγαγον	ἀγαγεῖν
-αἱρέω *take, capture*	-αἱρεῖν	-εῖλον (stem ἑλ-)	-ἑλεῖν
βάλλω *throw*	βάλλειν	ἔβαλον	βαλεῖν
ἐσθίω *eat*	ἐσθίειν	ἔφαγον	φαγεῖν
εὑρίσκω *find*	[εὑρίσκειν]	εὗρον	εὑρεῖν
ἔχω *have*	ἔχειν	ἔσχον	[σχεῖν]
λαμβάνω *take*	λαμβάνειν	ἔλαβον	λαβεῖν
λέγω *say*	λέγειν	εἶπον (stem εἰπ-)	εἰπεῖν

λείπω *leave*	[λείπειν]	-ἔλιπον	[λιπεῖν]
μανθάνω *learn*	[μανθάνειν]	ἔμαθον	μαθεῖν
ὁράω *see*	[ὁρᾶν]	εἶδον (stem ἰδ-)	ἰδεῖν
πάσχω *suffer*	πάσχειν	ἔπαθον	παθεῖν
πίπτω *fall*	-πίπτειν	ἔπεσον	πεσεῖν
τυγχάνω *happen*	-τυγχάνειν	ἔτυχον	τυχεῖν
φεύγω *flee*	[φεύγειν]	ἔφυγον	φυγεῖν

Notes

1 The aorists of -αἱρέω, ἐσθίω, λέγω, ὁράω are irregular as they come from roots entirely different from their presents (cf. English *go/went*). Their unaugmented aorist stems (ἑλ-, εἰπ-, ἰδ-) require particular attention.

2 The strong aorist ἦλθον *I came/went* is not listed above because it is peculiar in having an active aorist but a deponent present (ἔρχομαι 8.1/2 note).

3 The strong aorist endings are sometimes replaced by those of the weak aorist, although the strong aorist stem is kept. In some verbs this occurs erratically and we find the same strong aorist stem used with both sets of endings, e.g. εὕρομεν (Ac 5.23) and εὕραμεν (Lk 23.2). With other verbs the weak aorist endings predominate. An example is φέρω *carry, bring* whose aorist indicative active always has weak endings (e.g. ἤνεγκα, which was ἤνεγκον in earlier Greek); however, its aorist infinitive active has the normal strong aorist ending, -ἐνεγκεῖν.

4 In λαμβάνω, μανθάνω, τυγχάνω the suffix αν (cf. 6.1/4) is accompanied by a nasal infix (i.e. a nasal inserted before the final consonant of the root); neither αν nor the infix occur outside the present stem, e.g. λαμβάνω *take*, aor. stem λαβ-. In λα-μ-β-αν-ω the nasal infix takes the form of the labial nasal μ before the following labial; in μα-ν-θ-άν-ω *learn* (aor. stem μαθ-) it takes the form of the dental nasal ν; in τυ-γ-χ-άν-ω *happen* (aor. stem τυχ-) it takes the form of the guttural nasal γ (for this pronunciation of γ see 1.1/1)

5 By this stage you should be confident enough to consult the table of **Principal parts of verbs**, which sets out the principal parts of important verbs which have some irregularity. A normal transitive verb in Greek has six principal parts and from these all possible forms can be deduced. These parts are:

(i) 1st s. present indicative active (λύω; 2.1/5)
(ii) 1st s. future indicative active (λύσω; 2.1/5)
(iii) 1st s. aorist indicative active (ἔλυσα; 4.1/1; for strong aorist see above)

(iv) lst s. perfect indicative active (λέλυκα; 14.1/2)
(v) lst s. perfect indicative middle and passive (λέλυμαι; 16.1/3)
(vi) lst s. aorist indicative passive (ἐλύθην; 11.1/1).

This list is not as formidable as it might seem at first sight as some verbs do not exist in every possible part, while many (such as λύω) are completely regular and all their principal parts can be deduced from their present stem. However, do not, at this stage, try to digest the list in its entirety (in any case, we have not yet dealt with principal parts (iv) – (vi)), but familiarize yourself with its arrangement and get into the habit of using it. When individual principal parts are wildly irregular (e.g. εἶπον), they are given separate entries in the **Vocabulary**.

7.1/2 Direct and indirect speech

There are two ways of reporting what someone has said; we may either quote the speaker's words exactly: *'Greek,' said the teacher to his students, 'need have no terrrors for you'*; or we may subordinate what has been said to an introductory verb and make any adjustments required: *The teacher said to his students that Greek need have no terrors for them.* The former is called **direct speech,** the latter **indirect** (or **reported**) **speech**.

For grammatical purposes we may classify direct speech into statement, question and command, and to these there are three corresponding forms of indirect speech:

(a) **Indirect statement:** *The teacher said that learning Greek was pure joy.* (Direct *Learning Greek is pure joy.*)
(b) **Indirect question:** *The students asked if he was serious.* (Direct *Are you serious?*)
(c) **Indirect command:** *The teacher ordered them to adopt a more positive attitude.* (Direct *Adopt a more positive attitude!*)

These examples show the adjustments in pronouns that are nearly always necessary in English. Greek does the same with pronouns but does not, as we shall see, make the **tense** adjustments required by English in (a) and (b).

7.1/3 φημί *say* and direct speech

φημί is a -μι verb (2.1/4) which has survived in the New Testament only in the following forms:

		PRESENT	IMPERFECT
SINGULAR	1	φημί *I say*	
	3	φησί (ν) *he/she says*	ἔφη *he/she said*
PLURAL	3	φασί (ν) *they say*	

As indicated by the translation, the imperfect ἔφη has the sense of an aorist.

These four forms are often used to indicate the speaker in direct speech. They usually occur before the words quoted: ὁ ἑκατόνταρχος ἔφη, Κύριε, οὐκ εἰμὶ ἱκανός (Mt 8.8) *the centurion said, 'Lord, I am not worthy.'* (As this sentence illustrates, the normal convention in printing Greek is to introduce direct speech with a capital letter (Κύριε), but not to use inverted commas).

Κύριε, οὐκ εἰμὶ ἱκανός is a statement but φημί can introduce a question: ὁ δὲ ἔφη, Τί κακὸν ἐποίησεν; (*Mt 27.23) *and he said, 'What wrong did he do?'* although the normal words for puting a question are ἐρωτάω and ἐπερωτάω (both *ask*):

> ἐπερωτῶσιν αὐτὸν οἱ Φαρισαῖοι, Διὰ τί οὐ περιπατοῦσιν οἱ μαθηταί σου κατὰ τὴν παράδοσιν τῶν πρεσβυτέρων; (*Mk 7.5) *The Pharisees ask him, 'Why (lit. on account of what) do your disciples not walk according to the tradition of the elders?'*

φημί is also used to introduce direct commands but as these require verbal forms not yet treated (imperative and subjunctive) we may cite what is a virtual command (cf. 5.2.20): ὁ δὲ ἔφη αὐτῷ, Ἀγαπήσεις κύριον τὸν θεόν σου (Mt 22.37) *and he said to him, 'You shall love the Lord your God.'*

λέγω (aorist εἶπον or εἶπα – see above) can be used in the same way as φημί: οἱ μαθηταὶ εἶπαν αὐτῷ, Διὰ τί ἐν παραβολαῖς λαλεῖς αὐτοῖς; (Mt 13.10) *the disciples said to him, 'Why do you talk to them in parables?'*

7.1/4 Indirect command

After certain verbs of ordering Greek has the same construction as English, viz an infinitive: ἐκέλευσεν συνελθεῖν τοὺς ἀρχιερεῖς (Ac 22.30) *he ordered the high priests to assemble* (συνελθεῖν < συνέρχομαι, see 7.1/1 note 2); δεῖ αὐτοὺς παραγγέλλειν τηρεῖν τὸν νόμον Μωϋσέως. (*Ac 15.5) *it is necessary to order them to observe the law of Moses.* The tense of the infinitive is a matter of aspect (4.1/1). In the above examples the aorist συνελθεῖν is used because the high priests are to assemble on one particular occasion, whereas τηρεῖν indicates that those receiving the order must always observe the law of Moses. For the construction after other verbs of ordering see 13.1/3(b)(ii).

7.1/5 Numerals (see also Appendix 6)

There are three types of numerals in Greek (the range of each which occurs in the NT is restricted):

(a) **Cardinals** (in English *one, two, three, four,* etc.)

These function as adjectives. The numbers *one* to *four* are declined as follows:

	εἷς *one*			δύο *two*
	M.	F.	N.	M.F.N.
Nom.	εἷς	μία	ἕν	δύο
Acc.	ἕνα	μίαν	ἕν	δύο
Gen.	ἑνός	μιᾶς	ἑνός	δύο
Dat.	ἑνί	μιᾷ	ἑνί	δυσί(ν)

	τρεῖς *three*		τέσσαρες *four*	
	M. & F.	N.	M. & F.	N.
Nom.	τρεῖς	τρία	τέσσαρες	τέσσαρα
Acc.	τρεῖς	τρία	τέσσαρας	τέσσαρα
Gen.	τριῶν	τριῶν	τεσσάρων	τεσσάρων
Dat.	τρισί(ν)	τρισί(ν)	τέσσαρσι(ν)	τέσσαρσι(ν)

These must agree in gender and case with the noun qualified, e.g. ἐπὶ κλίνης μιᾶς (Lk 17.34) *on one bed*; ἀλεύρου σάτα τρία (Mt 13.33) *three measures* (σάτα) *of flour.*

The numbers *five* to *one hundred* are indeclinable (i.e. have no variable inflections), except when they contain any of the numbers *one* to *four,* e.g. εἴκοσι τέσσαρες *twenty-four,* where τέσσαρες would alter its ending as required: εἴκοσι τέσσαρας πρεσβυτέρους *twenty-four elders* (accusative).The words for *two hundred, three hundred,* etc. follow the plural of καλός (3.1/3): so διακόσιοι, -αι, -α, *two hundred.* Similarly the word for a *thousand* is an adjective χίλιοι (-αι, -α); for 2,000, 3,000 etc. χίλιοι is compounded with the numeral adverb (δίς *twice,* τρίς *three times* etc., see below) to give δισχίλιοι, τρισχίλιοι etc., but there are also alternatives which employ the noun χιλιάς (-άδος, ἡ) lit. *group of a thousand,* e.g. χιλιάδες πέντε *five thousand* (Ac 4.4; most examples are in Revelation). A word exists for *ten thousand,* viz μύριοι (-αι, -α), which has a corresponding noun μυριάς (-άδος, ἡ) lit. *group of a ten thousand.* Neither χιλιάς nor μυριάς is used in the singular.

(b) **Ordinals** (in English, *first, second, third,* etc.)These are first and second declension adjectives (3.1/3), e.g. ἡ πρώτη ἐντολή *the first commandment.*

(c) **Numeral adverbs** (in English, *once, twice, three times,* etc.)The following occur: ἅπαξ *once,* δίς *twice,* τρίς *three times,* τετράκις *four times,* πεντάκις *five times,* ἑπτάκις *seven times,* ἑβδομηκοντάκις *seventy times* (cf. πολλάκις *often,* lit. *many times*).

Note

Like εἷς is declined the pronoun οὐδείς (<οὐδέ + εἷς *not even one),* οὐδεμία, οὐδέν, gen. οὐδενός, οὐδεμιᾶς, οὐδενός *no one, nobody, none.* The neuter οὐδέν means *nothing,* but is often used adverbially in the sense *in no respect, not at all.* οὐδείς can also be used as an adjective meaning *no,* e.g. οὐδεμία γυνή *no woman.*

7.1/6 Phrases expressing time and space

In English many temporal phrases contain a preposition, e.g. *on Sunday, for three months* (but cf. *I will visit you next year*). Three common types are expressed in Greek as follows:

(a) *Time how long* can be expressed by the **accusative**: ἦν ἐν τῇ ἐρήμῳ τεσσαράκοντα ἡμέρας (Mk 1.13) *he was in the desert for forty days.* Very occasionally the dative is used in the same way: χρόνῳ ἱκανῷ οὐκ ἐνεδύσατο ἱμάτιον (Lk 8.27) *he did not put on* (ἐνεδύσατο is middle voice; see 8.1/1) *a garment for a long time.*

(b) *Time when* can be expressed by the **dative** without a preposition: τῇ ἐνάτῃ ὥρᾳ (Mk 15.34) *at the ninth hour;* but the preposition ἐν (+ dat.) is used in the same sense: ἐν τῇ ἡμέρᾳ τῇ ὀγδόῃ (Lk 1.59) *on the eighth day.*

(c) *Time within which (something happened)* is expressed by the **genitive**: Νικόδημος ἦλθεν πρὸς αὐτὸν νυκτός (*Jn 3.2) *Nicodemus came to him by night* (or *during the night*). Here too a preposition is found: διὰ νυκτός (with the same meaning as νυκτός alone).

(d) *Spatial extent* is expressed by the **accusative**: ἡ κώμη ἀπέχει σταδίους ἑξήκοντα ἀπὸ Ἰερουσαλήμ (cf. Lk 24.13) *the village is distant sixty stades from Jerusalem.*

7.2 Greek reading

1 ὁ χιλίαρχος ἐκέλευσεν τὸ στράτευμα ἁρπάσαι τὸν Παῦλον ἐκ μέσου αὐτῶν, ἄγειν τε εἰς τὴν παρεμβολήν. (*Ac 22.24)

2 εἶπεν οὖν αὐτοῖς ὁ Ἰησοῦς, Ἔτι μικρὸν χρόνον τὸ φῶς ἐν ὑμῖν ἐστιν. (Jn 12.35)

3 ὁ δὲ παρέλαβεν τὸ παιδίον καὶ τὴν μητέρα αὐτοῦ νυκτὸς καὶ ἀνεχώρησεν εἰς Αἴγυπτον. (*Mt 2.14)

4 εἶπεν δὲ Ἡρῴδης, Ἰωάννην ἐγὼ ἀπεκεφάλισα. (Lk 9.9)

5 τετάρτῃ δὲ φυλακῇ τῆς νυκτὸς ἦλθεν πρὸς αὐτοὺς περιπατῶν (*walking*) ἐπὶ τὴν θάλασσαν. (Mt 14.25)

6 οἱ δὲ ἐπέβαλον τὰς χεῖρας αὐτῷ καὶ ἐκράτησαν αὐτόν. (Mk 14.46)

7 ἐξῆλθεν οὖν ὁ Πιλᾶτος ἔξω πρὸς αὐτοὺς καὶ φησίν, Τίνα (*what*) κατηγορίαν φέρετε κατὰ τοῦ ἀνθρώπου; (Jn 18.29)

8 μετὰ ἡμέρας τρεῖς εὗρον αὐτὸν ἐν τῷ ἱερῷ. (Lk 2.46)

9 καὶ μεθ᾽ ἡμέρας ὀκτὼ πάλιν ἦσαν ἔσω οἱ μαθηταὶ αὐτοῦ καὶ Θωμᾶς μετ᾽ αὐτῶν. (Jn 20.26)

10 εἶπαν, Διδάσκαλε, καλῶς εἶπας· οὐκέτι γὰρ ἐτόλμων ἐπερωτᾶν αὐτὸν οὐδέν. (Lk 20.39f.)

11 Ἀβραὰμ δύο υἱοὺς ἔσχεν, ἕνα ἐκ τῆς παιδίσκης καὶ ἕνα ἐκ τῆς ἐλευθέρας. (Gal 4.22)

12 Ἀπὸ τότε ἤρξατο (*began*) ὁ Ἰησοῦς δεικνύειν τοῖς μαθηταῖς αὐτοῦ ὅτι δεῖ αὐτὸν εἰς Ἱεροσόλυμα ἀπελθεῖν καὶ πολλὰ παθεῖν ἀπὸ τῶν πρεσβυτέρων. (Mt 16.21)

13 νηστεύω δὶς τοῦ σαββάτου. (Lk 18.12)

14 εἰ θέλεις, ποιήσω ὧδε τρεῖς σκηνάς, σοὶ μίαν καὶ Μωϋσεῖ μίαν καὶ Ἠλίᾳ μίαν. (Mt 17.4)

15 ἦν Ἰωνᾶς ἐν τῇ κοιλίᾳ τοῦ κήτους τρεῖς ἡμέρας καὶ τρεῖς νύκτας. (Mt 12.40)

16 **The Magnificat**

Mary's song of praise takes its name from the first word of its translation in the Vulgate (the Latin translation of the Bible; see 17.3), *magnificat* being Latin for μεγαλύνει. The following are the first six of its nine verses, together with the introductory verse.

Καὶ εἶπεν Μαριάμ, Μεγαλύνει ἡ ψυχή μου τὸν κύριον, καὶ ἠγαλλίασεν τὸ πνεῦμά μου ἐπὶ τῷ θεῷ τῷ σωτῆρί μου, ὅτι ἐπέβλεψεν ἐπὶ τὴν ταπείνωσιν (*lowly station*) τῆς δούλης αὐτοῦ. ἰδοὺ γὰρ ἀπὸ τοῦ νῦν μακαριοῦσίν με πᾶσαι (*all*) αἱ

γενεαί, ὅτι ἐποίησέν μοι μεγάλα ὁ δυνατός. καὶ ἅγιον τὸ 5
ὄνομα αὐτοῦ, καὶ τὸ ἔλεος αὐτοῦ εἰς γενεὰς καὶ γενεὰς τοῖς
φοβουμένοις (*those fearing*) αὐτόν. ἐποίησεν κράτος ἐν
βραχίονι αὐτοῦ, διεσκόρπισεν ὑπερηφάνους διανοίᾳ καρδίας
αὐτῶν· καθεῖλεν δυνάστας ἀπὸ θρόνων καὶ ὕψωσεν ταπεινούς.
(Lk 1.46–52)

Notes

1 αὐτῶν refers to the mob that has surrounded Paul.
2 Translate ἐν by *among*.
5 φυλακή has a different sense here from that in 4.2.6 (*prison*)
and should be translated *watch* (the night was divided into
four equal periods which were called φυλακαί).
6 ἐπέβαλον could be 1 s. or 3 pl. but the context tells us it is
the latter – this is also the case in 8 (εὗρον) and 10 (ἐτόλμων).
7 ἔξω is superfluous after ἐξῆλθεν.
9 μεθ' ἡμέρας in this verse and μετὰ ἡμέρας in 8 illustrate the
inconsistency in elision (2.1/6(b)) we meet in the New Testament.
10 εἶπαν and εἶπας are strong aorists with weak aorist endings
(7.1/1 note 3); we tell from the capital of Διδάσκαλε that
direct speech is starting but only the sense tells us that it ends
with εἶπας; οὐκέτι ... οὐδέν the two negatives are for
emphasis and do not cancel each other as they would in
English (8.1/3(e)); γάρ *for* gives the reason why they did not
say anything else; ἐτόλμων (< τολμάω) lit. *they were not
daring* (their *not daring* is regarded as happening over a
period) but translate *they did not dare*; like the English *ask*
ἐπερωτάω can be followed by two accusatives.
12 Ἀπὸ τότε *from then*; ὅτι here introduces an indirect statement
(7.1/2) and must be translated *that* (in 6.2.11 we have already
seen ὅτι in the sense of *because*); translate δεῖ *it was necessary* as
in indirect speech Greek uses the tense employed in the original
direct speech (8.1/4(a); Jesus actually said δεῖ *it is necessary*).
13 σάββατον here means *week*, not *sabbath*.
16 *l*.2 ἠγαλλίασεν < ἀγαλλιάω; ἐπί trans. *in*. *l*.4 ἀπὸ τοῦ νῦν
from now. *ll*.5f. Supply ἐστί with ἅγιον and with τὸ ἔλεος;
εἰς γενεὰς καὶ γενεάς lit. *to generations and generations*, i.e.
from generation to generation. *l*.7 ἐποίησεν κράτος trans. *he
produced strength* – the meaning is that God showed his
strength and scattered his enemies. *ll*.8f. ὑπερηφάνους
διανοίᾳ καρδίας αὐτῶν lit. [*people*] *proud by reason of the
thought of their heart*, i.e. *the proud in the imagination of
their hearts* (some were proud because of high and ambitious
ideas about themselves but despite this God laid them low);
καθεῖλεν < καθαιρέω.

7.2/1 Vocabulary

ἀγαλλιάω *exult*
Αἴγυπτος, -ου, ἡ *Egypt*
ἀναχωρέω *go away*
ἀπελθεῖν aor. of ἀπέρχομαι
  go away
ἀπό (prep. + gen.) *from*
ἀποκεφαλίζω *behead*
ἁρπάζω *seize*
βραχίων, -ονος, ὁ *arm*
γενεά, -ᾶς, ἡ *generation*
δεικνύω *indicate to*
διάνοια, -ας, ἡ *thought, imagination*
διασκορπίζω *scatter*
δίς (adv.) *twice*
δούλη, -ης, ἡ *female slave, bondmaid*
δυνάστης, -ου, ὁ *ruler*
δυνατός, -ή, -όν *mighty*
ἔλεος, -ους, τό *mercy*
ἐξῆλθεν aor. of ἐξέρχομαι
  come out
ἔξω (adv.) *outside*
ἐπερωτάω *ask*
ἐπί (prep. + acc.) *on, on top of*; (+ dat.) *in, because of*
ἐπιβάλλω *put* (acc.) ... *on* (dat.)
ἐπιβλέπω *look upon*
ἔσω (adv.) *inside, within*
Ἡρῴδης, -ου, ὁ *Herod*
θέλω *wish*
θρόνος, -ου, ὁ *throne*
Θωμᾶς, -ᾶ, ὁ *Thomas*
Ἰωνᾶς, -ᾶ, ὁ *Jonah*
καθαιρέω *bring down, destroy*
καλῶς (adv.) *well*
κατηγορία, -ας, ἡ *charge*

κελεύω *order*
κῆτος, -ους, τό *sea monster*
κοιλία, -ας, ἡ *belly*
κρατέω *apprehend*
κράτος, -ους, τό *power, strength*
μακαρίζω *call blessed*
Μαριάμ, ἡ (indecl.) *Mary*
μεγαλύνω *magnify*
μέσος, -η, -ον *middle*
  ἐκ μέσου *from the midst (of)*
μικρός, -ά, -όν *small, little*
ὀκτώ (indecl.) *eight*
ὅτι (conj.) *that* (see note on 12)
παιδίον, -ου, τό *child*
πάλιν (adv.) *again*
παραλαμβάνω *take*
παρεμβολή, -ῆς, ἡ *barracks*
πάσχω *suffer*
Παῦλος, -ου, ὁ *Paul*
πρεσβύτερος, -ου, ὁ *an elder*
σκηνή, -ῆς, ἡ *tabernacle*
στράτευμα, -ατος, τό *army*
σωτήρ, -ῆρος, ὁ *saviour*
ταπεινός, -ή, -όν *lowly, humble*
τέταρτος, -η, -ον *fourth*
τολμάω *dare*
ὑπερήφανος, -ον *proud, haughty*
ὑψόω *raise, exalt*
φέρω *bring*
φυλακή, -ῆς, ἡ *watch* (of the night)
φῶς, φωτός, τό *light*
χιλίαρχος, -ου, ὁ *captain*
ψυχή, -ῆς, ἡ *soul*

8.1 Grammar

8.1/1 Middle and passive voices

When the finite verb of a clause is **active** the subject is the doer (*the man bit the dog*; *the Egyptian is running towards the pyramid*); there may or may not be an object, depending on whether the verb is transitive or intransitive. When the finite verb of a clause is **passive** the subject is the sufferer (*the dog was bitten by the man*; *the tax-collector was ignored in the street*); the agent or instrument (11.1/2) may or may not be specified. In Greek these voices are used in much the same way as in English.

However, in addition to active and passive, Greek has a third voice, the **middle**, which has no English equivalent. Its forms coincide with those of the passive except in the future and aorist. In earlier Greek this mood was used in fairly well defined ways, but in NT Greek its exact nuances can sometimes be hard to discern, and one of its earlier uses (to express reflexive action, see below) has almost disappeared.

With normal verbs the middle generally indicates that the subject has an even greater involvement in the action than would be the case if the verb were active. Often it can be considered as meaning *to do something for oneself*. The active ἐνδύω means *I put [clothes] on [someone], I dress [someone]*; the middle ἐνδύομαι means *I put [clothes] on myself, I wear*: ὁ Ἡρῴδης ἐνδύεται ἐσθῆτα βασιλικήν *Herod is putting on a royal garment* (ἐνδύεται 3rd s. pres. middle). In a few cases the middle voice of a verb has developed a meaning different from that of the active: κόπτω *strike*, κόπτομαι *mourn for*; ἄρχω *rule*, ἄρχομαι *begin*. However, by far the greatest use of the middle is to be seen in deponent verbs, which will be described in the next subsection.

The forms of the middle and passive indicative are identical in the present and imperfect (and also in the perfect and pluperfect – 16.1/3). This does not create ambiguity as the context of a particular verb shows its voice. The future and aorist passive differ in form from the middle and will be treated separately in 11.1/1. The present and imperfect middle/passive and the future and aorist middle are as follows:

		PRESENT	IMPERFECT	FUTURE	AORIST
SINGULAR	1	λύ-ομαι	ἐλυ-όμην	λύσ-ομαι	ἐλυσ-άμην
	2	λύ-ῃ	ἐλύ-ου	λύσ-ῃ	ἐλύσ-ω
	3	λύ-εται	ἐλύ-ετο	λύσ-εται	ἐλύσ-ατο
PLURAL	1	λυ-όμεθα	ἐλυ-όμεθα	λυσ-όμεθα	ἐλυσ-άμεθα
	2	λύ-εσθε	ἐλύ-εσθε	λύσ-εσθε	ἐλύσ-ασθε
	3	λύ-ονται	ἐλύ-οντο	λύσ-ονται	ἐλύσ-αντο
INFINITIVE		λύ-εσθαι	————	————	λύσ-ασθαι

It is much easier to remember these forms if we note that:

(a) In each tense the stem is the same as for the active, and the link vowel between the stem and the ending proper (which is more easily distinguishable in these forms) is o/ε in the present, imperfect (and strong aorist) and future, but α in the weak aorist (on -ω of the 2nd s., see below).

(b) In each tense the 2nd s. ending has undergone contraction. The present and future ending was originally -εσαι, the imperfect -εσο and the aorist -ασο. With the loss of intervocal σ (cf. 6.1/1(c)) these became ῃ, ου, ω respectively (we have already met the second and third contractions with contracted verbs – 5.1/2)

(c) When allowance has been made for the 2nd s., the endings, except for the 1st pl. and 2nd pl. which do not vary, fall into two classes. For the primary tenses they are -μαι, -σαι, -ται, -νται and for the historic -μην, -σο, -το, -ντο (cf. 4.1/1 note 1)

(d) The endings of the strong aorist indicative middle are the same as those of the imperfect: αἰσθάνομαι *perceive,* impf. ᾐσθανόμην, aor. ᾐσθόμην; the infinitive ending of the strong aorist is the same as that of the present: αἰσθάνεσθαι (pres.), αἰσθέσθαι (aor.).

Notes

1 Some verbs have, for no perceptible reason, their future in the middle voice, not the active, e.g. φεύγω *flee,* φεύξομαι;

λαμβάνω *take*, λήμψομαι; τίκτω *give birth to*, τέξομαι. These are verbs which would not otherwise have had reason to be used in the middle.

2 The future of ἀκούω *hear*, ζάω *live* and κλαίω *weep* can be either active or middle: ἀκούσω or ἀκούσομαι *I shall hear*; ζήσω or ζήσομαι *I shall live*; κλαύσω or κλαύσομαι *I shall weep*.

3 For the future of εἰμί *be* middle endings are added to the stem ἐσ-: ἔσομαι, ἔσῃ, ἔσται, ἐσόμεθα, ἔσεσθε, ἔσονται, infinitive ἔσεσθαι (*to be going to be*; this is the only future middle infinitive in the NT, apart from εἰσελεύσεσθαι at Hb 3.18).

4 Contracted verbs form their present and imperfect middle/passive according to the rules given at 5.1/2, except that the 2nd s. present middle/passive of verbs in -αω has the irregular ending -ᾶσαι, e.g. τιμᾶσαι. (see **Appendix 2**).

5 The middle is also used in a causative sense, i.e. *to cause something to be done*, as in ἀπογράφεσθαι *to have oneself registered* from ἀπογράφω *register*.

6 The earlier use of the middle to indicate reflexive action occurs rarely, e.g. ἀπήγξατο (Mt 27.5) *he hanged himself* from ἀπάγχω *throttle*.The normal way of expressing reflexive action is by using the reflexive pronoun as in English; see 9.1/4.

8.1/2 Deponent verbs

Deponent verbs are a linguistic peculiarity for which English offers no parallel. These are **middle or passive in form** but **active in meaning** and may be transitive (as κτάομαι *acquire*) or intransitive (as πορεύομαι *go, travel*). In some cases the meaning of a deponent exemplifies one of the uses of the middle voice (κτάομαι originally meant *procure for oneself*), but elsewhere (as δέχομαι *receive*) no explanation seems possible, although these verbs are among the most commonly used in Greek.

Examples of middle deponents are:

τὸ γὰρ ἔργον κυρίου ἐργάζεται ὡς κἀγώ (= καὶ ἐγώ) (1 Cor 16.10) *For he carries out the work of the Lord as I [do] too.* (ἐργάζομαι *work, carry out, accomplish*)

ψυχικὸς δὲ ἄνθρωπος οὐ δέχεται τὰ τοῦ πνεύματος τοῦ θεοῦ (1 Cor 2.14) *And a worldly man does not receive the [things] of God's spirit.* (δέχομαι *receive*)

ἀγαπητέ, εὔχομαί σε εὐοδοῦσθαι καὶ ὑγιαίνειν. (*3 J 2) *Beloved, I pray [for] you to prosper and be healthy.* (εὔχομαι *pray*; εὐοδόομαι *prosper*).

For deponents with passive forms in the future and aorist see 11.1/11 note 1.

A common deponent is γίνομαι (fut. γενήσομαι) which has a strong aorist middle ἐγενόμην as well as an aorist passive ἐγενήθην (both forms have the same meaning). Its basic meaning is *be born, become, happen* but sometimes English requires a more specific word, e.g. φωνὴ ἐγένετο ἐκ τῶν οὐρανῶν (Mk 1.11) *a voice came* (lit. *came into existence, happened*) *from heaven*. Other examples of its use are:

> τὰ ἱμάτια ἐγένετο λευκὰ ὡς τὸ φῶς. (*Mt 17.2) *The garments became white as the light.*
> καὶ ἰδοὺ σεισμὸς μέγας ἐγένετο ἐν τῇ θαλάσσῃ. (Mt 8.24) *And behold! a great storm arose on the sea.*

The form ἐγένετο in the sense of *it happened* [*that*], *it came to pass* [*that*] is used to reproduce a Semitic expression employed to mark a new stage in a narrative. There are three forms of this contruction and in each ἐγένετο is usually accompanied by a phrase or subordinate clause which fixes the time of the event described:

(a) καὶ ἐγένετο or ἐγένετο δέ followed by a finite verb without any conjunction: καὶ ἐγένετο ἐν τῇ ἡμέρᾳ τῇ ὀγδόῃ ἦλθον περιτεμεῖν τὸ παιδίον (Lk 1.59) *and it happened on the eighth day* [*that*] *they came to circumcise the child.* Here the phrase ἐν τῇ ἡμέρᾳ τῇ ὀγδόῃ defines the time but there is no conjunction connecting the two finite verbs ἐγένετο and ἦλθον, and consequently we supply *that* in English; note, however, that we can say in English *it happened I was in the country last week.*

(b) καὶ ἐγένετο or ἐγένετο δέ followed by καί and a finite verb: καὶ ἐγένετο ἐν μιᾷ τῶν ἡμερῶν καὶ αὐτὸς ἦν διδάσκων (Lk 5.17) *and it happened on one of the days that* (lit. *and*) *he was teaching.* Despite the use of καί we translate in the same way as in (a).

(c) καὶ ἐγένετο or ἐγένετο δέ followed by an accusative and infinitive (see also below 8.1/4(b)). Here the noun or pronoun in the accusative is the subject of the infinitive: ἐγένετο δὲ ἐν σαββάτῳ διαπορεύεσθαι αὐτὸν διὰ σπορίμων (Lk 6.1) lit. *and it happened on the sabbath him to be going through standing grain* i.e *and it happened that on the sabbath he was going* etc.

The idiom is common in Luke and also occurs in the other gospels and in Acts.

Note

The deponent ἔρχομαι *come, go* has a middle future (ἐλεύσομαι *I shall come/go*) but a strong aorist active ἦλθον (*I came/went*; 7.1/1 note 2).

8.1/3 Negatives

Greek has two negatives οὐ (οὐκ, οὐχ, 2.1/6(a)(i)), which we have already met, and μή. Although they must both be translated by *not* their uses are quite distinct. μή is used in a number of constructions and contexts, the first of which is treated in the next subsection. The following should be noted:

(a) οὐ is used to negate statements and so is the negative used with a verb in the indicative in main clauses.
(b) μή is used to negate wishes, commands and in certain types of subordinate clauses.
(c) μή is the usual negative used with infinitives and participles.
(d) For every compound of οὐ (e.g. οὐδέ *nor*, οὐδείς *no-one*) there is a corresponding compound of μή (e.g. μηδέ, μηδείς). The latter are to be translated in the same way but are used, where appropriate, in constructions otherwise requiring μή.
(e) A second negative normally reinforces an earlier negative in the same clause: οὐκ ἔφαγεν οὐδέν (Lk 4.2) *he did not eat anything* (cf. 7.2.10).

8.1/4 Indirect statement

(For the term *indirect statement* see 7.1/2.)

In English we can say, with the same meaning, *he considers that I am clever* or *he considers me to be clever*. Both ways of expressing an indirect statement (a noun clause introduced by *that* or an infinitive phrase without *that*) have their equivalents in Greek, but Greek, like English, shows a distinct preference for the former after verbs of **saying**. Verbs of **thinking, seeing, hearing and knowing** such as νομίζω *think, consider*, ὁράω *see*, ἀκούω *hear*, γινώσκω *know* may also take this construction.

(a) *Construction with finite verb*
The noun clause expressing the indirect statement is introduced by ὅτι *that*:

λέγω ὑμῖν ὅτι πλούσιος δυσκόλως εἰσελεύσεται εἰς τὴν βασιλείαν τῶν οὐρανῶν. (Mt 19.23) *I tell you that with difficulty will a rich man enter the Kingdom of heaven.* (εἰσελεύσεται fut. of εἰσέρχομαι)

The only difference from the English construction is that the tense of the verb in the original statement is normally retained in the reported version if the introductory verb is in a past tense:

ἤκουσε ὅτι Ἀρχέλαος βασιλεύει τῆς Ἰουδαίας. (*Mt. 2.22). *He heard that Archelaos was king of Judaea* (original Ἀρχέλαος βασιλεύει τῆς Ἰουδαίας *Archelaos is king of Judaea*).

οἱ πρῶτοι ἐνόμισαν ὅτι πλεῖον λήμψονται. (Mt 20.10) *They first thought that they would receive more* (original πλεῖον λημψόμεθα *we will receive more*).

Notes

1 As we have already seen, ὅτι can also mean *because*; this meaning will be obvious from the context: οὐαὶ ὑμῖν τοῖς Φαρισαίοις, ὅτι ἀγαπᾶτε τὴν πρωτοκαθεδρίαν ἐν ταῖς συναγωγαῖς (Lk 11.43) *woe to you Pharisees* (lit. *to you the Pharisees*) *because you love the seat of honour in the synagogues.*

2 Often even a **direct** statement is introduced by ὅτι; here ὅτι is not to be translated and the quote should be put between inverted commas: εἶπεν γὰρ ὅτι Θεοῦ εἰμι υἱός (Mt 27.43) *for he said, 'I am the son of God'.*

(b) *Infinitive construction*

In this alternative construction, which is not so common as (*a*), the original direct statement is recast so that a finite verb becomes an infinitive and its subject is changed from nominative to accusative; the name given to this construction is the **accusative and infinitive**. No introductory word similiar to ὅτι is used:

λέγουσιν αὐτὸν ζῆν. (Lk 24.23) *They say that he is alive.* (lit. *him to be alive*).

ἔλεγον αὐτὸν εἶναι θεόν. (Ac 28.6) *They were saying that he was a god.* (lit. *him to be a god*)

If the original statement is negated, οὐ is replaced by μή when it is converted into an accusative and infinitive:

Σαδδουκαῖοι λέγουσιν μὴ εἶναι ἀνάστασιν (Ac 23.8) *Sadducees say that there is no resurrection* (original οὐκ ἔστιν ἀνάστασις *there is no resurrection*).

Note

A variation of this construction can be used when the subject of the infinitive is the same as the subject of the main verb (**nominative and infinitive**). If the statement σοφοί εἰμεν *we are wise* is reported as a claim made by others, the English version will be *they claim to be wise*; because the subject of *claim* and of *to be wise* is the same, Greek can use the nominative and infinitive: φάσκουσιν εἶναι σοφοί (cf. Ro 1.22). However, here too the accusative and infinitive is possible. In English we can say with the same meaning *they claim themselves to be wise* and we use the accusative *themselves*; Greek has the same construction, e.g. Θευδᾶς ἔλεγεν εἶναί τινα ἑαυτόν (*Ac 5.36) *Theudas was saying that he was an important person*, lit. *was saying himself* (ἑαυτόν 9.1/4) *to be somebody* (τινά 10.1/1).

8.1/5 Third declension nouns – stems in ι and υ

Stems in ι are feminine, except for ὄφις (m) *snake* and σίναπι (n) *mustard*. Many are abstract nouns ending in -σις, e.g. φύσις *nature*. The original ι of the stem has been lost in most forms. The genitive singular has the irregular ending -εως.

A few masculine and feminine nouns have a stem in υ, which is kept in all forms (except πηχῶν – see below).

In the accusative singular all masculine or feminine nouns with these stems have ν (not α as with stems in consonants 5.1/1, 6.1/1).

	πόλις (f) *city*		ἰχθύς (m) *fish*	
	SINGULAR	PLURAL	SINGULAR	PLURAL
Nom	πόλις	πόλεις	ἰχθύς	ἰχθύες
Acc.	πόλιν	πόλεις	ἰχθύν	ἰχθύας
Gen.	πόλεως	πόλεων	ἰχθύος	ἰχθύων
Dat.	πόλει	πόλεσι(ν)	ἰχθύϊ	ἰχθύσι(ν)

Other nouns declined like ἰχθύς are: ἰσχύς (f) *strength*; στάχυς (m) *ear of corn*; ὀσφῦς (f.) *loins*.

Notes

1 The sole ι stem neuter σίναπι *mustard* occurs only in the genitive singular: σινάπεως. δακρύων (gen. pl.) and δάκρυσι (dat. pl.) from δάκρυ (or δάκρυον) *tear* are the only forms from a υ stem neuter.

2 πῆχυς (m) *cubit* (measure of length) only occurs in the acc. s. πῆχυν and in the gen. pl. πηχῶν.

8.2 Greek reading

1 Ἰησοῦς Χριστὸς Θεοῦ Υἱὸς Σωτήρ (the name of an early Christian symbol is concealed in the initial letters of this formula).

2 ὁ δὲ Παῦλος, Οὐ μαίνομαι, φησίν, κράτιστε Φῆστε, ἀλλὰ ἀληθείας καὶ σωφροσύνης ῥήματα ἀποφθέγγομαι. (Ac 26.25)

3 διὰ τί οἱ μαθηταί σου παραβαίνουσιν τὴν παράδοσιν τῶν πρεσβυτέρων; οὐ γὰρ νίπτονται τὰς χεῖρας αὐτῶν. (Mt 15.2)

4 πῶς οὐ νοεῖτε ὅτι οὐ περὶ ἄρτων εἶπον ὑμῖν; (Mt 16.11)

5 λέγει αὐτοῖς ὁ Ἰησοῦς, Ἀμὴν λέγω ὑμῖν ὅτι οἱ τελῶναι καὶ αἱ πόρναι προάγουσιν ὑμᾶς εἰς τὴν βασιλείαν τοῦ θεοῦ. (Mt 21.31)

6 εἶδεν ὁ ὄχλος ὅτι Ἰησοῦς οὐκ ἔστιν ἐκεῖ. (Jn 6.24)

7 οὐκ ἠρνήσατο, καὶ ὡμολόγησεν ὅτι Ἐγὼ οὐκ εἰμὶ ὁ Χριστός. (Jn 1.20)

8 ἀπὸ δὲ ἕκτης ὥρας σκότος ἐγένετο ἐπὶ ὅλην τὴν γῆν ἕως ὥρας ἐνάτης. (*Mt 27.45)

9 καὶ ἐγένετο ὡς ἤγγισεν εἰς Βηθφαγὴ καὶ Βηθανιὰ πρὸς τὸ ὄρος τὸ καλούμενον Ἐλαιῶν, ἀπέστειλεν (dispatched) δύο τῶν μαθητῶν. (Lk 19.29)

10 ἐγὼ δὲ λέγω ὑμῖν μὴ ὀμόσαι (swear) ὅλως· μήτε ἐν τῷ οὐρανῷ, ὅτι θρόνος ἐστὶν τοῦ θεοῦ· μήτε ἐν τῇ γῇ, ὅτι ὑποπόδιόν ἐστιν τῶν ποδῶν αὐτοῦ. (Mt 5.34f.)

11 ἐγένετο φόβος μέγας ἐφ' ὅλην τὴν ἐκκλησίαν. (Ac 5.11)

12 εἶπεν δὲ πρὸς αὐτούς, Πῶς λέγουσιν τὸν Χριστὸν εἶναι Δαυὶδ υἱόν; (Lk 20.41)

13 ὁ γεωργὸς ἐκδέχεται τὸν τίμιον καρπὸν τῆς γῆς. (Js 5.7)

14 ἐγένετο ἐν τῷ προσεύχεσθαι αὐτὸν τὸ εἶδος τοῦ προσώπου αὐτοῦ ἕτερον. (Lk 9.29)

15 Καὶ ἐξῆλθεν πάλιν παρὰ τὴν θάλασσαν· καὶ ὅλος ὁ ὄχλος ἤρχετο πρὸς αὐτόν, καὶ ἐδίδασκεν αὐτούς. (*Mk 2.13)

16 καὶ ἐγένετο ὅτε ἐτέλεσεν ὁ Ἰησοῦς τοὺς λόγους τούτους (these) ἐξεπλήσσοντο οἱ ὄχλοι ἐπὶ τῇ διδαχῇ αὐτοῦ. (Mt 7.28)

17 λέγει αὐτοῖς Σίμων Πέτρος, Ὑπάγω ἁλιεύειν. λέγουσιν αὐτῷ, Ἐρχόμεθα καὶ ἡμεῖς σὺν σοί. (Jn 21.3)

18 οἱ δὲ μαθηταὶ αὐτοῦ ἐπείνασαν, καὶ ἤρξαντο τίλλειν στάχυας καὶ ἐσθίειν. (Mt 12.1)

19 καὶ ἐγένετο ἐν τῷ καθεξῆς καὶ αὐτὸς διώδευεν κατὰ πόλιν καὶ κώμην. (Lk 8.1)

20 τότε ἐξεπορεύετο πρὸς αὐτὸν Ἱεροσόλυμα καὶ ὅλη ἡ Ἰουδαία καὶ ὅλη ἡ περίχωρος τοῦ Ἰορδάνου, καὶ ἐβαπτίζοντο ἐν τῷ Ἰορδάνῃ ποταμῷ ὑπ' αὐτοῦ. (*Mt 3.5f.)

Notes

5 λέγει is a vivid present (2.1/4 note 2) and should be translated by the English simple past (*said*); οἱ τελῶναι καὶ αἱ πόρναι are meant as general classes and do not require the definite article in English (2.1/2 note 1(ii)).

6 ἐστίν translate by *was*; although the main verb (εἶδεν) is not a verb of saying, the same construction is used (8.1/4(a)) because the thought in the crowd's mind was *Jesus is not there*.

7 ἠρνήσατο < ἀρνέομαι; ὡμολόγησεν < ὁμολογέω; do not translate ὅτι (8.1/4(a) note 2).

8 The time of day was divided in twelve equal parts starting with sunrise, so that at the equinox the sixth hour corresponded to our twelve noon and the ninth hour to our 3 p.m.; correspondence with our system of time reckoning varied at other times of the year.

9 τὸ ὄρος τὸ καλούμενον Ἐλαιῶν lit. *the mountain, the [one] called [that] of Olives*, i.e. *the Mount of Olives* (καλούμενον is a participle and will be treated at 12.1/1).

10 The full context shows that δέ here is to be translated by *but*; ἐν τῷ οὐρανῷ and ἐν τῇ γῇ lit. *on the heaven, on the earth* but English requires *by*; ὅτι *because*; predicates (see **Glossary of grammatical and other terms**) such as θρόνος and ὑποπόδιον do not have the definite article but it is required in English.

12 πρός + acc. can be used with the same meaning as the dat. without a preposition after verbs of saying (21.1/1(a)(i)); λέγουσιν is here followed by the accusative and infinitive construction (8.1/4(b)); the sense shows that the indeclinable Δαυίδ must be taken as genitive.

14 εγένετο has εἶδος as its subject (it is not used here in the sense *it happened*); ἐν τῷ προσεύχεσθαι αὐτόν see 5.1/3 (αὐτὸν is the subject of the infinitive).

15 ἤρχετο < ἔρχομαι (the impf. of ἄρχομαι would be the same); ἤρχετο and ἐδίδασκεν are imperfect because the actions are regarded as happening over a period, but trans. *came ... taught*.

16 Take τοὺς λόγους τούτους together *these words* (for τούτους see 9.1/1); ἐξεπλήσσοντο < ἐκπλήσσω.

17 ἁλιεύειν the infinitive in Greek is used to express purpose just as it is in English (11.1/3(b)(i)) – trans. *to fish*.

18 ἤρξαντο < ἄρχομαι.

19 Translate the second καί by *that* (8.1/2(b)).

20 ἐξεπορεύετο (<ἐκπορεύομαι) is singular because it agrees only with the nearest subject (Ἱεροσόλυμα which is neut. pl.

and so can take a singular verb – 2.1/2 note 3) – this is a common idiom; ὑπ' = ὑπό.

8.2/1 Vocabulary

ἀλήθεια, -ας, ἡ   *truth*
ἁλιεύω   *fish*
ἀμήν (adv.)   *truly*
ἀποφθέγγομαι   *speak*
ἀρνέομαι   *deny*
ἄρτος, -ου, ὁ   *loaf of bread*
ἄρχομαι   *begin*
Βηθανιά, (indecl.), ἡ   *Bethany*
   (village on Mt. of Olives)
Βηθφαγη, ἡ (indecl.)
   Bethphage (place on Mt. of
   Olives)
Δαυίδ, (indecl.), ὁ   *David*
διδαχή, -ῆς, ἡ   *teaching*
διοδεύω   *journey, travel*
ἐγγίζω   *come near*
εἶδος, -ους, τό   *appearance*
ἐκδέχομαι   *wait for*
ἐκεῖ (adv.)   *there, in that*
   place
ἐκπλήσσω   *amaze*
ἐκπορεύομαι   *come out*
ἕκτος, -η, -ον   *sixth*
ἐλαία, -ας, ἡ   *olive tree*
ἔνατος, -η, -ον   *ninth*
ἔρχομαι   *come*
ἕτερος, -α, -ον   *different*
ἕως (prep. + gen.)   *up to*
Ἰορδάνης, -ου, ὁ   *Jordan*
   (largest river in Palestine)
Ἰουδαία, -ας, ἡ   *Judaea*
καθεξῆς (adv.)   *next in order*
   ἐν τῷ καθεξῆς   *in the next*
   in order i.e. *afterwards*
κατά (prep. + acc.)   *through*
κράτιστος, -η, -ον   *most*
   excellent

κώμη, -ης, ἡ   *village*
μαίνομαι   *be mad*
μήτε ... μήτε (conj.)   *neither*
   ... nor
νίπτω   *wash*
νοέω   *understand*
ὅλος, -η, -ον   *all*
ὅλως (adv.)   *at all*
ὁμολογέω   *admit*
ὄρος, -ους, τό   *mountain*
παρά (prep. + acc.)   *to*
παραβαίνω   *transgress*
παράδοσις, -εως, ἡ   *tradition*
πεινάω   *be hungry*
περίχωρος, -ον   *neighbouring*
   ἡ περίχωρος (sc. γῆ)
   neighbourhood
πόρνη, -ης, ἡ   *prostitute*
ποταμός, -οῦ, ὁ   *river*
προάγω   *go before, precede*
προσεύχομαι   *pray*
στάχυς, -υος, ὁ   *ear of corn*
σύν (prep. + dat.)   *with, in*
   the company of
σωφροσύνη, -ης, ἡ   *rationality*
τελέω   *finish*
τίλλω   *pick*
τίμιος, -α, -ον   *precious*
ὑπάγω   *go out*
ὑπό (prep. + gen.)   *by* (used
   of an agent)
ὑποπόδιον, -ου, τό   *footstool*
Φῆστος, -ου, ὁ   *Festus* (Roman
   procurator of Palestine)
ὡς (conj.)   *when*

8.3 Excursus

Books in antiquity – the codex

As we have seen (4.3), the traditional form of the book in antiquity, the papyrus roll, was not a user-friendly production. It was awkward to read and cumbersome to consult. Whereas today we simply flick through a book's pages for a reference or to check the accuracy of a quotation, an ancient scholar was obliged to work through a roll until the necessary passage appeared; there was no equivalent to pagination. The limited amount of material which a roll could contain was also a grave disadvantage. It could not accommodate what today we would consider a book of medium size, such as the New Testament; anything as large as the whole Bible was completely unthinkable.

In the first century of the Christian era a new type of book was beginning to appear, the codex. An earlier form had already existed for several centuries and consisted of a small number of thin wooden boards smeared on each side with wax and held together by a leather thong which was threaded through holes in one side of each board, in much the same way as what we call spirex binding. This allowed the user to turn the boards over and inscribe a message on either side with a sharp-pointed stylus into the wax. The original codex was not meant for anything like the amount of text that even a papyrus roll could hold. It was for letters, messages and the like, and it could be re-used simply by applying a new coating of wax to the boards. When papyrus was substituted for wood, recycling became more difficult, but the modern form of the book was born. Sheets of papyrus were folded in two and a number of such foldings were held together by stitching along the spine, just as in better quality books today. Front, back and spine were protected by what we now call binding. With this new form of book, readers had something which was considerably easier to use, more convenient to consult when a particular reference or passage was required, and capable of holding the contents of many rolls. It is not surprising that it was soon adopted by Christians, since a single codex could hold the entire New Testament and more. From the second century AD it was by far the preferred form of book for producing copies of the Scriptures.

However, papyrus had one disadvantage when used as the leaves of a codex. Because of its inflexibility the folds which formed the spine of the codex tended to crack and split. Fortunately, a superior substitute was available. The ancient world had long known of parchment (also called vellum), which was the result of a special treatment of animal skins. It was not only thin and white but also extremely strong and durable, superior in this to any form of modern paper. It was ideal for the codex.

A few codices of the Scriptures dating from before AD 500 have survived, all unfortunately in a fragmentary state. One of the most celebrated is the Codex Sinaiticus (c. AD 350), a parchment codex which originally contained the entire Greek Bible (on the Septuagint, the name given to the Greek Old Testament, see 12.3). Its original length was over 700 pages of 380 x 343 mm (15 x 13.5 inches), each of which contained three or four narrow columns; the use of a narrow column goes back to the old papyrus roll. Part of one of the surviving sections of this codex is reproduced on the cover of the present volume and gives an idea of how an ancient scribe presented a text. What we have here is from the first chapter of John's gospel, and the middle column from immediately under the title box reads:

ΑΥΤΟΥΔΟΞΑΝΩϹ
ΜΟΝΟΓΕΝΟΥϹΠΑ
ΡΑΠΑΤΡΟϹΠΛΗΡΥϹ
ΧΑΡΙΤΟϹΚΑΙΑΛΗΘΕΙΑϹ

A modern reader might be forgiven for preferring a modern presentation, which would be αὐτοῦ, δόξαν, ὡς μονογενοῦς παρὰ πατρός, πλήρης χάριτος καὶ ἀληθείας (part of Jn 1.14) [*and the word became flesh and dwelt among us and we saw the glory*] *of him, glory of the only begotten* [*son*] *of his father, full of love and truth* (the translation is of the full verse). As well as using the old conventions mentioned in 4.3 (capitals including the different form of sigma, no word division, no punctuation, no accents or breathings) the scribe reduced the size of the final letters of the third and fourth lines in order to prevent the last words of each from running into the next line, although he had no compunction in splitting παρά between lines two and three. It is odd to learn that the Codex Sinaiticus is considered by experts to be particularly easy to read.

By the fourth and fifth centuries AD the codex had superseded the papyrus roll. The many copies of the Scriptures dating from later centuries are in the codex form. Styles of writing developed and in the Middle Ages we find a cursive script of a kind similar to normal handwriting today. In this period greater attention was given to produce a text which could be more easily read; spaces were left between words, and accents and breathings were added. But the basic failing that had always plagued the production of books remained: no two copies were exactly identical. Indeed, in the course of centuries the mistakes of scribes accumulated and often became worse. Consequently the oldest surviving texts of the New Testament are the most valuable; because they are closer in time to the original authors we can usually assume that they reproduce the words of the authors more faithfully.

The codex is, of course, still with us in the form of the modern book, but the middle of the fifteenth century saw a change which revolutionized scholarship and book production alike, viz the invention of printing. When in 1456 Gutenberg used movable type to print the Latin version of the Bible (the Vulgate, 20.3), the possibility of having multiple identical copies of a particular edition came into being. The text used by a printer may have contained corruptions inherited from the earlier period, but further scribal error was eliminated. Technology enabled every type of book to be transmitted in a completely accurate form, and a new era of scholarship came into being.

It was not until 1516 that the Greek New Testament appeared under the editorship of Desiderius Erasmus (1466–1536). From then on scholars could have in front of them a printed edition of the NT and be sure that, except for the odd misprint, it contained exactly what its editor had intended.

unit 09

9.1 Grammar

9.1/1 Demonstrative pronouns

Demonstratives draw our attention to persons and things. Both Greek and English have two: οὗτος *this* and ἐκεῖνος *that*. In both languages these words can function as pronouns or adjectives, although the pronominal use of *this* and *that* is more restricted than their Greek equivalents (*this* in *this horse* is an adjective, *that* in *I do not like that* is a pronoun).

ἐκεῖνος is declined as a first and second declension adjective (3.1/3), except that the neuter nom. and acc. s. is ἐκεῖνο (for other words with this ending -o see 4.1/2). οὗτος is similarly declined but the first syllable undergoes changes according to the following rules:

(a) an initial vowel with a rough breathing occurs in the same forms as in the definite article (2.1/2, 3.1/1);
(b) an initial τ occurs in the same forms as in the definite article;
(c) where the ending contains α or η the diphthong of the first syllable changes from ου to αυ.

	SINGULAR			PLURAL		
	M.	F.	N.	M.	F.	N.
Nom.	οὗτος	αὕτη	τοῦτο	οὗτοι	αὗται	ταῦτα
Acc.	τοῦτον	ταύτην	τοῦτο	τούτους	ταύτας	ταῦτα
Gen.	τούτου	ταύτης	τούτου	τούτων	τούτων	τούτων
Dat.	τούτῳ	ταύτῃ	τούτῳ	τούτοις	ταύταις	τούτοις

When a demonstrative is used as an adjective, the noun which it qualifies must retain the definite article and the demonstrative must not be placed between them: ἐκεῖνος ὁ νεανίας *that young man*; ἡ γυνὴ αὕτη *this woman*.

A demonstrative is used as a pronoun when emphasis is required and it is to be translated in the singular as *this/that man, woman, thing* and in the plural *these/those men, women, things* or simply by a third person pronoun (*he, she, it, they* etc.): οὐ θέλομεν τοῦτον βασιλεῦσαι ἐφ᾽ ἡμᾶς (Lk 19.14) *we do not want him* (or *this man*) *to be king over us*; ἐκεῖνον δεῖ αὐξάνειν (Jn 3.30) *he* (or *that man*) *must become great* (lit. *it is necessary for him to increase*).

Note

Earlier Greek had a third demonstrative ὅδε lit. *this near me*. This has survived in the NT in only two forms, τῇδε *for her* (only at Lk 10.39) and τάδε *these things* (eight occurrences, always in the expression τάδε λέγει *he says this*, lit. *these things*).

9.1/2 The relative pronoun ὅς and adjectival clauses

Adjectival clauses qualify nouns or pronouns, and so perform the same function as adjectives. They are introduced by a relative pronoun (in English *who, whom, whose, which, that*):

*I am the man **who** met you at Jerusalem.*
*The horse **which** you then sold me has since died.*

An adjectival clause normally has an antecedent, i.e. a noun or pronoun to which the clause refers and which it qualifies (in the above examples *man* and *horse*). In English the forms of the relative pronoun are not interchangeable but are influenced by the antecedent (*the man which* or *the horse who* are clearly impossible). Further, we cannot say *I know the man whom visited Bethlehem* because, although *man,* the antecedent of the adjectival clause, is the object of *know* (and so would be in the accusative in Greek), the relative pronoun is the subject of the clause it introduces and must take the nominative form *who,* not the accusative form *whom.* The same holds for Greek, where the rule is **a relative pronoun takes its number and gender from its antecedent but its case from the function it performs in its own clause** (but see note 3 below). Greek cannot, moreover, omit the relative pronoun as we so often do in English (*the man you visited cannot come into my house*; Greek must say *the man whom*).

The normal relative pronoun in Greek is ὅς, which is declined as a first and second declension adjective (3.1/3) except that the neuter s. nom. and acc. is ὅ without ν (for other words with this ending see 4.1/2):

	SINGULAR			PLURAL		
	M.	F.	N.	M.	F.	N.
Nom.	ὅς	ἥ	ὅ	οἵ	αἵ	ἅ
Acc.	ὅν	ἥν	ὅ	οὕς	ἅς	ἅ
Gen.	οὗ	ἧς	οὗ	ὧν	ὧν	ὧν
Dat.	ᾧ	ᾗ	ᾧ	οἷς	αἷς	οἷς

The Greek relative pronoun, unlike its English equivalent, cannot be used as an interrogative (in *which is your horse?* *which* introduces a question and therefore is an interrogative).

Examples of adjectival clauses are (the relative pronouns are in bold type):

> μακάριαι αἱ στεῖραι καὶ αἱ κοιλίαι αἳ οὐκ ἐγέννησαν καὶ μαστοὶ οἳ οὐκ ἔθρεψαν. (Lk 23.29) *Fortunate are the infertile and the wombs **that** have not given birth and breasts **that** have not nourished.*

> καὶ ἰδοὺ ὁ ἀστήρ, **ὃν** εἶδον ἐν τῇ ἀνατολῇ, προῆγεν αὐτούς. (Mt 2.9) *And behold, the star **which** they saw in the east was leading them.*

> καὶ ἔρχονται εἰς χωρίον **οὗ** τὸ ὄνομα Γεθσημανί. (Mk 14.32) *And they came to a place **whose** name [was] Gethsemane.* (ἔρχονται vivid present 2.1/5 note 2)

> ἐξελέξατο ἀπ᾽ αὐτῶν δώδεκα, **οὓς** καὶ ἀποστόλους ὠνόμασεν. (*Lk 6.13) *From them he chose twelve, **whom** he also called apostles.*

Notes

1 Greek has an alternative relative pronoun which is a combination of the normal relative pronoun and the indefinite τις (10.1/1). Its use is almost wholly restricted to the nominative forms, which are:

	MASCULINE	FEMININE	NEUTER
SINGULAR	ὅστις	ἥτις	ὅ τι
PLURAL	οἵτινες	αἵτινες	ἅτινα

The neuter singular is written ὅ τι to distinguish it from ὅτι *that* and ὅτι *because*.

ὅστις can be used as a relative pronoun in the same way as ὅς: ἄνθρωπος ἦν οἰκοδεσπότης ὅστις ἐφύτευσεν ἀμπελῶνα (Mt

21.33) *there was a man, a master of a house, who planted a vineyard.* For other uses of ὅστις see 14.1/1(c). The only other part of ὅστις in the NT is the genitive ὅτου which appears as the second element in ἕως ὅτου *until* (lit. *up to whatever*; see 14.1/1(b)(ii)).

2 The antecedent of an adjectival clause, if a pronoun, can be omitted: εἰσὶν ἔσχατοι οἳ ἔσονται πρῶτοι καὶ εἰσὶν πρῶτοι οἳ ἔσονται ἔσχατοι (Lk 13.30) [*Those*] *who will be first are last and* [*those*] *who will be last are first.*

3 Contrary to the rule given above, the Greek relative pronoun is sometimes put into the same case as its antecedent. This quite illogical attraction is most frequent when a relative pronoun in the accusative case has an antecedent in the genitive or dative: θάμβος περιέσχεν Πέτρον ἐπὶ τῇ ἄγρᾳ τῶν ἰχθύων ὧν (for οὓς) συνέλαβον (*Lk 5.9) *amazement seized Peter on the catch of fish which they took.* Sometimes the antecedent, if a pronoun, is omitted (cf. note 2); οὐδὲν εὗρον ἐν τῷ ἀνθρώπῳ τούτῳ αἴτιον ὧν (for τούτων ἃ) κατηγορεῖτε κατ᾽ αὐτοῦ (Lk 23.14) *I found this man not guilty of the charges which you bring against him* (lit. *I found in this man no* [οὐθέν] *guilt of which things you bring as charges* [κατηγορεῖτε] *against him*).

4 Sometimes when both the relative and its antecedent are in the same case the latter is put into the adjectival clause: οἱ ἄνθρωποι εἶδον ὃ ἐποίησεν σημεῖον (for τὸ σημεῖον ὃ ἐποίησεν) (*Jn 6.14) *the people saw the miracle which he performed*; here the relative is used as an adjective.

9.1/3 Other uses of αὐτός

For the terms **attributive position** and **predicative position** see 3.1/3(b).

We have already seen αὐτός as a pronoun (4.1/2). It has two other uses:

(a) As an **emphasizing adjective** meaning *self.* Greek has no separate words corresponding to the English emphatic *myself, yourself* etc. (as opposed to the **reflexive** *myself, yourself* etc., see 9.1/4) and instead uses αὐτός for all persons. When used with a noun it stands in the **predicative** position (i.e. it is not placed between the noun and the article): αὐτὸς ὁ ἀνήρ *the man himself,* περὶ τῆς γυναικὸς αὐτῆς *concerning the woman herself.*

(b) ὁ αὐτός means *the same*. In the **attributive** position (i.e. between the article and the noun) αὐτός **always** has this meaning: τὸν αὐτὸν ἀγῶνα (Phil 1.30) *the same contest* (acc. s.); τὸν αὐτὸν λόγον (Mt 26.44) *the same speech* (acc. s.). Examples in the neuter are: καὶ οἱ ἁμαρτωλοὶ τὸ αὐτὸ ποιοῦσιν (Lk 6.33) *even sinners do the same* [*thing*]; τὰ αὐτὰ ἐπάθετε (1 Th 2.14) *you suffered the same* [*things*].

9.1/4 Reflexive and reciprocal pronouns

(a) A **reflexive pronoun** refers back to the subject of a sentence or clause, as in *he killed himself*. In English all reflexive pronouns end in -*self* (*myself, yourself, himself, themselves,* etc.) and are to be carefully distinguished from the emphatic adjectives of the same form, e.g. *he himself killed the soldier.*

In the singular the reflexives of the first and second persons are formed by joining the stems of the personal pronouns (4.1/2) to the appropriate parts of αὐτός. The third person reflexive is formed by prefixing αὐτός with ἑ; this formation is also used in all persons of the plural. Reflexive pronouns can occur only in the oblique cases and the possibility of a neuter exists only in the third person forms.

SINGULAR

	First person		Second person		Third person		
	M.	F.	M.	F.	M.	F.	N.
Acc.	ἐμαυτόν	ἐμαυτήν	σεαυτόν	σεαυτήν	ἑαυτόν	ἑαυτήν	ἑαυτό
Gen.	ἐμαυτοῦ	ἐμαυτῆς	σεαυτοῦ	σεαυτῆς	ἑαυτοῦ	ἑαυτῆς	ἑαυτοῦ
Dat.	ἐμαυτῷ	ἐμαυτῇ	σεαυτῷ	σεαυτῇ	ἑαυτῷ	ἑαυτῇ	ἑαυτῷ

PLURAL **All persons**

	M.	F.	N.
Acc.	ἑαυτούς	ἑαυτάς	ἑαυτά
Gen.	ἑαυτῶν	ἑαυτῶν	ἑαυτῶν
Dat.	ἑαυτοῖς	ἑαυταῖς	ἑαυτοῖς

Examples of these pronouns in use are:

οὐδὲ ἐμαυτὸν ἠξίωσα πρὸς σὲ ἐλθεῖν. (Lk 7.7) *Nor did I think myself worthy to come to you.*

τί λέγεις περὶ σεαυτοῦ; (Jn 1.22) *What do you say about yourself?*

οὐκ ἔχει ῥίζαν ἐν ἑαυτῷ ἀλλὰ πρόσκαιρός ἐστιν. (*Mt 13. 21) *He has no root in himself but lasts only for a time* (lit. *is short-lasting*).

πάντοτε γὰρ τοὺς πτωχοὺς ἔχετε μεθ᾽ ἑαυτῶν. (Mt 26.11)
For you have the poor with you (lit. yourselves) always.

The third singular reflexive has alternative forms in which the first two syllables are contracted: αὑτόν (< ἑαυτόν), etc. In the manuscripts of the New Testament (21.3) these contracted forms (which have a rough breathing) are sometimes confused with the corresponding forms of αὐτός (which do not have a rough breathing). As it is difficult in some cases, if not impossible, to judge whether this confusion is a scribal error in the manuscripts or goes back to the original author, modern editors sometimes print αὐτόν etc, where strict grammar requires αὑτόν etc. An example is Jn 2.24 where the recommended edition prints Ἰησοῦς οὐκ ἐπίστευεν αὑτὸν αὐτοῖς, which clearly means *Jesus did not entrust himself to them*; other editions print αὐτὸν, which is required by strict grammar. The question is made more complex by passages where the normal personal pronouns are used instead of reflexives, e.g. εὑρήσετε ἀνάπαυσιν ταῖς ψυχαῖς ὑμῶν (Mt 11.29) *you will find rest for your souls* (strict grammar would require ταῖς ψυχαῖς ἑαυτῶν *the souls of you yourselves* because the pronoun refers back to the understood subject *you*).

(b) **Reciprocal** action can be expressed by the pronoun ἀλλήλους (acc. pl.) *each other* (gen. pl. ἀλλήλων, dat. pl. ἀλλήλοις are the only other forms that occur), e.g. ἔλεγον πρὸς ἀλλήλους (Mk 4.41) *they were saying to each other*. However, the reflexive pronoun can be used in the same sense: κρίματα ἔχετε μεθ᾽ ἑαυτῶν (1 Cor 6.7) *you have lawsuits with each other* (μετ᾽ ἀλλήλων would have the same meaning).

9.1/5 Possessive adjectives and pronouns

English has possessive adjectives of two types: attributive (*my, your, his, her, its; our, your, their,* which occur in phrases such as *my house*) and predicative (*mine, yours, his, hers; ours, yours, theirs,* which occur in clauses such as *the house is mine*). Greek has similar possessive adjectives for the first and second persons only, and these may be used either attributively or predicatively (we have already seen σός in 6.2.9). These are:

ἐμός *my*	ἡμέτερος *our*
σός *your* (with ref. to one person)	ὑμέτερος *your* (with ref. to two or more persons)

In the attributive use the possessive adjective is preceded by the definite article, and this can take two forms: τὸ ἐμὸν ὄνομα (Mt 18.20) or τὸ ὄνομα τὸ ἐμόν *my name*; ἡ χαρὰ ἡ ἐμή (Jn 3.29) or ἡ ἐμή χαρά *my joy*.

An example of the predicative use, where the possessive is **not** preceded by the definite article, is: ὁ λόγος ὃν ἀκούετε οὐκ ἔστιν ἐμός (Jn 14.24) *the word which you hear is not mine*.

To indicate possession Greek also uses the genitive of pronouns, e.g. ὁ πατὴρ ἡμῶν lit. *the father of us*, i.e. *our father*. This type of expression is the only one possible with the third person as Greek has no third person possessive adjectives, but in the NT it has also largely replaced the first and second person possessive adjectives described above. The forms involved are μου, *of me*; σου *of you* (s.) (the unemphatic forms are used; see 4.1/2); αὐτοῦ *of him*, αὐτῆς *of her*, αὐτοῦ *of it*; ἡμῶν *of us*; ὑμῶν *of you* (pl.); αὐτῶν *of them*. In this context these pronouns are to be translated *my, your, his, her, its, our, your, their* respectively. They normally (but not always) follow the noun qualified and are not preceded by the definite article. Examples with αὐτοῦ have already occurred in the reading (as 4.2.13). Examples with other pronouns are:

οὗτός ἐστιν ὁ υἱός μου. (Mt 3.17) *This is my son.*

ἀγαπήσεις τὸν πλησίον σου καὶ μισήσεις τὸν ἐχθρόν σου. (Mt 5.43) *You will love your neighbour and hate your enemy.*

If, however, the noun is also qualified by an attributive adjective (i.e. we have definite article + adjective + noun), then the pronoun is put after the adjective, e.g. εἰ ἡ δεξιά σου χεὶρ σκανδαλίζει σε ... (Mt 5.30) *if your right hand offends you ...* (lit. *the right of you hand*).

The genitive of reflexive pronouns is used when ownership is referred back to the subject of a clause; this use is almost wholly confined to ἑαυτοῦ and ἑαυτῶν, which can be placed in the attributive or predicative position. Examples are:

ἐπορεύοντο ἀπογράφεσθαι, ἕκαστος εἰς τὴν ἑαυτοῦ πόλιν. (Lk 2.3) *They went to have themselves registered, each to his own city.*

εἴ τις ἔρχεται πρός με καὶ οὐ μισεῖ τὸν πατέρα ἑαυτοῦ ... (Lk 14.26) *If anyone comes to me and does not hate his own father ...*

ὀφείλουσιν καὶ οἱ ἄνδρες ἀγαπᾶν τὰς ἑαυτῶν γυναῖκας ὡς τὰ ἑαυτῶν σώματα. (Eph 5.28) *Men too are obliged to love their wives (lit. their own women) as their own bodies.*

However, as noted in the previous subsection, the simple pronoun is sometimes used in place of the reflexive, e.g. ὃς οὐ λαμβάνει τὸν σταυρὸν αὐτοῦ... (Mt 10.38) [*He*] *who does not take up his cross* ... (we would expect ἑαυτοῦ as the reference is to the subject of λαμβάνει).

9.2 Greek reading

1 ὁ δὲ ἔφη αὐτοῖς, Ἐχθρὸς ἄνθρωπος τοῦτο ἐποίησεν. (Mt 13.28)

2 ἔστιν δὲ καὶ ἄλλα πολλὰ ἃ ἐποίησεν ὁ Ἰησοῦς. (Jn 21.25)

3 οἶδεν γὰρ ὁ πατὴρ ὑμῶν ὧν χρείαν ἔχετε πρὸ τοῦ ὑμᾶς αἰτῆσαι αὐτόν. (Mt 6.8)

4 ἀγαπήσεις τὸν πλησίον σου ὡς σεαυτόν. (Mt 19.19)

5 ὁ λόγος ὁ σὸς ἀλήθειά ἐστιν. (Jn 17.17)

6 αὐτὸ τὸ πνεῦμα συμμαρτυρεῖ τῷ πνεύματι ἡμῶν ὅτι ἐσμὲν τέκνα θεοῦ. (Ro 8.16)

7 ᾗ δὲ ἡμέρᾳ ἐξῆλθεν Λὼτ ἀπὸ Σοδόμων, ἔβρεξεν πῦρ καὶ θεῖον ἀπ' οὐρανοῦ. (Lk 17.29)

8 εἰσὶν εὐνοῦχοι οἵτινες εὐνούχισαν ἑαυτοὺς διὰ τὴν βασιλείαν τῶν οὐρανῶν. (Mt 19.12)

9 ὑμεῖς ἐκ τούτου τοῦ κόσμου ἐστέ, ἐγὼ οὐκ εἰμὶ ἐκ τοῦ κόσμου τούτου. (Jn 8.23)

10 καὶ ἐγὼ δέ σοι λέγω ὅτι σὺ εἶ Πέτρος, καὶ ἐπὶ ταύτῃ τῇ πέτρᾳ οἰκοδομήσω μου τὴν ἐκκλησίαν, καὶ πύλαι ᾅδου οὐ κατισχύσουσιν αὐτῆς. (*Mt 16.18)

11 ἐκεῖνοι δὲ οἱ γεωργοὶ πρὸς ἑαυτοὺς εἶπαν ὅτι Οὗτός ἐστιν ὁ κληρονόμος. (Mt 21.38)

12 σὺ δὲ ὁ αὐτὸς εἶ καὶ τὰ ἔτη σου οὐκ ἐκλείψουσιν. (Hb 1.12)

13 τότε γνώσεσθε ὅτι ἐγώ εἰμι, καὶ ἀπ' ἐμαυτοῦ ποιῶ οὐδέν, ἀλλὰ καθὼς ἐδίδαξέν με ὁ πατὴρ ταῦτα. (Jn 8.28)

14 οἱ οὖν Ἰουδαῖοι ἐζήτουν αὐτὸν ἐν τῇ ἑορτῇ καὶ ἔλεγον, Ποῦ ἐστιν ἐκεῖνος; (Jn 7.11)

15 εἰ οὖν ἐγὼ ἔνιψα ὑμῶν τοὺς πόδας ὁ κύριος καὶ ὁ διδάσκαλος, καὶ ὑμεῖς ὀφείλετε ἀλλήλων νίπτειν τοὺς πόδας. (Jn 13.14)

16 λέγει οὖν αὐτοῖς ὁ Ἰησοῦς, Ὁ καιρὸς ὁ ἐμὸς οὔπω πάρεστιν, ὁ δὲ καιρὸς ὁ ὑμέτερος πάντοτέ ἐστιν ἕτοιμος. (Jn 7.6)

17 ὁ οὖν Ἰησοῦς πρὸ ἓξ ἡμερῶν τοῦ πάσχα ἦλθεν εἰς Βηθανίαν, ὅπου ἦν Λάζαρος, ὃν ἤγειρεν ἐκ νεκρῶν Ἰησοῦς. (Jn 12.1)

18 παράκλητον ἔχομεν πρὸς τὸν πατέρα, Ἰησοῦν Χριστὸν δίκαιον· καὶ αὐτὸς ἱλασμός ἐστιν περὶ τῶν ἁμαρτιῶν ἡμῶν, οὐ περὶ τῶν ἡμετέρων δὲ μόνον ἀλλὰ καὶ περὶ ὅλου τοῦ κόσμου. (1 J 2.1f.)

19 Ὁμοία γάρ ἐστιν ἡ βασιλεία τῶν οὐρανῶν ἀνθρώπῳ οἰκοδεσπότῃ ὅστις ἐξῆλθεν ἅμα πρωῒ μισθώσασθαι ἐργάτας εἰς τὸν ἀμπελῶνα αὐτοῦ. (Mt 20.1)

20 ἐγώ εἰμι ὁ ποιμὴν ὁ καλός, καὶ γινώσκω τὰ ἐμὰ πρόβατα καὶ γινώσκουσί με τὰ ἐμά. (*Jn 10.14)

21 τοὺς πτωχοὺς γὰρ πάντοτε ἔχετε μεθ᾽ ἑαυτῶν, ἐμὲ δὲ οὐ πάντοτε ἔχετε. (Jn 12.8)

Notes

2 The neuter pl. subject (ἄλλα πολλα) has a singular verb ἐστί (2.1/2 note 3).

3 ὧν χρείαν ἔχετε lit. *of what [things] you have need*, i.e. *the things of which you have need* (9.1./2 note 2); we must tell from the context that ὑμᾶς is the subject of αἰτῆσαι and αὐτόν the object.

7 ᾖ δὲ ἡμέρᾳ lit. *and on what day*, i.e. *and on the day on which* (9.1/2 note 2).

10 καὶ ἐγὼ δέ *and* (δέ) *I also* (καί); there is a play on the words Πέτρος/πέτρᾳ; ᾅδης *Hades* was the Underworld of the Greeks and Romans to which all the dead were consigned, regardless of how they had spent their lives – here it is probably meant to be synonymous with death.

11 ὅτι should be ignored for purposes of translation (8.1/4(a) note 2).

13 The context of this verse shows that δέ should be translated *but*.

13 γνώσεσθε < γινώσκω which has a middle future (8.1/1 note 1); ἐγώ is predicative, so trans. ἐγώ εἰμι *it is I*.

15 ὁ κύριος καὶ ὁ διδάσκαλος (translate *your*, not *the*) is in apposition to ἐγώ; καὶ ὑμεῖς *you too*

16 λέγει vivid present (2.1/5 note 2).

17 πρὸ ἓξ ἡμερῶν τοῦ πάσχα idiomatic for *six days before the Passover*; ἤγειρεν < ἐγείρω.

18 παράκλητον is in apposition to Ἰησοῦν Χριστόν, translate as *intercessor*; take δίκαιον attributively with Ἰησοῦν Χριστόν.

19 μισθώσασθαι *to hire* the infinitive in Greek is used to express purpose just as in English (11.1/3(b)(i)); εἰς *for*, i.e. to work in his vineyard.

9.2/1 Vocabulary

ᾅδης, -ου, ὁ   Hades, the
  Underworld
ἄλλος, -η, -ο   other
ἅμα   see πρωΐ
ἀμπελών, -ῶνος, ὁ   vineyard
βρέχω   rain
δίκαιος, -α, -ον   just
ἐκλείπω   fail, come to an end
ἕξ (indecl.)   six
ἑορτή, -ῆς, ἡ   feast
ἐργάτης, -ου, ὁ   labourer
ἕτοιμος, -η, -ον   ready, at
  hand
εὐνουχίζω   emasculate
εὐνοῦχος, -ου, ὁ   eunuch
ἐχθρός, -ά, -όν   hostile
θεῖον, -ου, τό   sulphur
ἱλασμός, -οῦ, ὁ   expiation,
  remedy
κατισχύω (+ gen.)   win a
  victory over
Λάζαρος, -ου, ὁ   Lazarus
μισθόομαι   hire
οἰκοδεσπότης, -ου, ὁ   master
  of the house

οἰκοδομέω   build
ὅμοιος, -α, -ον (+ dat.)   like,
  resembling
οὔπω (adv.)   not yet
ὀφείλω   be obligated, must,
  ought
παράκλητος, -ου, ὁ   mediator,
  intercessor
πάρειμι   be present, be here
πάσχα, τό (indecl.)   Passover
πέτρα, -ας, ἡ   rock
ποιμήν, -ένος, ὁ   shepherd
πρωΐ (adv.)   early
  ἅμα πρωΐ   early in the
  morning
πύλη, -ης, ἡ   gate
πῦρ, πυρός, τό   fire
Σόδομα, -ων, τά   Sodom
συμμαρτυρέω (+ dat.)   testify
  with
φοβέομαι   fear
χρεία, -ας, ἡ   need

10.1 Grammar

10.1/1 Interrogative τίς and indefinite τις

The interrogative and indefinite pronouns belong to the third declension. They have identical forms except for the accent: when the first syllable is accented (always an acute), we have the interrogative, viz τίς *who*, τί *what*; when the first syllable has no accent, we have the indefinite, viz τις *someone, anyone*, τι *something, anything*. The forms of two syllables in the latter have an accent (as shown below) in certain circumstances (see **Appendix 7, (d)**); since τις is enclitic it does not normally stand as first word in its clause, and when used as an adjective (see below) it follows the word it qualifies.

		Interrogative		**Indefinite**	
		M. & F.	N.	M. & F.	N.
SINGULAR	*Nom.*	τίς	τί	τις	τι
	Acc.	τίνα	τί	τινά	τι
	Gen.	τίνος	τίνος	τινός	τινός
	Dat.	τίνι	τίνι	τινί	τινί
PLURAL	*Nom.*	τίνες	τίνα	τινές	τινά
	Acc.	τίνας	τίνα	τινάς	τινά
	Gen.	τίνων	τίνων	τινῶν	τινῶν
	Dat.	τίσι(ν)	τίσι(ν)	τισί(ν)	τισί(ν)

Both the interrogative and the indefinite pronouns may also be used as adjectives: τίς (τίς ἀνὴρ) τοῦτο ἐποίησεν; *who (what man) did this?* λέγει τις τοῦτο *someone says this*; κλέπτης τις τοῦτο ἐποίησεν *some thief did this*. Used in this way, indefinite τις is often little more than the equivalent of the English indefinite article (the singular is sometimes translated *a certain*). Examples of both words are:

Interrogative

τίς ἐκ τῶν δύο ἐποίησεν τὸ θέλημα τοῦ πατρός; (Mt 21.31) *Who of* (lit. *from*) *the two did the will of their father?* (pronominal use)

ὁ δὲ εἶπεν αὐτοῖς, Τίς ἔσται ἐξ ὑμῶν ἄνθρωπος ...; (Mt 12.11) *And he said to them, 'What man is there among you ...?'* (adjectival use)

τίνος υἱός ἐστιν; (Mt 22.42) *Whose son is he?* (lit. *of whom is he the son?*) (pronominal use)

τίνες εἰσὶν καὶ πόθεν ἦλθον; (Rv 7.13) *Who are they and from where did they come?* (pronominal use)

Indefinite

οὐδὲ ἀκούσει τις ἐν ταῖς πλατείαις τὴν φωνὴν αὐτοῦ. (Mt 12.19) *Nor will anyone hear his voice in the streets.* (pronominal use)

ἀποστέλλουσιν πρὸς αὐτόν τινας τῶν Φαρισαίων. (Mk 12.13) *They send some of the Pharisees to him.* (pronominal use)

ἑκατοντάρχου τινος δοῦλος. (*Lk 7.2) *A slave of some centurion* (or *a certain centurion*). (adjectival use)

Μετὰ δέ τινας ἡμέρας εἶπεν πρὸς Βαρναβᾶν Παῦλος. (Ac 15.36) *After some days Paul said to Barnabas.* (adjectival use)

Note

1 As we have already seen, the neuter τί often means *why*: περὶ ἐνδύματος τί μεριμνᾶτε; (Mt 6.28) *Why do you care about clothing?*

2 Phrases involving τί are: διὰ τί...; (lit. *on account of what...?*), εἰς τί...; (lit. *for what...?*), τί ὅτι...; (lit. *why [is it] that...?*) all to be translated *why...?*; τί γὰρ...;, τί οὖν...; both *why then...?*

10.1/2 Questions, direct and indirect

(a) Direct questions

Direct questions are those which are directly asked of someone else. In Greek, as in English, they are, where appropriate, introduced by an interrogative pronoun, adjective or adverb. The most common pronoun and adjective is τίς; others which can function as a pronoun or adjective are:

ποῖος,-α, -ον *of what kind?* or simply *who?*, *what?* (in the latter meaning virtually the same as τίς)

ποταπός, -ή, -όν *of what kind?*

πόσος, η, -ον *how much, how many?*

There are also the interrogative adverbs πότε *when*, πῶς *how*, ποῦ *where, to where*, πόθεν *from where*. These introduce questions but cannot be used in adverbial clauses as *when* and *where* can in English, e.g. *when we go to Jerusalem I always visit the Dome of the Rock* (Greek here uses the conjunction ὅταν, 14.1/1(b)(i)).

Notice that all interrogatives except τίς begin with a π (cf. *wh* in the English interrogatives: *who, when, why, what*, etc.).

Examples of direct questions introduced by an interrogative are (for examples with τίς see above):

ποταπός ἐστιν οὗτος ὅτι καὶ οἱ ἄνεμοι καὶ ἡ θάλασσα αὐτῷ ὑπακούουσιν; (Mt 8.27) *What kind of person is this that both the winds and the sea obey him?* (ὑπακούω takes the dative, 15.1/1)

ποῦ ἡ πίστις ὑμῶν; (Lk 8.25) *Where [is] your faith?*

πόσον ὀφείλεις τῷ κυρίῳ μου; (Lk 16.5) *How much do you owe to my lord?*

διδάσκαλε, πότε οὖν ταῦτα ἔσται; (Lk 21.7) *Master, so when will these things be?*

Where there is no interrogative word and English uses inversion (*are you sick?*) spoken Greek used some variation in tone to indicate a question, as we can also do in English: *you have been sick?* In written Greek this is shown by the punctuation: ἦλθες ὧδε πρὸ καιροῦ βασανίσαι ἡμᾶς; (Mt 8.29) *did you come here before [the right] time to torture us?*

Questions not introduced by an interrogative can also be framed in such a way as to invite (but not necessarily receive) a negative answer: *you didn't say this, did you?* or *surely you didn't say this?* In Greek such a question is prefixed with μή or μήτι:

μήτι συλλέγουσιν ἀπὸ ἀκανθῶν σταφυλάς; (Mt 7.16) *Surely they do not pick bunches of grapes from thorn-bushes?*

μὴ καὶ σὺ ἐκ τῆς Γαλιλαίας εἶ; (Jn 7.52) *You too aren't from Galilee, are you?* (here the question is sarcastic; the Pharisees wish to imply that the speaker could very well be a Galilean).

Sometimes, however, μή or μήτι is used to introduce what is simply a hesitant question: μήτι οὗτός ἐστιν ὁ Χριστός; (Jn 4.29) *Isn't this the Anointed One?* Μήτι οὗτός ἐστιν ὁ υἱὸς Δαυίδ; (Mt 12.23) *Isn't this the son of David?*

Translations often leave the exact nuance in questions introduced by μή/μήτι to be implied. The AV, for example, translates Mt 7.16 by *Do men gather grapes of thorns?*

We may also have a question which invites a positive answer: *you did say this, didn't you?* or *surely you said this?* In Greek such questions begin with οὐ or οὐχί:

οὐχὶ καὶ οἱ ἐθνικοὶ τὸ αὐτὸ ποιοῦσιν; (Mt 5.47) *Even* (καί) *the heathen do the same thing, don't they?*

οὐχὶ δώδεκα ὧραί εἰσιν τῆς ἡμέρας; (Jn 11.9) *There are twelve hours in the day, aren't there?*

(b) Indirect questions

Indirect questions are another form of indirect speech (7.1/2) and are expressed in Greek by a subordinate clause, just as in English. If the original question began with an interrogative, this is kept. As with indirect statement (8.1/4(a)) the tense of the original is also retained:

ἐπυνθάνετο παρ᾽ αὐτῶν ποῦ ὁ Χριστὸς γεννᾶται. (Mt 2.4) *He asked of them where the Anointed One was being born.* (original ποῦ ὁ Χριστὸς γεννᾶται; *where is the Anointed One being born?*)

If the original question did not contain an interrogative, its indirect form is introduced by εἰ *if* (cf. the English *he asked if I was sick*; original *are you sick?*):

Πιλᾶτος ἐπηρώτησεν εἰ ὁ ἄνθρωπος Γαλιλαῖός ἐστιν· (*Lk 23.6) *Pilate asked if the man was Galilean.* (original ὁ ἄνθρωπος Γαλιλαῖός ἐστιν; *is the man Galilean?*)

εἶπεν δὲ ὁ Ἰησοῦς πρὸς αὐτούς, Ἐπερωτῶ ὑμᾶς, εἰ ἔξεστιν τῷ σαββάτῳ ἀγαθοποιῆσαι ἢ κακοποιῆσαι. (Lk 6.9) *And Jesus said to them, 'I ask you if it is permitted to do good or to do evil on the sabbath.'*

Indirect questions can be introduced by ἐρωτάω (or its compound ἐπερωτάω) and πυνθάνομαι both *ask, inquire* (αἰτέω is also to be translated *ask* but it is used in the context of asking requests or favours).

Note

Just as a direct statement can be introduced by ὅτι (8.1/4(a) note 2) so a direct question can be introduced by εἰ (example at 21.2.2); in these cases neither ὅτι nor εἰ should be translated.

10.1/3 First and third declension adjectives

The masculine and neuter of adjectives in this category belong to the third declension, but their feminine to the first. There are two classes:

(a) *Stems in υ*

In this class the nom. s. ends in -ύς, -εῖα, -ύ (always so accented). ταχύς *swift* is declined:

	SINGULAR			PLURAL		
	M.	F.	N.	M.	F.	N.
Nom.	ταχύς	ταχεῖα	ταχύ	ταχεῖς	ταχεῖαι	ταχέα
Acc.	ταχύν	ταχεῖαν	ταχύ	ταχεῖς	ταχείας	ταχέα
Gen.	ταχέως	ταχείας	ταχέως	ταχέων	ταχειῶν	ταχέων
Dat.	ταχεῖ	ταχείᾳ	ταχεῖ	ταχέσι(ν)	ταχείαις	ταχέσι(ν)

(b) *Stems in ντ*

This class contains only a few adjectives but very many participles (12.1/1). The ντ of the stem is lost in all feminine forms and in the masculine and neuter dat. pl. (cf. ἱμάς 5.1/1(b)). πᾶς *all* is declined:

	SINGULAR			PLURAL		
	M.	F.	N.	M.	F.	N.
Nom.	πᾶς	πᾶσα	πᾶν	πάντες	πᾶσαι	πάντα
Acc.	πάντα	πᾶσαν	πᾶν	πάντας	πάσας	πάντα
Gen.	παντός	πάσης	παντός	πάντων	πασῶν	πάντων
Dat.	παντί	πάσῃ	παντί	πᾶσι(ν)	πάσαις	πᾶσι(ν)

Like πᾶς is declined its emphatic form ἅπας (which we must also translate by *all*).

Notes

1 In the predicative position πᾶς means *all*: πᾶσαι αἱ γενεαί (Mt 1.17) *all the generations* or *all generations*; πᾶσα ἡ Ἰουδαία (Mt 3.5) *all Judea*. In the attributive position it means *whole*: ὁ πᾶς χρόνος (*Ac 20.18) *the whole time.* Without the article it means *every* in the singular, but *all* in the plural: πᾶσα βασιλεία (Mt 12.25) *every kingdom*; πάντες ἄνθρωποι (*Ac 22.15) *all men.* Unfortunately these distinctions are not always rigidly observed.

πᾶς may also stand alone: πᾶς ἔσται ὡς ὁ διδάσκαλος αὐτοῦ (Lk 6.40) *everyone will be as his teacher*; καὶ ἔφαγον πάντες (Mt 14.20) *and all ate.*

2 μέλας, μέλαινα, μέλαν *black* has a stem in ν (not ντ); gen. s. μέλανος, μελαίνης, μέλανος; dat. pl. μέλασι(ν), μελαίναις, μέλασι(ν).

10.1/4 Third declension adjectives

Third declension adjectives are declined wholly within the third declension and fall into two classes. In both, the masculine and feminine have the same form.

(a) *Stems in* εσ

This large class resembles neuter nouns in -ος (6.1/1(c)), as is most obvious in the genitive and dative, where we find similar endings. ἀληθής *true* (stem ἀληθεσ-) is declined:

	SINGULAR		PLURAL	
	M. & F.	N.	M. & F.	N.
Nom.	ἀληθής	ἀληθές	ἀληθεῖς	ἀληθῆ
Acc.	ἀληθῆ	ἀληθές	ἀληθεῖς	ἀληθῆ
Gen.	ἀληθοῦς	ἀληθοῦς	ἀληθῶν	ἀληθῶν
Dat.	ἀληθεῖ	ἀληθεῖ	ἀληθέσι(ν)	ἀληθέσι(ν)

ἀληθῆ, ἀληθεῖς are contractions of ἀληθέ(σ)α, ἀληθέ(σ)ες. ἀληθεῖς as acc. pl. (m. and f.) is irregular – we would have expected ἀληθῆς (< -ε(σ)ας). The n. pl. nom. and acc. ἀληθῆ are only an apparent exception to the rule given at 3.1/1 (cf. γένος: pl. γένη < γένεσ-α, 6.1/1(c)).

συγγενής *related by family* is used as a noun in the sense *relative*. Its dative plural is irregular συγγενεῦσι(ν).

(b) *Stems in* ον

These are declined like ἡγεμών (6.1/1(a)) in the masculine and feminine forms; in the neuter the nom. and acc. ends in -ον in the singular and -ονα in the plural. An example is σώφρων *sensible, modest*:

	SINGULAR		PLURAL	
	M. & F.	N.	M. & F.	N.
Nom.	σώφρων	σῶφρον	σώφρον-ες	σώφρον-α
Acc.	σώφρον-α	σῶφρον	σώφρον-ας	σώφρον-α
Gen.	σώφρον-ος	σώφρον-ος	σωφρόν-ων	σωφρόν-ων
Dat.	σώφρον-ι	σώφρον-ι	σώφρο-σι(ν)	σώφρο-σι(ν)

Comparative adjectives in -ων (17.1/2(b)) are similarly declined, as well as ἄφρων *foolish*. ἄρσην *male* differs only in having η/ε instead of ω/ο.

10.2 Greek reading

Starting with this unit no separate vocabularies will be given and you should look up all unfamiliar words in the vocabulary at the end of the book.

1 οὐχὶ καὶ οἱ τελῶναι τὸ αὐτὸ ποιοῦσιν; (Mt 5.46)

2 καὶ λέγει αὐτοῖς ὁ Ἰησοῦς, Πόσους ἄρτους ἔχετε; (Mt 15.34)

3 Τίς ἐστιν ἡ μήτηρ μου, καὶ τίνες εἰσὶν οἱ ἀδελφοί μου; (Mt 12.48)

4 εἴ τις θέλει πρῶτος εἶναι ἔσται πάντων ἔσχατος καὶ πάντων διάκονος. (Mk 9.35)

5 κατεδίωξεν αὐτὸν Σίμων καὶ οἱ μετ᾽ αὐτοῦ, καὶ εὗρον αὐτὸν καὶ λέγουσιν αὐτῷ ὅτι Πάντες ζητοῦσίν σε. (Mk 1.36f.)

6 ἐν ποίᾳ δυνάμει ἢ ἐν ποίῳ ὀνόματι ἐποιήσατε τοῦτο ὑμεῖς; (Ac 4.7)

7 μήτι ἡ πηγὴ ἐκ τῆς αὐτῆς ὀπῆς βρύει τὸ γλυκὺ καὶ τὸ πικρόν; (Js 3.11)

8 ἤρξαντο λέγειν αὐτῷ εἷς ἕκαστος, Μήτι ἐγώ εἰμι, κύριε; (Mt 26.22)

9 δεῖ οὖν τὸν ἐπίσκοπον ἀνεπίλημπτον εἶναι, μιᾶς γυναικὸς ἄνδρα, νηφάλιον, σώφρονα. (1 Ti 3.2)

10 τί γὰρ οἶδας, γύναι, εἰ τὸν ἄνδρα σώσεις; ἢ τί οἶδας, ἄνερ, εἰ τὴν γυναῖκα σώσεις; (1 Cor 7.16)

11 διδάσκαλε, οἴδαμεν ὅτι ἀληθὴς εἶ καὶ τὴν ὁδὸν τοῦ θεοῦ ἐν ἀληθείᾳ διδάσκεις. (Mt 22.16)

12 θυγάτηρ μονογενὴς ἦν αὐτῷ ὡς ἐτῶν δώδεκα καὶ αὐτὴ ἀπέθνῃσκεν. (Lk 8.42)

13 τίνα λέγουσιν οἱ ἄνθρωποι εἶναι τὸν υἱὸν τοῦ ἀνθρώπου; (Mt 16.13)

14 τότε λέγει αὐτῷ ὁ Πιλᾶτος, Οὐκ ἀκούεις πόσα σου καταμαρτυροῦσιν; (Mt 27.13)

15 ἐγὼ οἶδα ὅτι εἰσελεύσονται μετὰ τὴν ἄφιξίν μου λύκοι βαρεῖς εἰς ὑμᾶς. (Ac 20.29)

16 ἐν δὲ τῷ πορεύεσθαι αὐτοὺς αὐτὸς εἰσῆλθεν εἰς κώμην τινά· γυνὴ δέ τις ὀνόματι Μάρθα ὑπεδέξατο αὐτόν. (Lk 10.38)

17 ξένος ἤμην καὶ οὐ συνηγάγετέ με, γυμνὸς καὶ οὐ περιεβάλετέ με, ἀσθενὴς καὶ ἐν φυλακῇ καὶ οὐκ ἐπεσκέψασθέ με. (Mt 25.43)

18 κατ' ἐκεῖνον δὲ τὸν καιρὸν ἐπέβαλεν Ἡρῴδης ὁ βασιλεὺς τὰς χεῖρας κακῶσαί τινας τῶν ἀπὸ τῆς ἐκκλησίας. (Ac 12.1)

19 Ταῦτα πάντα ἐλάλησεν ὁ Ἰησοῦς ἐν παραβολαῖς τοῖς ὄχλοις, καὶ χωρὶς παραβολῆς οὐδὲν ἐλάλει αὐτοῖς. (Mt 13.34)

20 ὁ Ἰησοῦς λέγει αὐτοῖς, Οὐδὲ ἐγὼ λέγω ὑμῖν ἐν ποίᾳ ἐξουσίᾳ ταῦτα ποιῶ. (Mk 11.33)

Notes

2 λέγει vivid present (2.1/5 note 2), as also in 14 and 20 below.

5 λέγουσιν vivid present (2.1/5 note 2) although two aorists precede – trans. all three verbs by the English past.

6 Translate ποίᾳ *what*; ποίῳ ὀνόματι *in what name* is the equivalent of *in whose name*.

7 ἡ πηγή because the definite article is used, a general class is meant (2.1/2 note 1(ii)) – translate *a fountain*; with τὸ γλυκύ and τὸ πικρόν supply ὕδωρ *water*.

8 ἤρξαντο is plural but the subject εἷς ἕκαστος is singular (agreement according to the sense; *each one* indicates that a group is involved); such grammatical irregularities are typical of the colloquial language of the NT.

10 γύναι and ἄνερ are vocative; Paul is here saying that those in a mixed marriage of a Christian and pagan should live peacefully together as one might be the salvation of the other.

12 ἦν αὐτῷ lit. *there was to him* i.e. *he had*.

17 συνηγάγετε < συνάγω; with γυμνός and ἀσθενὴς καὶ ἐν φυλακῇ supply ἤμην *I was*.

18 ἐπέβαλεν ... τὰς χεῖρας lit. *put his hands on* i.e. *set about* (cf. the English *put his hand to*).

20 The overall context shows that οὐδέ here means *neither*.

unit 11

11.1 Grammar

11.1/1 Aorist passive, root aorist, and future passive

As noted above (8.1/1), the aorist passive and future passive differ in form from the aorist middle and future middle. The stem of the aorist passive is formed by adding θη to a form of the verbal root, and in λύω this gives us λυθη (as the aorist is an historic tense the indicative requires the augment ἐλυθη-). To this are added **active** endings (-ν, -ς, -, -μεν, -τε, -σαν). This odd and confusing anomaly extends throughout all the aorist passive. The indicative of the aorist passive is:

	SINGULAR	PLURAL
1	ἐλύθην *I was loosened*	ἐλύθημεν
2	ἐλύθης	ἐλύθητε
3	ἐλύθη	ἐλύθησαν
INFINITIVE	λυθῆναι	

The form of the verbal root to which θη is added cannot always be predicted from the present (or any other) stem; for this reason the aorist passive is one of the parts of a Greek verb that must be learnt (7.1/1). However, the following guidelines will be of help:

(a) Most verbs with a present stem ending in a vowel or diphthong simply add θη to this: λύω *loosen, free* > ἐλύθην *I was freed*, μνηστεύω *betroth* > ἐμνηστεύθην *I was betrothed*. Two common verbs of this type add σθη: ἀκούω *hear* > ἠκούσθην *I was heard*; κλείω *shut* > ἐκλείσθην (ἐκλείσθη ἡ θύρα *the door was shut*). In regular contracted verbs the final vowel of the present stem is lengthened in the same way as in the aorist active (5.1/2), e.g. ἐπλανήθην *I was led astray* (πλανάω); ὠφελήθην *I was helped* (ὠφελέω); ἐπληρώθην *I was filled* (πληρόω).

(b) In both palatal and labial stems the final consonant of the stem is assimilated to the θ of the aorist passive ending by becoming an aspirate, i.e. κ and γ > χ; π and β > φ, (stems ending in χ and φ have no need to change). An example of a palatal stems is ἐκηρύχθην *I was announced* (κηρύσσω, stem κηρυκ-; verbs of this type have a present in -σσω, see 6.1/4(b)). An example of a labial stem is ἐπέμφθην *I was sent* (πέμπω, stem πέμπ-); some labial-stem verbs have a present in -πτω (6.1/4(b)), e.g. ἀποκαλύπτω, stem ἀποκαλυπ-, aor. pass. ἀπεκαλύφθην *I was revealed*.

(c) In dental stems the final consonant (whether τ, δ or θ) becomes σ, e.g. ἐπείσθην *I was persuaded* (πείθω, stem πειθ); many dental stems have a present in -ζω (6.1/4(b)), e.g. ἁγιάζω *sanctify*, stem ἁγιαδ-, aor. pass. ἡγιάσθην *I was sanctified*.

A further complication is what we term the root aorist. In earlier Greek a few verbs have an **active** aorist form which differs from both the weak and strong aorist of other verbs, and this is called the root aorist because the endings, which either are a single consonant or begin with a consonant, are added directly to the basic stem (also known as the root) of the verb. It differs from the other aorists in having neither suffix (σ as in the weak aorist) nor link vowel as in both weak and strong aorist (α in weak and ο/ε in strong). Some of these verbs survive in New Testament Greek. Prominent examples are γινώσκω *ascertain, know* (root γνω-) and compounds of -βαίνω *go*[1] (root βη-). The active aorist of these verbs is as follows:

	SINGULAR	PLURAL	SINGULAR	PLURAL
1	ἔγνων *I ascertained*	[ἔγνωμεν]	-έβην *I went*	-έβημεν
2	ἔγνως	[ἔγνωτε]	[-έβης]	[-έβητε]
3	ἔγνω	ἔγνωσαν	-έβη	-έβησαν
INFINITIVE	γνῶναι		-βῆναι	

ἔβην is to be analysed as ἔ-βη-ν (augment + stem + ending). As with the aorist passive the endings -ν, -ς, -, -μεν, -τε, -σαν are added to a stem ending in a long vowel. All forms of the root aorist of these two verbs will be found in **Appendix 4**.

---

[1] A dash before a verb indicates that it only occurs in compounds in the NT; forms in square brackets do not occur in the NT.

A second class of aorist **passive** follows ἔβην and does not contain the characteristic θ of ἐλύθην, but there is no difference in meaning. There are fewer verbs of this type and they cannot be identified by their present form. Examples are: ἐξεπλάγην *I was astounded* (ἐκπλήσσω); ἀπεστάλην *I was sent* (ἀποστέλλω). For convenience, these forms are called root aorist passives.

The future tense in Greek resembles the aorist in distinguishing between the middle and passive. The future passive is formed by adding σ to the stem of the aorist passive and then applying the same endings as for the future (and present) middle. As the future is a primary tense there is no augment, and from λύω we have a future passive stem λυθησ- (λυθη + σ-); this is conjugated:

SINGULAR	PLURAL
1 λυθήσομαι *I shall be freed*	λυθησόμεθα
2 λυθήσῃ	λυθήσεσθε
3 λυθήσεται	λυθήσονται

A future passive infinitive does not occur in the NT.

Notes

1 Some deponents are passive in both the future and the aorist, e.g. κοιμάομαι *sleep*; fut. κοιμηθήσομαι; aor. ἐκοιμήθην. Others have a future middle but an aorist passive, e.g. πορεύομαι *go, travel*; fut. πορεύσομαι; aor. ἐπορεύθην. Others again show both middle and passive forms, e.g. ἀποκρίνομαι *answer*; fut. ἀποκριθήσομαι; aor. ἀπεκρινάμην or ἀπεκρίθην (the latter is by far the more common). βούλομαι *wish* has a passive aorist ἐβουλήθην but its future does not occur in the NT. The difference between the different types of deponents is simply one of **form**; all are active in **meaning**.

2 The deponent δύναμαι *be able* (fut. δυνήσομαι; aor. ἐδυνήθην and ἠδυνήθην) has α (not ο/ε) as a link vowel in the present tense: -αμαι, -ασαι, -αται etc., not -ομαι -ῃ, -εται etc. (a full treatment of its forms is given at 19.1/3).

3 Some aorist passives appear to defy classification, e.g. ἐτύθην < θύω *sacrifice*; ἐτάφην < θάπτω *bury*.

4 Compounds of -βαίνω which occur frequently are ἀναβαίνω *go up*, ἐμβαίνω *embark*, καταβαίνω *come/go down*, συμβαίνω *happen*.

11.1/2 Agent and instrument

We have already met examples of both agent and instrument in the reading (agent 8.2.20, instrument 6.2.20).

In English we can say *the tax-collector was hit **by** a peasant* and *the tax-collector was hit **by** (or **with**) a pitchfork* but Greek makes a distinction between agent (*peasant*) and instrument (*pitchfork*).

An agent is a living being and agency is normally expressed by ὑπό with the genitive: ἐβαπτίσθη εἰς τὸν Ἰορδάνην ὑπὸ Ἰωάννου (Mk 1.9) *he was baptized in the Jordan by John*. Sometimes ἀπό and διά (both with the genitive) are used in the same sense: ἀπεστάλη ὁ ἄγγελος Γαβριὴλ ἀπὸ τοῦ θεοῦ (Lk 1.26) *the angel Gabriel was sent by God*; πιστὸς ὁ θεὸς δι' οὗ ἐκλήθητε εἰς κοινωνίαν τοῦ υἱοῦ αὐτου (1 Cor 1.9) *faithful [is] God, by whom you were called into the fellowship of his Son*.

On the other hand, an instrument is nearly always inanimate. It may be expressed by the dative alone; ἐγὼ ὕδατι βαπτίζω ὑμᾶς (Lk 3.16) *I am baptizing you with water*. More commonly, however, ἐν with the dative is used: ἐν αἵματι πάντα καθαρίζεται (Hb 9.22) *everything is cleansed with blood*.

11.1/3 -ω verbs with stems in λ, ν, ρ

The present stem of most verbs of this type was originally formed with a *y* suffix (6.1/4(b)). This combined with a preceding λ to give λλ; it disappeared after ν and ρ, but a preceding α or ε was lengthened to αι or ει respectively. These verbs have a contracted future (-ῶ < -έω; 5.1/2 note 3), and where a *y* suffix has been used in the present the future reverts to the original stem (e.g. βάλλω *throw*, future stem βαλ-). In the weak aorist (which occurs in all common verbs of this group, except βάλλω) the sigma is dropped with a preceding α lengthened to η (if not following a vowel or ρ) and a preceding ε to ει. The υ of stems in -υνω does not undergo any change. The following table shows the different possibilities:

PRESENT			FUTURE	AORIST
βάλλω	*throw*	(< βάλ-y ω)	βαλῶ	ἔβαλον
-στέλλω	*send*	(< στέλ-y ω)	-στελῶ	-έστειλα
μένω	*wait*	(no *y* suffix)	μενῶ	ἔμεινα
ἀποκτείνω	*kill*	(<ἀποκτέν-y ω)	ἀποκτενῶ	ἀπέκτεινα
μιαίνω	*stain*	(< μιάν-y ω)	μιανῶ	ἐμίανα
μεγαλύνω	*magnify*	(<μεγαλύν-y ω)	[μεγαλυνῶ]	[ἐμεγάλυνα]
αἴρω	*lift*	(< ἄρ-y ω)	ἀρῶ	ἦρα

Notes

1 ἀποκτείνω has an alternative present form ἀποκτεννύω.
2 The aorist passive of verbs in -αίνω and -ύνω ends in -άνθην
  and -ύνθην, e.g. ἐμεγαλύνθην (μεγαλύνω). Likewise, we have
  ἤρθην from αἴρω, but the aorist passive of βάλλω and -στέλλω
  are irregular: ἐβλήθην, -εστάλην (the latter is a root aorist
  passive).
3 ἐλαύνω *drive* and φέρω *carry* belong here but are highly
  irregular; see **Principal parts of verbs**.
4 For verbs with a present stem in -αν such as λαμβάνω and
  μανθάνω see 7.1/1 note 4.

11.1/4 Third declension nouns – stems in εu and ou

A number of masculine nouns end in -εύς (always so accented);
most involve male occupations, e.g. βασιλεύς *king*, ἱερεύς
priest, ἀρχιερεύς *high priest*, γραμματεύς *doctor of law*. The
genitive and dative singular endings are the same as for stems in
ι (8.1/5). βασιλεύς is declined:

	SINGULAR	PLURAL
Nom.	βασιλεύ-ς	βασιλεῖς
Voc.	βασιλεῦ	βασιλεῖς
Acc.	βασιλέ-α	βασιλεῖς
Gen.	βασιλέ-ως	βασιλέ-ων
Dat.	βασιλεῖ	βασιλεῦ-σι(ν)

Μωϋσῆς *Moses* is declined as βασιλεύς (with two alternative
forms): *acc.* Μωϋσέα (or Μωϋσῆν), *gen.* Μωϋσέως, dat. Μωϋσεῖ
(or Μωϋσῇ).

Four nouns end in -ους: βοῦς *ox*, νοῦς *mind*, πλοῦς *voyage*, χοῦς
dust. βοῦς may be masculine or feminine, depending on the sex
of the animal; the other three are masculine but follow βοῦς in
their declension:

	SINGULAR	PLURAL
Nom.	βοῦ-ς	βόες
Acc.	βοῦ-ν	βοῦς
Gen.	βο-ός	βο-ῶν
Dat.	βο-ΐ	βου-σί(ν)

11.1/5 Crasis

Crasis (κρᾶσις *mixing, blending*) is the contraction of a vowel or diphthong at the end of one word with a vowel at the beginning of the following word. It can occur in the NT when the first word is καί or the definite article, but it is not consistently applied. The two words are written together and the contraction is marked by ' (technically called **coronis** but identical in form with a smooth breathing). We find the following examples with καί:

κἀγώ (καὶ ἐγώ) *and I*

κἀμοί (καὶ ἐμοί) *and to/for me*

κἀκεῖ (καὶ ἐκεῖ) *and there*

κἀκεῖθεν (καὶ ἐκεῖθεν) *and from there*

κἀκεῖνος (καὶ ἐκεῖνος) *and that man*

κἄν (καὶ ἐάν) *and if, even if*

With the definite article we have only: τοὐναντίον (τὸ ἐναντίον) *on the other hand* (lit. *the opposite*) and τοὔνομα (τὸ ὄνομα) *by name* (lit. *the name*).

11.2 Greek reading

1 οὐκ ἀνέγνωτε ἐν τῷ νόμῳ ὅτι οἱ ἱερεῖς ἐν τῷ ἱερῷ τὸ σάββατον βεβηλοῦσιν καὶ ἀναίτιοί εἰσιν; (*Mt 12.5)

2 κύριε, τοὺς προφήτας σου ἀπέκτειναν, τὰ θυσιαστήριά σου κατέσκαψαν, κἀγὼ ὑπελείφθην μόνος, καὶ ζητοῦσιν τὴν ψυχήν μου. (Ro 11.3)

3 λέγω γὰρ ὑμῖν ὅτι δύναται ὁ θεὸς ἐκ τῶν λίθων τούτων ἐγεῖραι τέκνα τῷ Ἀβραάμ. (Mt 3.9)

4 ἀπεκρίθη δὲ αὐτῷ ὁ κύριος καὶ εἶπεν, Ὑποκριταί, ἕκαστος ὑμῶν τῷ σαββάτῳ οὐ λύει τὸν βοῦν αὐτοῦ ἢ τὸν ὄνον ἀπὸ τῆς φάτνης; (Lk 13.15)

5 νῦν μεγαλυνθήσεται Χριστὸς ἐν τῷ σώματί μου, εἴτε διὰ ζωῆς εἴτε διὰ θανάτου. (Phil 1.20)

6 τίς γὰρ ἔγνω νοῦν κυρίου; ἢ τίς σύμβουλος αὐτοῦ ἐγένετο; (Ro 11.34)

7 τότε ὁ Ἰησοῦς ἀνήχθη εἰς τὴν ἔρημον ὑπὸ τοῦ πνεύματος, πειρασθῆναι ὑπὸ τοῦ διαβόλου. (Mt 4.1)

8 καὶ κατέβη ἡ βροχὴ καὶ ἦλθον οἱ ποταμοὶ καὶ ἔπνευσαν οἱ ἄνεμοι καὶ προσέκοψαν τῇ οἰκίᾳ ἐκείνῃ, καὶ ἔπεσεν, καὶ ἦν ἡ πτῶσις αὐτῆς μεγάλη. (Mt 7.27)

9 τοῦτο οὖν λέγω καὶ μαρτύρομαι ἐν κυρίῳ, μηκέτι ὑμᾶς περιπατεῖν, καθὼς καὶ τὰ ἔθνη περιπατεῖ ἐν ματαιότητι τοῦ νοὸς αὐτῶν. (Eph 4.17)

10 ἐγένετο δὲ ἐν μιᾷ τῶν ἡμερῶν καὶ αὐτὸς ἐνέβη εἰς πλοῖον καὶ οἱ μαθηταὶ αὐτοῦ. (Lk 8.22)

11 πολλοὶ ἐροῦσίν μοι ἐν ἐκείνῃ τῇ ἡμέρᾳ, Κύριε κύριε, οὐ τῷ σῷ ὀνόματι ἐπροφητεύσαμεν, καὶ τῷ σῷ ὀνόματι δαιμόνια ἐξεβάλομεν, καὶ τῷ σῷ ὀνόματι δυνάμεις πολλὰς ἐποιήσαμεν; (Mt 7.22)

12 ἔμεινεν δὲ Μαριὰμ σὺν αὐτῇ ὡς μῆνας τρεῖς, καὶ ὑπέστρεψεν εἰς τὸν οἶκον αὐτῆς. (Lk 1.56)

13 ὅτε δὲ ἤγγισεν ὁ καιρὸς τῶν καρπῶν, ἀπέστειλεν τοὺς δούλους αὐτοῦ πρὸς τοὺς γεωργοὺς λαβεῖν τοὺς καρποὺς αὐτοῦ. (Mt 21.34)

14 Φωνὴ ἐν Ῥαμὰ ἠκούσθη, κλαυθμὸς καὶ ὀδυρμὸς πολύς. (Mt 2.18)

15 ἔσται γὰρ ἀνάγκη μεγάλη ἐπὶ τῆς γῆς καὶ ὀργὴ τῷ λαῷ τούτῳ, καὶ πεσοῦνται στόματι μαχαίρης καὶ αἰχμαλωτισθήσονται εἰς τὰ ἔθνη πάντα. (Lk 21.23f.)

16 Οἱ δὲ ἔνδεκα μαθηταὶ ἐπορεύθησαν εἰς τὴν Γαλιλαίαν εἰς τὸ ὄρος οὗ ἐτάξατο αὐτοῖς ὁ Ἰησοῦς. (Mt 28.16)

17 καὶ ἀπεκρίθησαν αὐτῷ οἱ μαθηταὶ αὐτοῦ ὅτι Πόθεν τούτους δυνήσεταί τις ὧδε χορτάσαι ἄρτων ἐπ᾽ ἐρημίας; (Mk 8.4)

18 ἀνέβη δὲ καὶ Ἰωσὴφ ἀπὸ τῆς Γαλιλαίας ἐκ πόλεως Ναζαρὲθ εἰς τὴν Ἰουδαίαν εἰς πόλιν Δαυὶδ ἥτις καλεῖται Βηθλέεμ, διὰ τὸ εἶναι αὐτὸν ἐξ οἴκου καὶ πατριᾶς Δαυίδ. (Lk 2.4)

19 ἐγὼ χρείαν ἔχω ὑπὸ σοῦ βαπτισθῆναι, καὶ σὺ ἔρχῃ πρός με; (Mt 3.14)

20 ἐπὶ τῆς Μωϋσέως καθέδρας ἐκάθισαν οἱ γραμματεῖς καὶ οἱ Φαρισαῖοι. (Mt 23.2)

Notes

1 ἀνέγνωτε < ἀναγινώσκω.

2 κἀγώ crasis for καί ἐγώ (11.1/5).

3 ἐγεῖραι aor. act. inf. of ἐγείρω *raise*; trans. τῷ Ἀβραάμ *for Abraham*.

5 μεγαλυνθήσεται fut. pass. of μεγαλύνω.

7 ἀνήχθη aor. pass. ind. of ἀνάγω; πειρασθῆναι aor. pass. inf. of πειράζω.

8 κατέβη < καταβαίνω; ἔπνευσαν < πνέω; προσέκοψαν < προσκόπτω; ἦν ἡ πτῶσις αὐτῆς μεγάλη presumably the house made a loud noise when it fell.

9 ἐν κυρίῳ *in* [*the name of the*] *Lord*; μηκέτι, not οὐκέτι, is used because it qualifies the infinitive περιπατεῖν (8.1/3(c)); trans. νοός by the plural.

10 ἐγένετο etc. see 8.1/2(b); ἐν μιᾷ τῶν ἡμερῶν lit. *on one of the days* but trans. *one day*; ἐνέβη < ἐμβαίνω.

11 ἐροῦσιν < λέγω; ἐπροφητεύσαμεν the augment is not placed after προ- because the verb προφητεύω is not regarded as a compound but as formed from προφήτης *prophet*.

12 ἔμεινεν < μένω; ὑπέστρεψεν < ὑποστρέφω.

13 ἤγγισεν < ἐγγίζω; ὁ καιρὸς τῶν καρπῶν trans. *harvest time*; λαβεῖν < λαμβάνω.

14 ἠκούσθη < ἀκούω.

15 αἰχμαλωτισθήσονται fut. pass. of αἰχμαλωτίζω; πεσοῦνται and αἰχμαλωτισθήσονται are pl. but the understood subject is the singular collective noun λαός (agreement according to the sense; cf. note on 10.2.8) – trans. *they will fall ... will be taken ...*

16 οὗ *when*.

17 χορτάζω takes the acc. of the person fed and the gen. of the food given; trans. ἄρτων by the singular *bread*.

18 καί *too, also* the previous verse states that everyone was going to be registered – Joseph *too* went; Δαυίδ is to be taken as genitive in both places; trans. διὰ τὸ εἶναι αὐτὸν ... as a clause *because he was ...* (5.1/3).

19 βαπτισθῆναι aor. pass. inf.; only the second clause is a question.

20 γραμματεῖς used to be translated by *scribes*, which reflects the meaning of the word in earlier Greek; in the NT the term refers to experts in Jewish law who were associated with the high priests (ἀρχιερεῖς) and the elders (πρεσβύτεροι) – it is better translated by *doctors of law*.

12.1 Grammar

12.1/1 Participles

Participles are those parts of verbs which function as adjectives.
They have tense (*killing* is present, *going to kill* future) and voice
(*killing* is active, *being killed* passive). In Greek there are
participles for all three voices in the present, future, and aorist
(and also the perfect, 16.1/4), and they use the same stem as the
corresponding indicatives (but the augment is dropped in the
historic tenses). For the sake of completeness the following table
includes perfect participles, which can be ignored until we treat
these in 16.1/4.

ACTIVE

Present m. λύ-ων (gen. λύ-οντος), f. λύ-ουσα, n. λῦ-ον
    loosening

Future m. λύσ-ων (gen. λύσ-οντος), f. λύσ-ουσα, n. λῦσ-ον
    going to loosen, about to loosen

Aorist m. λύσ-ας (gen. λύσ-αντος), f. λύσ-ασα, n. λῦσ-αν
    having loosened, after loosening

Perfect m. λελυκ-ώς (gen. λελυκ-ότος), f. λελυκ-υῖα, n. λελυκ-
    ός (*in a state of*) *having loosened*

MIDDLE

Present λυ-όμενος, -ομένη, -όμενον *loosening for oneself*

Future λυσ-όμενος, -ομένη, -όμενον *going to loosen for
    oneself, about to loosen for oneself*

Aorist λυσ-άμενος, -αμένη, -άμενον *having loosened for
    oneself, after loosening for oneself*

Perfect λελυ-μένος, -μένη, -μένον (*in a state of*) *having
    loosened for oneself*

PASSIVE

Present λυ-όμενος, -ομένη, -όμενον *being loosened*
Aorist   m. λυθ-είς (gen. λυθ-έντος), f. λυθεῖσα, n. λυθέν
           having been loosened, after being loosened
Perfect λελυ-μένος, -μένη, -μένον (*in a state of*) *having been
           loosened*

All active participles, together with that of the aorist passive, are declined like first and third declension adjectives (10.1/3). The declension of the aorist active participle is identical with that of πᾶς (10.1/3(b)). The present active and aorist passive are declined as follows:

SINGULAR

	M.	F.	N.	M.	F.	N.
Nom.	λύων	λύουσα	λῦον	λυθείς	λυθεῖσα	λυθέν
Acc.	λύοντα	λύουσαν	λῦον	λυθέντα	λυθεῖσαν	λυθέν
Gen.	λύοντος	λυούσης	λύοντος	λυθέντος	λυθείσης	λυθέντος
Dat.	λύοντι	λυούσῃ	λύοντι	λυθέντι	λυθείσῃ	λυθέντι

PLURAL

	M.	F.	N.	M.	F.	N.
Nom.	λύοντες	λύουσαι	λύοντα	λυθέντες	λυθεῖσαι	λυθέντα
Acc.	λύοντας	λυούσας	λύοντα	λυθέντας	λυθείσας	λυθέντα
Gen.	λυόντων	λυουσῶν	λυόντων	λυθέντων	λυθεισῶν	λυθέντων
Dat.	λύουσι(ν)	λυούσαις	λύουσι(ν)	λυθεῖσι(ν)	λυθείσαις	λυθεῖσι(ν)

All middle participles follow καλός (3.1/3). The present (and perfect) participle passive has the same form as the middle. The future active participle follows λύων.

Notes

1 The present participle of εἰμί (*I am*) is ὤν, which is declined:

	SINGULAR			PLURAL		
	M.	F.	N.	M.	F.	N.
Nom.	ὤν	οὖσα	ὄν	ὄντες	οὖσαι	ὄντα
Acc.	ὄντα	οὖσαν	ὄν	ὄντας	οὖσας	ὄντα
Gen.	ὄντος	οὔσης	ὄντος	ὄντων	οὐσῶν	ὄντων
Dat.	ὄντι	οὔσῃ	ὄντι	οὖσι(ν)	οὔσαις	οὖσι(ν)

Its future participle is ἐσόμενος, -η, -ον (cf. 8.1/1 note 3); it has no other participles.

2 In tenses where they differ from λύω, contracted verbs, verbs with a contracted future, and verbs with stems in λ, ν, ρ form their participles according to the rules already given for those tenses, e.g. the present active participle of φιλέω is φιλῶν, -οῦσα, -οῦν; the aorist active participle of μένω is μείν-ας, -ασα, -αν.

3 Strong aorists take the participial endings of the present (cf. 7.1/1), e.g. active λαβών, -οῦσα, -όν;[1] middle λαβόμενος (< λαμβάνω).

4 The participles of root aorists are similar to those of the weak aorist active and the aorist passive:

ἔγνων (γινώσκω): m. γνούς (gen. γνόντος), f. γνοῦσα, n. γνόν.
-ἔβην (βαίνω): m. -βάς (gen. -βάντος), f. -βᾶσα, n. -βάν (cf. ἔστην 19.1/2).

5 The future passive participle occurs once in the NT (Hb 3.5 λαληθησομένων [< λαληθησόμενος]) and can be ignored.

12.1/2 Uses of participles

The tense of a participle reflects the temporal relationship between the action it expresses and that of the finite verb of its clause, e.g. οἱ μαθηταὶ αὐτοῦ ἤρξαντο ὁδὸν ποιεῖν τίλλοντες τοὺς στάχυας (Mk 2.23) *his disciples began to make a journey [while] plucking ears of wheat*; the participle τίλλοντες is present because the action it describes happened at the same time as that of the finite verb ἤρξαντο (in English we often add *while* to a participle used in this way). Similarly an aorist participle can be used for an action which took place before that of the main verb: καὶ ἐλθόντες πρὸς τοὺς μαθητὰς εἶδον ὄχλον πολὺν περὶ αὐτοὺς καὶ γραμματεῖς συζητοῦντας πρὸς αὐτούς. (Mk 9.14) *and having come to the disciples they saw a large crowd around them and doctors of law disputing with them*; here ἐλθόντες is aorist because it describes an action that occurred before that of the finite verb εἶδον, but συζητοῦντας is present because the doctors of law were disputing with the disciples when the new arrivals saw them.

However, the aorist participle can be used in another way, which involves the concept of aspect (4.1/1). A type of expression frequently used in the NT is ἀποκριθεὶς δὲ ὁ Ἰησοῦς εἶπεν πρὸς αὐτόν (Mt 3.15), which must be translated *and Jesus replying* (or *in reply*) *said to him* as what Jesus went on to say was in fact his reply; to understand the sentence as meaning *and Jesus having replied said to him* would be contrary to the sense of the passage. An aorist participle so used simply denotes the action itself; the time when it occurred is shown by the finite verb of its

---

[1] Unlike the present active participle, the strong aorist active participle is always accented on the first syllable of its ending, hence λαμβάνων (pres.) but λαβών (aor.).

clause. In the sentence quoted above it is used because the writer, Matthew, regarded the reply of Jesus as a single simple act, rather than a continuous one (which would have required the present participles as τίλλοντες and συζητοῦντας above). It is only from the context that we can distinguish between the two functions of aorist participles.

For the future participle see below. The perfect participle will be treated at 16.1/4.

The negative used with participles is μή. The twenty or so exceptions in the New Testament (where a participle is negated by οὐ) have been explained in various ways but do not reflect any regular uses or distinctions.

Bearing in mind that there is always a temporal relation between the participle and the finite verb of its clause, we may describe the main uses of participles as follows:

(a) **Adjective equivalent**
   Participles can function as ordinary adjectives and qualify a noun: ὁ κοπιῶν γεωργός (*2 Tim 2.6) *the hard-working farmer*; Σίμων ὁ λεγόμενος Πέτρος (Mt 10.2) *Simon, the* [so-] *called Peter,* i.e *the one called Peter.* A participle used in this way may also take an accusative: ὁ πέμψας με πατήρ (Jn 8.18) lit. *the having-sent-me father,* i.e. *the father who sent me.*

(b) **Noun equivalent**
   Participles can function as nouns in the same way as adjectives: ὁ κλέπτων (Eph 4.28) lit. *the stealing* [*person*], i.e *the thief.* Here too the participle may govern a word or phrase: ἐγώ εἰμι ὁ μαρτυρῶν περὶ ἐμαυτοῦ (Jn 8.18) lit. *I am the witnessing-about-myself* [*person*], i.e. *I am one that bears witness of myself.* Both uses (a) and (b) are often to be translated by an adjectival clause.

(c) **Adverbial clause equivalent**
   Participles can perform the same function as an adverbial clause, and are often best translated as such. The two sentences given above could be rendered *his disciples began to make a journey while they were plucking ears of wheat* (οἱ μαθηταὶ αὐτοῦ ἤρξαντο ὁδὸν ποιεῖν τίλλοντες τοὺς στάχυας) and *when they had come to the disciples they saw ...* (ἐλθόντες πρὸς τοὺς μαθητὰς εἶδον ...). In both cases the participle indicates the time when the action of the finite verb took place, and consequently if we decide to translate by a clause, we shall use an adverbial clause of time (**temporal**

use). There are other possibilities. At Mt 1.19 Ἰωσὴφ, ... δίκαιος ὢν καὶ μὴ θέλων αὐτὴν δειγματίσαι ... a literal translation is *Joseph, being just and not wishing to expose her* ...; the context shows that the participle phrases give the reason for Joseph's intended action, and so we may translate *Joseph, because he was just and did not want to expose her*... (causal use). At Lk 9.25 τί γὰρ ὠφελεῖται ἄνθρωπος κερδήσας τὸν κόσμον ὅλον the literal meaning is *for how is a man benefited having gained the the whole world*; here the participial phrase clearly expresses a condition and the AV elegantly translates *for what is a man advantaged if he gain the whole world* (conditional use). Finally, a participle can express a concession: ἐλεύθερος ὢν ἐκ πάντων πᾶσιν ἐμαυτὸν ἐδούλωσα (*1 Cor 9.19), lit. *being free from everyone I enslaved myself to everyone*. The sense indicates that ἐλεύθερος ὢν ἐκ πάντων is a concession; although Paul was without obligations to anyone he made himself the servant of everyone, and we should translate *although I was independent of everyone, I made myself the servant of everyone* (concessive use). This use is occasionally reinforced by prefixing the participle with καίπερ *although*: καίπερ ὢν υἱὸς (Hb 5.8) lit. *although being a son*, i.e. *although he was a son*.

(d) The future participle (which is by no means common) can be used to express purpose: εἰς Δαμασκὸν ἐπορευόμην ἄξων καὶ τοὺς ἐκεῖσε ὄντας (Ac 22.5) *I was travelling to Damascus in order to bring those there as well* (lit. *I was travelling to Damascus going-to-bring those being there as well*); on other ways of expressing purpose see 13.1/3(b)(i). Elsewhere it refers to something which is going to happen: ἰδόντες δὲ οἱ περὶ αὐτὸν τὸ ἐσόμενον ... (Lk 22.49) *and those around him, seeing what was going to happen* (lit. *seeing the going-to-be [thing]*).

(e) Verbs of knowing and perceiving can be followed by a participle. In English we have this construction with verbs of perceiving but not with those of knowing:

ὄψονται τὸν υἱὸν τοῦ ἀνθρώπου ἐρχόμενον. (Mt 24.30) *They will see the Son of Man coming.* (ὄψονται < ὁράω, which counts as a verb of perceiving).

ἐθεώρουν τὸν Σατανᾶν ὡς ἀστραπὴν ἐκ τοῦ οὐρανου πεσόντα. (Lk 10.18) *I was watching Satan falling like lightning from the sky.*

τίς γάρ ἐστιν ἀνθρώπων ὃς οὐ γινώσκει τὴν Ἐφεσίων πόλιν
νεωκόρον οὖσαν τῆς μεγάλης Ἀρτέμιδος; (Ac 19.35) *For
what man is there who does not know that the city of
the Ephesians is guardian of mighty Artemis?* (lit. *know
the city of the Ephesians being guardian* ...).

εὐθὺς ὁ Ἰησοῦς ἐπιγνοὺς ἐν ἑαυτῷ τὴν ἐξ αὐτοῦ δύναμιν
ἐξελθοῦσαν... (Mk 5.30) *Straightway Jesus, knowing
in himself that the power had gone from him* ... (lit.
knowing the power having gone).

(f) **Genitive absolute**

This construction (*absolute* here means *independent*), in its
simplest form, involves a noun or pronoun and a participle
which are both in the genitive case and which stand apart
from (i.e. are **grammatically** independent of) the rest of the
sentence; there is, of course, a connection in **sense** as
otherwise there would be no point in putting the two
together. We have an absolute construction (the nominative
absolute) in English. Although it is a little clumsy, we can say
*the messengers of John having gone away, he began to talk
to the crowds.* In Greek this is ἀπελθόντων τῶν ἀγγέλων
Ἰωάννου ἤρξατο λέγειν πρὸς τοὺς ὄχλους (*Lk 7.24); a better
translation would be *when the messengers of John had gone
away,* etc. Genitive absolutes are almost always to be
translated by a clause. Other examples are:

πορευομένων αὐτῶν ἐν τῇ ὁδῷ εἶπέν τις πρὸς αὐτόν. (Lk
9.57) *As they were travelling on the road a certain
[man] said to him.*

χρονίζοντος δὲ τοῦ νυμφίου ἐνύσταξαν πᾶσαι καὶ
ἐκάθευδον. (Mt 25.5) *And when the bridegroom failed
to come, all [the maidens] became drowsy and began to
sleep.*

When the subject of the participle in the genitive is a
pronoun, it is sometimes omitted: καὶ ἐλθόντων πρὸς τὸν
ὄχλον προσῆλθεν αὐτῷ ἄνθρωπος (Mt 17.14) *when [they] had
come to the crowd a man came up to him* (we might have
expected ἐλθόντων αὐτῶν). Often the subject of the participle
is mentioned elsewhere in the clause in another case:
καταβάντος δὲ αὐτοῦ ἀπὸ τοῦ ὄρους ἠκολούθησαν αὐτῷ ὄχλοι
πολλοί (Mt 8.1) *when he had come down from the mountain
many crowds followed him* (ἀκολουθέω takes the dative,
15.1/1); here αὐτοῦ and αὐτῷ refer to the same person, viz
Jesus, and according to strict grammar we should have

καταβάντι δὲ αὐτῷ ἀπὸ τοῦ ὄρους ἠκολούθησαν ὄχλοι πολλοί (lit. ... *followed him having come down* ...).

(g) **Composite tenses**

A composite tense is one formed with an auxiliary verb, and we have many in English (*I was going, we were praying*). In the same way εἰμί *be* is often combined with a participle as a substitute for the finite form of a verb: ἦν γὰρ διδάσκων αὐτούς (Mt 7.29) *for he was teaching them* (ἦν διδάσκων is the equivalent of the imperfect ἐδίδασκε).

Notes

1 Various expressions occur in the NT similar to ἀποκριθεὶς ... εἶπεν (discussed above) where the action expressed by the participle is involved in the action of the finite verb. Most cases contain a verb of saying and require some change in English, e.g. ἔγραψεν λέγων (Lk 1.63) *he wrote saying*, i.e. *he wrote as follows*; εἶπεν μαρτυρήσας (Ac 13.22) *he spoke approving* i.e. *he said in approval*.

2 We sometimes meet an accumulation of participles in one clause with no connecting word between them, e.g. ποιήσας χρόνον τινὰ ἐξῆλθεν διερχόμενος καθεξῆς τὴν Γαλατικὴν χώραν καὶ Φρυγίαν, ἐπιστηρίζων πάντας τοὺς μαθητάς (Ac 18.23) lit. *after making [i.e. spending] a certain time he went out, going successively through the Galatian country and Phrygia strengthening all the disciples*. English idiom requires us to break such a sentence up into at least two clauses: *after spending a certain time [there]* (or *after he had spent a certain time [there]*) *he went out and travelled through the Galatian country and Phrygia in succession, strengthening all the disciples*.

12.2 Greek reading

From this point the reading will include longer passages. Some of these will contain sentences already given in previous reading exercises or as illustrations of points of grammar.

1 ὑπάρχων πανοῦργος δόλῳ ὑμᾶς ἔλαβον. (2 Cor 12.16)
2 ἀνέβην προσκυνήσων εἰς Ἰερουσαλήμ. (Ac 24.11)
3 ἀκούσας δὲ ὁ νεανίσκος τὸν λόγον ἀπῆλθεν λυπούμενος, ἦν γὰρ ἔχων κτήματα πολλά. (Mt 19.22)
4 **Paul on the road to Damascus**
ἐγένετο δέ μοι πορευομένῳ καὶ ἐγγίζοντι τῇ Δαμασκῷ περὶ

μεσημβρίαν ἐξαίφνης ἐκ τοῦ οὐρανοῦ περιαστράψαι φῶς
ἱκανὸν περὶ ἐμέ, ἔπεσά τε εἰς τὸ ἔδαφος καὶ ἤκουσα φωνῆς
λεγούσης μοι, Σαοὺλ Σαούλ, τί με διώκεις· ἐγὼ δὲ ἀπεκρίθην,
Τίς εἶ, κύριε; εἶπέν τε πρός με, Ἐγώ εἰμι Ἰησοῦς ὁ Ναζωραῖος
ὃν σὺ διώκεις. (Ac 22.6ff.)

5 **The parable of the sower**

ἐλάλησεν αὐτοῖς πολλὰ ἐν παραβολαῖς λέγων, Ἰδοὺ ἐξῆλθεν ὁ
σπείρων τοῦ σπείρειν. καὶ ἐν τῷ σπείρειν αὐτὸν ἃ μὲν (*some*
[*seeds*]) ἔπεσεν παρὰ τὴν ὁδόν, καὶ ἐλθόντα τὰ πετεινὰ
κατέφαγεν αὐτά. ἄλλα δὲ ἔπεσεν ἐπὶ τὰ πετρώδη ὅπου οὐκ
εἶχεν γῆν πολλήν, καὶ εὐθέως ἐξανέτειλεν διὰ τὸ μὴ ἔχειν 5
βάθος γῆς. ἡλίου δὲ ἀνατείλαντος ἐκαυματίσθη καὶ διὰ τὸ μὴ
ἔχειν ῥίζαν ἐξηράνθη. ἄλλα δὲ ἔπεσεν ἐπὶ τὰς ἀκάνθας, καὶ
ἀνέβησαν αἱ ἄκανθαι καὶ ἔπνιξαν αὐτά. ἄλλα δὲ ἔπεσεν ἐπὶ
τὴν γῆν τὴν καλὴν καὶ ἐδίδου (*produced*) καρπόν. (Mt 13.3ff.)

6 **The widow's mite**

Ἀναβλέψας δὲ εἶδεν τοὺς βάλλοντας εἰς τὸ γαζοφυλάκιον τὰ
δῶρα αὐτῶν πλουσίους. εἶδεν δέ τινα χήραν πενιχρὰν
βάλλουσαν ἐκεῖ λεπτὰ δύο, καὶ εἶπεν, Ἀληθῶς λέγω ὑμῖν ὅτι ἡ
χήρα αὕτη ἡ πτωχὴ πλεῖον πάντων ἔβαλεν· πάντες γὰρ οὗτοι
ἐκ τοῦ περισσεύοντος αὐτοῖς ἔβαλον εἰς τὰ δῶρα, αὕτη δὲ ἐκ
τοῦ ὑστερήματος αὐτῆς πάντα τὸν βίον ὃν εἶχεν ἔβαλεν. (Lk
21.1ff.)

7 **Paul sails for Rome**

As the result of a dispute with the Jewish authorities in
Jerusalem, Paul was held prisoner by the Roman governor.
Because he was a Roman citizen Paul had the right to appeal
to the Emperor, and when his request to do so was granted
he was dispatched under guard for Rome. He left in the
company of Luke, who, in the Acts of the Apostles, describes
the journey from Caesarea, the capital of the Roman
province at the time.

There is a map of Paul's journey inside the back cover of the
recommended edition of the NT.

Ὡς δὲ ἐκρίθη τοῦ ἀποπλεῖν ἡμᾶς εἰς τὴν Ἰταλίαν, παρεδίδουν
(*they handed over*) τόν τε Παῦλον καί τινας ἑτέρους
δεσμώτας ἑκατοντάρχῃ ὀνόματι Ἰουλίῳ σπείρης Σεβαστῆς.
ἐπιβάντες δὲ πλοίῳ Ἀδραμυττηνῷ μέλλοντι πλεῖν εἰς τοὺς
κατὰ τὴν Ἀσίαν τόπους ἀνήχθημεν, ὄντος σὺν ἡμῖν 5
Ἀριστάρχου Μακεδόνος Θεσσαλονικέως· τῇ τε ἑτέρᾳ
κατήχθημεν εἰς Σιδῶνα, φιλανθρώπως τε ὁ Ἰούλιος τῷ Παύλῳ
χρησάμενος ἐπέτρεψεν πρὸς τοὺς φίλους πορευθέντι
ἐπιμελείας τυχεῖν. κἀκεῖθεν ἀναχθέντες ὑπεπλεύσαμεν τὴν

Κύπρον διὰ τὸ τοὺς ἀνέμους εἶναι ἐναντίους, τό τε πέλαγος τὸ 10
κατὰ τὴν Κιλικίαν καὶ Παμφυλίαν διαπλεύσαντες κατήλθομεν
εἰς Μύρα τῆς Λυκίας. κἀκεῖ εὑρὼν ὁ ἑκατοντάρχης πλοῖον
Ἀλεξανδρῖνον πλέον εἰς τὴν Ἰταλίαν ἐνεβίβασεν ἡμᾶς εἰς
αὐτό. ἐν ἱκαναῖς δὲ ἡμέραις βραδυπλοοῦντες καὶ μόλις
γενόμενοι κατὰ τὴν Κνίδον, μὴ προσεῶντος ἡμᾶς τοῦ ἀνέμου, 15
ὑπεπλεύσαμεν τὴν Κρήτην κατὰ Σαλμώνην, μόλις τε
παραλεγόμενοι αὐτὴν ἤλθομεν εἰς τόπον τινὰ καλούμενον
Καλοὺς Λιμένας, ᾧ ἐγγὺς πόλις ἦν Λασαία. (Ac 27.1ff.)

Notes

1 The participial phrase ὑπάρχων πανοῦργος gives the reason
for δόλῳ ὑμᾶς ἔλαβον, and should be translated accordingly.

2 προσκυνήσων 12.1/2(d).

3 τὸν λόγον here refers to what had just been said, trans. *this*;
ἦν … ἔχων 12.1/2(g).

4 The subject of ἐγένετο is φῶς (ἐγένετο is not used here in the
way described at 8.1/2); μοι πορευομένῳ etc. is dat. after
ἐγένετο, *for me travelling … a great light happened to flash
…*, but the phrase should be translated by a clause; ἀκούω
takes the gen. of what is heard, hence φωνῆς.

5 *ll.*1f. ὁ σπείρων *the sowing* [*man*], i.e. *the sower* but trans. *a
sower* – a general class is meant (2.1/2 note 1(ii)) as the
parable is about sowers generally and what always happens
in sowing a crop (likewise the article with πετεινά, πετρώδη,
ἀκάνθας and γῆν is not to be translated); τοῦ σπείρειν we
have already seen the infinitive used alone to express purpose
(e.g. 9.2.19) but it may be preceded by τοῦ with the same
meaning (13.1/3(b)(i)); trans. ἐν τῷ σπείρειν αὐτόν by a
clause (5.1/3, αὐτόν is the subject of the infinitive); the seeds
are not mentioned by name but simply referred to in the
neuter plural (ἅ, αὐτά, ἄλλα) – this is in keeping with the
colloquial tone; the neut. pl. subject (ἅ) is correctly followed
by a singular verb ἔπεσεν (2.1/2 note 3) – likewise we have
the singular verbs κατέφαγεν (<κατεσθίω), εἶχεν (<ἔχω),
ἐξανέτειλεν (<ἐξανατέλλω), etc., all of which are governed
by a neut. pl. subject; in the phrase ἃ μέν the neut. pl. relative
pronoun (ἅ) is the equivalent of the article (τά) when used as
a pronoun (cf. ὁ δέ 5.1/3) – here, in conjunction with μέν
(15.1/2(b)), it introduces a slight contrast with the three
following instances of ἄλλα δέ, i.e. *some* [*seed*] … *and other*
[*seed*] … *and other* [*seed again*] etc. (on μὲν … δέ see
15.1.2(b)). *l.*4 The subject of κατέφαγεν is τὰ πετεινά; τὰ
πετρώδη lit. *the stoney* [*parts*], i.e *stoney ground*. *ll.*6f. διὰ τὸ
μὴ ἔχειν lit. *on account of* [*them* i.e. the seeds] *not having*

(the same construction occurs in the next sentence); ἡλίου ... ἀνατείλαντος (<ἀνατέλλω) gen. absolute 12.1/2f.

6 τινά trans. *a* (10.1/1); πάντων trans. *than all* (17.1/4(a)); ἐκ τοῦ περισσεύοντος αὐτοῖς lit. *from the [state of] being abundant for them* i.e. *from their abundance, from their ample wealth* (the neuter pple. τὸ περισσεῦον is used as a noun); ἐκ τοῦ ὑστερήματος αὐτῆς *in* (lit. *from*) *her poverty.*

7 *l.*1 ὡς *when*; τοῦ is idiomatically used with the infinitive after ἐκρίθη (*it was decided*) and can be ignored for purposes of translation; ἡμᾶς is the subject of ἀποπλεῖν *us to sail* i.e. *that we sail. l.*3 ὀνόματι *by name*; Ἰουλίῳ is in apposition to ἑκατοντάρχῃ and hence in the same case; σπείρης Σεβαστῆς *of the Imperial cohort* the unit of the Roman army to which Julius belonged. *l.*7 τῷ Παύλῳ is governed by χρησάμενος (<χράομαι) and ἐπέτρεψεν (<ἐπιτρέπω; both verbs take the dat.). *ll.*8f. πορευθέντι agrees with τῷ Παύλῳ; take ἐπιμελείας with τυχεῖν (which takes the gen., 15.1/1); κἀκεῖθεν = καὶ ἐκεῖθεν (crasis 11.1/5 cf. κἀκεῖ in *l.*12); ἀναχθέντες aor. pass. pple. of ἀνάγω; ὑπεπλεύσαμεν (<ὑποπλέω) they sail to the east of Cyprus to avoid the strong westerly winds. *l.*10 The τε of τό τε πέλαγος joins the clause which begins here with the preceding one. *l.*12 εἰς Μύρα τῆς Λυκίας lit. *to Myra of Lycia*, i.e. *at Myra in Lycia. l.*13 Take πλέον (<πλέω) with πλοῖον. *l.*14 δέ can be put after the second word when the first word is a preposition. *l.*15 γενόμενοι κατὰ τὴν Κνίδον *getting to*; προσεῶντος < προσεάω.

12.3 Excursus

The Septuagint

Ptolemy Philadelphus (308–246 BC), the second Greek king of Egypt, did much to foster Greek culture in the alien environment where he ruled, and one of his most significant initiatives was to found the famous library at Alexandria. In the course of building up its holdings he commissioned the librarian to obtain for the library a Greek translation of the Pentateuch, the first five books of what we now call the Old Testament; perhaps his motive was to win the support of his Jewish subjects. According to an early account the librarian applied to the high priest at Jerusalem for scholars to do the work and was sent seventy-two, who completed the task in seventy-two days. Whatever the truth of this, the translation of the remainder of the Hebrew scriptures was continued in subsequent generations and by the beginning of the Christian era there existed a Greek version of the whole. The work came to be known as the Ἑβδομήκοντα *Seventy* (the English name, Septuagint, comes from the Latin **septuaginta** *seventy*); this appears to be a distorted folk memory of the number of scholars originally employed. A story subsequently became current that of these seventy thirty knew Greek but not Hebrew, thirty Hebrew but not Greek, while the remaining ten were administrators with no knowledge of either language. This slander may have been prompted by the colloquial nature of the Septuagint's language.

As would be expected given its history, the Septuagint shows variations in style and methods of translation; some sections are a free rendering, while others are overlaid with Hebrew idioms and expressions in an attempt to give a close translation of the original. Its language is the Greek koine (see pp. 7f.) of the three centuries before the beginning of the Christian era, and is very close to that of the New Testament.

The Septuagint played an important part in Jewish communities which had developed beyond the traditional boundaries of Palestine and which had forgotten their ancestral language, Hebrew. With the rise of Christianity early Christians also had this version to read if they wished to consult the Hebrew scriptures, and it is the source of the many quotations from the Old Testament in the Gospels. Jewish scholars, however, were exasperated by the use made by this new sect of what was only a translation of their holy writings and finally rejected it as inadequate, but the Septuagint continued to be used in eastern Christianity. The western church, centred on Rome, adopted the Latin translation of St Jerome (c. AD 400) which, together with his translation of the New Testament, forms the Vulgate (see 17.3). The Septuagint remains the version of the Old Testament used by the Greek Orthodox Church.

The Septuagint contains more than what is accepted today as the Old Testament. The extra material, known as the Old Testament Apocrypha (from ἀπόκρυφος *hidden, spurious*), was rejected by Protestants at the time of the Reformation because no original existed in the canonical form of the Hebrew Bible (it is interesting that the Hebrew text of some parts of the Apocrypha has been discovered in the Dead Sea scrolls). Despite its lack of authority, the Apocrypha contains passages of considerable literary merit; perhaps the most famous is from Ecclesiasticus (44.1ff.) *Let us now praise famous men and our fathers that begat us,* etc.

13.1 Grammar

13.1/1 Moods of the Greek verb

All finite forms of the Greek verb can be classified according to mood. Up to now we have dealt only with the indicative, the mood used for facts. There are three other moods, the imperative, which expresses commands (17.1/1), and the subjunctive and optative.

The original distinction between the subjunctive and optative appears to have been between what is **willed** or **expected** (subjunctive) and what is **desired** or considered **possible** (optative); for example, in a main clause the subjunctive can express the will of the speaker, e.g. ἄγωμεν (pres. subj. act. of ἄγω) ἀλλαχοῦ εἰς τὰς ἐχομένας κωμοπόλεις (Mk 1.38) *let us go elsewhere to the neighbouring towns*, while the optative can express the speaker's wish, e.g. ὁ δὲ θεὸς τῆς ἐλπίδος πληρώσαι (aor. opt. act. of πληρόω) ὑμᾶς πάσης χαρᾶς (Ro 15.13) *and may the God of hope fill you with every joy!* Both are used in subordinate clauses but in ways that go far beyond any original meaning.

In English we still possess some single-word subjunctive forms (*be that as it may*; *if I were you*). Apart from these few relics, we use auxiliary verbs (*let, may, would* etc.) for uses covered by the subjunctive (and optative) in Greek.

In earlier times both subjunctive and optative were an integral part of Greek, but in the Koine of the first century AD the latter was almost extinct, surviving only in a few fossilized expressions and in writers with literary pretensions. It occurs sixty-seven times in the NT (mainly in Luke and Acts) but a significant proportion of these consists of the time-honoured clichés γένοιτο *may it happen* and μὴ γένοιτο *may it not happen*. As a result the total number of different optative forms found in the NT is small.

13.1/2 Subjunctive mood

The subjunctive exists in the present and aorist (and perfect, 16.1/4 note). There is only one set of endings, which are applied to the present and aorist stems (the latter without the augment). The endings are formed by lengthening all the initial short vowels (even when the first element of a diphthong) of the present indicative endings:

> **Active:** -ω, -ῃς, -ῃ, -ωμεν, -ητε, -ωσι(ν).
> **Middle and passive:** -ωμαι, -ῃ, -ηται, -ωμεθα, -ησθε, -ωνται.

Note that in ου > ω (3rd pl. act.) the second element of the diphthong disappears. As in all its other forms, the aorist passive has active endings.

The subjunctive forms of λύω are:

		PRESENT ACTIVE	PRESENT MID./PASS.	AORIST ACTIVE	AORIST MIDDLE	AORIST PASSIVE
SINGULAR	1	λύω	λύωμαι	λύσω	λύσωμαι	λυθῶ[1]
	2	λύῃς	λύῃ	λύσῃς	λύσῃ	λυθῇς
	3	λύῃ	λύηται	λύσῃ	λύσηται	λυθῇ
PLURAL	1	λύωμεν	λυώμεθα	λύσωμεν	λυσώμεθα	λυθῶμεν
	2	λύητε	λύησθε	λύσητε	λύσησθε	λυθῆτε
	3	λύωσι(ν)	λύωνται	λύσωσι(ν)	λύσωνται	λυθῶσι(ν)

In the present subjunctive of contracted verbs the rules of contraction apply as for the indicative (5.1/2). Paradigms will be found in **Appendix 2**.

The endings for the subjunctive are classified as **primary** (4.1/1 note 1 and 8.1/1(c); we have -σι(ν) in the 3rd pl. act., -μαι in the 1st s. mid./pass., etc.).

Notes

1 The indicative and subjunctive coincide in a few forms, e.g. λύω, τιμῶ, τιμᾷς.

---

[1] The aorist passive subjunctive is always accented with a circumflex on the first syllable of the ending (the circumflex indicates contraction, λυθῶ < λυθέω etc.).

2 Strong aorists and root aorists have the normal subjunctive endings, except for the root aorist ἔγνων (< γινώσκω), whose subjunctive is γνῶ, γνῷς, γνῷ, γνῶμεν, γνῶτε, γνῶσι(ν) (cf. the present and aorist subjunctive active of δίδωμι, 18.1/2).

3 The subjunctive of εἰμί is identical with the endings of the present subjunctive of λύω, viz ὦ, ᾖς, ᾖ, ὦμεν, ἦτε, ὦσι(ν).

4 The difference between the present and aorist subjunctive is one of **aspect**, not time, just as with infinitives (4.1/1).

13.1/3 Uses of the subjunctive (1)

The subjunctive is used in both main and subordinate clauses; the latter use is far more common than the former.

(a) *Subjunctive in main clauses*

    (i) The **jussive** subjunctive (negated by μή) is used for giving orders but, because we also have the imperative (17.1/1), its use is limited. In the first person plural (the singular is possible but not as common) it expresses self-exhortation or self-encouragement: φάγωμεν καὶ πίωμεν, αὔριον γὰρ ἀποθνῄσκομεν (1 Cor 15.32) *let us eat and drink for tomorrow we die.* The use of the second and third persons of the jussive subjunctive complements the imperative mood in the aorist. Both are treated at 17.1/1.

    (ii) The **deliberative** subjunctive (negated by μή) is used exclusively in questions and indicates the uncertainty of the speaker about the future and what must be done (in English we use the verb *to be* followed by an infinitive): τί φάγωμεν; τί πίωμεν; τί περιβαλώμεθα; (*Mt 6.31) *what are we to eat? what are we to drink? what are we to clothe ourselves in?*

    (iii) A **strong denial** is expressed by οὐ μή and the subjunctive: οὐ μὴ εἰσέλθητε εἰς τὴν βασιλείαν τῶν οὐρανῶν (Mt 5.20) *you **shall not** enter into the kingdom of heaven.*

(b) *Subjunctive in subordinate clauses*

    In uses (i) and (ii) the verb in the subjunctive can be literally translated by *may* or *might.* In (iii) it is to be translated by an indicative in English:

    (i) **Purpose clauses**

        These can be expressed by ἵνα or ὅπως (both conjunctions meaning *in order that, so that*) and the subjunctive.[2] The negative is μή (sometimes a negated purpose clause is introduced by μή alone).

---

[2] Very occasionally ἵνα is used with the future indicative to express purpose.

Διδάσκαλε, τί ἀγαθὸν ποιήσω ἵνα σχῶ ζωὴν αἰώνιον; (Mt
  19.16) *Master, what good shall I do so that I may
  gain eternal life?* (σχῶ 1st s. aor. subj. act. of ἔχω)
ἐξελθόντες δὲ οἱ Φαρισαῖοι συμβούλιον ἔλαβον κατʼ
  αὐτοῦ ὅπως αὐτὸν ἀπολέσωσιν. (Mt 12.14) *And the
  Pharisees went out and took counsel against him so
  that they might destroy him.* (ἀπολέσωσιν 3rd pl. aor.
  subj. act. of ἀπόλλυμι)
ἔρχεται ὁ διάβολος καὶ αἴρει τὸν λόγον ἀπὸ τῆς καρδίας
  αὐτῶν, ἵνα μὴ πιστεύσαντες σωθῶσιν. (Lk 8.12) *The
  devil comes and takes the word from their hearts so
  that they are not saved [by] believing.* (σωθῶσιν 3rd
  pl. aor. subj. pass. of σῴζω)

As we have already seen in the reading exercises, Greek,
like English, can use an infinitive to express purpose: ὁ
υἱὸς τοῦ ἀνθρώπου οὐκ ἦλθεν διακονηθῆναι ἀλλὰ
διακονῆσαι (Mt 20.28) *the Son of Man did not come to
be served but to serve*; other examples occur at 9.2.19
(μισθώσασθαι), 11.2.7 (πειρασθῆναι), 11.2.13 (λαβεῖν).
Sometimes an infinitive used in this way is preceded by
τοῦ with no difference in meaning: μετέβη ἐκεῖθεν τοῦ
διδάσκειν καὶ κηρύσσειν ἐν ταῖς πόλεσιν αὐτῶν (Mt
11.1) *he went from there to instruct and preach in their
cities* (another example at 12.2.5). The infinitive may
also be introduced by εἰς τό or πρός τό: πάντα τὰ ἔργα
αὐτῶν ποιοῦσιν πρὸς τὸ θεαθῆναι (*Mt 23.5) *they do all
their works [in order] to be seen* (another example at
5.2.11).

(ii) **Other subordinate clauses expressed by ἵνα and the
subjunctive**
Verbs of **wishing**, **requesting**, **encouraging** and some
verbs of **ordering** are followed by ἵνα and the subjunctive
(on verbs of ordering see also 7.1/4). Here the ἵνα clause
is to be translated by an infinitive phrase (or occasionally
a *that* clause).

ἀπῆλθεν πρὸς αὐτὸν καὶ ἠρώτα ἵνα καταβῇ καὶ ἰάσηται
  αὐτοῦ τὸν υἱόν (Jn 4.47) *He went out to him and
  asked him to go down and heal his son.* (καταβῇ 3rd
  s. aor. subj. of καταβαίνω; ἰάσηται 3rd s. aor. subj. of
  ἰάομαι)
παρήγγειλεν αὐτοῖς ἵνα μηδὲν ἄρωσιν εἰς ὁδὸν εἰ μὴ
  ῥάβδον μόνον. (Mk 6.8) *He ordered them to take
  nothing for the journey except a staff.* (παραγγέλλω

takes the dative, 15.1/1(b); we could translate *that they take* ...; ἄρωσιν 3rd pl. aor. subj. act. of αἴρω)

Explanatory ἵνα is used to explain, or give more information about, what precedes: τοῦτό ἐστιν τὸ ἔργον τοῦ θεοῦ, ἵνα πιστεύητε εἰς ὃν ἀπέστειλεν ἐκεῖνος (Jn 6.29) *this is the work of* (i.e. *required by*) *God [namely] that you should believe in him whom he sent.*

Consecutive ἵνα gives the consequence or result: τίς ἥμαρτεν, οὗτος ἢ οἱ γονεῖς αὐτοῦ, ἵνα τυφλὸς γεννηθῇ; (Jn 9.2) *who sinned, this man or his parents, that he should be born blind?* The dividing line between this use and purpose clauses is blurred and some examples have been interpreted in both ways; is the meaning of ἦν ἐκεῖ ἕως τῆς τελευτῆς Ἡρῴδου, ἵνα πληρωθῇ τὸ ῥηθὲν ὑπὸ κυρίου (Mt 2.15) *he was there until the death of Herod, so that the word of the Lord* (lit. *the [thing] said by the Lord) was fulfilled* ... (result), or does it mean *so that the word of the Lord should be fulfilled* ... (purpose)? We cannot decide on linguistic grounds. (On consecutive expressions see also 16.1/1).

13.1/4 Optative mood and its uses

(a) *Optative in main clauses*
The optative to express a **wish** is the use most frequently found in the NT (negated by μή). Apart from μὴ γένοιτο *may it not happen!* (a favourite expression of Paul) we may instance:

Ὁ δὲ κύριος κατευθύναι ὑμῶν τὰς καρδίας εἰς τὴν ἀγάπην τοῦ θεοῦ. (2 Th 3.5) *And may the Lord direct your hearts towards the love of God.* (κατευθύναι 3 s. aor. opt. act. of κατευθύνω).

The **potential** optative (negated by οὐ) expresses something that could happen and is accompanied by the particle ἄν (see 18.1/4):

τί ἂν θέλοι ὁ σπερμολόγος οὗτος λέγειν; (Ac 17.18) *What would this chatterer want to say?* (θέλοι 3 s. pres. opt. act. of θέλω).

(b) *Optative in subordinate clauses*
In indirect speech introduced by a verb in a historic tense (*he said that ...; he asked if ...* etc.) it was optional in the older

language for all finite verbs to be put into the optative. A few examples of this occur in the writings of Luke (both in his gospel and Acts). There is no change in sense, and optatives of this sort are to be translated as indicatives:

> ἡ δὲ ἐπὶ τῷ λόγῳ διεταράχθη καὶ διελογίζετο ποταπὸς εἴη ὁ ἀσπασμὸς οὗτος. (Lk 1.29) *And she was perplexed by the statement and wondered what sort of greeting this was.* (εἴη 3 s. pres. opt. of εἰμί; instead of εἴη we could have ἐστί; on the tense see 10.1/2(b)).

Because of the extremely limited use of the optative there is obviously no point in giving full paradigms as the vast majority of possible forms are not found in the NT. A complete list of the forms that do occur is given below. A characteristic of the optative is that all endings contain a diphthong with an iota as its second element (αι, ει, οι, ῳ). Forms marked with asterisks occur more than once; those marked with two asterisks should be committed to memory.

PRESENT	ACTIVE	MIDDLE	
SINGULAR 1		δυναίμην (δύναμαι 19.1/3)	
3	εἴη** (εἰμί)	βούλοιτο (βούλομαι)	
	ἔχοι* (ἔχω)		
	θέλοι (θέλω)		
PLURAL 2	πάσχοιτε (πάσχω)		
3	ἔχοιεν (ἔχω)	δύναιντο* (δύναμαι)	

AORIST	ACTIVE	MIDDLE	PASSIVE
SINGULAR 1		εὐξαίμην (εὔχομαι)	
		ὀναίμην (ὀνίναμαι)	
		γένοιτο** (γίνομαι)	
3	ἁγιάσαι (ἁγιάζω)		λογισθείη (λογίζομαι)
	δῴη** (δίδωμι 18.1/2)		πληθυνθείη (πληθύνω)
	καταρτίσαι (καταρτίζω)		τηρηθείη (τηρέω)
	κατευθύναι* (κατευθύνω)		
	παρακαλέσαι (παρακαλέω)		
	πλεονάσαι (πλεονάζω)		
	περισσεύσαι (περισσεύω)		
	πληρώσαι (πληρόω)		
	στηρίξαι (στηρίζω)		
	φάγοι (ἐσθίω)		
PLURAL 3	εὕροιεν (εὑρίσκω)		
	ποιήσαιεν (ποιέω)		
	ψηλαφήσειαν (ψηλαφάω)		

Of these twenty-seven forms three come from -μι verbs (εἴη, δῴη, ὀναίμην); there are none from the present tense of contracted verbs. The endings of the optative are historic (8.1/1(c)), hence -μην and -(ν)το in the middle.

Further knowledge of this mood is not necessary to read the NT, but the curious will find full tables in any grammar of classical Greek.

13.2 Greek reading

1 Τί οὖν; ἁμαρτήσωμεν ὅτι οὐκ ἐσμὲν ὑπὸ νόμον ἀλλὰ ὑπὸ χάριν; μὴ γένοιτο. (Ro 6.15)
2 ὁ οὐρανὸς καὶ ἡ γῆ παρελεύσεται, οἱ δὲ λόγοι μου οὐ μὴ παρέλθωσιν. (Mt 24.35)
3 Τότε πορευθέντες οἱ Φαρισαῖοι συμβούλιον ἔλαβον ὅπως αὐτὸν παγιδεύσωσιν ἐν λόγῳ. (Mt 22.15)
4 Κύριε, οὐκ εἰμὶ ἱκανὸς ἵνα μου ὑπὸ τὴν στέγην εἰσέλθῃς. (Mt 8.8)
5 τοῦτο γάρ ἐστιν τὸ θέλημα τοῦ πατρός μου, ἵνα πᾶς ὁ θεωρῶν τὸν υἱὸν καὶ πιστεύων εἰς αὐτὸν ἔχῃ ζωὴν αἰώνιον. (Jn 6.40)
6 νυκτὸς καὶ ἡμέρας ἐργαζόμενοι πρὸς τὸ μὴ ἐπιβαρῆσαί τινα ὑμῶν ἐκηρύξαμεν εἰς ὑμᾶς τὸ εὐαγγέλιον τοῦ θεοῦ. (1 Th 2.9)
7 Καὶ λέγει αὐτοῖς ἐν ἐκείνῃ τῇ ἡμέρᾳ ὀψίας γενομένης, Διέλθωμεν εἰς τὸ πέραν. (Mk 4.35)
8 οὐ γὰρ ἀπέστειλεν ὁ θεὸς τὸν υἱὸν εἰς τὸν κόσμον ἵνα κρίνῃ τὸν κόσμον, ἀλλ᾽ ἵνα σωθῇ ὁ κόσμος δι᾽ αὐτοῦ. (Jn 3.17)
9 εἶπεν τοῖς μαθηταῖς αὐτοῦ ἵνα πλοιάριον προσκαρτερῇ αὐτῷ διὰ τὸν ὄχλον ἵνα μὴ θλίβωσιν αὐτόν. (Mk 3.9)
10 ὑμεῖς δέ, ἀδελφοί, οὐκ ἐστὲ ἐν σκότει, ἵνα ἡ ἡμέρα ὑμᾶς ὡς κλέπτης καταλάβῃ, πάντες γὰρ ὑμεῖς υἱοὶ φωτός ἐστε καὶ υἱοὶ ἡμέρας. οὐκ ἐσμὲν νυκτὸς οὐδὲ σκότους. (1 Th 5.4f.)
11 ἡ δὲ γυνὴ ἦν Ἑλληνίς, Συροφοινίκισσα τῷ γένει· καὶ ἠρώτα αὐτὸν ἵνα τὸ δαιμόνιον ἐκβάλῃ ἐκ τῆς θυγατρὸς αὐτῆς. (Mk 7.26)
12 ὄφεις, γεννήματα ἐχιδνῶν, πῶς φύγητε ἀπὸ τῆς κρίσεως τῆς γεέννης; (Mt 23.33)
13 **The mob demands that Jesus be crucified**
λέγει αὐτοῖς ὁ Πιλᾶτος, Τί οὖν ποιήσω Ἰησοῦν τὸν λεγόμενον Χριστόν; λέγουσιν πάντες, Σταυρωθήτω (*let him be crucified*).
ὁ δὲ ἔφη, Τί γὰρ κακὸν ἐποίησεν; οἱ δὲ περισσῶς ἔκραζον λέγοντες, Σταυρωθήτω. ἰδὼν δὲ ὁ Πιλᾶτος ὅτι οὐδὲν ὠφελεῖ ἀλλὰ μᾶλλον θόρυβος γίνεται, λαβὼν ὕδωρ ἀπενίψατο τὰς 5 χεῖρας ἀπέναντι τοῦ ὄχλου λέγων, Ἀθῷός εἰμι ἀπὸ τοῦ αἵματος

τούτου· ὑμεῖς ὄψεσθε. καὶ ἀποκριθεὶς πᾶς ὁ λαὸς εἶπεν, Τὸ αἷμα αὐτοῦ ἐφ᾽ ἡμᾶς καὶ ἐπὶ τὰ τέκνα ἡμῶν. τότε ἀπέλυσεν αὐτοῖς τὸν Βαραββᾶν, τὸν δὲ Ἰησοῦν φραγελλώσας παρέδωκεν (*handed over*) ἵνα σταυρωθῇ. (Mt 27.22ff.)   1

14 Lazarus

Ἦν δέ τις ἀσθενῶν, Λάζαρος ἀπὸ Βηθανίας, ἐκ τῆς κώμης Μαρίας καὶ Μάρθας τῆς ἀδελφῆς αὐτῆς. ἦν δὲ Μαριὰμ ἡ ἀλείψασα τὸν κύριον μύρῳ καὶ ἐκμάξασα τοὺς πόδας αὐτοῦ ταῖς θριξὶν αὐτῆς, ἧς ὁ ἀδελφὸς Λάζαρος ἠσθένει. ἀπέστειλαν οὖν αἱ ἀδελφαὶ πρὸς αὐτὸν λέγουσαι, Κύριε, ἴδε ὃν φιλεῖς 5 ἀσθενεῖ. ἀκούσας δὲ ὁ Ἰησοῦς εἶπεν, Αὕτη ἡ ἀσθένεια οὐκ ἔστιν πρὸς θάνατον ἀλλ᾽ ὑπὲρ τῆς δόξης τοῦ θεοῦ, ἵνα δοξασθῇ ὁ υἱὸς τοῦ θεοῦ δι᾽ αὐτῆς. ἠγάπα δὲ ὁ Ἰησοῦς τὴν Μάρθαν καὶ τὴν ἀδελφὴν αὐτῆς καὶ τὸν Λάζαρον. ὡς οὖν ἤκουσεν ὅτι ἀσθενεῖ, τότε ἔμεινεν ἐν ᾧ ἦν τόπῳ δύο ἡμέρας· ἔπειτα μετὰ 1 τοῦτο λέγει τοῖς μαθηταῖς, Ἄγωμεν εἰς τὴν Ἰουδαίαν πάλιν. λέγουσιν αὐτῷ οἱ μαθηταί, Ῥαββί, νῦν ἐζήτουν σε λιθάσαι οἱ Ἰουδαῖοι, καὶ πάλιν ὑπάγεις ἐκεῖ; (*Jn 11.1–8)

Notes

1 ἁμαρτήσωμεν (<ἁμαρτάνω) deliberative subj. (13.1/3(a)(ii)).

2 παρελεύσεται singular because it agrees with the closer subject; οὐ μή 13.1/3(a)(iii).

6 νυκτὸς καὶ ἡμέρας gen. of time within which (7.1/6(c)); πρός introduces a phrase of purpose; τινά is the object of the infinitive ἐπιβαρῆσαι.

7 λέγει vivid present, trans. *he said* (also in 13 and 14); ὀψίας γενομένης gen. absolute (12.1/2(f)), lit. *evening having become*, i.e. *when it had become evening*; διέλθωμεν jussive subj. (13.1/3(a)(i)).

8 ἀπέστειλεν < ἀποστέλλω; σωθῇ < σῴζω.

9 εἶπεν the following construction (ἵνα + subj.) shows that the verb is used here in the sense of *tell* [*someone to do something*], *order* (13.1/3(b)(ii)); πλοιάριον is the subject of the ἵνα clause.

10 The ἵνα clause expresses what would happen if the people addressed were in fact in the dark – it should be translated by a phrase *for the day to catch you* ...

12 φύγητε deliberative subj. (13.1/3(a)(iii)), trans. *are you to flee?*

13 *l*.1 ποιήσω could be either fut. (*what shall I do with* ...) or aor. subj. (what *am I to do with* ...). *l*.3 γάρ has the sense of *well* [*granted that this is what you want*], *what wrong* etc.; ἔκραζον inceptive impf. (4.1/1 note 3) *started to shout*. *l*.4 οὐδὲν ὠφελεῖ lit. *he was accomplishing nothing* (on the tense

of ὠφελεῖ and γίνεται see 8.1/4(a)). *l.*5 γίνεται lit. *was being born*, i.e. *was starting. l.*7 ὑμεῖς ὄψεσθε lit. *you will see [to it yourselves]*, an idiomatic expression meaning *it is your business.*

14 *l.*3 ἐκμάξασα < ἐκμάσσω. *l.*4 ἀπέστειλαν < ἀποστέλλω. *l.*5 ὃν φιλεῖς the antecedent is not expressed (9.1/2 note 2), trans. [*the man*] *whom* ... *ll.*6f. οὐκ ἔστιν πρὸς θάνατον lit. *is not towards death* a condensed expression for *is not leading/extending up to death*, i.e will not cause his death. *l.*8 δι' αὐτῆς i.e. the sickness (ἀσθένεια is feminine, and a pronoun referring back to it must also be feminine); ἠγάπα because in English we use the verb *love* for an emotion extending over a period, we can translate the impf. by *loved*, rather than *was loving. l.*9 οὖν here has the rarer sense of *however. l.*10 ἐν ᾧ ἦν τόπῳ lit. *in what place he was*, i.e. *in the place where he was* (9.1/4 note 4).

unit 14

14.1 Grammar

14.1/1 Uses of the subjunctive (2)

(a) **Noun clauses after verbs of fearing and taking precautions**
The deponent φοβέομαι can be followed by a noun in the accusative: ὁ Ἡρῴδης ἐφοβεῖτο τὸν Ἰωάννην (*Mk 6.20) *Herod was afraid of John*. It may also be followed by a clause which performs the same function as a noun (and hence is called a noun clause): *Herod was afraid that there might be a revolt*. Most (but not all) clauses of this sort have reference to a time subsequent to that of the main verb and in Greek are expressed by μή and the subjunctive; μή here, and elsewhere when used as a conjunction, can be literally translated by *lest*. The same construction is used after verbs meaning *take precautions, take heed*.

> φοβηθεὶς ὁ χιλίαρχος μὴ διασπασθῇ ὁ Παῦλος ὑπ᾽ αὐτῶν ἐκέλευσεν τὸ στράτευμα καταβὰν ἁρπάσαι αὐτόν. (Ac 23.10) *The captain, fearing lest* (or *that*) *Paul might be torn apart by them, ordered the soldiers to go down and seize him.* (lit. *having gone down to seize him*)

The negative used to negate the μή clause is οὐ:

> φοβοῦμαι γὰρ μή πως ἐλθὼν οὐχ οἵους θέλω εὕρω ὑμᾶς. (2 Cor 12.20) *For I am afraid lest when I come I may perhaps not find you such as* (οἵους) *I wish.*

φοβέομαι is followed by an infinitive where English has the same construction: ἐφοβήθη ἐκεῖ ἀπελθεῖν (Mt 2.22) *he was afraid to go there*.

As well as meaning *see* βλέπω can also mean *take precautions, take heed* (cf. our *see to it*). In this use βλέπω is normally in the imperative mood (17.1/1): βλέπετε μή τις ὑμᾶς πλανήσῃ (Mt 24.4) *take heed lest anyone lead you astray* (or *that no-one*).

(b) **Indefinite adverbial clauses**

  (i) Certain temporal conjunctions (e.g. ὅτε *when*) may introduce a subordinate clause and be followed by the indicative. Greek idiom here is very similar to that of English and we have already met examples (4.2.12; 5.2.10; 8.2.16; 11.2.13). Such a clause refers to a single definite event. Another type of adverbial clause is that with an indefinite sense and is often expressed in English by the addition of *ever*. In *when I went to the Middle East I visited the remains of Crusader castles* the subordinate clause refers to a specific event (viz the occasion of my visit to the Middle East), but in *whenever I go to the Middle East I visit the remains of Crusader castles* the subordinate clause refers to a number of events, and so is called **indefinite**. To express this in Greek the particle ἄν, which is here the equivalent of *ever,* is added to the subordinate clause; in addition its verb is put into the subjunctive if the reference is to the **present** or **future**. ἄν coalesces with certain conjunctions, the most common being ὅτε *when*; the resulting ὅταν (ὅτε + ἄν) means *whenever*:

  μακάριοί ἐστε ὅταν ὀνειδίσωσιν ὑμᾶς καὶ διώξωσιν. (Mt 5.11) *Blessed are you whenever they abuse and persecute you.*

  οὐ νίπτονται τὰς χεῖρας αὐτῶν ὅταν ἄρτον ἐσθίωσιν. (*Mt 15.2) *They do not wash their hands whenever they eat bread.*

In both sentences we would normally say *when* in English but the sense would be the same. Compare the following where a single event is described in the subordinate clause:

  ὅτε ἐγένετο ἡμέρα, προσεφώνησεν τοὺς μαθητὰς αὐτοῦ. (Lk 6.13) *When it became day he summoned his disciples.*

If the reference of a sentence involving repeated action is to the **past**, the verb of the ὅταν clause is in the indicative:

τὰ πνεύματα τὰ ἀκάθαρτα, ὅταν αὐτὸν ἐθεώρουν, προσέπιπτον αὐτῷ. (Mk 3.11) *Whenever they used to see him, the unclean spirits used to fall down before him.*

There are, however, variations in use of these conjunctions and we find examples of ὅτε with the subjunctive and ὅταν with the indicative where we would expect the reverse. NT usage is inconsistent here, and we must judge from the context whether a single event or repeated action is involved; to translate both ὅτε and ὅταν by *when* is generally satisfactory.

ὡς, which has other meanings (see **Vocabulary**), can also be used as a conjunction in the sense of *when*: ὡς ἐπλήσθησαν αἱ ἡμέραι τῆς λειτουργίας αὐτοῦ, ἀπῆλθεν εἰς τὸν οἶκον αὐτοῦ (Lk 1.23) *when the days of his service were completed, he went away to his house* (other examples at 8.2.9, 12.2.7).

(ii) ἕως (also ἕως οὗ, ἕως ὅτου with no difference in sense) *until* is used with the indicative when the clause it introduces describes an event that actually happened: οὐκ ἐγίνωσκεν αὐτὴν ἕως οὗ ἔτεκεν υἱόν (Mt 1.25) *he did not know her until she bore a son.* When its clause refers to something expected, the subjunctive is used, with or without ἄν; most clauses of this sort refer to the future:

οὐ μὴ παρέλθῃ ἡ γενεὰ αὕτη ἕως ἂν πάντα ταῦτα γένηται. (Mt 24.34) *This generation shall not pass away until all these things happen.*

οὐ μὴ ἀλέκτωρ φωνήσῃ ἕως οὗ ἀρνήσῃ με τρίς. (Jn 13.38) *A cock shall not crow until you deny me three times.*

ἕως can also function as a preposition (+ gen.):

In a temporal sense *until*: ἦν ἐκεῖ ἕως τῆς τελευτῆς Ἡρῴδου (Mt 2.15) *he was there until the death of Herod.*

In a spatial sense: ἕως τῆς αὐλῆς τοῦ ἀρχιερέως (Mt 26.58) *up to the courtyard of the high priest.*

To indicate degree or measure: ἕως ἑπτάκις *up to seven times.*

There is an overlap in meaning between ἕως and two other words, ἄχρι and μέχρι (sometimes written ἄχρις, μέχρις). As prepositions (+ gen.) they mean *until, up to*: ἄχρι τῆς ἡμέρας ταύτης (Ac 2.29) *up to this day*; μέχρι ταύτης τῆς ὥρας (Ac 10.30) *until this hour* but they can also be used as conjunctions (sometimes in the form ἄχρις οὗ, μέχρις οὗ): ἄχρις οὗ ἔλθῃ (1 Cor 11.26) *until he comes*; μέχρις οὗ ταῦτα πάντα γένηται (Mk 13.30) *until all these things happen*.

(iii) πρίν (also πρὶν ἤ) *before* can be conveniently treated here. With two exceptions in the NT it is followed, not by a clause, but by the **accusative and infinitive** (8.1/4(b)); this must be translated by a clause in English: ὁ ἥλιος μεταστραφήσεται εἰς σκότος καὶ ἡ σελήνη εἰς αἷμα πρὶν ἐλθεῖν ἡμέραν κυρίου τὴν μεγάλην (Ac 2.20) *the sun will be changed to darkness and the moon to blood before the great day of the Lord comes.*

(c) Indefinite adjectival clauses

Adjectival clauses also can be given an indefinite sense by using the subjunctive with ἄν. In the sentence ὃς ἀπολύει τὴν γυναῖκα αὐτοῦ καὶ γαμεῖ ἄλλην, μοιχᾶται we are referring to a particular person and we must translate [*the man*] *who is divorcing his wife and marrying another, is committing adultery.* But if we wish to make a general statement and refer to all such men we must say ὃς ἂν ἀπολύσῃ τὴν γυναῖκα αὐτοῦ καὶ γαμήσῃ ἄλλην μοιχᾶται (*Mt 19.9) *whoever divorces his wife and marries another, commits adultery*; here the adjectival clause ὃς ἂν ἀπολύσῃ τὴν γυναῖκα αὐτοῦ καὶ γαμήσῃ ἄλλην is given an indefinite meaning by the subjunctives ἀπολύσῃ, γαμήσῃ and ἄν.

ὅστις, which we have already seen at 9.1/2 note 1 as an alternative for the normal relative pronoun (ὅς, ἥ, ὅ), was originally an indefinite relative in its own right in the sense *whoever* and it is sometimes so used in the NT. It can be followed by the indicative (and we must judge from the context whether it means *who* or *whoever*): ὅστις ὑψώσει ἑαυτὸν ταπεινωθήσεται (*Mt 23.12) *whoever exalts himself will be humbled.* It is also used with ἄν and the subjunctive in the the same sense: ὅστις γὰρ ἂν ποιήσῃ τὸ θέλημα τοῦ πατρός μου τοῦ ἐν οὐρανοῖς, αὐτός μου ἀδελφὸς καὶ ἀδελφὴ καὶ μήτηρ ἐστίν (Mt 12.50) *for whoever does the will of my Father in heaven, he is my brother and sister and mother.*

Notes

1 ἄν has an alternative form ἐάν: ὃς ἐὰν δέξηται ἒν παιδίον τοιοῦτο ἐπὶ τῷ ὀνόματί μου, ἐμὲ δέχεται (Mt 18.5) *whoever receives one such child in my name receives me*; this ἐάν is more frequent as a substitute for ἄν in indefinite adjectival clauses. It must not be confused with the other ἐάν, which has the meaning *if ever* (18.1/3 note 2).

2 The negative for indefinite clauses is μή: ὃς ἂν μὴ δέξηται τὴν βασιλείαν τοῦ θεοῦ ὡς παιδίον, οὐ μὴ εἰσέλθῃ εἰς αὐτήν (Mk 10.15) *whoever does not accept the kingdom of God as a child will not enter into it.*

3 The ἄν of indefinite clauses has a completely different sense and use from the ἄν which we shall meet in potential clauses (18.1/3).

14.1/2 Perfect indicative active

The perfect tense in both Greek and English expresses a present state resulting from an action in the past. κέκλεικα τὴν θύραν *I have closed the door* means that the door is now closed as a result of my past action of closing it. The aorist ἔκλεισα τὴν θύραν *I closed the door* describes a single past action, but tells us nothing about the present state of the door, not even whether it is still in existence. Because the perfect tense describes a present state it is classified as a **primary** tense (4.1/1 note 1). The perfect is by no means as common as the aorist and does not exist in every Greek verb.

The perfect active is formed in two ways, called **strong** and **weak**. These have a common set of endings (in the indicative -α, -ας, -ε(ν), -αμεν, -ατε, -ασι(ν)), but, whereas the strong perfect, like the strong aorist, has no suffix, the weak perfect has a suffixed κ which is attached in a way similar to that of the σ of the weak aorist (see below). There is no difference in meaning between the two, and in NT Greek no verb has both.

The stems of both strong and weak perfects must have either reduplication or an augment.

(a) **Reduplication**
This occurs with most verbs beginning with a consonant. If a verb begins with a single consonant (except ρ) or with two consonants of which the second is λ, μ, ν, or ρ, the initial consonant is doubled with the insertion of ε; hence **weak** λέλυκα (λύω) *I have loosened*; πεπίστευκα (πιστεύω) *I have trusted*; **strong** γέγραφα (γράφω) *I have written*. When,

however, the initial consonant is an aspirate (θ, φ, χ), it is reduplicated in its unaspirated form: τέθυκα (θύω) I *have sacrificed*; πέφευγα (φεύγω) I *have fled*.

(b) **Augment**

(i) The **temporal augment** (4.1/1 note 2(ii)) is used with verbs with an initial vowel or diphthong: ἡμάρτηκα (ἁμαρτάνω) I *have sinned*.

(ii) The **syllabic augment** (4.1/1 note 2(i)) is used with verbs beginning with ρ, a double consonant (ζ, ξ, ψ), or two consonants (the second not being λ, μ, ν, ρ): -ἔσταλκα (-στέλλω) I *have sent*; ἔρριμμαι (ρίπτω) I *have been thrown*; ἐζώγρημαι (ζωγρέω) I *have been captured alive* (the last two examples are perfect passive as perfect active forms of these types of verb do not occur in the NT; see 16.1/3).

The perfect indicative active of λύω (weak) and γράφω (strong) is:

1 S. λέλυκα	PL. λελύκαμεν	S. γέγραφα	PL. γεγράφαμεν
I *have loosened*		I *have written*	
2 λέλυκας	λελύκατε	γέγραφας	γεγράφατε
3 λέλυκε(ν)	λελύκασι(ν)	γέγραφε(ν)	γεγράφασι(ν)

The weak perfect occurs mostly in:

(a) Stems ending in vowels or diphthongs. Here the κ suffix is added to the present stem: πεπίστευκα (πιστεύω *trust*). As in the aorist, the final vowel of most contracted verbs is lengthened: πεποίηκα (ποιέω *do, make*).

(b) Stems ending in λ and ρ, where the κ suffix must be added to the original stem (i.e. the present stem stripped of any suffix, cf. 11.1/3): ἦρκα (αἴρω *lift*, i.e. ἄρ-γω, stem ἀρ-).

(c) Dental stems (6.1/4), where the final dental is lost before the κ suffix: ἤλπικα (ἐλπίζω *hope*, stem ἐλπιδ-).

The strong perfect occurs in other consonant stems: πέφευγα (φεύγω *flee*); γέγραφα (γράφω *write*). Sometimes a final unaspirated consonant is aspirated, e.g. γ/κ > χ, πέπραχα (πράσσω *do* stem πραγ-). An o appears in some strong perfects: πέποιθα (πείθω *persuade*); πέπονθα (πάσχω *suffer*); γέγονα (γίνομαι *become* – note change in voice).

Notes

1 Some strong perfects have an intransitive sense although their other active tenses are transitive, e.g. πέποιθα (< πείθω

persuade) which takes the dative and has a **present** sense *I have confidence in*, i.e. *I trust*.

2 A few perfects are highly irregular, e.g. ἀκήκοα (ἀκούω *hear* – the only common verb in a vowel stem which has a strong perfect); εἴληφα (λαμβάνω *take*); many are less anomalous, e.g. βέβληκα (βάλλω *throw*); κέκληκα (καλέω *call*); πέπτωκα (πίπτω *fall*). The perfect of ἀποθνῄσκω *die* is always τέθνηκα (without the ἀπο- prefix) *I have died*, i.e. *I am dead*.

14.2 Greek reading

1 εὑρίσκει οὗτος πρῶτον τὸν ἀδελφὸν τὸν ἴδιον Σίμωνα καὶ λέγει αὐτῷ, Εὑρήκαμεν τὸν Μεσσίαν. (Jn 1.41)

2 ὃς ἐὰν οὖν λύσῃ μίαν τῶν ἐντολῶν τούτων τῶν ἐλαχίστων καὶ διδάξῃ οὕτως τοὺς ἀνθρώπους, ἐλάχιστος κληθήσεται ἐν τῇ βασιλείᾳ τῶν οὐρανῶν· ὃς δ᾽ ἂν ποιήσῃ καὶ διδάξῃ, οὗτος μέγας κληθήσεται ἐν τῇ βασιλείᾳ τῶν οὐρανῶν. (Mt 5.19)

3 φοβοῦμαι δὲ μή πως, ὡς ὁ ὄφις ἐξηπάτησεν Εὕαν ἐν τῇ πανουργίᾳ αὐτοῦ, φθαρῇ τὰ νοήματα ὑμῶν. (2 Cor 11.3)

4 ἀλλὰ ταῦτα λελάληκα ὑμῖν ἵνα ὅταν ἔλθῃ ἡ ὥρα αὐτῶν μνημονεύητε αὐτῶν. (Jn 16.4)

5 ὅτε γέγονα ἀνήρ, κατήργηκα τὰ τοῦ νηπίου. (1 Cor 13.11)

6 ὃς ἂν βλασφημήσῃ εἰς τὸ πνεῦμα τὸ ἅγιον, οὐκ ἔχει ἄφεσιν εἰς τὸν αἰῶνα. (*Mk 3.29)

7 ἀμὴν γὰρ λέγω ὑμῖν, ἕως ἂν παρέλθῃ ὁ οὐρανὸς καὶ ἡ γῆ, ἰῶτα ἓν ἢ μία κεραία οὐ μὴ παρέλθῃ ἀπὸ τοῦ νόμου ἕως ἂν πάντα γένηται. (Mt 5.18)

8 λέγω δὲ ὑμῖν, οὐ μὴ πίω ἀπ᾽ ἄρτι ἐκ τούτου τοῦ γενήματος τῆς ἀμπέλου ἕως τῆς ἡμέρας ἐκείνης ὅταν αὐτὸ πίνω μεθ᾽ ὑμῶν καινὸν ἐν τῇ βασιλείᾳ τοῦ πατρός μου. (Mt 26.29)

9 Καὶ ὅταν ὀψὲ ἐγένετο, ἐξεπορεύοντο ἔξω τῆς πόλεως. (Mk 11.19)

10 ὅστις δ᾽ ἂν ἀρνήσηταί με ἔμπροσθεν τῶν ἀνθρώπων, ἀρνήσομαι κἀγὼ αὐτὸν ἔμπροσθεν τοῦ πατρός μου. (Mt 10.33)

11 **Peter denies Christ**
Συλλαβόντες δὲ αὐτὸν ἤγαγον καὶ εἰσήγαγον εἰς τὴν οἰκίαν τοῦ ἀρχιερέως· ὁ δὲ Πέτρος ἠκολούθει μακρόθεν. περιαψάντων δὲ πῦρ ἐν μέσῳ τῆς αὐλῆς καὶ συγκαθισάντων ἐκάθητο (*sat*) ὁ Πέτρος μέσος αὐτῶν. ἰδοῦσα δὲ αὐτὸν παιδίσκη τις καθήμενον (*sitting*) πρὸς τὸ φῶς καὶ ἀτενίσασα 5 αὐτῷ εἶπεν, Καὶ οὗτος σὺν αὐτῷ ἦν· ὁ δὲ ἠρνήσατο λέγων, Οὐκ οἶδα αὐτόν, γύναι. καὶ μετὰ βραχὺ ἕτερος ἰδὼν αὐτὸν ἔφη, Καὶ σὺ ἐξ αὐτῶν εἶ· ὁ δὲ Πέτρος ἔφη, Ἄνθρωπε, οὐκ εἰμί. καὶ

διαστάσης ὡσεὶ ὥρας μιᾶς (*when about an hour had passed*)
ἄλλος τις διϊσχυρίζετο λέγων, Ἐπ' ἀληθείας καὶ οὗτος μετ' 10
αὐτοῦ ἦν, καὶ γὰρ Γαλιλαῖός ἐστιν· εἶπεν δὲ ὁ Πέτρος,
Ἄνθρωπε, οὐκ οἶδα ὃ λέγεις. καὶ παραχρῆμα ἔτι λαλοῦντος
αὐτοῦ ἐφώνησεν ἀλέκτωρ. καὶ στραφεὶς ὁ κύριος ἐνέβλεψεν
τῷ Πέτρῳ, καὶ ὑπεμνήσθη ὁ Πέτρος τοῦ ῥήματος τοῦ κυρίου ὡς
εἶπεν αὐτῷ ὅτι Πρὶν ἀλέκτορα φωνῆσαι σήμερον ἀπαρνήσῃ με 15
τρίς· καὶ ἐξελθὼν ἔξω ἔκλαυσεν πικρῶς. (Lk 22.54–62)

12 **The crucifixion**

Παρέλαβον οὖν τὸν Ἰησοῦν· καὶ βαστάζων ἑαυτῷ τὸν σταυρὸν
ἐξῆλθεν εἰς τὸν λεγόμενον Κρανίου Τόπον, ὃ λέγεται
Ἑβραϊστὶ Γολγοθᾶ, ὅπου αὐτὸν ἐσταύρωσαν, καὶ μετ' αὐτοῦ
ἄλλους δύο ἐντεῦθεν καὶ ἐντεῦθεν, μέσον δὲ τὸν Ἰησοῦν.
ἔγραψεν δὲ καὶ τίτλον ὁ Πιλᾶτος καὶ ἔθηκεν (*put*) ἐπὶ τοῦ 5
σταυροῦ· ἦν δὲ γεγραμμένον (*written*), ΙΗΣΟΥΣ Ο
ΝΑΖΩΡΑΙΟΣ Ο ΒΑΣΙΛΕΥΣ ΤΩΝ ΙΟΥΔΑΙΩΝ. τοῦτον οὖν τὸν
τίτλον πολλοὶ ἀνέγνωσαν τῶν Ἰουδαίων, ὅτι ἐγγὺς ἦν ὁ τόπος
τῆς πόλεως ὅπου ἐσταυρώθη ὁ Ἰησοῦς· καὶ ἦν γεγραμμένον
Ἑβραϊστί, Ῥωμαϊστί, Ἑλληνιστί. ἔλεγον οὖν τῷ Πιλάτῳ οἱ 10
ἀρχιερεῖς τῶν Ἰουδαίων, Μὴ γράφε (*do not write*), Ὁ
βασιλεὺς τῶν Ἰουδαίων, ἀλλ' ὅτι ἐκεῖνος εἶπεν, Βασιλεύς εἰμι
τῶν Ἰουδαίων. ἀπεκρίθη ὁ Πιλᾶτος, Ὃ γέγραφα, γέγραφα.
(John 19.16–22)

Notes

2 μίαν τῶν ἐντολῶν τούτων τῶν ἐλαχίστων lit. *one of the least of
these commandments*, but trans. *the least of these
commandments*; the second half of the sentence has its main
verb in the future, κληθήσεται, and so we must supply ἔσται
will be (not ἐστί) as the main verb in the first; with ποιήσῃ
καὶ διδάξῃ we must supply an object *them*, i.e. these
commandments.

3 The n. pl. subject τὰ νοήματα has a singular verb φθαρῇ (2.1/2
note 3; also below in 7).

4 μνημονεύω takes the gen. (here αὐτῶν), 15.1/1.

5 ὅτε γέγονα ἀνήρ lit. *when I have become a man* but trans.
now that I have become a man; τοῦ νηπίου represents a
general class and should be translated *a child* (2.1/2 note 1
(ii)).

8 πίω 1 s. aor. subj. act. of πίνω; take καινόν with αὐτό, *drink
it new* (presumably it will be a new wine).

9 ὀψέ is an adverb *in the evening* but trans. the clause *when it
became evening*; ἐξεπορεύοντο is best taken as an inceptive
impf. *started to go* (4.1/1 note 3).

10 κἀγώ = καὶ ἐγώ *I too* (crasis 11.1/5).

11 *l.*3 The subject of the gen. absol. περιαψάντων ... συγκαθισάντων is those who had arrested Jesus – if expressed it would be αὐτῶν (12.1/2*f*). *l.*4 μέσος αὐτῶν lit. *middle of them*, i.e. *in the middle of them*; ἰδοῦσα nom. fem. s. of the aor. act. pple. of ὁράω. *l.*7 μετὰ βραχύ *after a little (while)*. *l.*10 καὶ οὗτος *this man too*. *l.*11 καὶ γάρ *for indeed*. *l.*13 ἐμβλέπω takes the dat. (15.1/1).

12 *l.*4 ἐντεῦθεν καὶ ἐντεῦθεν lit. *from here and from there*, i.e. *on each side*. *l.*6 Accents are not used with capitals. *ll.*7f. Take πολλοί with τῶν Ἰουδαίων and ἐγγύς with τῆς πόλεως; ἀνέγνωσαν < ἀναγινώσκω. *l.*10 ἔλεγον *said* the imperfect is used because the subject is an unspecified number of individuals.

unit 15

15.1 Grammar

15.1/1 Verbs used with the genitive or dative

A transitive verb is one that can be followed by the accusative case. Both the Greek πέμπω and the English *send* are transitive, and in the clause ἔπεμψεν φίλους ὁ ἑκατοντάρχης (Lk 7.6) and its English translation *the centurion sent friends* both φίλους and *friends* are direct objects and therefore accusative. We might at first assume that if a verb is transitive in English its Greek equivalent will be the same. However, although this is true for the greater number of verbs, there are some which are transitive in one language but intransitive in the other.

The verb βλέπω is used transitively in πᾶς ὁ βλέπων γυναῖκα πρὸς τὸ ἐπιθυμῆσαι αὐτὴν (Mt 5.28) because it governs the accusative γυναῖκα, and we would translate it by *every [man] looking at a woman with a view to* (πρός) *desiring her*. However, we could not say *every man looking a woman* because the English verb *look* is intransitive (the word *woman* in *looking at a woman* is accusative after the proposition *at*). Similarly, there are verbs which are transitive in English but not in Greek, but, whereas in English the logical object of an intransitive verb is always preceded by a preposition (*looking at a woman*), in Greek it can sometimes be preceded by a preposition, sometimes be put into the genitive or dative.

Greek verbs that take the genitive or dative can, to a large extent, be classified according to their meaning. We have already seen some examples (with gen. τυγχάνω 12.2.7, μνημονεύω 14.2.4; with dat. ὑπακούω 5.2.15, ἐμβλέπω 14.2.11). The following are the main groups:

(a) *Verbs followed by the genitive*

  (i) Verbs of **ruling** and **prevailing**, e.g. ἄρχω *rule*; βασιλεύω lit. *be king* (βασιλεύς) *of*; κυριεύω *rule, control*; κατισχύω *prevail over*:

πύλαι ἄδου οὐ κατισχύσουσιν αὐτῆς (Mt 16.18) [*The*] *gates of hell will not prevail over it* (viz τῆς ἐκκλησίας *the church*).

 (ii) Some verbs of **emotion** or **concern** and their opposites, e.g. ἐπιθυμέω *desire* (which can also take the acc.; see example quoted above); ἐπιμελέομαι *care for*; φείδομαι *spare*; ἀμελέω *neglect*:

φειδόμενος ὑμῶν οὐκ ἦλθον εἰς Κόρινθον. (*2 Cor 1.23) *to spare you* (lit. *sparing you*) *I did not come to Corinth.*
κἀγὼ ἠμέλησα αὐτῶν. (Hb 8.9) *I too neglected them.*

(iii) Verbs of **perceiving, remembering, forgetting,** e.g. ἀκούω *hear, listen to* (+ acc. of thing heard, gen. of person heard; also with gen. of thing heard); μιμνήσκομαι, μνημονεύω *remember*; ἐπιλανθάνομαι *forget*:

οἱ δὲ ἀκούσαντες τοῦ βασιλέως ἐπορεύθησαν. (Mt 2.9) *And they, having heard the king, departed.*
ἡ γυνὴ οὐκέτι μνημονεύει τῆς θλίψεως. (*Jn 16.21) *The woman no longer remembers her affliction.*

(iv) Verbs of **laying hold of, obtaining,** e.g. τυγχάνω *receive, attain*; ἀντέχομαι *hold fast to*; ἅπτομαι *touch*:

ἀντεχόμενος τοῦ πιστοῦ λόγου. (*Tit 1.9) *Holding fast to the trustworthy word.*
πολλῆς εἰρήνης τυγχάνοντες διὰ σοῦ. (Ac 24.2) *Receiving long peace through you.*

 (v) Verbs of **sharing,** e.g. μετέχω, μεταλαμβάνω *share, have a share in*:

μετελάμβανον τροφῆς. (Ac 2.46) *They used to share food.*

(b) *Verbs followed by the dative*

  (i) Verbs indicating that **the subject is asserting himself in some way over someone else,** e.g.

βοηθέω *help, assist*; ἐπιτιμάω *rebuke, censure*; παραγγέλλω *order*; ἐπιτρέπω *allow*:

παρήγγειλεν ἡμῖν κηρύξαι τῷ λαῷ. (Ac 10.42) *He ordered us to preach to the people.*

(ii) Verbs indicating that **the subject is submitting himself in some way to somebody else**, e.g. ὑπακούω *obey*; πιστεύω *believe in*; δουλεύω *serve*; λατρεύω *worship*:

δουλεύων τῷ κυρίῳ μετὰ πάσης ταπεινοφροσύνης. (Ac 20.19) *Serving the Lord with all humility.*

(iii) Verbs indicating **association of some sort**, e.g. ἀκολουθέω *follow*; ἐντυγχάνω *fall in with*; ἐγγίζω *approach*; χράομαι *use*; ὁμοιόομαι *be like*:

ἀκολουθοῦσιν αὐτῷ οἱ μαθηταὶ αὐτοῦ. (Mk 6.1) *His disciples followed him.*
οὐκ ἐχρησάμεθα τῇ ἐξουσίᾳ ταύτῃ. (1 Cor 9.12) *we did not use that right.*

(iv) Verbs **compounded with the prepositional prefixes** ἀντι, εἰσ-, ἐν-, ἐπι-, παρα-, περι-, προσ-, συν-, ὑπο- are sometimes followed by the dative, sometimes by a preposition:

τότε προσέρχονται αὐτῷ οἱ μαθηταὶ Ἰωάννου. (Mt 9.14) *Then the disciples of John come to him.*
καὶ ἰδοὺ ἄνδρες δύο συνελάλουν αὐτῷ (Lk 9.30) *And behold! two [men] were talking with him.*
ὁ Φῆστος συλλαλήσας μετὰ τοῦ συμβουλίου ἀπεκρίθη. (Ac 25.12) *Festos having talked with his council replied.*

Not all verbs which, by virtue of their meaning, we would expect to belong to these groups do in fact take the genitive or dative without a preposition; e.g. σπλαγχνίζομαι *pity,* which we might have expected to come under verbs of emotion or concern, is followed by ἐπί with the accusative or dative: σπλαγχνίζομαι ἐπὶ τὸν ὄχλον (Mt 15.32) *I feel pity for the crowd.*

Apart from those given in (b)(iv), other verbs listed above are sometimes used with prepositions, e.g. ὅτε ἤγγισαν εἰς Ἰεροσόλυμα καὶ ἦλθον εἰς Βηθφαγὴ εἰς τὸ Ὄρος τῶν Ἐλαιῶν (Mt 21.1) *when they approached Jerusalem and went to Bethphage on* [lit. *to*] *the Mount of Olives.* The same variation can be seen with λέγω *say, speak,* which normally takes the accusative for what is said and the dative for the person addressed: ἔλεγεν δὲ παραβολὴν αὐτοῖς (Lk 18.1) *and he began to tell them a parable;*

but in the same gospel we have ἔλεγεν δὲ καὶ παραβολὴν πρὸς αὐτούς (Lk 5.36) *and he began to tell them a parable as well* (other examples at 8.2.12 and 9.2.11).

15.1/2 Further particles

We have already seen the more common particles at 4.1/4. We can classify the remaining examples into two groups:

(a) Particles which convey **shades of tone, colour or emphasis**

- **ἀμήν**, which we have already met (14.2.7), is a Hebrew word taken over into NT Greek with the meaning *truly, verily*. It is always combined with λέγω (ἀμὴν λέγω, ἀμὴν δὲ λέγω, ἀμὴν γὰρ λέγω, ἀμὴν ἀμὴν λέγω) and is used only by Christ. When used at the end of prayers in Christian practice it has a secondary meaning, *so be it.*

- **γε#** is an emphasizing and restrictive particle which affects the preceding word. Its literal meaning is *at least, at any rate, certainly, indeed,* and it is nearly always used in combination with conjunctions: εἴ γε *if indeed*, ἄρα γε strengthened form of ἄρα (see below); ἀλλά γε *but at any rate*.

- **μέντοι#** has an adversative sense, *however*: παρακύψας βλέπει κείμενα τὰ ὀθόνια, οὐ μέντοι εἰσῆλθεν (Jn 20.5) *he stooped and saw the linen bandages lying [there]; he did not, however, go in.*

- **ποτέ#** *formerly, once*: ὃ ποτε τυφλός (*Jn 9.13) *the man [who was] once blind*; after a negative it has the sense *ever*: οὐδεὶς γάρ ποτε τὴν ἑαυτοῦ σάρκα ἐμίσησεν (Eph 5.29) *for no-one ever hated his own flesh.*

(b) Other **connecting** particles

- **ἄρα** *so, then, consequently* introduces the result of what has preceded: εἰ δὲ ὑμεῖς Χριστοῦ, ἄρα τοῦ Ἀβραὰμ σπέρμα ἐστέ (Gal 3.29) *and if you [are] of Christ, then you are the seed of Abraham.* It is frequently used in questions which pose a problem arising from what has happened or been said immediately before; in Lk 8.22ff. when Christ has amazed the apostles by calming a storm in the Sea of Galilee, they are at a loss and say τίς ἄρα οὗτός ἐστιν ὅτι καὶ τοῖς ἀνέμοις ἐπιτάσσει καὶ τῷ ὕδατι, καὶ ὑπακούουσιν αὐτῷ; (Lk 8.25) *so who is this man that he commands both the winds and the water, and they obey him?*

- **καὶ γάρ** *for even, for indeed* gives a justification of what has preceded. When Zechariah has regained his speech at the circumcision of his son, John the Baptist, the populace is amazed and says τί ἄρα τὸ παιδίον τοῦτο ἔσται; καὶ γὰρ χεὶρ κυρίου ἦν μετ᾽ αὐτοῦ. (Lk 1.66) *so what will this child be? for indeed the hand of the Lord was with him* (the second clause gives the reason for posing the question of what the child will be).

- **μέν#… δέ#** when used together present two parallel balanced or contrasted items, which may be words, phrases or clauses. We may think of the pair as meaning *on the one hand … and/but on the other hand,* but in most cases such a translation would be heavy or clumsy. For example, ὁ μὲν θερισμὸς πολύς, οἱ δὲ ἐργάται ὀλίγοι (Mt 9.37) should not be translated by *the harvest on the one hand [is] great but on the other hand the workers [are] few* but by *the harvest is great but the workers are few* or by *although the harvest is great the workers are few.* In ὁ μὲν … ὁ δέ *one man … but another man* the article is used as a pronoun (cf. 5.1/3). When μέν occurs alone (except in the combination μὲν οὖν; see below) a contrast is implied; as we have seen, δέ is very commonly used by itself in the sense of *and* or *but* (4.1/4).

- **μὲν# οὖν** as a combination is most frequently used to resume or redirect the narrative; it is to be translated *so, and so.* At Mk 16.14ff. Christ gives his final instructions to the disciples; when he has finished the narrative is taken up again with the verse ὁ μὲν οὖν κύριος Ἰησοῦς μετὰ τὸ λαλῆσαι αὐτοῖς ἀνελήμφθη εἰς τὸν οὐρανόν (Mk 16.19) *and so the Lord Jesus after talking to them was taken up into heaven.* When the two are written together, μενοῦν (also with the addition of γε as μενοῦνγε), the sense is *rather, on the contrary.*

15.2 Greek reading

1 οἱ γὰρ τοιοῦτοι τῷ κυρίῳ ἡμῶν Χριστῷ οὐ δουλεύουσιν ἀλλὰ τῇ ἑαυτῶν κοιλίᾳ. (Ro 16.18)

2 εἰσελεύσονται μετὰ τὴν ἄφιξίν μου λύκοι βαρεῖς εἰς ὑμᾶς μὴ φειδόμενοι τοῦ ποιμνίου. (Ac 20.29)

3 τὸ μὲν πνεῦμα πρόθυμον ἡ δὲ σὰρξ ἀσθενής. (Mt 26.41)

4 εἰ ἀγαπᾶτε τοὺς ἀγαπῶντας ὑμᾶς, ποία ὑμῖν χάρις ἐστίν; καὶ γὰρ οἱ ἁμαρτωλοὶ τοὺς ἀγαπῶντας αὐτοὺς ἀγαπῶσιν. (Lk 6.32)

5 παραγγείλας τῷ ὄχλῳ ἀναπεσεῖν ἐπὶ τὴν γῆν ἔλαβεν τοὺς ἑπτὰ ἄρτους καὶ τοὺς ἰχθύας. (Mt 15.35f.)

6 ὁ διώκων ἡμᾶς ποτε νῦν εὐαγγελίζεται τὴν πίστιν ἥν ποτε ἐπόρθει. (Gal 1.23)

7 **Paul escapes from Jerusalem but the Church enjoys peace**
καὶ ἦν μετ' αὐτῶν εἰσπορευόμενος καὶ ἐκπορευόμενος εἰς Ἱερουσαλήμ, παρρησιαζόμενος ἐν τῷ ὀνόματι τοῦ κυρίου, ἐλάλει τε καὶ συνεζήτει πρὸς τοὺς Ἑλληνιστάς, οἱ δὲ ἐπεχείρουν ἀνελεῖν αὐτόν. ἐπιγνόντες δὲ οἱ ἀδελφοὶ κατήγαγον αὐτὸν εἰς Καισάρειαν καὶ ἐξαπέστειλαν αὐτὸν εἰς Ταρσόν. ἡ μὲν οὖν ἐκκλησία καθ' ὅλης τῆς Ἰουδαίας καὶ Γαλιλαίας καὶ Σαμαρείας εἶχεν εἰρήνην. (Ac 9.28ff.)

8 πᾶν δένδρον μὴ ποιοῦν καρπὸν καλὸν ἐκκόπτεται καὶ εἰς πῦρ βάλλεται. ἄρα γε ἀπὸ τῶν καρπῶν αὐτῶν ἐπιγνώσεσθε αὐτούς. (Mt 7.19f.)

9 ἦλθαν οἱ μαθηταὶ αὐτοῦ, καὶ ἐθαύμαζον ὅτι μετὰ γυναικὸς ἐλάλει· οὐδεὶς μέντοι εἶπεν, Τί ζητεῖς; ἤ, Τί λαλεῖς μετ' αὐτῆς; (Jn 4.27)

10 ἔχωμεν χάριν, δι' ἧς λατρεύωμεν εὐαρέστως τῷ θεῷ μετὰ εὐλαβείας καὶ δέους· καὶ γὰρ ὁ θεὸς ἡμῶν πῦρ καταναλίσκον. (Hb 12.28f.)

11 εἰς τοῦτο γὰρ Χριστὸς ἀπέθανεν καὶ ἔζησεν, ἵνα καὶ νεκρῶν καὶ ζώντων κυριεύσῃ. (Ro 14.9)

12 εἰ ἄλλοις οὐκ εἰμὶ ἀπόστολος, ἀλλά γε ὑμῖν εἰμι. (1 Cor 9.2)

13 ὅτε δὲ ἐξεβλήθη ὁ ὄχλος, εἰσελθὼν ἐκράτησεν τῆς χειρὸς αὐτῆς, καὶ ἠγέρθη τὸ κοράσιον. καὶ ἐξῆλθεν ἡ φήμη αὕτη εἰς ὅλην τὴν γῆν ἐκείνην. (Mt 9.25)

14 **The good Samaritan**
ἄνθρωπός τις κατέβαινεν ἀπὸ Ἱερουσαλὴμ εἰς Ἱεριχὼ καὶ λῃσταῖς περιέπεσεν, οἳ καὶ ἐκδύσαντες αὐτὸν καὶ πληγὰς ἐπιθέντες (*inflicting*) ἀπῆλθον ἀφέντες (*leaving*) ἡμιθανῆ. κατὰ συγκυρίαν δὲ ἱερεύς τις κατέβαινεν ἐν τῇ ὁδῷ ἐκείνῃ, καὶ ἰδὼν αὐτὸν ἀντιπαρῆλθεν· ὁμοίως δὲ καὶ Λευίτης κατὰ τὸν 5 τόπον ἐλθὼν καὶ ἰδὼν ἀντιπαρῆλθεν. Σαμαρίτης δέ τις ὁδεύων ἦλθεν κατ' αὐτὸν καὶ ἰδὼν ἐσπλαγχνίσθη, καὶ προσελθὼν κατέδησεν τὰ τραύματα αὐτοῦ ἐπιχέων ἔλαιον καὶ οἶνον, ἐπιβιβάσας δὲ αὐτὸν ἐπὶ τὸ ἴδιον κτῆνος ἤγαγεν αὐτὸν εἰς πανδοχεῖον καὶ ἐπεμελήθη αὐτοῦ. καὶ ἐπὶ τὴν αὔριον 10 ἐκβαλὼν ἔδωκεν (*he gave*) δύο δηνάρια τῷ πανδοχεῖ καὶ εἶπεν, Ἐπιμελήθητι (*look after* as an order) αὐτοῦ, καὶ ὅ τι ἂν προσδαπανήσῃς ἐγὼ ἐν τῷ ἐπανέρχεσθαί με ἀποδώσω (*I shall give*) σοι. (Lk 10.30–5)

Notes

3 Supply ἐστί with both halves of the sentence (legend has it that in the 1960s a computer translated this famous verse into Russian as *the whisky's OK but the meat's a bit off*).

4 ποία ὑμῖν χάρις ἐστίν; lit. *what thanks are there to you?* i.e *what thanks do you have?*

6 ἐπόρθει conative impf. *tried to destroy* (4.1/1 note 3).

7 The understood subject of the first two clauses is Paul; εἰς Ἰερουσαλήμ lit. *into Jerusalem* only applies to εἰσπορευόμενος (and not to ἐκπορευόμενος) but Paul was going in and coming out of Jerusalem, and in English we would say *in and out of Jerusalem*; πρός lit. *to* is normal after both λαλέω and συζητέω but in English we would say *talk and argue with*; ἀνελεῖν aor. inf. act. of ἀναιρέω; ἀδελφοί not Paul's brothers but his fellow Christians, trans. *brethren* (ἀδελφός was the term used by Christians in addressing each other); μὲν οὖν (15.1/2(b)) resumes the narrative of what is happening to the Church – trans. here *meanwhile*.

8 ποιοῦν nom. s. n. of the present act. pple. of ποιέω.

10 ἔχωμεν jussive subj. (13.1/3(a)(i)) *let us possess*; χάριν here *grace* – the idea is that we should obtain and keep divine grace so that we may worship God acceptably; λατρεύωμεν the subj. can be used in an adjectival clause to express purpose, lit. *through which we may worship*; after καί γάρ supply ἐστί; καταναλίσκον nom. s. n. of pres. pple. act. of καταναλίσκω, agreeing with πῦρ.

11 εἰς τοῦτο *for this* [*purpose*] anticipates the ἵνα clause.

12 εἰ here *although*; ἀλλά γε lit. *but at any rate* (15.1/2(a)), here trans. *at least*.

13 αὐτῆς lit. *of her*, although the word used here for *girl* (κοράσιον) is neuter she is referred to by her proper gender (agreement according to the sense).

14 *l*.2 περιέπεσεν < περιπίπτω. l.3 ἡμιθανῆ i.e. αὐτόν. *l*.5 ἀντιπαρῆλθεν < ἀντιπαρέρχομαι. *l*.7 ἦλθεν κατ᾽ αὐτόν *came upon him*. *l*.10 αὐτοῦ gen. after ἐπεμελήθη (<ἐπίμελέομαι; the same construction in the next line but one); ἐπὶ τὴν αὔριον lit. *on the tomorrow* i.e. *on the next day*. *l*.12 ὅ τι ἂν + subj. to express an indefinite clause *whatever* ... (14.1/1(c)). *l*.13 ἐν τῷ ἐπανέρχεσθαί με take these words together (5.1/3), lit. *on me returning*, i.e. *when I return*.

16.1 Grammar

16.1/1 Uses of ὥστε

ὥστε is a conjunction which is used in two ways:

(a) To express result. In English we normally use a subordinate clause introduced by *that*, *so that* or *with the result that*: *I was so tired yesterday that I could not do any work*. In Greek this is expressed by ὥστε and the accusative and infinitive (8.1/4(b)):

λέγουσιν αὐτῷ οἱ μαθηταί, πόθεν ἡμῖν ἐν ἐρημίᾳ ἄρτοι τοσοῦτοι ὥστε χορτάσαι ὄχλον τοσοῦτον; (Mt 15.33) *The disciples say to him, 'From where do we have* (lit. *[are there] to us) so many loaves in the desert that we can feed* (lit. *so as to feed*) *so large a multitude?'*

καὶ ἰδοὺ σεισμὸς μέγας ἐγένετο ἐν τῇ θαλάσσῃ, ὥστε τὸ πλοῖον καλύπτεσθαι ὑπὸ τῶν κυμάτων. (Mt 8.24) *And behold! a great storm arose on the sea so that the boat was covered by the waves* (the literal translation *so as the boat to be covered* is not idiomatic English).

ὁ δὲ Ἰησοῦς οὐκέτι οὐδὲν ἀπεκρίθη, ὥστε θαυμάζειν τὸν Πιλᾶτον. (Mk 15.5) *And Jesus said nothing further, with the result that Pilate was amazed* (on the double negative οὐκέτι οὐδέν see 8.1/3(e)).

If required, the infinitive is negated by **μή**:

ὑπήντησαν αὐτῷ δύο δαιμονιζόμενοι ἐκ τῶν μνημείων ἐξερχόμενοι, χαλεποὶ λίαν, ὥστε μὴ ἰσχύειν τινὰ παρελθεῖν διὰ τῆς ὁδοῦ ἐκείνης. (Mt 8.28) *Two [men] possessed of evil spirits, who came* (lit. *coming*) *out from the tombs, met him; [they were] exceedingly violent with the result that no-one was able to pass through that road.*

(b) To introduce a sentence which gives the result or consequence of what has gone before. Here we translate ὥστε by *therefore, accordingly, and so*:

ἐξαπέστειλεν ὁ θεὸς τὸ πνεῦμα τοῦ υἱοῦ αὐτοῦ εἰς τὰς καρδίας ἡμῶν ... ὥστε οὐκέτι εἶ δοῦλος ἀλλὰ υἱός. (Gal 4.6f.) *God sent the spirit of his Son into our hearts. Therefore you are no longer a slave but a son.*

The negative here is **οὐ**:

ὥστε οὐκέτι εἰσὶν δύο ἀλλὰ σὰρξ μία. (Mt 19.6) *And so they are no longer two but one flesh.*

Note

The normal construction for purpose (ἵνα and the subjunctive) can also be used for result (13.1/3(b)(ii)). In a similar reversal ὥστε and the infinitive sometimes express purpose: συμβούλιον ἔλαβον πάντες οἱ ἀρχιερεῖς καὶ οἱ πρεσβύτεροι τοῦ λαοῦ κατὰ τοῦ Ἰησοῦ ὥστε θανατῶσαι αὐτόν (Mt 27.1) *all the high priests and the elders of the people took counsel against Jesus to kill him.* The infinitive by itself or preceded by τοῦ is used in the same meaning (13.1/3(b)(i)).

16.1/2 Pluperfect indicative active

Like the imperfect, the pluperfect tense is a **historic** tense (4.1/1 note 1) and exists only in the indicative mood. It is normally to be translated by the same tense in English (*I had washed before you came*) but its use is much more restricted than that of its English equivalent (see below).

The stem of the pluperfect active is the same as that of the perfect, except that where the latter contains reduplication (14.1/2) the augment is sometimes added; this is optional and does not follow any regular pattern:

PERFECT ACTIVE STEM	PLUPERFECT ACTIVE STEM
λελυκ- (λύω)	(ἐ)λελυκ-
γεγραφ- (γράφω)	(ἐ)γεγραφ-
πεπομφ- (πέμπω)	(ἐ)πεπομφ-

Where, however, the perfect active stem is already augmented it is also used for the pluperfect without change, e.g. ἠχ- (ἄγω).

The pluperfect active endings are: -ειν, -εις, -ει, -ειμεν, -ειτε, -εισαν. The pluperfect active of λύω is conjugated:

SINGULAR	PLURAL
1 (ἐ)λελύκειν *I had loosened*	(ἐ)λελύκειμεν
2 (ἐ)λελύκεις	(ἐ)λελύκειτε
3 (ἐ)λελύκει	(ἐ)λελύκεισαν

The pluperfect is the past version of the perfect and thus expresses a state that existed in the past (cf. 14.1/2): ἦν δὲ ὁ λεγόμενος Βαραββᾶς μετὰ τῶν στασιαστῶν δεδεμένος οἵτινες ἐν τῇ στάσει φόνον πεποιήκεισαν (Mk 15.7) *and there was the man called Barabbas, in custody* (lit. *bound*, on the form see next subsection) *with the rebels who had committed murder during the uprising.*

The pluperfect is relatively uncommon in Greek. In English we often use the pluperfect in subordinate clauses to denote an action which happened before the action described by the main verb but Greek normally regards both actions as single past events and uses two aorists. In the verse ὅτε ἦλθον ἐπὶ τὸν τόπον τὸν καλούμενον Κρανίον, ἐκεῖ ἐσταύρωσαν αὐτὸν (Lk 23.33) *when they came to the place called The Skull, there they crucified him* the arrival of the group obviously preceded the crucifixion and we could translate *when they had come* . . . In Greek it would be possible for the author to regard the group as being in a state of having come and so use the pluperfect tense, but in subordinate clauses of time and reason this is rarely done.

16.1/3 Perfect and pluperfect indicative middle/passive

In both the perfect and pluperfect the middle and passive voices coincide. As the middle use of both tenses is rare, only the passive meaning is given below.

Perfect

The stem of the strong perfect active is retained in the middle/passive, but that of the weak perfect active loses its κ. Consequently the distinction between strong and weak perfects is not maintained. As, however, the stem of the perfect middle/passive is not always predictable, the first person perfect indicative middle/passive is included in the principal parts of irregular verbs (7.1/1 note 5 and **Principal parts of verbs**).

When a perfect middle/passive stem ends in a vowel or diphthong (e.g. λελυ-, νενικη-) the endings -μαι, -σαι, -ται, -μεθα, -σθε, -νται are added:

S. 1 λέλυμαι *I have been loosened*   PL. λελύμεθα
   2 λέλυσαι   λέλυσθε
   3 λέλυται   λέλυνται

When a perfect middle/passive stem ends in a consonant, a sound change is necessary in certain cases to assimilate the final consonant of the stem to the initial consonant of the ending. With consonant stems a succession of three consonants in the second and third plural is avoided, except in (d); in the second plural the σ of the ending (-σθε) is dropped, but in the third plural Greek sidesteps the difficulty by using a two-word periphrasis consisting of the perfect middle/passive participle (see 16.1/4) and the third plural present of εἰμί.

Consonant stems are classified in the same way as for the present tense (6.1/4 and 11.1/3):

(a) **Palatal stems**
    The final palatal of the stem appears as γ before -μαι and -μεθα (and -μένος of the participle), and as κ before -σαι (giving -ξαι) and -ται. In the second pl. κ + σθε > κθε > χθε (the κ is aspirated to assimilate it to θ). From τάσσω *appoint, ordered* (perf. mid./pass. stem τεταγ-) we have:

S. 1 τέταγμαι *I have been*   PL. τετάγμεθα
      appointed
   2 τέταξαι   τέταχθε
   3 τέτακται   τεταγμένοι εἰσί(ν)

The participle used in the third plural varies in gender according to the subject. This applies to all forms of this type.

(b) **Labial stems**
    The final labial of the stem appears as μ before -μαι and -μεθα (and -μένος of the participle), and as π before -σαι (giving -ψαι) and -ται. In the second pl. π + σθε > πθε > φθε. From κρύπτω *hide* (perf. mid./pass. stem κεκρυπ-) we have:

S. 1 κέκρυμμαι *I have been*   PL. κεκρύμμεθα
      hidden
   2 κέκρυψαι   κέκρυφθε
   3 κέκρυπται   κεκρυμμένοι εἰσί(ν)

(c) *Dental stems*

The final dental of the stem becomes σ before all endings. In the second person s. and pl. σσ > σ. From πείθω *persuade* (perf. mid./pass. stem πεπειθ-) we have:

S. 1 πέπεισμαι *I have been* PL. πεπείσμεθα
  persuaded
 2 πέπεισαι   πέπεισθε
 3 πέπεισται   πεπεισμένοι εἰσί(ν)

(d) *Stems in* λ, ρ *and* ν

The final consonant of λ and ρ stems remains unchanged, but the final consonant of κρίνω (the only ν stem occurring more than once in the perfect middle/passive) is dropped. From ἐγείρω *raise* and κρίνω *judge* we have:

S. 1 ἐγήγερμαι *I have been* κέκριμαι *I have been*
  raised   *judged*
 2 ἐγήγερσαι   κέκρισαι
 3 ἐγήγερται   κέκριται
PL. 1 ἐγηγέρμεθα   κεκρίμεθα
 2 ἐγήγερσθε   κέκρισθε
 3 ἐγηγερμένοι εἰσι(ν) κεκριμένοι εἰσι(ν)

Pluperfect

The pluperfect indicative middle/passive uses the perfect middle/passive stem; just as in the pluperfect active (16.1/2), the syllabic augment may added when the latter is reduplicated, e.g. (ἐ)λελυ- (λύω), (ἐ)τεταγ- (τάσσω). Because the pluperfect is a historic tense, we have the historic middle/passive endings: -μην, -σο, -το, -μεθα, -σθε, -ντο (cf. 8.1/1(c)). With stems ending in a consonant the same sound changes are involved as with the perfect indicative middle/passive, and the perfect middle/passive participle with ἦσαν is used for the third plural.

S. 1 (ἐ)λελύμην   (ἐ)κεκρύμμην
  I had been loosened *I had been hidden*
 2 (ἐ)λέλυσο   (ἐ)κέκρυψο
 3 (ἐ)λέλυτο   (ἐ)κέκρυπτο
PL. 1 (ἐ)λελύμεθα   (ἐ)κεκρύμμεθα
 2 (ἐ)λέλυσθε   (ἐ)κέκρυφθε
 3 (ἐ)λέλυντο   κεκρυμμένοι ἦσαν

Note

Composite forms consisting of the perfect middle/passive participle and the verb εἰμί also occur as alternatives for the normal third person singular of the perfect middle/passive: ἔστιν γεγραμμένον (Jn 6.31) *it has been written*; here we could simply have γέγραπται. Similarly the perfect subjunctive of both the active and middle/passive is formed with the perfect participle and the subjunctive of εἰμί; see note on 16.1/4.

16.1/4 Other parts of the perfect tense

The perfect infinitives and participles are formed from the same stem as the corresponding indicatives (the reduplication or the temporal/syllabic augment of the perfect indicative stem is **not** dropped). The infinitive endings are -έναι (act.) and -σθαι (mid./pass.; with consonantal stems this ending undergoes the same changes as -σθε). The active participle is a first and third declension adjective (10.1/3) in -ώς, -υῖα, -ός (see below), and the middle/passive participle is a first and second declension adjective (3.1/3) in -μένος, -μένη, -μένον.[1] In the following table for λύω, τάσσω, κρύπτω, πείθω, κρίνω only the masculine forms of the participles are given.

Infinitives		**Participles**	
ACTIVE	MIDDLE/PASSIVE	ACTIVE	MIDDLE/PASSIVE
λελυκέναι	λελύσθαι	λελυκώς	λελυμένος
to have loosened	*to have been loosened*	*having loosened*	*having been loosened*
τεταχέναι	τετάχθαι	τεταχώς	τεταγμένος
κεκρυφέναι	κεκρύφθαι	κεκρυφώς	κεκρυμμένος
πεποιθέναι	πεπεῖσθαι	πεποιθώς	πεπεισμένος
κεκρικέναι	κεκρίσθαι	κεκρικώς	κεκριμένος

Note that the perfect active and the perfect middle/passive of πείθω have different stems.

The corresponding forms of the aorist are sometimes to be translated in the same way as those of the perfect, but the meanings and uses of the two tenses are quite distinct. The perfect always expresses a state (on the meaning of the aorist see 4.1/1, 12.1/2).

---

[1] The accent of all forms of the perfect middle/passive participle is on the second syllable from the end (paroxytone, see **Appendix 7**, (b)(v)).

λελυκώς is declined:

SINGULAR

	M.	F.	N.
Nom.	λελυκώς	λελυκυῖα	λελυκός
Acc.	λελυκότα	λελυκυῖαν	λελυκός
Gen.	λελυκότος	λελυκυίας	λελυκότος
Dat.	λελυκότι	λελυκυίᾳ	λελυκότι

PLURAL

	M.	F.	N.
Nom.	λελυκότες	λελυκυῖαι	λελυκότα
Acc.	λελυκότας	λελυκυίας	λελυκότα
Gen.	λελυκότων	λελυκυιῶν	λελυκότων
Dat.	λελυκόσι(ν)	λελυκυίαις	λελυκόσι(ν)

Note

The perfect active subjunctive consists of the perfect active participle and the appropriate part of εἰμί: λελυκὼς ὦ, etc. The perfect middle/passive subjunctive follows the same pattern: λελυμένος ὦ etc.

16.2 Greek reading

1 Καὶ ἐγένετο ὅτε ἐτέλεσεν ὁ Ἰησοῦς τὰς παραβολὰς ταύτας, μετῆρεν ἐκεῖθεν. καὶ ἐλθὼν εἰς τὴν πατρίδα αὐτοῦ ἐδίδασκεν αὐτοὺς ἐν τῇ συναγωγῇ αὐτῶν, ὥστε ἐκπλήσσεσθαι αὐτοὺς καὶ λέγειν, Πόθεν τούτῳ ἡ σοφία αὕτη καὶ αἱ δυνάμεις; (Mt 13.53f.)

2 ὁ θεὸς ἐν ἡμῖν μένει καὶ ἡ ἀγάπη αὐτοῦ ἐν ἡμῖν τετελειωμένη ἐστιν. (1 J 4.12)

3 οὐδὲν δὲ συγκεκαλυμμένον ἐστὶν ὃ οὐκ ἀποκαλυφθήσεται, καὶ κρυπτὸν ὃ οὐ γνωσθήσεται. (Lk 12.2)

4 τὸ σάββατον διὰ τὸν ἄνθρωπον ἐγένετο καὶ οὐχ ὁ ἄνθρωπος διὰ τὸ σάββατον· ὥστε κύριός ἐστιν ὁ υἱὸς τοῦ ἀνθρώπου καὶ τοῦ σαββάτου. (Mk 2.27f.)

5 ἀναχωρήσαντες ἐλάλουν πρὸς ἀλλήλους λέγοντες ὅτι Οὐδὲν θανάτου ἢ δεσμῶν ἄξιον πράσσει ὁ ἄνθρωπος οὗτος. Ἀγρίππας δὲ τῷ Φήστῳ ἔφη, Ἀπολελύσθαι ἐδύνατο ὁ ἄνθρωπος οὗτος εἰ μὴ ἐπεκέκλητο Καίσαρα. (Ac 26.31f.)

6 κατέβη ἡ βροχὴ καὶ ἦλθον οἱ ποταμοὶ καὶ ἔπνευσαν οἱ ἄνεμοι καὶ προσέπεσαν τῇ οἰκίᾳ ἐκείνῃ, καὶ οὐκ ἔπεσεν, τεθεμελίωτο γὰρ ἐπὶ τὴν πέτραν. (Mt 7.25)

7 Christ walks on water

ὡς δὲ ὀψία ἐγένετο κατέβησαν οἱ μαθηταὶ αὐτοῦ ἐπὶ τὴν
θάλασσαν, καὶ ἐμβάντες εἰς πλοῖον ἤρχοντο πέραν τῆς
θαλάσσης εἰς Καφαρναούμ. καὶ σκοτία ἤδη ἐγεγόνει καὶ οὔπω
ἐληλύθει πρὸς αὐτοὺς ὁ Ἰησοῦς, ἥ τε θάλασσα ἀνέμου
μεγάλου πνέοντος διεγείρετο. ἐληλακότες οὖν ὡς σταδίους 5
εἴκοσι πέντε ἢ τριάκοντα θεωροῦσιν τὸν Ἰησοῦν
περιπατοῦντα ἐπὶ τῆς θαλάσσης καὶ ἐγγὺς τοῦ πλοίου
γινόμενον, καὶ ἐφοβήθησαν. (Jn 6.16–19)

8 μακάριοι οἱ δεδιωγμένοι ἕνεκεν δικαιοσύνης, ὅτι αὐτῶν ἐστιν
ἡ βασιλεία τῶν οὐρανῶν. (Mt 5.10)

9 Paul's experience in the gaol of Philippi

Κατὰ δὲ τὸ μεσονύκτιον Παῦλος καὶ Σίλας προσευχόμενοι
ὕμνουν τὸν θεόν, ἐπηκροῶντο δὲ αὐτῶν οἱ δέσμιοι· ἄφνω δὲ
σεισμὸς ἐγένετο μέγας ὥστε σαλευθῆναι τὰ θεμέλια τοῦ
δεσμωτηρίου, ἠνεῴχθησαν δὲ παραχρῆμα αἱ θύραι πᾶσαι, καὶ
πάντων τὰ δεσμὰ ἀνέθη (were unfastened). ἔξυπνος δὲ 5
γενόμενος ὁ δεσμοφύλαξ καὶ ἰδὼν ἀνεῳγμένας τὰς θύρας τῆς
φυλακῆς, σπασάμενος μάχαιραν ἤμελλεν ἑαυτὸν ἀναιρεῖν,
νομίζων ἐκπεφευγέναι τοὺς δεσμίους. ἐφώνησεν δὲ μεγάλῃ
φωνῇ Παῦλος λέγων, Μηδὲν πράξῃς (do not do anything)
σεαυτῷ κακόν, ἅπαντες γάρ ἐσμεν ἐνθάδε. αἰτήσας δὲ φῶτα 10
εἰσεπήδησεν, καὶ ἔντρομος γενόμενος προσέπεσεν τῷ Παύλῳ
καὶ Σίλᾳ, καὶ προαγαγὼν αὐτοὺς ἔξω ἔφη, Κύριοι, τί με δεῖ
ποιεῖν ἵνα σωθῶ; οἱ δὲ εἶπαν, Πίστευσον (trust as an order)
ἐπὶ τὸν κύριον Ἰησοῦν, καὶ σωθήσῃ σὺ καὶ ὁ οἶκός σου. καὶ
ἐλάλησαν αὐτῷ τὸν λόγον τοῦ κυρίου σὺν πᾶσιν τοῖς ἐν τῇ 15
οἰκίᾳ αὐτοῦ. καὶ παραλαβὼν αὐτοὺς ἐν ἐκείνῃ τῇ ὥρᾳ τῆς
νυκτὸς ἔλουσεν ἀπὸ τῶν πληγῶν, καὶ ἐβαπτίσθη αὐτὸς καὶ οἱ
αὐτοῦ πάντες παραχρῆμα, ἀναγαγών τε αὐτοὺς εἰς τὸν οἶκον
παρέθηκεν (set) τράπεζαν, καὶ ἠγαλλιάσατο πανοικεὶ
πεπιστευκὼς τῷ θεῷ. (Ac 16.25–34)

Notes

1 μετῆρεν aor. of μεταίρω; τὴν πατρίδα αὐτοῦ the town where
Jesus had lived, Nazareth; ἐδίδασκεν inceptive impf. (4.1/1
note 3); αὐτούς i.e. the people of Nazareth.
2 Both τετελειωμένη … ἐστί and συγκεκαλυμμένον ἐστί (in 3
below) are composite forms (16.1/3 note) for τετελείωται
and συγκεκάλυπται.
4 καὶ τοῦ σαββάτου of the sabbath too.
5 ἀπολελύσθαι < ἀπολύω.
6 κατέβη aor. of καταβαίνω; προσέπεσαν aor. of προσπίπτω;
because θεμελιόω means lay the foundation of, a change of

construction is necessary to translate the passive τεθεμελίωτο.

7 ἤρχοντο inceptive impf. (4.1/1 note 3) of ἔρχομαι *they began to go*; ἐληλύθει plpf. of ἔρχομαι – this verb and ἐγεγόνει (<γίνομαι) are plpf. because they describe the state existing when the disciples were rowing; ἐληλακότες < ἐλαύνω; θεωροῦσιν vivid present.

8 οἱ δεδιωγμένοι (<διώκω) lit. *those being in a state of being persecuted*, trans. *those persecuted*.

9 *l.*2 ἐπηκροῶντο < ἐπακροάομαι. *l.*8. τοὺς δεσμίους is the subject of ἐκπεφευγέναι. *ll.*11f. προσέπεσεν < προσπίπτω; προαγαγών < προάγω. *l.*13 σωθῶ < σώζω. *l.*17 ἔλουσεν ἀπὸ τῶν πληγῶν trans. *washed their wounds* (ἀπό is used idiomatically with λούω and can be ignored in translation). *l.*18 ἀναγαγών < ἀνάγω. *l.*19 ἠγαλλιάσατο < ἀγαλλιάω; πεπιστευκώς is best translated by a phrase such as *having put his faith*.

17.1 Grammar

17.1/1 Imperative mood – commands and prohibitions

The imperative mood is used for **commands**. In Greek it exists in the present and aorist tenses. The stem used is the same as that of the corresponding indicative. As well as second person imperatives (which we have in English), Greek also has imperatives in the **third** person with the meanings given below.

The imperative of λύω is:

Present

		ACTIVE		MIDDLE/PASSIVE	
S.	2	λῦε	loosen!	λύου	mid. *loosen for yourself!* pass. *be loosened!*
	3	λυέτω	let him loosen!	λυέσθω	mid. *let him loosen for himself!* pass. *let him be loosened!*
PL.	2	λύετε	loosen!	λύεσθε	mid. *loosen for yourselves!* pass. *be loosened!*
	3	λυέτωσαν	let them loosen!	λυέσθωσαν	mid. *let them loosen for themselves!* pass. *let them be loosened!*

Aorist

		ACTIVE	MIDDLE	PASSIVE
S.	2	λῦσον	λῦσαι	λύθητι
	3	λυσάτω	λυσάσθω	λυθήτω
PL.	2	λύσατε	λύσασθε	λύθητε
	3	λυσάτωσαν	λυσάσθωσαν	λυθήτωσαν

The aorist is usually to be translated in the same way as the present but the two are not interchangeable. The difference, as elsewhere, is one of aspect. The present is used for an action which is seen as going on, in the process of happening or being repeated, the aorist for an action which is seen simply as an event: ἀσθενοῦντας θεραπεύετε (pres.), νεκροὺς ἐγείρετε (pres.) (Mt 10.8) *heal the sick, raise the dead* (the reference is to repeated action); λύσατε (aor.) τὸν ναὸν τοῦτον (Jn 2.19) *destroy this temple* (a single act would be involved; note this other sense of λύω).

The middle imperative is found with middle deponents: δέξαι τὸ πνεῦμά μου (Ac 7.59) *receive my spirit* (δέξαι 2nd s. aor. imp. mid. of δέχομαι); it is sometimes required with normal verbs: ὑπόδησαι τὰ σανδάλιά σου (Ac 12.8) lit. *put on your sandals for yourself*, i.e. *put on your sandals* (ὑπόδησαι 2nd s. aor. imp. mid. of ὑποδέω).

Prohibitions (negative commands) are expressed with μή, e.g. μὴ θησαυρίζετε (pres.) ὑμῖν θησαυροὺς ἐπὶ τῆς γῆς (Mt 6.19) *do not store up for yourselves treasures upon the earth*; μὴ κρίνετε (Mt 7.1) *do not judge,* but if the **aorist** aspect is appropriate the mood employed is always the **subjunctive**, not the imperative: Ἰωσήφ, υἱὸς Δαυίδ, μὴ φοβηθῇς παραλαβεῖν Μαρίαν τὴν γυναῖκά σου (Mt 1.20) *Joseph, son of David, do not be afraid to take Mary [as] your wife.* For the other use of this type of subjunctive (jussive) see 13.1/3(a)(i).

Only occasionally can the Greek present/aorist distinction be made in English: πείθεσθε τοῖς ἡγουμένοις (Hb 13.17) *be obedient to* (lit. *keep obeying*; the present indicates continual action) *the leaders*; here the aorist imperative πείσασθε would have reference to a single act and be simply translated by *obey*.

Notes

1 The imperative of the strong aorist has the same endings as the present. From μανθάνω (aor. ἔμαθον) the aor. imp. act. is μάθε, μαθέτω, μάθετε, μαθέτωσαν.

2 The imperative of the root aorist (11.1/1) follows that of the aorist passive except that the ending for the 2nd s. is -θι, not

-τι: from ἔγνων (γινώσκω) we have γνῶθι, γνώτω, γνῶτε, γνώτωσαν. ἀνάβηθι (<ἀναβαίνω) and μετάβηθι (<μεταβαίνω) have alternatives ἀνάβα and μετάβα.

3 The present imperative of contracted verbs is regular but, because of contraction, the 2nd s. forms are easily confused:

Active   τίμα (τίμαε)   ποίει (ποίεε)   δήλου (δήλοε)
Mid./pass. τιμῶ (τιμάου) ποιοῦ (ποιέου) δηλοῦ (δηλόου)

The position of the accent can be important for distinguishing between different forms, e.g. ποίει (imp.), ποιεῖ (ind.).

4 The imperative of εἰμί is ἴσθι *be!*, ἔστω or ἤτω, [ἔστε], ἔστωσαν.

5 An order can also be expressed by:
   (i) the future tense οὐ φονεύσεις (Mt 5.21) *you shall not kill!* (another example at 5.2.20).
   (ii) ἵνα and the subjunctive: ἡ δὲ γυνὴ ἵνα φοβῆται τὸν ἄνδρα (Eph 5.33) *and let a wife fear her husband.* This use of ἵνα and the subjunctive is easily distinguished from others because it stands as main clause, as shown in the example by δέ.

17.1/2 Comparison of adjectives and adverbs

Adjectives (and adverbs) have three degrees: **positive** *bad, sick, wonderful*; **comparative** *worse, sicker, more wonderful*; **superlative** *worst, sickest, most wonderful.* To give the three degrees of an adjective is to **compare** it. Some adjectives in English are compared regularly (*sick, wonderful*), some irregularly (*bad*). The same applied in earlier Greek, where adjectives were compared by the addition of suffixes, of which there were two sets -ων (compar.), -ιστος (supl.) and -τερος (compar.), -τατος (supl.). However, in NT Greek, while we find comparative forms in -ων and -τερος, the old superlative ending -τατος has almost disappeared, and -ιστος is generally used to give emphasis (e.g. τὰ μέγιστα ἐπαγγέλματα (2 Pt 1.4) *the very great promises*). On how the superlative is normally expressed see 17.1/3.

(a) *Comparative in -τερος*
   Comparatives in -τερος (f. -τερα, n. -τερον) are first and second declension adjectives (3.1/3). All regularly compared adjectives belong here. The way in which -τερος is attached to the stem of an adjective depends on the category of its positive form:

(i) First and second declension adjectives (3.1/3) add -οτερος if the last syllable of their stem is long, but -ωτερος if this is short (the stem is obtained by subtracting -ος from the nom. m. s., e.g. σοφός, stem σοφ-). A syllable is long if it contains a long vowel, or a diphthong, or a short vowel followed by two consonants; a syllable is short if it contains a short vowel followed by a single consonant. Examples are: σοφός *wise*, σοφώτερος *wiser*; ἀνεκτός *bearable*, ἀνεκτότερος *more endurable*.

Some first and second declension adjectives are irregular and belong to type (b) below.

(ii) Third declension adjectives (10.1/4) with a stem in ον add -εστερος, e.g. δεισιδαίμων (stem δεισιδαιμον-) *religious,* δεισιδαιμονέστερος *more religious*. Those with a stem in ες add -τερος, e.g. εὐγενής (stem εὐγενες) *high-minded,* εὐγενέστερος *more high-minded*.

(iii) First and third declension adjectives (10.1/3) in -υς follow βαρύς *heavy,* βαρύτερος *heavier*. πολύς *much,* which is a first and second declension adjective, is irregular; see below.

The old superlative ending for this class (-τατος) has only survived in four places: ἀκριβέστατος *strictest* (Ac 26.5), ἁγιώτατος *most sacred* (Jd 20), and τιμιώτατος *most/very precious* (Rev 18.12; 21.11).

We may summarize these formations as follows:

POSITIVE	COMPARATIVE	SUPERLATIVE
σοφός *wise*	σοφώτερος *wiser*	
ἀνεκτός *endurable*	ἀνεκτότερος *more endurable*	
ἅγιος *sacred*	ἁγιώτερος *more sacred*	ἁγιώτατος *most sacred*
εὐγενής *high-minded*	εὐγενέστερος *more high-minded*	
βαρύς *heavy*	βαρύτερος *heavier*	

(b) *Comparative in* -ων, *superlative in* -ιστος

Irregular adjectives from all categories belong here. The stem of the positive form is sometimes changed for the other degrees of comparison. The following are the most common examples:

POSITIVE	COMPARATIVE	SUPERLATIVE
ἀγαθός *good*	κρείττων *better*	κράτιστος *most excellent*[1]
κακός *bad*	(1) χείρων *worse*	
	(2) ἥσσων *lesser, inferior*	
μέγας *great*	μείζων *greater*	μέγιστος *greatest*
μικρός *small, young*	(1) μικρότερος *smaller*	
	(2) ἐλάσσων *younger, inferior*	ἐλάχιστος *smallest, least*
πολύς *much*	πλείων (n. πλείον or πλέον) *more*	πλεῖστος *greatest (of quantity)*

Comparatives in -ων are declined as third declension adjectives in ον (10.1/4(b)), but with some important alternative contracted forms where the uncontracted forms end in -ονα (m. and f. s. acc.; n. pl. nom. and acc.), -ονες (m. and f. pl. nom.) and -ονας (m. and f. pl. acc.): here -ονα > -ω, -ονες > -ους, and -ονας > -ους The second is confusing as it resembles an accusative and the third involves an irregular contraction (α + ο normally give ω as in the first). The uncontracted and contracted forms from μείζων are:

	SINGULAR		PLURAL	
	M. & F.	N.	M. & F.	N.
Nom.	μείζων	μεῖζον	μείζονες/μείζους	μείζονα/μείζω
Acc.	μείζονα/μείζω	μεῖζον	μείζονας/μείζους	μείζονα/μείζω
Gen.	μείζονος		μειζόνων	
Dat.	μείζονι		μείζοσι(ν)	

In earlier Greek, **adverbs** formed from adjectives (e.g. σοφῶς *wisely*; ἡδέως *pleasantly*) had as their comparative the neuter **singular** nom./acc. of the comparative of the adjective (σοφώτερον *more wisely*; ἥδιον *more pleasantly*). The -τερον ending survives in a few cases, e.g. πρότερον *earlier*, ὕστερον *later, afterwards*, but the most common comparative adverbs are of the ἥδιον type:

POSITIVE	COMPARATIVE
εὖ *well*	(1) κρεῖττον *better*
	(2) βέλτιον *better*
κακῶς *badly*	(1) χεῖρον *worse*
	(2) ἧσσον *less* (in degree), *worse*

---

[1] Only used as a term of address, κράτιστε Θεόφιλε (Lk 1.3) *most excellent Theophilus* (voc.).

καλῶς *well, rightly* κάλλιον *better*
[μάλα] μᾶλλον *to a greater degree, more*
μικρόν *a little* ἔλασσον *less* (in quantity)
πολύ *much, greatly* πλεῖον or πλέον *more*

Notes

1 In earlier Greek superlative adverbs had the same form as the neuter **plural** nom./acc. of the superlative adjective. Of the few remaining NT examples we may note μάλιστα *most of all*, ἥδιστα *most gladly*.

2 The adverb of περισσότερος *greater, more* can be either περισσότερον or περισσοτέρως (both *even more, to a greater degree*).

3 Comparatives with σσ sometimes have a form in ττ and vice-versa, e.g. ἐλάσσων or ἐλάττων, κρείττων or κρείσσων.

17.1/3 Meaning of the comparative and superlative

Comparatives in Greek are not always to be understood in the sense *more X*. A comparative adjective is sometimes used where no comparison is expressed, and indicates a higher degree than the positive. English here uses *very, rather, too*: ὃ ποιεῖς ποίησον τάχιον *what you are doing do very quickly* (Jn 13.27; most translations have simply *do quickly*); ἄνδρες Ἀθηναῖοι, κατὰ πάντα ὡς δεισιδαιμονεστέρους ὑμᾶς θεωρῶ (Ac 17.22) *men of Athens* (lit. *Athenian men*) *I see you as very religious in every way*.

The comparative can also be used as a superlative with the meaning *most X*: ὁ μείζων ἐν ὑμῖν γινέσθω ὡς ὁ νεώτερος (Lk 22.26) *let the greatest among you become as the youngest*.

What is left of the old superlative can mean *most X*: οὗτοι οἱ ἄνθρωποι δοῦλοι τοῦ θεοῦ τοῦ ὑψίστου εἰσίν (Ac 16.17) *these people are slaves of God the Most High*. More often, however, it is used to express a very high degree: ὁ πιστὸς ἐν ἐλαχίστῳ καὶ ἐν πολλῷ πιστός ἐστιν (Lk 16.10) *the [person who is] trustworthy in a very little [matter] is trustworthy also in an important [matter]*.

17.1/4 Constructions involving the comparative

(a) In comparisons in English a comparative adjective or adverb is followed by *than*. In Greek ἤ *than* (which also means *or*) is used in the same way: Ἰησοῦς πλείονας μαθητὰς ποιεῖ καὶ βαπτίζει ἢ Ἰωάννης (Jn 4.1) *Jesus is making and baptizing more disciples than John.* ἤ is here a conjunction and what follows must be in the same case as what precedes. The first member of the comparison, Ἰησοῦς, is nominative and therefore the second member must also be nominative, hence Ἰωάννης.

There is, however, another construction, the **genitive of comparison**, in which the second member of the comparison is put into the genitive and ἤ is omitted: μείζω (=μείζονα) τούτων ὄψῃ (Jn 1.50) *you will see greater things than these.*

(b) A comparative may be strengthened by πολύ or πολλῷ, e.g. πολλῷ πλείους (=πλείονες) ἐπίστευσαν (Jn 4.41) *very many more believed* (lit. *many more by much*); this use is very common with μᾶλλον: ὁ δὲ πολλῷ μᾶλλον ἔκραζεν, Υἱὲ Δαυίδ, ἐλέησόν με (Mk 10.48) *and he began crying out all the more* (lit. *more by much*) *'Son of David, have mercy on me!'* πολλῷ here is a dative of measure of difference (21.1/1(j)).

17.2 Greek reading

1 Ἰατρέ, θεράπευσον σεαυτόν. (Lk 4.23)

2 ὁ δὲ ὀπίσω μου ἐρχόμενος ἰσχυρότερός μού ἐστιν. (Mt 3.11)

3 Καὶ σὺ Βηθλέεμ οὐδαμῶς ἐλαχίστη εἶ ἐν τοῖς ἡγεμόσιν Ἰούδα. (*Mt 2.6)

4 ὁ μικρότερος ἐν τῇ βασιλείᾳ τοῦ θεοῦ μείζων αὐτοῦ ἐστιν. (Lk 7.28)

5 τὸ φῶς ἐλήλυθεν εἰς τὸν κόσμον καὶ ἠγάπησαν οἱ ἄνθρωποι μᾶλλον τὸ σκότος ἢ τὸ φῶς, ἦν γὰρ αὐτῶν πονηρὰ τὰ ἔργα. (Jn 3.19)

6 μὴ σὺ μείζων εἶ τοῦ πατρὸς ἡμῶν Ἰακώβ; (Jn 4.12)

7 μηκέτι ὑδροπότει, ἀλλὰ οἴνῳ ὀλίγῳ χρῶ διὰ τὸν στόμαχον καὶ τὰς πυκνάς σου ἀσθενείας. (1 Tim 5.23)

8 μετὰ ταῦτα εὑρίσκει αὐτὸν ὁ Ἰησοῦς ἐν τῷ ἱερῷ καὶ εἶπεν αὐτῷ, Ἴδε ὑγιὴς γέγονας· μηκέτι ἁμάρτανε, ἵνα μὴ χεῖρόν σοί τι γένηται. (Jn 5.14)

9 ἐγὼ δὲ ἔχω τὴν μαρτυρίαν μείζω τοῦ Ἰωάννου. (Jn 5.36)

10 ἀμὴν λέγω ὑμῖν, ἀνεκτότερον ἔσται γῇ Σοδόμων καὶ Γομόρρων ἐν ἡμέρᾳ κρίσεως ἢ τῇ πόλει ἐκείνῃ. (Mt 10.15)

11 Ὁμοία ἐστὶν ἡ βασιλεία τῶν οὐρανῶν κόκκῳ σινάπεως, ὃν λαβὼν ἄνθρωπος ἔσπειρεν ἐν τῷ ἀγρῷ αὐτοῦ· ὃ μικρότερον μέν ἐστιν πάντων τῶν σπερμάτων, ὅταν δὲ αὐξηθῇ μεῖζον τῶν λαχάνων ἐστὶν καὶ γίνεται δένδρον, ὥστε ἐλθεῖν τὰ πετεινὰ

τοῦ οὐρανοῦ καὶ κατασκηνοῦν ἐν τοῖς κλάδοις αὐτοῦ. (Mt 13.31f.)

12 πάλιν δὲ λέγω ὑμῖν, εὐκοπώτερόν ἐστιν κάμηλον διὰ τρυπήματος ῥαφίδος διελθεῖν ἢ πλούσιον εἰσελθεῖν εἰς τὴν βασιλείαν τοῦ θεοῦ. (Mt 19.24)

13 λέγω ὑμῖν, μείζων ἐν γεννητοῖς γυναικῶν Ἰωάννου οὐδείς ἐστιν. (Lk 7.28)

14 ὅταν κληθῇς ὑπό τινος εἰς γάμους, μὴ κατακλιθῇς εἰς τὴν πρωτοκλισίαν, μήποτε ἐντιμότερός σου ᾖ κεκλημένος ὑπ’ αὐτοῦ. (Lk 14.8)

15 εἴ τις ἔχει οὖς, ἀκουσάτω. (Rev 13.9)

16 οὗτοι ἦσαν εὐγενέστεροι τῶν ἐν Θεσσαλονίκῃ. (Ac 17.11)

17 ἠλπίκαμεν ἐπὶ θεῷ ζῶντι ὅς ἐστιν σωτὴρ πάντων ἀνθρώπων, μάλιστα πιστῶν. (1 Ti 4.10)

18 **The Lord's prayer**

Πάτερ ἡμῶν ὁ ἐν τοῖς οὐρανοῖς, ἁγιασθήτω τὸ ὄνομά σου· ἐλθέτω ἡ βασιλεία σου· γενηθήτω τὸ θέλημά σου, ὡς ἐν οὐρανῷ καὶ ἐπὶ γῆς· τὸν ἄρτον ἡμῶν τὸν ἐπιούσιον δὸς (give) ἡμῖν σήμερον· καὶ ἄφες (forgive) ἡμῖν τὰ ὀφειλήματα ἡμῶν, ὡς καὶ ἡμεῖς ἀφήκαμεν (we forgave) τοῖς ὀφειλέταις ἡμῶν· καὶ μὴ εἰσενέγκῃς ἡμᾶς εἰς πειρασμόν, ἀλλὰ ῥῦσαι ἡμᾶς ἀπὸ τοῦ πονηροῦ. (Mt 6.9ff.)

19 **The destruction of Jerusalem foretold**

ὅταν δὲ ἴδητε κυκλουμένην ὑπὸ στρατοπέδων Ἰερουσαλήμ, τότε γνῶτε ὅτι ἤγγικεν ἡ ἐρήμωσις αὐτῆς. τότε οἱ ἐν τῇ Ἰουδαίᾳ φευγέτωσαν εἰς τὰ ὄρη καὶ οἱ ἐν μέσῳ αὐτῆς ἐκχωρείτωσαν καὶ οἱ ἐν ταῖς χώραις μὴ εἰσερχέσθωσαν εἰς αὐτήν. (Lk 21.20f.)

20 **The return of an unclean spirit**

Ὅταν δὲ τὸ ἀκάθαρτον πνεῦμα ἐξέλθῃ ἀπὸ τοῦ ἀνθρώπου, διέρχεται δι’ ἀνύδρων τόπων ζητοῦν ἀνάπαυσιν, καὶ οὐχ εὑρίσκει. τότε λέγει, Εἰς τὸν οἶκόν μου ἐπιστρέψω ὅθεν ἐξῆλθον· καὶ ἐλθὸν εὑρίσκει σχολάζοντα σεσαρωμένον καὶ κεκοσμημένον. τότε πορεύεται καὶ παραλαμβάνει μεθ’ ἑαυτοῦ ἑπτὰ ἕτερα πνεύματα πονηρότερα ἑαυτοῦ, καὶ εἰσελθόντα κατοικεῖ ἐκεῖ· καὶ γίνεται τὰ ἔσχατα τοῦ ἀνθρώπου ἐκείνου χείρονα τῶν πρώτων. (Mt 12.43–5)

Notes

2 The second μου is a gen. of comparison.

3 ἐλαχίστη is used as a true superlative *least, least important.* Ἰούδα (gen. of Ἰούδας) here the country belonging to the tribe of Judah.

4 ὁ μικρότερος *the least,*17.1/3; αὐτοῦ gen. of comparison.

5 ἐλήλυθεν perf. of ἔρχομαι. ἦν is sing. because of the neut. pl. subject (2.1/2 note 3); take αὐτῶν with τὰ ἔργα.

6 μή introduces a question expecting a negative answer (10.1/2(a)); Ἰακώβ indecl., in apposition to πατρός.

7 χρῶ 2nd s. pres. imp. of χράομαι, which takes the dative.

8 εὑρίσκει vivid present (2.1/5 note 2), trans. *found*; take τι with χεῖρον, *something worse*.

9 μείζω i.e. μείζονα 17.1/2(b); what we have here is a condensed form of *the testimony I have is greater than that of John* – trans. *I have a testimony...* with the indefinite article.

10 γῇ ... τῇ πόλει ἐκείνῃ are dative after ἀνεκτότερον.

11 ὁμοία takes the dative *similar to*; the antecedent of ὅν is κόκκῳ which is masculine, but the antecedent of ὅ is the neuter noun σινάπεως (with the latter, start a new sentence [*Mustard seed*] *is ...*); μέν ... δέ 15.1/2(b); κατασκηνοῦν pres. inf. act. of κατασκηνόω.

12 διελθεῖν < διέρχομαι.

14 γάμους trans. *wedding* (the pl. of γάμος is used of a single event); κατακλιθῇς aor. subj of κατακλίνομαι; μήποτε introduces a negative purpose clause (13.1/3(b)(i)); ᾖ κεκλημένος perf. pass. subj. of καλέω (16.1/4 note).

16 The context of this sentence shows that τῶν ... is a gen. of comparison.

17 ἠλπίκαμεν perf. of ἐλπίζω, used to express a state *we have set our hopes*.

18 The Lord's prayer also occurs at Lk 11.2ff. but in a slightly different form. ὁ ἐν τοῖς οὐρανοῖς is in apposition to the voc. Πάτερ, lit. *the [one] in the heavens* i.e. as opposed to one's earthly and biological father; ἐλθέτω < ἔρχομαι; γενηθήτω < γίνομαι; καὶ ἐπὶ γῆς *on earth as well*; ἡμῖν is dat. after ἄφες *forgive us*; ὀφείλημα here *sins*; τοῖς ὀφειλέταις (dat. after ἀφήκαμεν) ἡμῶν *those who sinned against us* (lit. *those guilty of sin against us*); εἰσενέγκῃς 2nd s. aor. subj. act of φέρω; the subj. is used here in an aorist prohibition (17.1/1); ῥῦσαι 2nd s. aor. imp. mid. of ῥύομαι; τοῦ πονηροῦ is ambiguous as it could be masculine (*the evil one*, i.e. the Devil) or neuter (*evil*).

19 ἴδητε 2nd pl. aor. subj. act. of ὁράω; κυκλουμένην agrees with Ἰερουσαλήμ (the indecl. form is feminine); γνῶτε aor. imp. act of γινώσκω (17.1/1 note 2); ἤγγικεν (perf. of ἐγγίζω) the perf. expresses a state; ταῖς χώραις trans. *the country*.

20 τὸ ἀκάθαρτον πνεῦμα the article is used to denote a general class (2.1/2 note 1(ii)), trans. *an unclean spirit*; ἐξέλθη < ἐξέρχομαι; ζητοῦν neut. s. nom. of the pres. act. pple. of

ζητέω, agreeing with πνεῦμα; ἐλθόν neut. s. nom. of the aor. pple. of ἔρχομαι; the three pples. σχολάζοντα, σεσαρωμένον, κεκοσμημένον agree with οἶκον, which is understood from the previous sentence; the subject of κατοικεῖ is [πνεύματα] εἰσελθόντα (<εἰσέρχομαι) and because this is neut. pl. the verb is singular (2.1/2 note 3); τὰ ἔσχατα ... τῶν πρώτων (gen. neut. pl.) lit. *the last things ... the first things*, i.e. *the final condition ... the original condition.*

17.3 Excursus

Translations of the Bible

It is pointless to consider translations of the New Testament in isolation. The Christian tradition has always considered the Old and the New Testament together as forming its core beliefs, and most translations are of both.

During the first four centuries of our era Christianity spread to communities which did not speak Greek, and so the need for translations arose. Versions of at least part of the Scriptures were made into a number of the languages then spoken in the Middle East and adjoining countries. From these we may instance translations made into:

- Syriac, one of the dialects of Aramaic which were spoken in Syria, Palestine and other regions immediately to the east. The Aramaic dialect of Palestine would have been the language used by Christ himself (this dialect has no special name).
- Armenian, the language of the people of what is now eastern Turkey.
- Coptic, the descendant of the language represented in Egyptian hieroglyphics. It was spoken by the native population of Egypt.

These versions have an historical value as they testify to the spread of the new religion. They are also important in another way. Because they were made from Greek originals before the earliest surviving Greek texts (as e.g. the Codex Sinaiticus) there is always the possibility that they preserve a more authentic version of a particular passage.

But the most important of these early translations appeared in the western half of the Roman empire, where the dominant language was Latin, not Greek. Christianity seems to have been established in Rome and the west soon after Christ's death, and many converts would have needed a Latin version of the Scriptures. The evidence we have indicates that such a version existed in Gaul and Carthage in the second century of our era, but over the next two centuries translations into Latin multiplied, and of them enough survives for us to form a judgement on their character. They are very literal, even to the point of word-for-word renderings of Greek idioms into Latin. The language they use is termed Vulgar Latin, the speech of the common people (Latin **vulgus** *mob*), and in this they reflect the type of Greek employed by the original authors (see 1.3). In east and west alike, Christianity was addressed to common people, not to the educated classes.

Towards the end of the fourth century the number of Latin translations in circulation was leading to such confusion that in AD 382 Pope Damascus commissioned a leading Christian scholar of the day, Jerome, to establish an authoritative Latin text. Jerome started by revising existing Latin versions of the Gospels; his method here, and elsewhere in the NT, was to correct particular passages which did not agree with the Greek, not to make a completely fresh translation. Jerome's work eventually extended to most of the Bible, but when he came to the Old Testament his method changed. Rather than revise existing versions, he made a new translation from the Hebrew original. The results of his work made up the greater part of what eventually came to be the official Latin version, the Vulgate (from the Latin **vulgata** *in common use*). The language of the Vulgate follows the norm established by the previous Latin versions. Jerome, although completely familiar with classical Latin, as is shown by his letters, did not depart from what had become the established tradition.

The Vulgate was undoubtedly the most influential translation ever made of the Bible. While the Greek-speaking East could use the NT in its original form and the Old Testament as presented by the Septuagint (12.3), the Western church, which was centred on Rome, had the Vulgate. This continued through the Middle Ages. The Greek Orthodox Church still uses the Greek Bible as it existed in antiquity (i.e. NT + Septuagint), not a translation in modern Greek, but the supremacy of the Vulgate in the West was upset during the Reformation when Luther translated the Bible into German (1534), thereby setting a precedent for versions in other European languages. However, the Vulgate continued as the official version of the Catholic church until recent times.

The history of the Bible in English up to the Authorized Version (1611) has been told often. The Authorized Version itself combined such accuracy and elegance of language that it soon gained a place in the annals of English literature and remained the standard translation of English Protestants for over two centuries. In the 1880s a revision of this appeared which retained the tone and language of the original but took into account developments in biblical scholarship and new textual evidence for the Greek and Hebrew originals.

Since then a large number of fresh translations have appeared and the Bible has been rendered into various styles of English aimed at satisfying the ideas or culture of a particular audience. As a result we have versions into varieties of contemporary English, slangy English, gender-neutral English, and so on.

However, it would be a mistake to imagine that accuracy goes hand in hand with modernity. Many recent translations show a tendency to paraphrase, which at times distorts the meaning of the original. As an example we may take Mt 19.12:

> εἰσὶν γὰρ εὐνοῦχοι οἵτινες ἐκ κοιλίας μητρὸς ἐγεννήθησαν οὕτως, καὶ εἰσὶν εὐνοῦχοι οἵτινες εὐνουχίσθησαν ὑπὸ τῶν ἀνθρώπων, καὶ εἰσὶν εὐνοῦχοι οἵτινες εὐνούχισαν ἑαυτοὺς διὰ τὴν βασιλείαν τῶν οὐρανῶν.

Compare the following versions:

> For there are some eunuchs, which were so born from their mother's womb: and there are some eunuchs, which were made eunuchs of men: and there be eunuchs, which have made themselves eunuchs for the kingdom of heaven's sake. (Authorized Version, 1611)

> For while some are incapable of marriage because they were born so, or were made so by men, there are others who have themselves renounced marriage for the sake of the kingdom of Heaven. (*The New English Bible*, OUP and CUP, second edition 1970)

> Some people are unable to marry because of birth defects or because of what someone has done to their bodies. Others stay single in order to serve God better. (*Today's New Testament and Psalms*, Bible Society, 1991)

The first is a literal and accurate rendering of the Greek. With a few slight changes to eliminate its archaisms it would pass as an example of clear, modern English.

As for the second and third translations, the reader should now be in a position to pass a judgement on both their accuracy and their closeness to the original Greek.

18.1 Grammar

18.1/1 -μι verbs

-μι verbs were very common in earlier Greek but in modern Greek they have disappeared completely. In NT Greek the type still exists but some are in the process of being converted to the -ω class, while a few have already vanished. What remains can be divided into two classes:

(a) The -νυμι class, where the stem of the present and imperfect has a νυ suffix, e.g. δείκνυμι *show* (19.1/1).

(b) The suffixless class, where the endings of the present and imperfect are added directly to the stem without any suffix or link vowel, e.g. εἰ-μί (3.1/6) and φη-μί (7.1/3). There are five other verbs in this type:

> δίδωμι *give* and τίθημι *put, place* (18.1/2)
> ἵστημι *make to stand* (19.1/2)
> -ἵημι *let go, send forth* (20.1/1)
> -εἶμι (to be distinguished from εἰμί *I am*), which originally meant *I shall go* and of which a few remnants remain (20.1/4(a)).

Both classes differ from -ω verbs in the present and imperfect; of class (b) δίδωμι, τίθημι, ἵστημι, ἵημι also differ from -ω verbs in the aorist active and middle (ἵστημι in the perfect and pluperfect as well). Elsewhere, -μι verbs take the same suffixes and endings as -ω verbs. πίμπλημι *fill*, which originally belonged to class (b), occurs in the NT only in the aor. act. ἔπλησα, aor. pass. ἐπλήσθην, fut. pass. πλησθήσομαι, which are all regular.

Verbs in -αμαι, which from a historical point of view belong to the -μι type, are treated at 19.1/3.

In the tables of -μι verbs the many forms which do not occur in the NT (and which, as elsewhere, are enclosed in square brackets) are included to give a fuller picture and to show the overall similarity between certain verbs. If you do not intend to read beyond the NT, there is obviously no point in learning them. However, a full knowledge of these verbs is necessary for a broader study of early Christian literature written in Greek.

18.1/2 δίδωμι *give,* τίθημι *put, place* (see Appendix 5)

These two -μι verbs are closely parallel. In nearly all their forms an ο/ου/ω in δίδωμι corresponds to an ε/ει/η in τίθημι; the only exceptions are the 1st s. impf. act. (ἐδίδουν/ἐτίθην), the present and aorist subjunctive and the perfect mid./pass. (δέδομαι etc. but τέθειμαι etc.). Both verbs form their present stem by reduplication with iota; as in the perfect tense (14.1/2), an aspirated consonant is reduplicated with the corresponding non-aspirate, hence τιθη- (not θιθη-). In both, the aorist active indicative is formed with κ (**not** σ) added to the long-vowel form of the root (δω-/θη-).

Their principal parts are:

PRESENT	FUTURE	AOR. ACT	PERF. ACT	PERF. MID./PASS	AOR. PASS
δίδωμι	δώσω	ἔδωκα	δέδωκα	δέδομαι	ἐδόθην
τίθημι	θήσω	ἔθηκα	τέθεικα	τέθειμαι/κεῖμαι	ἐτέθην
				(note 2)	

The future, perfect (act. and mid./pass.), and aorist passive are regular. The present, imperfect, and aorist active forms, which require the greatest attention and should be mastered first, are set out here. The middle and passive forms are easily recognized from their endings (for full tables see **Appendix 5**). Forms which do not occur in the NT are enclosed in square brackets, but those which appear only in compounds are not indicated.

	PRESENT		AORIST	
INDICATIVE				
S. 1	δίδωμι	τίθημι	ἔδωκα	ἔθηκα
2	δίδως	[τίθης]	ἔδωκας	ἔθηκας
3	δίδωσι(ν)	τίθησι(ν)	ἔδωκε(ν)	ἔθηκε(ν)
PL. 1	[δίδομεν]	τίθεμεν	ἐδώκαμεν	[ἐθήκαμεν]
2	[δίδοτε]	[τίθετε]	ἐδώκατε	[ἐθήκατε]
3	διδόασι(ν)	τιθέασι(ν)	ἔδωκαν	ἔθηκαν

INFINITIVE

διδόναι	τιθέναι	δοῦναι	θεῖναι

PARTICIPLE

διδούς, -όντος	τιθείς, -έντος	δούς, δόντος	θείς, θέντος
διδοῦσα, -ούσης	τιθεῖσα, -είσης	δοῦσα, δούσης	θεῖσα, θείσης
διδόν, -όντος	τιθέν, -έντος	δόν, δόντος	θέν, θέντος

IMPERATIVE

S. 2	δίδου	τίθει	δός	θές
3	διδότω	τιθέτω	δότω	θέτω
PL. 2	δίδοτε	[τίθετε]	δότε	θέτε
3	[διδότωσαν]	[τιθέτωσαν]	[δότωσαν]	[θέτωσαν]

SUBJUNCTIVE

S. 1	[διδῶ]	[τιθῶ]	δῶ	θῶ
2	[διδῷς]	[τιθῇς]	δῷς	θῇς
3	διδῷ	[τιθῇ]	δῷ, δοῖ or δώῃ	θῇ
PL. 1	διδῶμεν	[τιθῶμεν]	δῶμεν	θῶμεν
2	διδῶτε	[τιθῆτε]	δῶτε	[θῆτε]
3	διδῶσι(ν)	τιθῶσι(ν)	δῶσι(ν)	θῶσι(ν)

IMPERFECT ACTIVE

[ἐδίδουν], [ἐδίδους], ἐδίδου, [ἐδίδομεν], [ἐδίδοτε], [ἐδίδοσαν]
[ἐτίθην], [ἐτίθεις], ἐτίθει, [ἐτίθεμεν], [ἐτίθετε], ἐτίθεσαν

The irregular endings for the present and aorist subjunctive active of δίδωμι (-ῶ, -ῷς, -ῷ, -ῶμεν, -ῶτε, -ῶσι(ν)) also occur in the aorist subjunctive active of γίνωσκω (13.1/2 note 2 and **Appendix 4**).

Notes

1 Luke (1.2) has the older form παρέδοσαν (=παρέδωκαν, 3 pl aor. ind. act. of παραδίδωμι); this is in keeping with Luke's more literary style.

2 κεῖμαι *lie, be laid down* can be used in place of the perfect passive of τίθημι; see 19.1/3.

18.1/3 Conditional sentences

Conditional sentences contain at least one main clause and one adverbial clause of condition; the latter is introduced by εἰ *if*. They fall into two clearly defined categories in both English and Greek, and are clearly distinguished by the form of the main clause:

Category 1

In the main clause English has the auxiliary verb *would* or *should* (or occasionally *could*), and Greek has the particle ἄν (see below). An English example is: *I would go to Rome if I had sufficient money.*

Category 2

In the main clause English does **not** have the auxiliary *would* or *should,* and Greek does **not** have the particle ἄν. An English example is: *I shall go to Rome if I have sufficient money.*

There is a clear distinction between the two categories. The first is used in cases where something could have happened in the past, could be happening now, or could happen in the future. The cases covered by the second are also hypothetical (as all conditional sentences must be), but here, by not using *would* or *should* in English (or ἄν in Greek), we express ourselves in a more positive and confident way.

The particle ἄν, when used with the subjunctive in subordinate clauses (14.1/1(b)), can be represented in English by *ever.* Here, however, it has no semantic equivalent in English. When in English we wish to express potentiality we use an auxiliary verb (generally *would* or *should*), e.g. *I would have gone to Rome with you.* ἄν, however, which expresses potentiality in Greek, is an adverbial particle and modifies the verb to which it is attached: οὐκ ἐγένετο means *it did not happen*; οὐκ ἄν ἐγένετο means *it would not have happened.*

Conditional clauses of both categories can refer to the future, present, or past, and consequently there are six possibilities, three within the first category and three within the second. However, category 1 conditions with a future reference (*if you were to do this you would be wrong*), which in earlier Greek were expressed by putting both verbs into the optative mood (13.1/4) and adding ἄν to the main verb, are not represented in the NT in any complete example, and so this type is enclosed in square brackets in the table given below.The three time-frames of each category are as follows:

CATEGORY 1	CATEGORY 2
English *would/should* in the main clause	verb without *would/should* in the main clause
Greek ἄν in the main clause	no ἄν in the main clause

FUTURE

Conditional clause

[εἰ + optative]	ἐάν (see note 2) + subjunctive (pres. or aor.)

Main clause

[optative + ἄν]	future indicative
[εἰ τοῦτο πράξειας, ἁμάρτοις ἄν.]	ἐὰν τοῦτο πράξῃς, ἁμαρτήσεις.
[*If you were to do this you would sin.*]	*If you do this you will sin.*

PRESENT

Conditional clause

εἰ + imperfect indicative	εἰ + present indicative

Main clause

imperfect indicative + ἄν	present indicative
εἰ τοῦτο ἔπρασσες, ἡμάρτανες ἄν.	εἰ τοῦτο πράσσεις, ἁμαρτάνεις.
If you were [now] doing this you would be sinning.	*If you are doing this you are sinning.*

PAST

Conditional clause

εἰ + aorist indicative	εἰ + imperfect or aorist indicative (depending on the sense)

Main clause

aorist indicative + ἄν	imperfect or aorist indicative (depending on the sense)
εἰ τοῦτο ἔπραξας, ἥμαρτες ἄν.	εἰ τοῦτο ἔπρασσες, ἡμάρτανες.
If you had done this you would have sinned.	*If you used to do this you were sinning.*
	εἰ τοῦτο ἔπραξας, ἥμαρτες.
	If you did this you sinned.

ἄν never stands as the first word in the main clause of conditional clauses of the first category.

The negative in a category 1 conditional clause (i.e the clause beginning with εἰ) is μή; in a category 2 conditional clause (i.e the clause beginning with ἐάν or εἰ) it is usually μή when the reference is to the future, but elsewhere usually οὐ.

Notes

1 The meaning of εἰ … ἔπρασσες/ἔπραξας depends on what follows, i.e. on whether it is in a category 1 or category 2 sentence.

2 The conjunction ἐάν of the future time-frame of category 2 is a contraction of εἰ + ἄν (cf. ὅταν < ὅτε + ἄν, 14.1/1(b)(i)); this use of ἐάν can be easily distinguished from ἐάν when used as a particle in indefinite subordinate clauses (14.1/1 note 1) because, as a conjunction, it is almost always placed at the beginning of a clause.

3 The conjunction ἐάν is sometimes contracted to ἄν: ἄν τι αἰτήσητε τὸν πατέρα ἐν τῷ ὀνόματί μου, δώσει ὑμῖν (Jn 16.23) *if you ask the Father for something in my name, he will give [it] to you.* Just as with the two uses of ἐάν, this ἄν can be distinguished from the particle ἄν of indefinite subordinate clauses (which occurs far more often) and the particle ἄν of category 1 conditions by its position at the beginning of a clause.

4 It is possible to combine certain time references within one sentence:

εἰ τοῦτο ἔπραξας, ἐκινδύνευες ἄν. *If you had done that you would [now] be in danger.*

εἰ τοῦτο ἔπραξας, κινδυνεύεις. *If you did that you are [now] in danger.*

5 Occasionally ἄν is omitted with the verb in a category 1 main clause; this is always obvious from the sense: καλὸν ἦν αὐτῷ εἰ οὐκ ἐγεννήθη ὁ ἄνθρωπος ἐκεῖνος (Mt 26.24) *it would be better if that man had not been born.*[1] (cf. (b) of next subsection).

18.1/4 Other potential constructions

The main clauses of category 1 conditional sentences express something that could be happening now, could happen in the future or could have happened in the past. The term **potential**, which is applied to these clauses, is also used for clauses of the same type which are not qualified by any condition, i.e. are not accompanied by another clause introduced by εἰ in Greek or *if* in English; e.g. *I would have been glad to see her.* We distinguish two types:

[1] We would have expected μή, not οὐ, in the conditional clause.

(a) Where ἄν is added to the verb to express potentiality (i.e. the same contruction as in main clauses of category 1 conditionals). Examples are rare in the NT, and it is here that we very occasionally meet the optative, which is used for a future potential: τί ἂν θέλοι ὁ σπερμολόγος οὗτος λέγειν; (Ac 17.18) *what would this chatterer want to say?* (the reference is to the future).We also find a past potential in [αἱ θυσίαι] οὐκ ἂν ἐπαύσαντο προσφερόμεναι; (Hb 10.2) *would not [the sacrifices] have stopped being offered?*

(b) Where the imperfect indicative of a verb is used without ἄν but the sense shows that the verb must be understood potentially, i.e must be translated with the addition of *would/should/could*. This construction occurs mainly with ἔδει (imperfect of δεῖ *it is necessary*) which can mean either *it was necessary* (actual) or *it would/should have been necessary* (potential); only the context can show which we must choose.

When Christ is going from Judea to Galilee John tells us: ἔδει αὐτὸν διέρχεσθαι διὰ τῆς Σαμαρείας (*Jn 4.4); this can mean either *he had to go through Samaria* (lit. *it was necessary for him to go ...*) or *he should have gone through Samaria* (lit. *it should have been necessary for him to go ...*). As the next verse tells us that Christ came to a city in Samaria the first interpretation is the correct one.

When Paul is sailing to Rome, the ship on which he is travelling puts in at Fair Harbours in Crete (12.2.7). Those in command then decide, against Paul's advice, to continue despite approaching bad weather. When the ship is hit by a storm, Paul says: ἔδει, ὦ ἄνδρες, πειθαρχήσαντάς μοι μὴ ἀνάγεσθαι ἀπὸ τῆς Κρήτης and the context shows that we must interpret ἔδει in its other sense and translate *it should have been necessary, O men, listening to me not to put out from Crete*, i.e. *you should have listened to me and not put out from Crete*.

18.2 Greek reading

Place each conditional sentence within the appropriate category and time-frame as given above (e.g. category 1 future).

1 Οὐαί σοι, Χοραζίν· οὐαί σοι, Βηθσαϊδά· ὅτι εἰ ἐν Τύρῳ καὶ Σιδῶνι ἐγένοντο αἱ δυνάμεις αἱ γενόμεναι ἐν ὑμῖν, πάλαι ἂν ἐν σάκκῳ καὶ σποδῷ μετενόησαν. (Mt 11.21)

2 ἔρχεται Ἰησοῦς καὶ λαμβάνει τὸν ἄρτον καὶ δίδωσιν αὐτοῖς, καὶ τὸ ὀψάριον ὁμοίως. (Jn 21.13)

3 ἐάν τις φάγῃ ἐκ τούτου τοῦ ἄρτου ζήσει εἰς τὸν αἰῶνα. (Jn 6.51)

4 καὶ ἔλεγεν, Πῶς ὁμοιώσωμεν τὴν βασιλείαν τοῦ θεοῦ, ἢ ἐν τίνι αὐτὴν παραβολῇ θῶμεν; (Mk 4.30)

5 Εἰ ἤμεθα ἐν ταῖς ἡμέραις τῶν πατέρων ἡμῶν, οὐκ ἂν ἤμεθα αὐτῶν κοινωνοὶ ἐν τῷ αἵματι τῶν προφητῶν. (Mt 23.30)

6 ἡ οὖν Μαριάμ, ὡς ἦλθεν ὅπου ἦν Ἰησοῦς, ἰδοῦσα αὐτὸν ἔπεσεν αὐτοῦ πρὸς τοὺς πόδας, λέγουσα αὐτῷ, Κύριε, εἰ ἦς ὧδε οὐκ ἂν μου ἀπέθανεν ὁ ἀδελφός. (Jn 11.32)

7 προσετίθεντο πιστεύοντες τῷ κυρίῳ πλήθη ἀνδρῶν τε καὶ γυναικῶν, ὥστε καὶ εἰς τὰς πλατείας ἐκφέρειν τοὺς ἀσθενεῖς καὶ τιθέναι ἐπὶ κλιναρίων καὶ κραβάττων, ἵνα ἐρχομένου Πέτρου κἂν ἡ σκιὰ ἐπισκιάσῃ τινὶ αὐτῶν. (Ac 5.14f.)

8 εἰ οὖν τὴν ἴσην δωρεὰν ἔδωκεν αὐτοῖς ὁ θεὸς ὡς καὶ ἡμῖν πιστεύσασιν ἐπὶ τὸν κύριον Ἰησοῦν Χριστόν, ἐγὼ τίς ἤμην δυνατὸς κωλῦσαι τὸν θεόν; (Ac 11.17)

9 Πονηρὲ δοῦλε καὶ ὀκνηρέ, ᾔδεις (*you knew*) ὅτι θερίζω ὅπου οὐκ ἔσπειρα καὶ συνάγω ὅθεν οὐ διεσκόρπισα; ἔδει σε οὖν βαλεῖν τὰ ἀργύριά μου τοῖς τραπεζίταις, καὶ ἐλθὼν ἐγὼ ἐκομισάμην ἂν τὸ ἐμὸν σὺν τόκῳ. (Mt 25.26f.)

10 ἄρτι γὰρ ἀνθρώπους πείθω ἢ τὸν θεόν; ἢ ζητῶ ἀνθρώποις ἀρέσκειν; εἰ ἔτι ἀνθρώποις ἤρεσκον, Χριστοῦ δοῦλος οὐκ ἂν ἤμην. (Gal 1.10)

11 Ἰδοὺ ὁ παῖς μου ὃν ᾑρέτισα, ὁ ἀγαπητός μου εἰς ὃν εὐδόκησεν ἡ ψυχή μου· θήσω τὸ πνεῦμά μου ἐπ᾽ αὐτόν, καὶ κρίσιν τοῖς ἔθνεσιν ἀπαγγελεῖ. (Mt 12.18)

12 οὐδεὶς δὲ λύχνον ἅψας καλύπτει αὐτὸν σκεύει ἢ ὑποκάτω κλίνης τίθησιν. (Lk 8.16)

13 Εἰ οὕτως ἐστὶν ἡ αἰτία τοῦ ἀνθρώπου μετὰ τῆς γυναικός, οὐ συμφέρει γαμῆσαι. (Mt 19.10)

14 ὁ δὲ λέγει αὐταῖς, Μὴ ἐκθαμβεῖσθε· Ἰησοῦν ζητεῖτε τὸν Ναζαρηνὸν τὸν ἐσταυρωμένον· ἠγέρθη, οὐκ ἔστιν ὧδε· ἴδε ὁ τόπος ὅπου ἔθηκαν αὐτόν. (Mk 16.6)

15 **The death of John the Baptist**

Ὁ γὰρ Ἡρῴδης κρατήσας τὸν Ἰωάννην ἔδησεν καὶ ἐν φυλακῇ ἀπέθετο διὰ Ἡρῳδιάδα τὴν γυναῖκα Φιλίππου τοῦ ἀδελφοῦ αὐτοῦ· ἔλεγεν γὰρ ὁ Ἰωάννης αὐτῷ, Οὐκ ἔξεστίν σοι ἔχειν αὐτήν. καὶ θέλων αὐτὸν ἀποκτεῖναι ἐφοβήθη τὸν ὄχλον, ὅτι ὡς προφήτην αὐτὸν εἶχον. γενεσίοις δὲ γενομένοις τοῦ Ἡρῴδου 5 ὠρχήσατο ἡ θυγάτηρ τῆς Ἡρῳδιάδος ἐν τῷ μέσῳ καὶ ἤρεσεν τῷ Ἡρῴδῃ, ὅθεν μεθ᾽ ὅρκου ὡμολόγησεν αὐτῇ δοῦναι ὃ ἐὰν αἰτήσηται. ἡ δὲ προβιβασθεῖσα ὑπὸ τῆς μητρὸς αὐτῆς, Δός μοι, φησίν, ὧδε ἐπὶ πίνακι τὴν κεφαλὴν Ἰωάννου τοῦ βαπτιστοῦ. καὶ λυπηθεὶς ὁ βασιλεὺς διὰ τοὺς ὅρκους καὶ τοὺς 10 συνανακειμένους (*fellow diners*) ἐκέλευσεν δοθῆναι, καὶ πέμψας ἀπεκεφάλισεν τὸν Ἰωάννην ἐν τῇ φυλακῇ· καὶ ἠνέχθη ἡ κεφαλὴ αὐτοῦ ἐπὶ πίνακι καὶ ἐδόθη τῷ κορασίῳ, καὶ ἤνεγκεν τῇ μητρὶ αὐτῆς. (Mt 14.3–11)

Notes

2 Trans. the vivid presents by the English past tense.

4 ὁμοιώσωμεν and θῶμεν are deliberative subjunctives (13.1/3(a)(ii)); θῶμεν < τίθημι (here with the meaning *present*).

5 Because there is only one past tense of εἰμί (4.1/1 note 5) it must be used in both cat. 1 pres. and cat. 1 past conditions (here the sense indicates the latter is meant).

7 πλῆθος is a neuter noun but, because the large numbers (πλήθη) consist of men and women, the pple. (πιστεύοντες) which goes with it is masculine (the gender used where both men and women are involved); such agreement according to the sense rather than to the rules of strict grammar is common (cf. note on 11.2.8 and 12.1.15).

8 ἐγὼ τίς ἤμην δυνατός a condensed expression *who was I to be able* (i.e. *who was I that I was able*).

9 ἤδεις ... διεσκόρπισα; we must tell from the punctuation that this is a question (10.1/2(a)); ἔδει σε οὖν βαλεῖν lit. *then it should have been necessary for you to put* i.e. *you should have put* (8.1/4(b); the sense tells us that the potential use of ἔδει is involved because the slave had not done anything with his master's money); τὸ ἐμόν i.e. *what was mine*.

13 αἰτία here *relationship*: ἄνθρωπος here means *man* in the sense of *male* (in 10 the word has its normal meaning of *human being, person*).

14 αὐταῖς shows that those addressed are women but as English does not distinguish gender in the 3rd pers. pl. pronoun we must translate simply *them*; ἐκθαμβεῖσθε imp.

15 *ll.*1f. ἔδησεν < δέω; ἀπέθετο < ἀποτίθημι. *ll.*4f. τὸν ὄχλον (s.) and εἶχον (pl.) are another example of agreement according to the sense (see note on 8); we can use the same idiom here in English. *l.*5 γενεσίοις δέ ... trans. δέ by *but* as this sentence begins the story of how the situation changed; the dat. gives the time of Salome's dance (7.1/6(b)) – trans. *when H's birthday....* *l.*6 ἐν τῷ μέσῳ lit. *in the middle* [of the guests], trans. *in their midst*. *ll.*7f. ὃ ἐὰν (=ἄν) αἰτήσηται 14.1/1(c). *l.*10 τοὺς ὅρκους trans. by a singular noun. *l.*11

δοθῆναι lit. [*it* i.e. the head] *to be given*; πέμψας ἀπεκεφάλισεν lit. *sending he beheaded* a condensed expression; obviously Herod sent an order to the prison for John to be beheaded and this was done there (Herod did not do it himself); the use of a verb meaning *to do something* in the sense of *to have something done* is common in English (e.g. *last year I built a house in the suburbs*). *l.*13 ἡ κεφαλή is the subject of ἠνέχθη and ἐδόθη. *l.*14 Supply the subject [*she*] for ἤνεγκεν; note that we have αὐτῆς although κοράσιον is a neuter noun (agreement according to the sense, cf. note on 8 above).

unit 19

19.1 Grammar

19.1/1 Verbs in -νυμι

Verbs in -νυμι (and -ννυμι), where the present stem is formed with the suffix νυ, are not common in NT Greek as the transformation of this class into -ω verbs is far advanced.

The present indicative, infinitive and participle (and formerly the imperfect) have endings without the o/e characteristic of -ω verbs (cf. 2.1/5 note 5). The other tenses, which do not keep the νυ suffix, are formed in the same way as those of -ω verbs. An example is δείκνυμι *show*, which has the principal parts: pres. δείκνυμι, fut. δείξω, aor. act. ἔδειξα, perf. act. [δέδειχα], perf. mid./pass. δέδειγμαι, aor. pass. ἐδείχθην.

The present tense of δείκνυμι is:

PRESENT INDICATIVE

		ACTIVE	MIDDLE/PASSIVE
S.	1	δείκνυμι	[δείκνυμαι]
	2	[δείκνυς]	[δείκνυσαι]
	3	δείκνυσι(ν)	δείκνυται
PL.	1	[δείκνυμεν]	[δεικνύμεθα]
	2	[δείκνυτε]	[δείκνυσθε]
	3	[δεικνύασι]	δείκνυνται

IMPERATIVE   δείκνυτε (2 pl. act.)

INFINITIVES   ACTIVE δεικνύναι MIDDLE/PASSIVE δείκνυσθαι

PARTICIPLES   ACTIVE δεικνύς, δεικνῦσα, δεικνύν;
gen. δεικνύντος, δεικνύσης, δεικνύντος
MIDDLE/PASSIVE δεικνύμεν-ος, -η, -ον

Forms in brackets do not occur in δείκνυμι or any other -νυμι verb in the NT (the present subjunctive and the imperfect do not occur at all). Forms not in brackets occur in δείκνυμι or some other -νυμι verb.

Notes

1 δείκνυμι, like other remaining -νυμι verbs, also has present forms of an -ω verb, e.g. δεικνύειν (Mt 16.21 = δεικνύναι), δεικνύεις (Jn 2.18 = δείκνυς). In some cases a -νυμι verb has been almost wholly changed, e.g. ὀμνύω *swear, vow* from an earlier ὄμνυμι (the only old form occurring in the NT is the present infinitive active ὀμνύναι at Mk 14.71 but in the corresponding passage at Mt 26.74 we have the newer ὀμνύειν).

2 ἀπόλλυμι (originally ἀπο + ὄλ-νυμι) and its compound συναπόλλυμι are the only verbs in -λυμι. ἀπόλλυμι has complications beyond those of form. It means *destroy, ruin, lose* in its active forms (except the perfect), but its middle forms (and the perfect active) are intransitive and mean *perish, be lost*. Consequently we have:

Transitive tenses		**Intransitive tenses**
PRESENT	ἀπόλλυμι *I destroy,lose*	ἀπόλλυμαι *I perish*
FUTURE	ἀπολῶ or ἀπολέσω *I shall destroy, lose*	ἀπολοῦμαι *I shall perish*
AORIST	ἀπώλεσα *I destroyed, lost*	ἀπωλόμην *I perished*
PERFECT		ἀπόλωλα *I have perished*

19.1/2 ἵστημι and its compounds (see **Appendix 5**)

ἵστημι *make to stand, set up, place* was originally parallel to δίδωμι and τίθημι (i.e. reduplication with iota and no suffix) but this has been partly obscured by sound changes which occurred at an earlier stage of Greek. Consequently, where the alternation δω/δο occurs in δίδωμι and θη/θε in τίθημι we have στη/στα in ἵστημι.

The **present** and **imperfect** of ἵστημι are almost completely parallel to δίδωμι and τίθημι. Note that the imperative active, the imperfect active, the subjunctive middle/passive are totally absent from the NT and therefore not given.

		ACTIVE		MIDDLE/PASSIVE	
		PRES. IND.	PRES. SUBJ.	PRES. IND.	IMPERFECT
S.	1	ἵστημι	[ἱστῶ]	[ἵσταμαι]	[ἱστάμην]
	2	[ἵστης]	[ἱστῇς]	[ἵστασαι]	ἵστασο
	3	ἵστησι(ν)	[ἱστῇ]	ἵσταται	ἵστατο
PL.	1	[ἵσταμεν]	[ἱστῶμεν]	[ἱστάμεθα]	[ἱστάμεθα]
	2	[ἵστατε]	ἱστῆτε	[ἵστασθε]	[ἵστασθε]
	3	[ἱστᾶσι]	ἱστῶσι(ν)	ἵστανται	ἵσταντο

INFINITIVES ACTIVE ἱστάναι   MIDDLE/PASSIVE ἵστασθαι

PARTICIPLES ACTIVE ἱστάς, ἱστᾶσα, MIDDLE/PASSIVE ἱστάμενος,
         ἱστάν   -η, -ον
     (gen. ἱστάντος, ἱστάσης, ἱστάντος)

The only imperative form of the middle/passive is περιΐστασο (2 s.) in 2 Ti 2.16 and Tit 3.9.

ἵστημι is also parallel to δίδωμι and τίθημι in the following:

- **future active** στήσω *I shall set up, shall place*
- **future middle** στήσομαι *I shall set up for myself, shall place for myself*
- **future passive** σταθήσομαι *I shall be set up, shall be placed*
- **aorist passive** ἐτάθην *I was set up, was placed*

We meet a divergence from δίδωμι and τίθημι in the **aorist active.** ἵστημι has two sets of forms:

(a) A weak aorist ἔστησα, which is transitive and means *I set up, placed.* This is conjugated as ἔλυσα. The middle (ἐστησάμην) does not occur in the NT.

(b) A root aorist ἔστην (conjugated as ἔβην, 11.1/1), which is intransitive and means *I stood.*

		INDICATIVE	IMPERATIVE	SUBJUNCTIVE
S.	1	ἔστην		[στῶ]
	2	[ἔστης]	στῆθι	[στῇς]
	3	ἔστη	στήτω	στῇ
PL.	1	ἔστημεν		[στῶμεν]
	2	ἔστητε	στῆτε	στῆτε
	3	ἔστησαν	[στήτωσαν]	στῶσι(ν)

INFINITIVE   στῆναι
PARTICIPLE   στάς, στᾶσα, στάν gen. στάντος, στάσης, στάντος

Examples of these two aorists are:

Transitive

προσκαλεσάμενος παιδίον ἔστησεν αὐτὸ ἐν μέσῳ αὐτῶν (Mt 18.2) *He called a child and placed him in their midst* (lit. *having called a child ... in the middle of them*).

Intransitive

αὐτῶν λαλούντων αὐτὸς ἔστη ἐν μέσῳ αὐτῶν (Lk 24.36) *And as they were talking he stood in their midst.*

The two aorists are identical in the 3rd pl. indicative active, viz ἔστησαν (ἔστησ-αν from ἔστησα; ἔστη-σαν from ἔστην). The context will show whether the transitive or intransitive form is involved.

ἵστημι is also irregular in its **perfect** and **pluperfect**. Both tenses have a κ suffix in the indicative but a shorter form stem without κ is used in the perfect infinitive and sometimes in the perfect participle. Because these tenses are intransitive (see below) they occur only in the active voice. The subjunctive and imperative do not occur.

		PERFECT	PLUPERFECT
S.	1	ἕστηκα	[εἱστήκειν]
	2	ἕστηκας	[εἱστήκεις]
	3	ἕστηκε(ν)	εἱστήκει
PL.	1	ἑστήκαμεν	[εἱστήκειμεν]
	2	ἑστήκατε	[εἱστήκειτε]
	3	ἑστήκασι(ν)	εἱστήκεισαν

INFINITIVE ἑστάναι (but ἐξεστακέναι Ac 8.11)

PARTICIPLES (1) ἑστώς, ἑστῶσα, ἑστός gen. ἑστῶτος, ἑστώσης, ἑστῶτος

(2) ἑστηκώς, [ἑστηκυῖα], ἑστηκός gen. ἑστηκότος, [ἑστηκυίας], ἑστηκότος

Both perfect and pluperfect are intransitive and they are used as a **present** and **imperfect** tense respectively: ἕστηκα *I am standing* and εἱστήκειν *I was standing*.

We may summarize the different meanings of τίθημι as follows:

	Transitive tenses		Intransitive tenses
PRESENT	ἵστημι *I set up, place*	PERFECT	ἕστηκα *I am standing*
FUTURE	στήσω *I shall set up, shall place*		
IMPERFECT	active does not occur in the NT	PLUPERFECT	εἱστήκειν *I was standing*
WEAK AORIST	ἔστησα *I set up, placed*	ROOT AORIST	ἔστην *I stood*

A comprehensive table of ἵστημι is given in **Appendix 5**. The present, future and imperfect of the middle/passive (ἵσταται, στήσομαι, ἵστατο) occur very occasionally in compounds, always with an intransitive sense, but the middle voice of the transitive aorist (which would be ἐστησάμην) is totally absent.

ἵστημι has many compounds and these retain the same distinctions between transitive and intransitive tenses. Among the most common are:

	Transitive tenses	Intransitive tenses
ἀνίστημι	*raise up*	*rise up, stand up*
ἀφίστημι	*mislead, make to revolt*	*go away*
ἐξίστημι	*confuse, amaze*	*lose one's senses; be amazed*
καθίστημι	*ordain, appoint*	
συνίστημι	*commend, prove*	*stand with*

Examples of the above compounds are:

τοῦτον τὸν Ἰησοῦν ἀνέστησεν ὁ θεός. (Ac 2.32) *This Jesus God raised up* (sc. *from the dead*).

εὐθὺς ἀνέστη τὸ κοράσιον καὶ περιεπάτει. (Mk 5.42) *The girl immediately stood up and started to walk.*

ἐν ὑστέροις καιροῖς ἀποστήσονταί τινες τῆς πίστεως. (1Ti 4.1) *In later times some will depart from the faith.*

ἀπέστησεν λαὸν ὀπίσω αὐτοῦ. (Ac 5.37) *He made the people revolt under his leadership* (lit. *behind him*).

γυναῖκές τινες ἐξ ἡμῶν ἐξέστησαν ἡμᾶς. (Lk 24.22) *Some women from [among] us amazed us.*

ἔλεγον γὰρ ὅτι ἐξέστη. (Mk 3.21) *For they were saying that he was out of his mind.*

Notes

1 To distinguish the different forms of ἵστημι it is essential to remember that:

(i) ἱστ- occurs in all forms of the present and imperfect but nowhere else.

(ii) ἐστ- (with smooth breathing) occurs only in the aorist **indicative** both transitive and intransitive. It does not occur in aorist infinitives, participles or subjunctive, which all begin with στ-.

(iii) ἑστ- (with rough breathing) occurs in all forms of the perfect but nowhere else.

(iv) εἱστ- occurs only in the pluperfect.

2 Tenses formed from the present stem of some compounds of ἵστημι are in the process of passing over to -ω verbs. Consequently we find συνιστάνω as well as συνίστημι; and παριστάνω is always used instead of παρίστημι. However, the tenses of these verbs not formed from the present stem are not affected.

3 ἀνάστα is an alternative form for the intrans. aor. imp. ἀνάστηθι *rise!*.

19.1/3 Eccentric -μαι verbs

Two deponents end in -αμαι, not -ομαι, because they belong to the -μι class of verbs (18.1/1; cf. ἵσταμαι pres. mid./pass. of ἵστημι, 19.1/2). These are δύναμαι *be able* and ἐπίσταμαι *know how to, understand*. These differ from -ω verbs only in the present and imperfect (we have already met δύναμαι at 11.1/1 note 2). δύναμαι is conjugated as follows:

		PRES. IND.	PRES. SUBJ.	IMPERFECT	FUTURE	AOR. IND.
S.	1	δύναμαι	[δύνωμαι]	[ἐδυνάμην]	[δυνήσομαι]	ἠδυνήθην
	2	δύνασαι	δύνῃ	[ἐδύνω]	δυνήσῃ	[ἠδυνήθης]
	3	δύναται	δύνηται	ἐδύνατο / ἠδύνατο	δυνήσεται	ἠδυνήθη
PL.	1	δυνάμεθα	[δυνώμεθα]	[ἐδυνάμεθα]	δυνησόμεθα	ἠδυνήθημεν
	2	δύνασθε	[δύνησθε]	ἐδύνασθε	δυνήσεσθε	ἠδυνήθητε
	3	δύνανται	δύνωνται	ἠδύναντο	δυνήσονται	ἠδυνήθησαν

INFINITIVE δύνασθαι
PARTICIPLE δυνάμενος, -η, -ον

From δύναμαι we also find the 2 pl aor. subj. δυνηθῆτε; on the two forms of the optative that occur (δυναίμην, δύναιντο) see 13.1/4. Note that the augment in the imperfect is either ἐ- or ἠ- (only the latter appears in the aorist).

ἐπίσταμαι can be conveniently shown with two similar verbs, κεῖμαι *lie, be laid down* and κάθημαι *be seated, sit*. These are restricted to the following tenses:

		ἐπίσταμαι	κεῖμαι		κάθημαι	
		PRES. IND.	PRES. IND.	IMPERFECT	PRES. IND.	IMPERFECT
S.	1	ἐπίσταμαι	κεῖμαι	[ἐκείμην]	κάθημαι	[ἐκαθήμην]
	2	[ἐπίστασαι]	[κεῖσαι]	[ἔκεισο]	κάθῃ	[ἐκάθησο]
	3	ἐπίσταται	κεῖται	ἔκειτο	κάθηται	ἐκάθητο
PL.	1	[ἐπιστάμεθα]	κείμεθα	[ἐκείμεθα]	[καθήμεθα]	[ἐκαθήμεθα]
	2	ἐπίστασθε	[κεῖσθε]	[ἔκεισθε]	[κάθησθε]	[ἐκάθησθε]
	3	ἐπίστανται	κεῖνται	ἔκειντο	κάθηνται	[ἐκάθηντο]
INF.		[ἐπίστασθαι]	κεῖσθαι		καθῆσθαι	
PPLE.		ἐπιστάμενος, -η, -ον	κείμενος,		καθήμενος, -η, -ον	

κάθημαι has two other forms: κάθου *sit!* (2 pl. fut. imp.) and καθήσεσθε *you will sit* (2 pl. fut.).

Although δύναμαι, κεῖμαι and κάθημαι are defective verbs, the forms indicated above occur frequently in the NT; we meet ἐπίσταμαι slightly less often.

Notes

1 κεῖμαι has several compounds, e.g. ἀντίκειμαι *be opposed (to)*, ἐπίκειμαι *press upon, threaten*.

2 κεῖμαι can be used in place of the perfect passive of τίθημι with a basic meaning of *to have been placed/set up* (the context of a passage will give the exact nuance):

> ἔχεις πολλὰ ἀγαθὰ κείμενα εἰς ἔτη πολλά. (Lk 12.19) *You have many good things stored up for many years* (we might have expected τεθειμένα lit. *having been placed [aside]*).
>
> εἰς ἀπολογίαν τοῦ εὐαγγελίου κεῖμαι. (Phil 1.16) *I am appointed for the defence of the gospel* (we might have expected τέθειμαι lit. *I have been set up*).

3 κρέμαμαι *hang* (intr.), the passive of a defunct form κρεμάννυμι *hang* (tr.), is conjugated as ἐπίσταμαι. πίμπρημι *burn* occurs in the pres. inf. mid.pass. (πίμπρασθαι) and the aor. ind. act. (ἔπρησα).

19.2 Greek reading

1 περὶ δὲ τὴν ἑνδεκάτην (*sc.* ὥραν) ἐξελθὼν εὗρεν ἄλλους ἑστῶτας, καὶ λέγει αὐτοῖς, Τί ὧδε ἑστήκατε ὅλην τὴν ἡμέραν ἀργοί; λέγουσιν αὐτῷ, Ὅτι οὐδεὶς ἡμᾶς ἐμισθώσατο. (Mt 20.6f.)

2 τίς ἄρα ἐστὶν ὁ πιστὸς δοῦλος καὶ φρόνιμος ὃν κατέστησεν ὁ κύριος ἐπὶ τῆς οἰκετείας αὐτοῦ τοῦ δοῦναι αὐτοῖς τὴν τροφὴν ἐν καιρῷ; (Mt 24.45)

3 παραλαμβάνει αὐτὸν ὁ διάβολος εἰς ὄρος ὑψηλὸν λίαν, καὶ δείκνυσιν αὐτῷ πάσας τὰς βασιλείας τοῦ κόσμου καὶ τὴν δόξαν αὐτῶν. (Mt 4.8)

4 ὁ δὲ βασιλεὺς ὠργίσθη, καὶ πέμψας τὰ στρατεύματα αὐτοῦ ἀπώλεσεν τοὺς φονεῖς ἐκείνους καὶ τὴν πόλιν αὐτῶν ἐνέπρησεν. (Mt 22.7)

5 ἐν τῇ ἡμέρᾳ ἐκείνῃ ἐξελθὼν ὁ Ἰησοῦς τῆς οἰκίας ἐκάθητο παρὰ τὴν θάλασσαν· καὶ συνήχθησαν πρὸς αὐτὸν ὄχλοι

πολλοί, ὥστε αὐτὸν εἰς πλοῖον ἐμβάντα καθῆσθαι, καὶ πᾶς ὁ
ὄχλος ἐπὶ τὸν αἰγιαλὸν εἱστήκει. (Mt 13.1)
6 ἤδη δὲ ἡ ἀξίνη πρὸς τὴν ῥίζαν τῶν δένδρων κεῖται. (Mt 3.10)
7 τίς ἄνθρωπος ἐξ ὑμῶν ἔχων ἑκατὸν πρόβατα καὶ ἀπολέσας ἐξ
αὐτῶν ἓν οὐ καταλείπει τὰ ἐνενήκοντα ἐννέα ἐν τῇ ἐρήμῳ καὶ
πορεύεται ἐπὶ τὸ ἀπολωλὸς ἕως εὕρῃ αὐτό; (Lk 15.4)
8 Εἶπεν δέ τις ἐκ τοῦ ὄχλου αὐτῷ, Διδάσκαλε, εἰπὲ τῷ ἀδελφῷ
μου μερίσασθαι μετ᾽ ἐμοῦ τὴν κληρονομίαν. ὁ δὲ εἶπεν αὐτῷ,
Ἄνθρωπε, τίς με κατέστησεν κριτὴν ἐφ᾽ ὑμᾶς; (*Lk 12.13f.)
9 μετὰ τοῦτον ἀνέστη Ἰούδας ὁ Γαλιλαῖος ἐν ταῖς ἡμέραις τῆς
ἀπογραφῆς καὶ ἀπέστησεν λαὸν ὀπίσω αὐτοῦ· κἀκεῖνος
ἀπώλετο, καὶ πάντες ὅσοι ἐπείθοντο αὐτῷ διεσκορπίσθησαν.
(Ac 5.37)
10 συνίστημι δὲ ὑμῖν Φοίβην τὴν ἀδελφὴν ἡμῶν, οὖσαν διάκονον
τῆς ἐκκλησίας τῆς ἐν Κεγχρεαῖς, ἵνα αὐτὴν προσδέξησθε ἐν
κυρίῳ ἀξίως τῶν ἁγίων καὶ παραστῆτε αὐτῇ ἐν ᾧ ἂν ὑμῶν
χρῄζῃ πράγματι. (Ro 16.1f.)
11 While shepherds watch'd their flocks by night ...
καὶ ποιμένες ἦσαν ἐν τῇ χώρᾳ τῇ αὐτῇ ἀγραυλοῦντες καὶ
φυλάσσοντες φυλακὰς τῆς νυκτὸς ἐπὶ τὴν ποίμνην αὐτῶν. καὶ
ἄγγελος κυρίου ἐπέστη αὐτοῖς καὶ δόξα κυρίου περιέλαμψεν
αὐτούς, καὶ ἐφοβήθησαν φόβον μέγαν. καὶ εἶπεν αὐτοῖς ὁ
ἄγγελος, Μὴ φοβεῖσθε, ἰδοὺ γὰρ εὐαγγελίζομαι ὑμῖν χαρὰν 5
μεγάλην ἥτις ἔσται παντὶ τῷ λαῷ, ὅτι ἐτέχθη ὑμῖν σήμερον
σωτὴρ ὅς ἐστιν Χριστὸς κύριος ἐν πόλει Δαυίδ· καὶ τοῦτο ὑμῖν
τὸ σημεῖον, εὑρήσετε βρέφος ἐσπαργανωμένον καὶ κείμενον
ἐν φάτνῃ. καὶ ἐξαίφνης ἐγένετο σὺν τῷ ἀγγέλῳ πλῆθος
στρατιᾶς οὐρανίου αἰνούντων τὸν θεὸν καὶ λεγόντων, Δόξα ἐν 10
ὑψίστοις θεῷ καὶ ἐπὶ γῆς εἰρήνη ἐν ἀνθρώποις εὐδοκίας. (Lk
2.8–14)
12 Dorcas brought back to life
ἐν Ἰόππῃ δέ τις ἦν μαθήτρια ὀνόματι Ταβιθά, ἣ
διερμηνευομένη λέγεται Δορκάς· αὕτη ἦν πλήρης ἔργων
ἀγαθῶν καὶ ἐλεημοσυνῶν ὧν ἐποίει. ἐγένετο δὲ ἐν ταῖς
ἡμέραις ἐκείναις ἀσθενήσασαν αὐτὴν ἀποθανεῖν· λούσαντες
δὲ ἔθηκαν αὐτὴν ἐν ὑπερῴῳ. ἐγγὺς δὲ οὔσης Λύδδας τῇ Ἰόππῃ 5
οἱ μαθηταὶ ἀκούσαντες ὅτι Πέτρος ἐστὶν ἐν αὐτῇ ἀπέστειλαν
δύο ἄνδρας πρὸς αὐτὸν παρακαλοῦντες, Μὴ ὀκνήσῃς διελθεῖν
ἕως ἡμῶν. ἀναστὰς δὲ Πέτρος συνῆλθεν αὐτοῖς· ὃν
παραγενόμενον ἀνήγαγον εἰς τὸ ὑπερῷον, καὶ παρέστησαν
αὐτῷ πᾶσαι αἱ χῆραι κλαίουσαι καὶ ἐπιδεικνύμεναι χιτῶνας 10
καὶ ἱμάτια ὅσα ἐποίει μετ᾽ αὐτῶν οὖσα ἡ Δορκάς. ἐκβαλὼν δὲ
ἔξω πάντας ὁ Πέτρος καὶ θεὶς τὰ γόνατα προσηύξατο, καὶ
ἐπιστρέψας πρὸς τὸ σῶμα εἶπεν, Ταβιθά, ἀνάστηθι. ἡ δὲ

ἤνοιξεν τοὺς ὀφθαλμοὺς αὐτῆς, καὶ ἰδοῦσα τὸν Πέτρον ἀνεκάθισεν. (Ac 9.36–40)

Notes

1 ἑστῶτας and ἑστήκατε 19.1/2; λέγει vivid present, trans. *said* (further examples will not be noted).

2 κατέστησεν < καθίστημι; τοῦ δοῦναι expresses purpose (13.1/3(b)(i)).

4 ἀπώλεσεν < ἀπόλλυμι (19.1/1 note 2); ἐνέπρησεν < ἐμπίμπρημι.

5 τῆς οἰκίας is governed by the ἐξ- of ἐξελθών (we could also have ἐκ τῆς οἰκίας); συνήχθησαν < συνάγω; ἐμβάντα < ἐμβαίνω; εἱστήκει 19.1/2.

6 κεῖται is used here for the perf. pass. of τίθημι (19.1/3 note 2).

7 ἔχων here *possessing*; ἀπολέσας (and ἀπολωλός) < ἀπόλλυμι (19.1/1 note 2); ἐπί lit. *to, towards* but trans. here *after*; ἕως + subj. *until* (14.1/1(b)(ii)).

8 εἰπέ 2nd s. aor. imp. act. of λέγω; κατέστησεν < καθίστημι.

9 ἀνέστη < ἀνίστημι; ἀπέστησεν < ἀφίστημι; κἀκεῖνος i.e. καὶ ἐκεῖνος (11.1/5); ἀπώλετο < ἀπόλλυμι (19.1/1 note 2); πάντες ὅσοι *all who* (21.1/3(c)).

10 παραστῆτε 2nd pl. subj. of the intr. aor. of παρίστημι; ἄν + subj. makes the clause indefinite *in whatever matter* (14.1/1(c)).

11 *ll.*1f. ἀγραυλοῦντες lit. *being in the open air* but *being* can be omitted; φυλακὰς τῆς νυκτός the *watches of the night* were the divisions of time into which the night was divided (cf. 7.2.5). *l.*4 ἐφοβήθησαν φόβον μέγαν lit. *they feared a great fear*, i.e. *they were extremely afraid*. *ll.*7f. τοῦτο ὑμῖν τὸ σημεῖον supply ἐστί; ἐσπαργανωμένον perf. pple. pass. of σπαργανόω *wrap in swaddling clothes* (narrow lengths of cloth wrapped around a baby so that only its head was visible); ἐγένετο here *appeared*. *l.*10 αἰνούντων goes with στρατιᾶς (agreement according to the sense rather than strict grammar, cf. note on 18.2.8). *l.*11 ἀνθρώποις εὐδοκίας the traditional interpretation *men of good will* has now been abandoned for *people who enjoy God's good will* or *favour* (for the use of the genitive involved see 20.1/3(e)).

12 *l.*3 ὧν ἐποίει we would expect ἃ ἐποίει but the relative is attracted in the case of its antecedents ἔργων and ἐλεημοσυνῶν (9.1/2 note 3). *l.*4 ἀσθενήσασαν trans. *having fallen sick*. *l.*6 ἐστίν on the tense see 8.1/4(a); ἀπέστειλαν

< ἀποστέλλω. *ll.*8f. ἕως is here a preposition; ἀναστάς <
ἀνίστημι; ὃν παραγενόμενον ἀνήγαγον (<ἀνάγω) lit. *whom
having arrived they took up*; παρέστησαν (<παρίστημι) could
be either tr. or intr. (19.1/2) – here it is the latter. *l.*11 ὅσα lit.
as many as (21.1/3(c)), trans. *all the … which*. *l.*12 θείς
(< τίθημι) τὰ γόνατα idiomatic for *falling to his knees*;
προσηύξατο < προσεύχομαι. *l.*13 ἀνάστηθι < ἀνίστημι; ἤνοιξεν
< ἀνοίγω. *l.*14 ἰδοῦσα < ὁράω.

unit 20

20.1 Grammar

20.1/1 Compounds of -ἵημι

The last -μι verb that requires our attention is -ἵημι; most of its forms are exactly parallel to τίθημι. Unlike the latter, -ἵημι had become so moribund that in the NT it survives only in compounds. These are:

ἀνίημι	*loosen; stop; desert*	παρίημι	*neglect*
ἀφίημι	*forgive; allow; send away*	συνίημι	*understand*
καθίημι	*lower*		

Of these ἀφίημι is the most common but even it does not occur in all tenses.

The present and aorist of -ἵημι are given below (all -μι conjugation forms of -ἵημι in the imperfect middle/passive and in the aorist middle are missing from the NT):

PRESENT		ACTIVE		MID./PASS.
	PRES. IND.	PRES. SUBJ.	PRES. IMP.	PRES. IND.
S. 1	-ἵημι	[-ἰῶ]		[-ἵεμαι]
2	[-ἵης]	[-ἰῇς]	[-ἵει]	[-ἵεσαι]
3	-ἵησι(ν)	[-ἰῇ]	-ἱέτω	-ἵεται
PL. 1	[-ἵεμεν]	[-ἰῶμεν]		[-ἱέμεθα]
2	-ἵετε	[-ἰῆτε]	-ἵετε	[-ἵεσθε]
3	-ἱᾶσι	-ἰῶσι(ν)	[-ἱέτωσαν]	-ἵενται
INFINITIVES	ACT. -ἱέναι		MID./PASS.	[-ἵεσθαι]
PARTICIPLES	ACT. -ἱείς (gen. -ἱέντος),		MID./PASS.	-ἱέμενος,
	[-ἱεῖσα], [-ἱέν]			-η, -ον

AORIST		ACTIVE	
	INDICATIVE	SUBJUNCTIVE	IMPERATIVE
S. 1	-ἧκα	-ὧ	
2	[-ἧκας]	[-ῇς]	-ἕς
3	-ἧκε	-ῇ	[-ἕτω]
PL. 1	-ἥκαμεν	-ὧμεν	
2	-ἥκατε	-ἧτε	-ἕτε
3	-ἧκαν	-ὧσι	[-ἕτωσαν]

INFINITIVE -εἷναι
PARTICIPLES -εἷς (gen. -ἕντος), [-εἷσα], [-ἕν]

Compounds of -ἵημι also appear in the following tenses, where they follow λύω:

- future active -ήσω, e.g. ἀφήσω (Mt 18.21)
- future passive -ἐθήσομαι, e.g. ἀφεθήσεται (Mt 12.31)
- perfect middle indicative -ἕωμαι, e.g. ἀφέωνται (Lk 5.20)
- perfect middle participle -ειμένος, e.g. παρειμένας (Hb 12.12)
- aorist passive -ἕθην, e.g. ἀνέθη (Ac 16.26), ἀφεθῇ (subj.; Mt 24.2)

Note

As we have already seen with ἵστημι (19.1/2 note 2), tenses formed from the present stem of ἵημι compounds sometimes have the regular endings of -ω verbs, e.g. ἀφίομεν (Lk 11.4 = ἀφίεμεν). The 3rd s. impf. form ἤφιεν (Mk 1.34 = ἀφίει) shows a double augment (as noted above, no forms of the -μι conjugation occur for the imperfect).

20.1/2 Uses of cases (1) – nominative and accusative

All the Greek cases, except the vocative, can be used in more than one way, and many of these we have already met. In this unit and the next all the main uses are listed, together with a description of those not previously treated. This list is undoubtedly formidable, and an attempt to absorb it in its entirety on first reading could lead to severe indigestion. A better plan is to get a general idea of the range of uses of each case (particularly those where English idiom is different), and then to refer back when confronted with particular instances. The name given to each use is traditional and in most instances is an adequate short description.

Here, as elsewhere, it is necessary to fit linguistic phenomena into pigeonholes. This can give the impression that distinctions are more clear-cut than is sometimes the case. There is, in fact, an overlap between certain uses, and we frequently meet examples that can be classified in more than one way.

The **nominative** is the case used for the subject of a finite verb (and for a noun in apposition to the subject). It can also used for the vocative, in which case it is usually preceded by the article: Ἡ παῖς, ἔγειρε (Lk 8.54) [*my*] *child, get up.*

Apart from its use as the case of the direct object of transitive verbs (2.1/3(c)) and after certain prepositions (2.1/3(f); 3.1/5(a)), the **accusative** can function in a number of ways, some of which require rephrasing to be turned into normal English.

(a) *Accusative and infinitive* (see 8.1/4(b))
(b) *Accusative to express time how long* (see 7.1/6(a))
(c) *Accusative to express spatial extent* (see 7.1/6(d))
(d) *Accusative of respect (or specification) and adverbial accusative*

> The **accusative of respect** is used with an adjective to denote a thing with respect to which that adjective is relevant. A literal translation may be obtained by employing the words *with respect to* before the noun or pronoun involved, but, to produce an idiomatic translation, it will often be necessary to recast the expression somewhat in English:
>
> > ἀνέπεσαν οὖν οἱ ἄνδρες τὸν ἀριθμὸν ὡς πεντακισχίλιοι. (Jn 6.10) *So the men, about five thousand in* (lit. *with respect to*) *number, sat down.*
>
> An **adverbial accusative** performs the same function with verbs:
>
> > καὶ τὰ νῦν παραινῶ ὑμᾶς εὐθυμεῖν. (Ac 27.22) *In the present situation* (lit. *with respect to the* [*things*] *now*) *I advise you to keep your courage up.*
> > Ἰουδαίους οὐδὲν ἠδίκησα. (Ac 25.10) *I have wronged the Jews in no way* (lit. *with respect to nothing*).

(e) *Verbs taking two accusatives - retained accusative*

> Some verbs in English can take two accusatives (*we chose him leader; they asked us our opinion*). Such verbs in Greek can be divided into two categories:

(i) Verbs of **considering, naming, choosing** etc. (factitive verbs), which take a direct object and an object complement (also called a predicate):

Ἰουδαῖόν σε ἐπονομάζω. *I call you a Jew.*

When such expressions are put into the passive, both accusatives become nominative:

σὺ Ἰουδαῖος ἐπονομάζῃ. (Ro 2.17) *You are called a Jew.*

(ii) Verbs meaning **ask for** (αἰτέω), **teach** (διδάσκω), **remind** (ἀναμιμνήσκω), **make someone/something into something** (ποιέω), **put on** and **remove clothing** (ἐνδύω, ἐκδύω), **cause to drink** (ποτίζω), and a few others, which may take two accusatives (one accusative of the person and the other of the thing involved, but NT usage is not always consistent). The construction of the corresponding verbs in English is sometimes the same:

ἐρωτήσω ὑμᾶς κἀγὼ λόγον ἕνα. (Mt 21.24) *I too shall ask you one question.*

When such expressions are put into the passive, the thing involved remains in the accusative (**retained accusative**) while the person involved is put into the nominative:

πάντες ἓν πνεῦμα ἐποτίσθημεν. (1 Cor 12.13) *We were made to drink one spirit.*

The term **retained accusative** is also used to describe accusatives used after passive verbs which, when used in the active voice, do not take two accusatives. This use is very close to the adverbial accusative (see above):

ἐξῆλθεν ὁ τεθνηκὼς δεδεμένος τοὺς πόδας καὶ τὰς χεῖρας κειρίαις. (Jn 11.44) *The dead man came out with his feet and hands wrapped in bandages* (lit. *bound with respect to feet and hands with bandages*; δεδεμένος perf. pple pass. of δέω, which does not take two accusatives when used actively).

(f) *Cognate accusative*

This describes an expression in which a noun and the verb (usually otherwise intransitive) by which it is governed are both derived from the same root (as in English *sing a song*). Often some change is needed in translation:

ἰδόντες δὲ τὸν ἀστέρα ἐχάρησαν χαρὰν μεγάλην σφόδρα. (Mt 2.10) *And on seeing the star they rejoiced with very great joy* (lit. *they rejoiced a very great joy*).

20.1/3 Uses of cases (2) – genitive

Apart from its use as the case of possession (2.1/3(d)) and after certain prepositions (2.1/3(g), 3.1/5(b)), the genitive can function in a number of ways with another noun, or a verb, adjective or even adverb. Although the genitive is often to be translated by *of*, in some of its uses a different rendering in English is required.

(a) *Possessive genitive* (see 2.1/3(d))

In this use the genitive denotes possession or some looser association: τὰ Καίσαρος (Mt 22.21) *the things of Caesar*; ἐν ἡμέραις Ἡρῴδου τοῦ βασιλέως (Mt 2.1) *in the days of King Herod*; τὰ τῆς σαρκός (Ro 8.5) *the things of the flesh*. In certain very restricted contexts a possessive genitive qualifies a missing noun which can easily be supplied; the most common are *wife, son/daughter* (cf. 5.1/3 note 2), and *place of abode*: Ἰάκωβον τὸν τοῦ Ζεβεδαίου (Mt 4.21) *James, the [son] of Zebedee*; Μαρία ἡ τοῦ Κλωπᾶ (Jn 19.25) *Mary, the [wife] of Clopas*.

(b) *Objective and subjective genitive*

An **objective** genitive stands in the same relation to a noun or adjective as an object does to a transitive verb, but a **subjective** genitive stands in the same relation to a noun as a subject does to a verb; in some cases only the context tells us which use is involved. The phrase ἡ ἀγάπη τοῦ θεοῦ can mean *God's love* (i.e. ὁ θεὸς ἀγαπᾷ *God loves*) or *love for God* (i.e. Χ τὸν θεὸν ἀγαπᾷ *X loves God*). In τὴν ἀγάπην τοῦ θεοῦ οὐκ ἔχετε ἐν ἑαυτοῖς (Jn 5.42) the genitive τοῦ θεοῦ is objective because the context tells us that the meaning is *you do not have love for God in yourselves* (i.e. you do not love God); but in ἡ ἀγάπη τοῦ θεοῦ ἐκκέχυται ἐν ταῖς καρδίαις ἡμῶν (Ro 5.5) we have a subjective genitive as the meaning is *God's love* (i.e. the love God has for us) *has been poured out in our hearts*. In some contexts this phrase and others involving similar uses are ambiguous.

(c) *Partitive genitive*

In this construction the genitive denotes the whole, and the noun or pronoun on which it depends denotes a part of that whole; it is sometimes to be translated by *of*: οἱ λοιποὶ τῶν ἀνθρώπων (Rv 9.20) *the remainder of mankind*, sometimes by another preposition: τοὺς πτωχοὺς τῶν ἁγίων τῶν ἐν Ἰερουσαλήμ (Ro 15.26) *the poor among the Christians in Jerusalem.* NT Greek also uses prepositions to express this relationship: τίνα θέλετε ἀπὸ τῶν δύο ἀπολύσω; (Mt 27.21) *whom of the two shall I free?*

Under this heading also belongs the genitive of **geographic definition**: Ταρσὸς τῆς Κιλικίας (*Ac 22.3) *Tarsus in Cilicia.*

(d) *Genitive of explanation – genitive of content*
The genitive may be used as the equivalent of a noun in apposition which gives an explanation or definition of the preceding noun. The construction in English is generally the same: σημεῖον περιτομῆς (*Ro 4.11) *a sign of circumcision*, i.e *a sign that consists in circumcision.*

The genitive of content gives the content of the noun on which it depends. It too is usually rendered into English by *of*: ἀγέλη χοίρων (Mk 5.11) *a herd of pigs.*

(e) *Genitive of quality*
A quality of a person or thing can be expressed by the genitive, which is often the equivalent of an adjective: ὀνόματα βλασφημίας (Rv 17.3) *names of blasphemy*, i.e. *blasphemous names.* Sometimes there is a possible ambiguity: ὁ κριτὴς τῆς ἀδικίας (Lk 18.6) *the judge of injustice*, i.e. *the unjust judge* (ὁ ἄδικος κριτής). However, the words τῆς ἀδικίας could be an objective genitive (above (b)), with the phrase meaning *the person who judges injustice* (which would be the natural meaning of the English *judge of injustice*); the context in Luke tells us that the former interpretation is correct and for the sake of clarity we must translate *the unjust judge.*

(f) *Genitive of price or value*
The genitive is used to express price or value with verbs denoting **buying, selling, valuing**, and the like: οὐχὶ δύο στρουθία ἀσσαρίου πωλεῖται; (Mt 10.29) *Are not two sparrows sold for an as?* This genitive is also used after ἄξιος *worthy*: ἄξιος ὁ ἐργάτης τῆς τροφῆς αὐτοῦ. (*Mt 10.10) *a workman is worthy of his sustenance.*

(g) *Genitive of separation*
Verbs denoting **separation, cessation, prevention, hindrance, difference**, etc. can be followed by the genitive:

ἐκώλυσεν αὐτοὺς τοῦ βουλήματος. (Ac 27.43) *he prevented them from [carrying out] their intention.*

ἀποστήσονταί τινες τῆς πίστεως (1 Ti 4.1) *Some will depart from the faith.*

πολλῶν στρουθίων διαφέρετε. (Lk 12.7) *You are different from (i.e. worth more than) many sparrows.*

However, NT usage is inconsistent and we often find the simple genitive replaced by ἐκ or ἀπό and the genitive: παρήγγειλεν αὐτοῖς ἀπὸ Ἱεροσολύμων μὴ χωρίζεσθαι (Ac 1.4) *he ordered them not to go away from Jerusalem.*

(h) *Genitive with adjectives*

Some adjectives are followed by the genitive (sometimes the English idiom is the same): πλήρης πνεύματος ἁγίου (Lk 4.1) *full of the Holy Ghost*; ἔνοχος θανάτου (Mt 26.66) *deserving of death* (cf. ἄξιος above (f))

(i) *Genitive with verbs* (see 15.1/1)
(j) *Genitive of time within which* (see 7.1/6(c))
(k) *Genitive absolute* (see 12.1/2(f))
(l) *Genitive of comparison* (see 17.1/4(a))

20.1/4 Oddities in verbs

(a) **-εἶμι** *come/go*

-εἶμι, like -ἵημι, is a verb that survives only in compounds. When it existed as a verb independent of prefixes, the present 1st s. form, εἶμι, was differentiated that of εἰμί *I am* only by its accent. In earlier Greek its present tense had a future reference (*I shall go*), but in the NT its basic meaning is *come/go*.

It occurs in the following compounds:

ἄπειμι *go*	ἔπειμι *be next*
εἴσειμι *enter*	σύνειμι *come together*
ἔξειμι *depart, leave*	

We find the following forms:

-ἴασιν 3rd pl. pres. ind.	-ἰέναι pres. inf.
-ἤει 3rd s. impf. (but used as aor.)	-ἰών (gen. ἰόντος),
	-ἰοῦσα, -ἰόν pres. pple.
-ἤεσαν 3rd pl. impf. (but used as aor.)	

Most examples are in Luke and Acts. We may cite: τῇ τε ἐπιούσῃ ἡμέρᾳ (Ac 7.26) *and on the next day*; εἰς τὴν συναγωγὴν τῶν Ἰουδαίων ἀπῄεσαν (Ac 17.10) *they went to the synagogue of the Jews.*

(b) *Perfects with a present meaning*

As we have seen (14.1.2), the perfect expresses a state in the present resulting from an action in the past. The perfect of some Greek verbs is best expressed in English by the present tense of verbs which in themselves indicate a state. The most common examples are:

• μέμνημαι *I remember* (lit. *I have reminded myself*) from μιμνήσκομαι *remind oneself*. The aorist passive ἐμνήσθην means *I remembered*.

• τέθνηκα *I am dead* (lit. *I have died*) from ἀποθνῄσκω *die* (the perfect is exceptional in never having the prefix ἀπο-). The perfect participle is τεθνηκώς (gen. τεθνηκότος; only the masculine occurs) and the infinitive τεθνηκέναι.

• πέποιθα (+ dat.) *I trust* is the perfect of πείθω *persuade*.

• οἶδα *I know*, which we have already met at 6.1/2, requires special treatment. It exists only in the active of the perfect, pluperfect (which has the meaning of an aorist), and one form of the future. It is conjugated as follows:

INDICATIVE		SUBJUNCTIVE	PLUPERFECT	
S.	1	οἶδα *I know*	εἰδῶ	ᾔδειν *I knew*
	2	οἶδας	εἰδῇς	ᾔδεις
	3	οἶδε(ν)	[εἰδῇ]	ᾔδει
PL.	1	οἴδαμεν	εἰδῶμεν	[ᾔδειμεν]
	2	οἴδατε	εἰδῆτε	ᾔδειτε
	3	οἴδασι(ν)	[εἰδῶσι]	ᾔδεισαν

IMPERATIVE ἴστε (2 pl. act.) *know!*
INFINITIVE εἰδέναι *to know*
PARTICIPLE εἰδώς (gen. εἰδότος), εἰδυῖα, εἰδός *knowing*
FUTURE εἰδήσουσιν *they will know* (only at Hb 8.11)

20.2 Greek reading

1 In addition to translating the following, define the use of the genitive involved:

(i) κεράμιον ὕδατος. (Mk 14.13) (ii) ἡ πίστις ὑμῶν ἡ πρὸς τὸν θεόν. (1 Thes 1.8) (iii) ἀκούσατε τὴν παραβολὴν τοῦ σπείραντος. (Mt 13.18) (iv) καὶ ἰδού τινες τῶν γραμματέων εἶπαν ἐν ἑαυτοῖς, Οὗτος βλασφημεῖ. (Mt 9.3) (v) ἐπῄνεσεν ὁ κύριος τὸν οἰκονόμον τῆς ἀδικίας. (Lk 16.8) (vi) εἰς ὅλην τὴν περίχωρον τῆς Γαλιλαίας. (Mk 1.28) (vii) πάντες γὰρ ἥμαρτον καὶ ὑστεροῦνται τῆς δόξης τοῦ θεοῦ. (Ro 3.23) (viii) ἢ οὐκ οἴδατε ὅτι τὸ σῶμα ὑμῶν ναὸς τοῦ ἐν ὑμῖν ἁγίου πνεύματός ἐστιν, οὗ ἔχετε ἀπὸ θεοῦ, καὶ οὐκ ἐστὲ ἑαυτῶν; ἠγοράσθητε γὰρ τιμῆς. (1 Cor 6.19f.)

2 ἐκαυματίσθησαν οἱ ἄνθρωποι καῦμα μέγα. (Rev 16.9)

3 διὰ τοῦτο καὶ ἡμεῖς, ἀφ᾽ ἧς ἡμέρας ἠκούσαμεν, οὐ παυόμεθα ὑπὲρ ὑμῶν προσευχόμενοι καὶ αἰτούμενοι ἵνα πληρωθῆτε τὴν ἐπίγνωσιν τοῦ θελήματος αὐτοῦ. (Col 1.9)

4 δεῦτε ὀπίσω μου, καὶ ποιήσω ὑμᾶς ἁλιεῖς ἀνθρώπων. (Mt 4.19)

5 Ἐπαινῶ δὲ ὑμᾶς ὅτι πάντα μου μέμνησθε καὶ καθὼς παρέδωκα ὑμῖν τὰς παραδόσεις κατέχετε. (1 Cor 11.2)

6 ἐγὼ πέποιθα εἰς ὑμᾶς ὅτι οὐδὲν ἄλλο φρονήσετε· ὁ δὲ ταράσσων ὑμᾶς βαστάσει τὸ κρίμα, ὅστις ἐὰν ᾖ. (*Gal 5.10)

7 ἐπῆλθαν δὲ ἀπὸ Ἀντιοχείας καὶ Ἰκονίου Ἰουδαῖοι, καὶ πείσαντες τοὺς ὄχλους καὶ λιθάσαντες τὸν Παῦλον ἔσυρον ἔξω τῆς πόλεως, νομίζοντες αὐτὸν τεθνηκέναι. (Ac 14.19)

8 ἔχω οὖν καύχησιν τὰ πρὸς τὸν θεόν. (*Ro 15.17)

9 καὶ ἐθεράπευσεν πολλοὺς κακῶς ἔχοντας ποικίλαις νόσοις, καὶ δαιμόνια πολλὰ ἐξέβαλεν, καὶ οὐκ ἤφιεν λαλεῖν τὰ δαιμόνια, ὅτι ᾔδεισαν αὐτόν. (Mk 1.34)

10 **The healing of a paralytic**

καὶ ἰδοὺ προσέφερον αὐτῷ παραλυτικὸν ἐπὶ κλίνης βεβλημένον. καὶ ἰδὼν ὁ Ἰησοῦς τὴν πίστιν αὐτῶν εἶπεν τῷ παραλυτικῷ, Θάρσει, τέκνον· ἀφίενταί σου αἱ ἁμαρτίαι. καὶ ἰδού τινες τῶν γραμματέων εἶπαν ἐν ἑαυτοῖς, Οὗτος βλασφημεῖ. καὶ εἰδὼς ὁ Ἰησοῦς τὰς ἐνθυμήσεις αὐτῶν εἶπεν, 5 Ἱνατί ἐνθυμεῖσθε πονηρὰ ἐν ταῖς καρδίαις ὑμῶν; τί γάρ ἐστιν εὐκοπώτερον, εἰπεῖν, Ἀφίενταί σου αἱ ἁμαρτίαι, ἢ εἰπεῖν, Ἔγειρε καὶ περιπάτει; ἵνα δὲ εἰδῆτε ὅτι ἐξουσίαν ἔχει ὁ υἱὸς τοῦ ἀνθρώπου ἐπὶ τῆς γῆς ἀφιέναι ἁμαρτίας – τότε λέγει τῷ παραλυτικῷ, Ἐγερθεὶς ἆρόν σου τὴν κλίνην καὶ ὕπαγε εἰς τὸν 10 οἶκόν σου. καὶ ἐγερθεὶς ἀπῆλθεν εἰς τὸν οἶκον αὐτοῦ. (Mt 9.2–7)

11 **Moses in Egypt**

ὡς δὲ ἐπληροῦτο αὐτῷ τεσσαρακονταετὴς χρόνος, ἀνέβη ἐπὶ τὴν καρδίαν αὐτοῦ ἐπισκέψασθαι τοὺς ἀδελφοὺς αὐτοῦ τοὺς υἱοὺς Ἰσραήλ. καὶ ἰδών τινα ἀδικούμενον ἠμύνατο καὶ ἐποίησεν ἐκδίκησιν τῷ καταπονουμένῳ πατάξας τὸν Αἰγύπτιον. ἐνόμιζεν δὲ συνιέναι τοὺς ἀδελφοὺς αὐτοῦ ὅτι ὁ 5 θεὸς διὰ χειρὸς αὐτοῦ δίδωσιν σωτηρίαν αὐτοῖς, οἱ δὲ οὐ συνῆκαν. τῇ τε ἐπιούσῃ ἡμέρᾳ ὤφθη αὐτοῖς μαχομένοις καὶ συνήλλασσεν αὐτοὺς εἰς εἰρήνην εἰπών, Ἄνδρες, ἀδελφοί ἐστε· ἱνατί ἀδικεῖτε ἀλλήλους; ὁ δὲ ἀδικῶν τὸν πλησίον

ἀπώσατο αὐτὸν εἰπών, Τίς σε κατέστησεν ἄρχοντα καὶ 10
δικαστὴν ἐφ᾽ ἡμῶν; μὴ ἀνελεῖν με σὺ θέλεις ὃν τρόπον ἀνεῖλες
ἐχθὲς τὸν Αἰγύπτιον; ἔφυγεν δὲ Μωϋσῆς ἐν τῷ λόγῳ τούτῳ, καὶ
ἐγένετο πάροικος ἐν γῇ Μαδιάμ, οὗ ἐγέννησεν υἱοὺς δύο. (Ac
7. 23–29)

Notes

1 (v) ἐπήνεσεν < ἐπαινέω. (viii) οὗ = ὅ the relative pronoun is
   attracted into the case of its antecedent πνεύματος.
3 οὐ παυόμεθα trans. *have not ceased* – instead of *I have
   waited for you for five hours* Greek idiom (like French)
   requires *I wait for you since five hours*; τὴν ἐπίγνωσιν
   retained accusative (20.1/2(e)(ii)).
5 ὅτι *because*; πάντα μου *everything of me*, i.e. *everything
   about me* (μου is a broad use of the possessive genitive).
6 ἐάν = ἄν (14.1/1 note 1).
8 τὰ πρὸς τὸν θεόν adverbial accusative (20.1/2(d)) because ἔχω
   καύχησιν is the equivalent of a verb (*I am proud*).
9 κακῶς ἔχοντας *suffering* (ἔχω is used with adverbs to express
   a state).
10 *l.*2 βεβλημένον (< βάλλω) lit. [*in a state of*] *having been put*,
   i.e *lying. l.*3 θάρσει 2nd s. pres. imp. act. of θαρσέω; ἀφίενται
   (and ἀφιέναι in *l.*9) < ἀφίημι. *l.*5 εἰδώς (and εἰδῆτε in *l.*8) <
   οἶδα. *l.*10 ἐγερθείς aor. pass. pple. of ἐγείρω, lit. *having risen*
   (the passive has the intransitive sense of *rise*).
11 *l.*1 ἀνέβη impers. *it came. l.*3 ἠμύνατο < ἀμύνομαι. *l.*5
   ἐνόμιζεν the impf. indicates that this was Moses's thought
   during and after his action but in English we would use a
   simple past *he thought*; συνιέναι (and συνῆκαν) < συνίημι –
   the subject of συνιέναι is ἀδελφούς. *l.*7. ἐπιούσῃ 20.1/4(a);
   ὤφθη (<ὁράω) lit. *he appeared* but as this could imply that he
   appeared out of thin air, trans. *he came upon. l.*8
   συνήλλασσεν (<συναλλάσσω) conative impf. (4.1/1 note 3)
   tried to reconcile; εἰς εἰρήνην lit. *into peace* but English
   idiom requires a fuller expression such as *and put them at
   peace. l.*10 ἀπώσατο < ἀπωθέομαι; κατέστησεν < καθίστημι.
   *l.*11 μή here introduces a hesitant question (10.1/2(a));
   ἀνελεῖν (and ἀνεῖλες) < ἀναιρέω; ὃν τρόπον lit. *in respect of
   what way* (adverbial accusative qualifying ἀνελεῖν;
   20.1/2(d)), i.e. *in the way in which. l.*12 ἐν τῷ λόγῳ τούτῳ
   because of this remark ἐν + dat. is used to express cause as
   well as instrument (11.1/2); οὗ here *where*.

21.1 Grammar

21.1/1 Uses of cases (3) – dative

The Greek dative is an amalgam of three cases (dative proper, instrumental, locative), which existed in Indo-European, the language from which Greek is derived. From an early stage Greek started to employ prepositions to reduce the multiplicity of uses to which this case could be put, and the process continues in NT Greek. Consequently, in constructions where earlier Greek had used the dative exclusively, we find that it is sometimes retained (e.g. λέγω + dat. *to say to [someone]*), sometimes replaced by a preposition (e.g. λέγω πρός + acc. with the same meaning).

(a) *Verbs governing the dative*

   (i) Verbs of **giving, saying, promising** are followed by a direct object (accusative) and an indirect object (dative 2.1/3(e)): τίς σοι ἔδωκεν τὴν ἐξουσίαν ταύτην; (Mt 21.23) *who gave you this power?*; ἐλάλησεν αὐτοῖς πολλά (Mt 13.3) *he said many things to them*; ἡ ἐπαγγελία ἣν αὐτὸς ἐπηγγείλατο ἡμῖν (1 Jn 2.25) *the promise which he promised to us.* However, with verbs of saying we also find the indirect object expressed by a preposition: εἶπεν δὲ πρὸς αὐτὸν ὁ ἄγγελος (Lk 1.13) *and the angel said to him*; εἰς πάντα τὰ ἔθνη πρῶτον δεῖ κηρυχθῆναι τὸ εὐαγγέλιον (Mk 13.10) *the gospel must first be proclaimed to all nations.* (other examples at 8.2.12).

   Conversely, we sometimes find the dative used where we would expect a preposition: ἀποστέλλουσιν αὐτῷ τοὺς μαθητὰς αὐτῶν (Mt 22.16) *they sent his disciples to him* (with a verb of motion πρός + acc. would be more in accord with Greek usage).

(ii) **Intransitive verbs** followed by the dative (see 15.1/1(b)).
(iii) **Impersonal verbs** followed by the dative:

The impersonal verb δεῖ *it is necessary*, as we have seen, is followed by an accusative and infinitive (5.1/2 note 5).

The impersonal ἔξεστι *it is permitted/allowed* takes the dative and infinitive:

σάββατόν ἐστιν, καὶ οὐκ ἔξεστίν σοι ἆραι τὸν κράβαττόν σου. (Jn 5.10) *It is the sabbath and you are not allowed* (lit. *it is not permitted to you*) *to lift up your bed.* (another example at 18.2.16).

δοκεῖ *it seems good* takes the dative and generally some change is necessary for translation into idiomatic English:

εἰπὲ οὖν ἡμῖν τί σοι δοκεῖ· ἔξεστιν δοῦναι κῆνσον Καίσαρι ἢ οὔ; (Mt 22.17) *So tell us what you think* (lit. *what seems good to you*). *Is it lawful* (lit. *is it allowed*) *to give tribute to Caesar or not?*

δοκέω is also used as a normal verb with two basic meanings of *consider* and *seem*.

Another impersonal μέλει *it is of concern* is followed by the person concerned in the dative; the object of concern is usually expressed by περί + gen.: μισθωτός ἐστιν καὶ οὐ μέλει αὐτῷ περὶ τῶν προβάτων (Jn 10.13) *he is a hired labourer and is not concerned about the sheep.* (lit. *it is of no concern to him about the sheep*).

(b) *Dative with adjectives*

The dative is used with a few adjectives whose English equivalent is usually followed by *to* or *for*. These include ἐναντίος *opposed to*; ὅμοιος *like to, resembling*; πιστός *faithful to*: ἦν γὰρ ὁ ἄνεμος ἐναντίος αὐτοῖς (Mk 6.48) *for the wind was against* (lit. *opposed to*) *them*. Often, however, these adjectives are used in contexts where a dependent dative is not required: δοῦλε ἀγαθὲ καὶ πιστέ (Mt 25.21) *O good and faithful slave!*

(c) *Dative of possession*

The dative is used with εἶναι and γίνεσθαι to denote the owner or possessor: ἃ δὲ ἡτοίμασας, τίνι ἔσται; (Lk 12.20) *and who will have the things you have made ready?*; ἐὰν γένηταί τινι ἀνθρώπῳ ἑκατὸν πρόβατα . . . (Mt 18.12) *if a man has a hundred sheep . . .*

(d) **Dative of advantage and disadvantage**

The dative can indicate the person or thing for whose advantage or disadvantage something is done:

> ἠγόρασαν τὸν Ἀγρὸν τοῦ Κεραμέως εἰς ταφὴν τοῖς ξένοις. (*Mt 27.7) *They bought the Potter's Field for a burial place for strangers.* (τοῖς ξένοις dat. of advantage *for the benefit of strangers*).
>
> μαρτυρεῖτε ἑαυτοῖς ὅτι υἱοί ἐστε τῶν φονευσάντων τοὺς προφήτας. (Mt 23.31) *You bear witness against yourselves that you are the sons of those who murdered the prophets.* (ἑαυτοῖς dat. of disadvantage *to your own disadvantage*).

(e) **Dative of reference**

Similarly, the dative may be used to denote a person or thing to whose case a statement is limited:

> λογίζεσθε ἑαυτοὺς νεκροὺς μὲν τῇ ἁμαρτίᾳ ζῶντας δὲ τῷ θεῷ. (Ro 6.11) *Consider yourselves dead as far as sin goes but living in the eyes of God.* (i.e. dead if the reference point is sin but living if the reference point is God).

The distinction between this use and the dative of respect can be tenuous.

(f) **Dative of respect**

We have already met the accusative of respect (20.1/2(d)); more frequently, the dative is used with the same meaning: οἱ καθαροὶ τῇ καρδίᾳ (Mt 5.8) *the pure in heart* (lit. *in respect of their heart*); εὗρον ἄνθρωπον Κυρηναῖον ὀνόματι Σίμωνα (Mt 27.32) *they found a man of Cyrene* (lit. *Cyrenean man*), *Simon by name.* (lit. *in respect of his name*; other examples of this use of ὀνόματι at 10.2.16, 12.2.7, 19.2.12)

(g) **Dative of instrument** (see 11.1/2)

(h) **Dative of cause**

The dative may denote cause:

> οὗτοι ἀναγκάζουσιν ὑμᾶς περιτέμνεσθαι, μόνον ἵνα τῷ σταυρῷ τοῦ Χριστοῦ μὴ διώκωνται. (Gal 6.12) *These men are forcing you to be circumcised only so that they may not be persecuted by reason of Christ's cross.*

Often the noun in the dative denotes an emotional or mental condition: οὐ διεκρίθη τῇ ἀπιστίᾳ ἀλλ᾽ ἐνεδυναμώθη τῇ πίστει (Ro 4.20) *he did not waver through disbelief but he was strengthened through faith.*

This use is sometimes replaced by a preposition: ἐθαύμαζον ἐπὶ τοῖς λόγοις τῆς χάριτος τοῖς ἐκπορευομένοις ἐκ τοῦ στόματος αὐτοῦ (Lk 4.22) *they were amazed by the words of grace coming from his mouth.*

(i) *Dative of manner and attendant circumstances*
The noun or noun phrase describing the manner in which something is done is put into the dative:

> πᾶσα γυνὴ προσευχομένη ἢ προφητεύουσσα ἀκατακαλύπτῳ τῇ κεφαλῇ ... (*1 Cor 11.5) *Every woman praying or prophesying with head uncovered ...*

But here too we find prepositions being used in place of the plain dative: εἰσελθοῦσα εὐθὺς μετὰ σπουδῆς πρὸς τὸν βασιλέα ... (Mk 6.25) *she, immediately going in haste to the king ...* (earlier Greek would have preferred σπουδῇ); οὐ μετὰ βίας (Ac 5.26) *not forcibly* (= βίᾳ in earlier Greek).

In earlier Greek the dative of attendant circumstances, which is close in meaning to the dative of manner, gave the circumstances accompanying an action but this has been superseded in NT Greek by ἐν + dat.: ἦν ἐν τῇ συναγωγῇ αὐτῶν ἄνθρωπος ἐν πνεύματι ἀκαθάρτῳ (Mk 1.23) *in their synagogue there was a man with an unclean spirit.* (ἐν πνεύματι ἀκαθάρτῳ tells us the condition or circumstances the man was in; this use of ἐν is never to be translated by *in*).

(j) *Dative of measure of difference*
This dative is used with comparatives (17.1/4(b)) and in expressions involving some sort of comparison: πόσῳ διαφέρει ἄνθρωπος προβάτου. (*Mt 12.12) *how much better is a man than a sheep!* (lit. *by how much is a man different from a sheep*; on ποσῳ in exclamations see below 21.1/3(d)).

(k) *Dative of time when* (see 7.1/6(b))

21.1/2 First and second declension contracted adjectives

A very few first and second declension adjectives ending in -εος or -οος contract the final epsilon or omicron of their stem with the initial vowel of endings. χρυσοῦς (<χρύσεος) *golden* is declined as follows:

SINGULAR	M.		F.		N.	
Nom.	χρυσοῦς	(-εος)	χρυσῆ	(-έα)	χρυσοῦν	(-εον)
Acc.	χρυσοῦν	(-εον)	χρυσῆν	(-έαν)	χρυσοῦν	(-εον)
Gen.	χρυσοῦ	(-έου)	χρυσῆς	(-έας)	χρυσοῦ	(-έου)
Dat.	χρυσῷ	(-έῳ)	χρυσῇ	(-έᾳ)	χρυσῷ	(-έῳ)
PLURAL						
Nom.	χρυσοῖ	(-εοι)	χρυσαῖ	(-εαι)	χρυσᾶ	(-εα)
Acc.	χρυσοῦς	(-έους)	χρυσᾶς	(-έας)	χρυσᾶ	(-εα)
Gen.	χρυσῶν	(-έων)	χρυσῶν	(-έων)	χρυσῶν	(-έων)
Dat.	χρυσοῖς	(-έοις)	χρυσαῖς	(-έαις)	χρυσοῖς	(-έοις)

Notes

1 Contractions in the declension of χρύσεος follow the rules given for contracted verbs (5.1/2) with the addition that in the feminine singular ε + α > η, except where ε is preceded by ρ (see below), but in the neuter plural nom. and acc. ε + α > α (the combination ε + α does not occur in any form of contracted verbs). Adjectives in -οος (as ἁπλόος *sound, healthy*, διπλόος *double, twofold*, τετραπλόος *fourfold*) follow χρυσοῦς completely, even in the feminine.

2 Adjectives ending in -ρεος contract ε + α > α in the feminine singular. From ἀργυροῦς (-εος), -ᾶ (-έα), -οῦν, (-εον) [*made of*] *silver* the feminine singular forms are: nom. ἀργυρᾶ, acc. ἀργυρᾶν, gen. ἀργυρᾶς, dat. ἀργυρᾷ.

3 νέος *new* and στερεός *hard* do not contract.

21.1/3 Further demonstrative and relative adjectives/pronouns

Greek possesses two series of adjectives, each containing a demonstrative, relative and interrogative form. One series, with the element -οσ-, refers to **quantity**, the other, with the element -οι-, refers to **quality** (all forms can also function as pronouns):

DEMONSTRATIVE	RELATIVE	INTERROGATIVE
τοσοῦτος *so much/many*	ὅσος, -η, -ον *as much/many as*	πόσος -η, -ον *how big?* pl. *how many?*
τοιοῦτος *of this sort, such*	οἷος -α, -ον *of what sort*	ποῖος -α, -ον *of what sort?*

The relative and interrogative forms are first and second declension adjectives (3.1/3). τοσοῦτος and τοιοῦτος follow οὗτος (9.1/1) but with the omission of the latter's initial tau in the oblique forms and with alternative forms for the neuter singular nominative and accusative:

S.	M.	F.	N.	M.	F.	N.
Nom.	τοσοῦτος	τοσαύτη	τοσοῦτο(ν)	τοιοῦτος	τοιαύτη	τοιοῦτο(ν)
Acc.	τοσοῦτον	τοσαύτην	τοσοῦτο(ν)	τοιοῦτον	τοιαύτην	τοιοῦτο(ν)
Gen.	τοσούτου	τοσαύτης	τοσούτου	τοιούτου	τοιαύτης	τοιούτου
Dat.	τοσούτῳ	τοσαύτῃ	τοσούτῳ	τοιούτῳ	τοιαύτῃ	τοιούτῳ

PL.						
Nom.	τοσοῦτοι	τοσαῦται	τοσαῦτα	τοιοῦτοι	τοιαῦται	τοιαῦτα
Acc.	τοσούτους	τοσαύτας	τοσαῦτα	τοιούτους	τοιαύτας	τοιαῦτα
Gen.	τοσούτων	τοσούτων	τοσούτων	τοιούτων	τοιούτων	τοιούτων
Dat.	τοσούτοις	τοσαύταις	τοσούτοις	τοιούτοις	τοιαύταις	τοιούτοις

The uses to which these can be put are:

(a) τοσοῦτος and τοιοῦτος can be used as simple attributive adjectives:

> παρ' οὐδενὶ τοσαύτην πίστιν ἐν τῷ Ἰσραὴλ εὗρον. (Mt 8.10) *I found such great* (lit. *so much*) *faith in no-one in Israel.*
>
> ἐδόξασαν τὸν θεὸν τὸν δόντα ἐξουσίαν τοιαύτην τοῖς ἀνθρώποις. (Mt 9.8) *They praised God for giving such power to men.*

In this use τοιοῦτος sometimes has the definite article: ἐν τῶν τοιούτων παιδίων (Mk 9.37) *one of such children.*

(b) τοσοῦτος/ὅσος and τοιοῦτος/οἷος are used in sentences where ὅσος and οἷος introduce a comparison. As English does not have relatives of this sort some change is needed in translation:

> οἷοί ἐσμεν τῷ λόγῳ δι' ἐπιστολῶν ἀπόντες, τοιοῦτοι καὶ παρόντες τῷ ἔργῳ. (2 Cor 10.11) lit. *of what sort we are in word through letters* [*when we are*] *absent, of this sort* [*are we*] *also in deed* [*when we are*] *present* i.e. *when I am present my actions show me just the same as my words do through letters when I am absent* (Paul is using the writer's plural).

The relatives alone, without the corresponding demonstratives, may be used in this way:

τὰ ἱμάτια αὐτοῦ ἐγένετο στίλβοντα λευκὰ λίαν οἷα γναφεὺς ἐπὶ τῆς γῆς οὐ δύναται οὕτως λευκᾶναι. (Mk 9.3) lit. *his clothes became shining [and] exceedingly white, of what sort a fuller on earth cannot so whiten* i.e. *of a sort that a fuller on earth cannot match.*

(c) πάντες ὅσοι is used in the sense *all who* (lit. *all as many as*) instead of the expected πάντες οἵ:

πάντες ὅσοι ἦλθον πρὸ ἐμοῦ κλέπται εἰσὶν καὶ λῃσταί. (Jn 10.8) *All who came before me are thieves and robbers.*

Very often ὅσος is used by itself in this sense:

ὅσοι ἥψαντο διεσώθησαν. (Mt 14.36) *All who touched were cured.*

(d) The interrogatives (πόσος, ποῖος) are used in direct or indirect questions:

πόσους ἄρτους ἔχετε; (Mt 15.34) *How many loaves of bread do you have?*

θεωρεῖς, ἀδελφέ, πόσαι μυριάδες εἰσὶν ἐν τοῖς Ἰουδαίοις τῶν πεπιστευκότων. (Ac 21.20) *You see, my brother, how many myriads of those who have faith there are among the Jews.*

τοῦτο δὲ ἔλεγεν σημαίνων ποίῳ θανάτῳ ἤμελλεν ἀποθνήσκειν. (Jn 12.33) *And he said this, indicating by what sort of death he was going to die.*

However, ποῖος is often used as a simple interrogative with the same sense as τίς:

οὐκ οἴδατε ποίᾳ ἡμέρᾳ ὁ κύριος ὑμῶν ἔρχεται. (Mt 24.42) *You do not know on what day your lord is coming.*

διὰ ποῖον αὐτῶν ἔργον ἐμὲ λιθάζετε; (Jn 10.32) *For which of these works* (lit. *for which work of these*) *are you stoning me?*

πόσος and ποῖος are also used to introduce exclamations (note that these are not indicated by an exclamation mark in Greek):

εἰ οὖν τὸ φῶς τὸ ἐν σοὶ σκότος ἐστίν, τὸ σκότος πόσον. (Mt 6.23) *So if the light in you is darkness, how great is the darkness!*

21.2 Greek reading

1 In addition to translating the following, define the use of the dative involved:

(i) ἐὰν οὖν μὴ εἰδῶ τὴν δύναμιν τῆς φωνῆς, ἔσομαι τῷ λαλοῦντι βάρβαρος. (1 Cor 14.11) (ii) ὁ παθὼν σαρκί. (1 Pt 4.1) (iii) ἀναπληροῦται αὐτοῖς ἡ προφητεία Ἡσαΐου. (Mt 13.14) (iv) εἰδότες τὰ αὐτὰ τῶν παθημάτων τῇ ἐν τῷ κόσμῳ ὑμῶν ἀδελφότητι ἐπιτελεῖσθαι. (1 Pt 5.9) (v) ὑμῖν γάρ ἐστιν ἡ ἐπαγγελία καὶ τοῖς τέκνοις ὑμῶν. (Ac 2.39) (vi) τῇ ἀπιστίᾳ ἐξεκλάσθησαν, σὺ δὲ τῇ πίστει ἕστηκας. (Ro 11.20) (vii) ὁ ἀρχιερεὺς εἰσέρχεται εἰς τὰ ἅγια κατ᾽ ἐνιαυτὸν ἐν αἵματι ἀλλοτρίῳ. (Hb 9.25) (viii) παντὶ τρόπῳ, εἴτε προφάσει εἴτε ἀληθείᾳ, Χριστὸς καταγγέλλεται. (Phil 1.18) (ix) τὸν δὲ ἀσθενοῦντα τῇ πίστει προσλαμβάνεσθε. (Ro 14.1) (x) φανερὸν ἐγένετο τῷ Φαραὼ τὸ γένος τοῦ Ἰωσήφ. (Ac 7.13)

2 καὶ προσῆλθον αὐτῷ Φαρισαῖοι πειράζοντες αὐτὸν καὶ λέγοντες, Εἰ ἔξεστιν ἀνθρώπῳ ἀπολῦσαι τὴν γυναῖκα αὐτοῦ κατὰ πᾶσαν αἰτίαν; (Mt 19.3)

3 καὶ αὐτὸς ἦν ἐν τῇ πρύμνῃ ἐπὶ τὸ προσκεφάλαιον καθεύδων· καὶ ἐγείρουσιν αὐτὸν καὶ λέγουσιν αὐτῷ, Διδάσκαλε, οὐ μέλει σοι ὅτι ἀπολλύμεθα; (Mk 4.38)

4 διελθόντες δὲ πρώτην φυλακὴν καὶ δευτέραν ἦλθαν ἐπὶ τὴν πύλην τὴν σιδηρᾶν τὴν φέρουσαν εἰς τὴν πόλιν. (Ac 12.10)

5 Συνηγμένων δὲ τῶν Φαρισαίων ἐπηρώτησεν αὐτοὺς ὁ Ἰησοῦς λέγων, Τί ὑμῖν δοκεῖ περὶ τοῦ Χριστοῦ; τίνος υἱός ἐστιν; λέγουσιν αὐτῷ, Τοῦ Δαυίδ. (Mt 22.41f.)

6 ἐὰν οὖν ᾖ ὁ ὀφθαλμός σου ἁπλοῦς, ὅλον τὸ σῶμά σου φωτεινὸν ἔσται. (Mt 6.22)

7 οἱ γὰρ τοιοῦτοι τῷ κυρίῳ ἡμῶν Χριστῷ οὐ δουλεύουσιν ἀλλὰ τῇ ἑαυτῶν κοιλίᾳ, καὶ διὰ τῆς χρηστολογίας καὶ εὐλογίας ἐξαπατῶσιν τὰς καρδίας τῶν ἀκάκων. (Ro 16.18)

8 ὁ πρῶτος ἄνθρωπος ἐκ γῆς χοϊκός, ὁ δεύτερος ἄνθρωπος ἐξ οὐρανοῦ. οἷος ὁ χοϊκός, τοιοῦτοι καὶ οἱ χοϊκοί, καὶ οἷος ὁ ἐπουράνιος, τοιοῦτοι καὶ οἱ ἐπουράνιοι. (1 Cor 15.47f.)

9 Ὁμοία ἐστὶν ἡ βασιλεία τῶν οὐρανῶν θησαυρῷ κεκρυμμένῳ ἐν ἀγρῷ, ὃν εὑρὼν ἄνθρωπος ἔκρυψεν, καὶ ἀπὸ τῆς χαρᾶς αὐτοῦ ὑπάγει καὶ πωλεῖ πάντα ὅσα ἔχει καὶ ἀγοράζει τὸν ἀγρὸν ἐκεῖνον. (*Mt 13.44)

10 εἰ οὖν ὑμεῖς πονηροὶ ὄντες οἴδατε δόματα ἀγαθὰ διδόναι τοῖς τέκνοις ὑμῶν, πόσῳ μᾶλλον ὁ πατὴρ ὑμῶν ὁ ἐν τοῖς οὐρανοῖς δώσει ἀγαθὰ τοῖς αἰτοῦσιν αὐτόν. (Mt 7.11)

11 ὅσοι γὰρ πνεύματι θεοῦ ἄγονται, οὗτοι υἱοὶ θεοῦ εἰσιν. (Ro 8.14)

12 **The prodigal son**

ἄνθρωπός τις εἶχεν δύο υἱούς. καὶ εἶπεν ὁ νεώτερος αὐτῶν τῷ
πατρί, Πάτερ, δός μοι τὸ ἐπιβάλλον μέρος τῆς οὐσίας. ὁ δὲ
διεῖλεν αὐτοῖς τὸν βίον. καὶ μετ᾽ οὐ πολλὰς ἡμέρας συναγαγὼν
πάντα ὁ νεώτερος υἱὸς ἀπεδήμησεν εἰς χώραν μακράν, καὶ
ἐκεῖ διεσκόρπισεν τὴν οὐσίαν αὐτοῦ ζῶν ἀσώτως. 5
δαπανήσαντος δὲ αὐτοῦ πάντα ἐγένετο λιμὸς ἰσχυρὰ κατὰ τὴν
χώραν ἐκείνην, καὶ αὐτὸς ἤρξατο ὑστερεῖσθαι. καὶ πορευθεὶς
ἐκολλήθη ἑνὶ τῶν πολιτῶν τῆς χώρας ἐκείνης, καὶ ἔπεμψεν
αὐτὸν εἰς τοὺς ἀγροὺς αὐτοῦ βόσκειν χοίρους· καὶ ἐπεθύμει
χορτασθῆναι ἐκ τῶν κερατίων ὧν ἤσθιον οἱ χοῖροι, καὶ οὐδεὶς 10
ἐδίδου αὐτῷ. εἰς ἑαυτὸν δὲ ἐλθὼν ἔφη, Πόσοι μίσθιοι τοῦ
πατρός μου περισσεύονται ἄρτων, ἐγὼ δὲ λιμῷ ὧδε ἀπόλλυμαι.
ἀναστὰς πορεύσομαι πρὸς τὸν πατέρα μου καὶ ἐρῶ αὐτῷ,
Πάτερ, ἥμαρτον εἰς τὸν οὐρανὸν καὶ ἐνώπιόν σου, οὐκέτι εἰμὶ
ἄξιος κληθῆναι υἱός σου. ποίησόν με ὡς ἕνα τῶν μισθίων σου. 15
καὶ ἀναστὰς ἦλθεν πρὸς τὸν πατέρα ἑαυτοῦ. ἔτι δὲ αὐτοῦ
μακρὰν ἀπέχοντος εἶδεν αὐτὸν ὁ πατὴρ αὐτοῦ καὶ
ἐσπλαγχνίσθη καὶ δραμὼν ἐπέπεσεν ἐπὶ τὸν τράχηλον αὐτοῦ
καὶ κατεφίλησεν αὐτόν. εἶπεν δὲ ὁ υἱὸς αὐτῷ, Πάτερ, ἥμαρτον
εἰς τὸν οὐρανὸν καὶ ἐνώπιόν σου, οὐκέτι εἰμὶ ἄξιος κληθῆναι 20
υἱός σου. εἶπεν δὲ ὁ πατὴρ πρὸς τοὺς δούλους αὐτοῦ, Ταχὺ
ἐξενέγκατε στολὴν τὴν πρώτην καὶ ἐνδύσατε αὐτόν, καὶ δότε
δακτύλιον εἰς τὴν χεῖρα αὐτοῦ καὶ ὑποδήματα εἰς τοὺς πόδας,
καὶ φέρετε τὸν μόσχον τὸν σιτευτόν, θύσατε καὶ φαγόντες
εὐφρανθῶμεν, ὅτι οὗτος ὁ υἱός μου νεκρὸς ἦν καὶ ἀνέζησεν, ἦν 25
ἀπολωλὼς καὶ εὑρέθη. καὶ ἤρξαντο εὐφραίνεσθαι. (Lk 15.
11–24)

Notes

1 (iv) τὰ αὐτὰ τῶν παθημάτων lit. *the same [types] of sufferings*,
trans. *the same sufferings*. (vi) ἐξεκλάσθησαν < ἐκκλάω; The
sentence is from a passage where disbelievers are compared
to branches broken off trees. (vii) The blood is that of a
sacrificed animal. (ix) προσλαμβάνεσθε imp.

2 εἰ here introduces a direct question (10.1/2(b) note).

3 τὸ προσκεφάλαιον trans. *a pillow* (the article implies that it
was normal to have a pillow in the stern).

5 συνηγμένων perf. mid. pple. of συνάγω; ἐπηρώτησεν <
ἐπερωτάω.

9 The man who discovers the treasure hides it in the same
field, which he then proceeds to buy in order to legitimize his
find.

10 It is better to take this sentence as an exclamation than as a

question; translate the pples. ὄντες and αἰτοῦσιν by adjectival clauses; οἴδατε ... διδόναι *know [how] to give.*

11 ὅσοι is used here in the sense *all who* (21.1/3(c)) but our translation must also take account of οὗτοι.

12 *l.*2 δός < δίδωμι. *l.*3 διεῖλεν < διαιρέω; αὐτοῖς dat. of advantage *for them,* trans. *between them* (the two brothers); τὸν βίον here *his possessions;* συναγαγών < συνάγω. *l.*6 δαπανήσαντος ... αὐτοῦ gen. absol. (12.1/2(f)). *l.*10 τῶν κερατίων ὧν the relative (ὧν) has been attracted into the case of the antecedent (9.1/2 note 3); carob pods resemble large French beans and their interior lining is by no means inedible. *l.*13 ἀναστάς < ἀνίστημι. *l.*15 κληθῆναι aor. pass. inf. of καλέω. *ll.*16f. ἑαυτοῦ refers to the subject as prescribed by traditional Greek grammar, but in *l.*5 we have [τὴν οὐσίαν] αὐτοῦ where strict grammar requires ἑαυτοῦ; αὐτοῦ μακρὰν ἀπέχοντος (gen. absol.) lit. *him being distant far off* (μακράν is here an adverb); this gen. absol. is not independent of the clause in which it stands because its subject and αὐτόν are the same person (the prodigal son) – such violations of the rule given at 12.1/2(f) sometimes occur. *l.*18 δραμών < τρέχω; ἐπέπεσεν < ἐπιπίπτω. *l.*22 ἐξενέγκατε < ἐκφέρω; τὴν πρώτην (lit. *the first*) here obviously means *the best;* δότε < δίδωμι. *ll.*24f. φαγόντες < ἐσθίω; εὐφρανθῶμεν aor. subj. of εὐφραίνομαι; ἦν ἀπολωλώς is a composite tense (12.1/2(g)) and the equivalent of a pluperfect.

21.3 Excursus

The text of the New Testament

During the Renaissance the study of ancient texts developed rapidly. Scholars searched everywhere for manuscripts of works in Greek and Latin. (The term *manuscript* here means a book written out by hand and at this time it was used only of codices which had survived from late antiquity and the Middle Ages. Later, its meaning was extended to include the ancient papyrus rolls discovered in Egypt since they too were handwritten.)

As we have seen, it was impossible for two manuscripts to be identical. When scholars began to compare one with another they realized that any attempt to recover the author's original words must involve collecting variants in places where the surviving manuscripts differed. Only then could a judgement be reached on which variant, if any at all, represented what the author wrote.

As printing grew more sophisticated it became possible for scholarly editions of works in Greek and Latin to be equipped with a set of notes at the bottom of each page which gave the different readings (i.e manuscript variants) for the section of the text presented above. This is called the textual (or critical) apparatus, and it has long been a standard feature of editions of ancient works.

The recommended edition of the NT (see **Suggestions for further study**) goes further still in the information given for each page of text; its arrangement is as follows:

- Immediately under the text and separated from it by a broad horizontal line is the textual apparatus.
- Below this, and separated from the textual apparatus by a short horizontal line, is the punctuation apparatus, which shows the differences in punctuation between the Greek text given above and various other editions of the NT as well as translations.
- Below this again is the list of references for quotations from elsewhere in the Bible and from other sources; references for allusions and parallel passages are also given.

When you begin to read the NT for yourself it is not necessary to bother about this information, although it can often be interesting to chase up quotations and parallel passages. If you take your studies further you will probably become interested in the textual apparatus as the meaning of a particular passage can vary significantly according to the reading adopted.

On completing the present book you will want to read further in the NT. If you do not feel confident enough to make an immediate start on a full text, the following contains selected passages with vocabularies on facing pages:

J.A.C.T., *New Testament Greek – A Reader,* Cambridge University Press 2001 (a volume in Joint Association of Classical Teachers' Greek course)

When you do start on the NT itself, the recommended edition is:

The Greek New Testament, edited by K. Aland and others, United Bible Societies, Stuttgart, 1966+

Parallel to this edition is:

Newman, Barclay M. Jr., *A Concise Greek–English Dictionary of the New Testament*, United Bible Societies, Stuttgart, 1971.

This excellent small dictionary can be obtained separately or bound together with the Greek text. For practical purposes the separate version of each is to be preferred. You should start with the gospels; it is easy to pick out favourite passages in the recommended edition as English headings are provided for each section. If you have made yourself familiar with the contents of the present book you will have no trouble with points of grammar.

The standard dictionary for NT Greek is:

Danker, F. W. (editor), *A Greek–English Lexicon of the New Testament and Other Early Christian Literature,* University of Chicago Press, 3rd edition 2000 (originally published in German by W. Bauer and translated into English by W. F. Arndt and F. W. Ginrich).

This very large work is obviously not for beginners working their way through the NT, but you may find it profitable to consult a library copy in order to get the full range of meanings of particular words.

An interesting book on the text of the whole of the Greek Bible is:

Kenyon, F. G., *The Text of the Greek Bible*, third edition revised and augmented by A. W. Adams, Duckworth, 1975.

Appendix 1

Conjugation of λύω *loosen*

ACTIVE

		Pres. Indicative	Impf.	Future	Aorist	Perfect	Pluperfect
s.	1	λύ-ω *I loosen,* etc.	ἔλυ-ον *I was* *loosening,* etc.	λύσ-ω *I will* *loosen*	ἔλυσ-α *I loosened*	λέλυκ-α *I have* *loosened*	(ἐ)λελύκ-ει *I had* *loosened*
	2	λύ-εις	ἔλυ-ες	λύσ-εις	ἔλυσ-ας	λέλυκ-ας	(ἐ)λελύκ-εις
	3	λύ-ει	ἔλυ-ε(ν)	λύσ-ει	ἔλυσ-ε(ν)	λέλυκ-ε(ν)	(ἐ)λελύκ-ει
pl.	1	λύ-ομεν	ἐλύ-ομεν	λύσ-ομεν	ἐλύσ-αμεν	λελύκ-αμεν	(ἐ)λελύκ-ειμεν
	2	λύ-ετε	ἐλύ-ετε	λύσ-ετε	ἐλύσ-ατε	λελύκ-ατε	(ἐ)λελύκ-ειτε
	3	λύ-ουσι(ν)	ἔλυ-ον	λύσ-ουσι(ν)	ἔλυσ-αν	λελύκ-ασι(ν)	(ἐ)λελύκ-εισαν

Subjunctive

s.	1	λύ-ω		λύσ-ω	λελυκὼς ὦ
	2	λύ-ῃς		λύσ-ῃς	λελυκὼς ᾖς
	3	λύ-ῃ		λύσ-ῃ	λελυκὼς ᾖ
pl.	1	λύ-ωμεν		λύσ-ωμεν	λελυκότες ὦμεν
	2	λύ-ητε		λύσ-ητε	λελυκότες ἦτε
	3	λύ-ωσι(ν)		λύσ-ωσι(ν)	λελυκότες ὦσι(ν)

Imperative

s.	2	λῦ-ε	λῦσ-ον
	3	λυ-έτω	λυσ-άτω
pl.	2	λύ-ετε	λύσ-ατε
	3	λυ-έτωσαν	λυσ-άτωσων

Infinitive

λύ-ειν	λῦσ-αι	λελυκ-έναι

Participle

λύ-ων	λύσ-ας	λελυκ-ώς
λύ-ουσα	λύσ-ασα	λελυκ-υῖα
λῦ-ον	λῦσ-αν	λελυκ-ός

MIDDLE

	Pres.	Impf.	Future	Aorist	Perfect	Pluperfect
Indicative						
s. 1	λύ-ομαι	ἐλυ-όμην	λύσ-ομαι	ἐλυσ-άμην	λέλυ-μαι	(ἐ)λελύ-μην
2	λύ-ῃ	ἐλύ-ου	λύσ-ῃ	ἐλύσ-ω	λέλυ-σαι	(ἐ)λέλυ-σο
3	λύ-εται	ἐλύ-ετο	λύσ-εται	ἐλύσ-ατο	λέλυ-ται	(ἐ)λέλυ-το
pl. 1	λυ-όμεθα	ἐλυ-όμεθα	λυσ-όμεθα	ἐλυσ-άμεθα	λελύ-μεθα	(ἐ)λελύ-μεθα
2	λύ-εσθε	ἐλύ-εσθε	λύσ-εσθε	ἐλύσ-ασθε	λέλυ-σθε	(ἐ)λέλυ-σθε
3	λύ-ονται	ἐλύ-οντο	λύσ-ονται	ἐλύσ-αντο	λέλυ-νται	(ἐ)λέλυ-ντο

	Pres.		Aorist	Perfect
Subjunctive				
s. 1	λύ-ωμαι		λύσ-ωμαι	λελυμένος ὦ
2	λύ-ῃ		λύσ-ῃ	λελυμένος ᾖς
3	λύ-ηται		λύσ-ηται	λελυμένος ᾖ
pl. 1	λυ-ώμεθα		λυσ-ώμεθα	λελυμένοι ὦμεν
2	λύ-ησθε		λύσ-ησθε	λελυμένοι ἦτε
3	λύ-ωνται		λύσ-ωνται	λελυμένοι ὦσι(ν)

	Pres.		Aorist	Perfect
Imperative				
s. 2	λύ-ου		λῦσ-αι	λέλυ-σο
3	λυ-έσθω		λυσ-άσθω	λελύ-σθω
pl. 2	λύ-εσθε		λύσ-ασθε	λέλυ-σθε
3	λυ-έσθωσαν		λυσ-άσθωσαν	λελύ-σθωσαν

	Pres.		Aorist	Perfect
Infinitive				
	λύ-εσθαι		λύσ-ασθαι	λελύ-σθαι

Participle

λυ-όμενος,	λυσ-όμενος, λυσ-άμενος, λελυ-μένος,		
-ομένη,	-ομένη,	-αμένη,	-μένη,
-όμενον	-όμενον	-άμενον	-μένον

Note

In all forms of the perfect which are made up of a perfect participle and εἰμί the participle must agree with the subject of the verb in number and gender.

PASSIVE

The forms for the present, imperfect, perfect and pluperfect are the same as for the middle.

	Future	Aorist		
	Indicative	Indicative	Subjunctive	Imperative
s. 1	λυθήσ-ομαι	ἐλύθη-ν	λυθ-ῶ	
2	λυθήσ-ῃ (-ει)	ἐλύθη-ς	λυθ-ῇς	λύθη-τι
3	λυθήσ-εται	ἐλύθη	λυθ-ῇ	λυθή-τω
pl. 1	λυθησ-όμεθα	ἐλύθη-μεν	λυθ-ῶμεν	
2	λυθήσ-εσθε	ἐλύθη-τε	λυθ-ῆτε	λύθη-τε
3	λυθήσ-ονται	ἐλύθη-σαν	λυθ-ῶσι(ν)	λυθήτωσαν

Infinitive *lacking*   λυθῆ-ναι

Participle [λυθήσ-ομενος][1]   λυθ-είς, λυθ-εῖσα, λυθ-έν

---

[1] The future passive particle occurs only once in the NT (λαληθησόμενος Hb 3.5).

Appendix 2

Conjugation of contracted verbs

τιμάω *honour*

Rules for contracting -αω verbs:

- α + an e-sound (ε, η) > α: ἐτίμα (ἐτίμα-ε)
- α + an o-sound (o, ου, ω) > ω: τιμῶσι (τιμά–ουσι); τιμῶμεν (τιμά–ομεν)
- α + an ι-diphthong (ει, ῃ, οι) obeys the above rules but retains the iota as a subscript in the contracted form: τιμᾷ (τιμά–ει)

	ACTIVE		MIDDLE/PASSIVE	
	Present	Imperfect	Present	Imperfect
	Indicative			
s. 1	τιμῶ	ἐτίμων	τιμῶμαι	ἐτιμώμην
2	τιμᾷς	ἐτίμας	τιμᾶσαι[1]	ἐτιμῶ
3	τιμᾷ	ἐτίμα	τιμᾶται	ἐτιμᾶτο
pl. 1	τιμῶμεν	ἐτιμῶμεν	τιμώμεθα	ἐτιμώμεθα
2	τιμᾶτε	ἐτιμᾶτε	τιμᾶσθε	ἐτιμᾶσθε
3	τιμῶσι(ν)	ἐτίμων	τιμῶνται	ἐτιμῶντο
	Subjunctive			
s. 1	τιμῶ		τιμῶμαι	
2	τιμᾷς		τιμᾷ	
3	τιμᾷ		τιμᾶται	
pl. 1	τιμῶμεν		τιμώμεθα	
2	τιμᾶτε		τιμᾶσθε	
3	τιμῶσι(ν)		τιμῶνται	
	Imperative			
s. 2	τίμα		τιμῶ	
3	τιμάτω		τιμάσθω	
pl. 2	τιμᾶτε		τιμᾶσθε	
3	τιμάτωσαν		τιμάσθωσαν	
	Infinitive			
	τιμᾶν		τιμᾶσθαι	
	Participle			
	τιμῶν, τιμῶσα, τιμῶν		τιμώμεν-ος, -η, -ον	

Other tenses of τιμάω:

	ACTIVE	MIDDLE	PASSIVE
Future	τιμήσω	τιμήσομαι	τιμηθήσομαι
Aorist	ἐτίμησα	ἐτιμησάμην	ἐτιμήθην
Perfect	τετίμηκα	τετίμημαι	τετίμημαι

---

[1] τιμᾶσαι (2nd s. pres. mid./pass.) is irregular as we would expect τιμᾷ (<τιμά+η); the other contracted verbs do not show this peculiarity.

ποιέω *make, do*

Rules for contracting -εω verbs:

- ε + ε > ει: ποιεῖτε (ποιέ-ετε)
- ε + ο > ου: ἐποίουν (ἐποίε-ον)
- ε disappears before a long vowel or diphthong: ποιῶ (ποιέ-ω); ποιοῦσι (ποιέ-ουσι).

		ACTIVE		**MIDDLE/PASSIVE**	
		Present	**Imperfect**	**Present**	**Imperfect**
	Indicative				
s.	1	ποιῶ	ἐποίουν	ποιοῦμαι	ἐποιούμην
	2	ποιεῖς	ἐποίεις	ποιῇ	ἐποιοῦ
	3	ποιεῖ	ἐποίει	ποιεῖται	ἐποιεῖτο
pl.	1	ποιοῦμεν	ἐποιοῦμεν	ποιούμεθα	ἐποιούμεθα
	2	ποιεῖτε	ἐποιεῖτε	ποιεῖσθε	ἐποιεῖσθε
	3	ποιοῦσι(ν)	ἐποίουν	ποιοῦνται	ἐποιοῦντο

		Subjunctive		
s.	1	ποιῶ		ποιῶμαι
	2	ποιῇς		ποιῇ
	3	ποιῇ		ποιῆται
pl.	1	ποιῶμεν		ποιώμεθα
	2	ποιῆτε		ποιῆσθε
	3	ποιῶσι(ν)		ποιῶνται

		Imperative		
s.	2	ποίει		ποιοῦ
	3	ποιείτω		ποιείσθω
pl.	2	ποιεῖτε		ποιεῖσθε
	3	ποιείτωσαν		ποιείσθωσαν

Infinitive

ποιεῖν   ποιεῖσθαι

Participle

ποιῶν, ποιοῦσα, ποιοῦν   ποιούμεν-ος, -η, -ον

Other tenses of ποιέω:

	ACTIVE	**MIDDLE**	**PASSIVE**
Future	ποιήσω	ποιήσομαι	ποιηθήσομαι
Aorist	ἐποίησα	ἐποιησάμην	ἐποιήθην
Perfect	πεποίηκα	πεποίημαι	πεποίημαι

δηλόω *make clear, show*

Rules for contracting -οω verbs:
- ο + ε/ο/ου > ου: ἐδήλου (ἐδήλο-ε); δηλοῦμεν (δηλό-ομεν); δηλοῦσι (δηλό-ουσι)
- ο + η/ω > ω: δηλῶ (δηλό-ω)
- ο + an ι-diphthong (ει, οι, ῃ) > οι: δηλοῖ (δηλό-ει)

	ACTIVE		MIDDLE/PASSIVE	
	Present	**Imperfect**	**Present**	**Imperfect**
Indicative				
s. 1	δηλῶ	ἐδήλουν	δηλοῦμαι	ἐδηλούμην
2	δηλοῖς	ἐδήλους	δηλοῖ	ἐδηλοῦ
3	δηλοῖ	ἐδήλου	δηλοῦται	ἐδηλοῦτο
pl. 1	δηλοῦμεν	ἐδηλοῦμεν	δηλούμεθα	ἐδηλούμεθα
2	δηλοῦτε	ἐδηλοῦτε	δηλοῦσθε	ἐδηλοῦσθε
3	δηλοῦσι(ν)	ἐδήλουν	δηλοῦνται	ἐδηλοῦντο

Subjunctive		
s. 1	δηλῶ	δηλῶμαι
2	δηλοῖς	δηλοῖ
3	δηλοῖ	δηλῶται
pl. 1	δηλῶμεν	δηλώμεθα
2	δηλῶτε	δηλῶσθε
3	δηλῶσι(ν)	δηλῶνται

Imperative		
s. 2	δήλου	δηλοῦ
3	δηλούτω	δηλούσθω
pl. 2	δηλοῦτε	δηλοῦσθε
3	δηλούτωσαν	δηλούσθωσαν

Infinitive		
	δηλοῦν	δηλοῦσθαι

Participle		
	δηλῶν, δηλοῦσα, δηλοῦν	δηλούμεν-ος, -η, -ον

Other tenses of δηλόω:

	ACTIVE	MIDDLE	PASSIVE
Future	δηλώσω	δηλώσομαι	δηλωθήσομαι
Aorist	ἐδήλωσα	ἐδηλωσάμην	ἐδηλώθην
Perfect	δεδήλωκα	δεδήλωμαι	δεδήλωμαι

Appendix 3

Conjugation of εἰμί be

	Present ind.	Present subj.	Present imp.	Future	Imperfect
s. 1	εἰμί	ὦ		ἔσομαι	ἤμην
2	εἶ	ᾖς	ἴσθι	ἔσῃ	ἦς or ἦσθα
3	ἐστί(ν)	ᾖ	ἔστω or ἤτω	ἔσται	ἦν
pl. 1	ἐσμέν	ὦμεν		ἐσόμεθα	ἦμεν or ἤμεθα
2	ἐστέ	ἦτε	[ἔστε]	ἔσεσθε	ἦτε
3	εἰσί(ν)	ὦσι(ν)	ἔστωσαν	ἔσονται	ἦσαν

Present optative εἴη (3 s., the only occurring form)
Present infinitive εἶναι   Present participle ὤν, οὖσα, ὄν
Future infinitive ἔσεσθαι   Future participle ἐσόμενος, -η, -ον

Appendix 4

Root aorist (11.1/1)

-ἔβην (-βαίνω go) and ἔγνων (γινώσκω ascertain, know) are conjugated:

		Ind.	Subj.	Imp.	
s.	1	-ἔβην	[-βῶ]		
	2	[-ἔβης]	[-βῇς]	-βηθι	Infinitive -βῆναι
	3	-ἔβη	-βῇ	[-βήτω]	
pl.	1	-ἔβημεν	[-βῶμεν]		
	2	[-ἔβητε]	[-βῆτε]	-βῆτε	Participle -βάς, -βᾶσα, -βάν
	3	-ἔβησαν	[-βῶσι]	[-βάτωσαν]	

s.	1	ἔγνων	γνῶ		
	2	ἔγνως	γνῷς	γνῶθι	Infinitive γνῶναι
	3	ἔγνω	γνῷ	γνώτω	
pl.	1	[ἔγνωμεν]	[γνῶμεν]		
	2	[ἔγνωτε]	γνῶτε	γνῶτε	Participle γνούς,
	3	ἔγνωσαν	γνῶσι(ν)	[γνώτωσαν]	γνοῦσα, γνόν

Note: Alternative forms for the 2nd s. aor. imp. of -βαίνω are ἀνάβα (<ἀνάβαινω) and μετάβα (<μετάβαινω).

Appendix 5

Conjugation of δίδωμι *give*, τίθημι *put, place*, ἵστημι *make stand*

Forms which occur only in compounds are not indicated. For full details of which tenses of ἵστημι are transitive and which are intransitive see 19.1/2.

		δίδωμι	τίθημι	ἵστημι
			ACTIVE	
Present indicative				
s.	*1*	δίδωμι	τίθημι	ἵστημι
	2	δίδως	[τίθης]	[ἵστης]
	3	δίδωσι(ν)	τίθησι(ν)	ἵστησι(ν)
pl.	*1*	[δίδομεν]	τίθεμεν	[ἵσταμεν]
	2	[δίδοτε]	τίθετε	[ἵστατε]
	3	διδόασι(ν)	τιθέασι(ν)	[ἱστᾶσι]
Present subjunctive				
s.	*1*	[διδῶ]	[τιθῶ]	[ἱστῶ]
	2	[διδῷς]	[τιθῇς]	[ἱστῇς]
	3	διδῷ	[τιθῇ]	[ἱστῇ]
pl.	*1*	διδῶμεν	[τιθῶμεν]	[ἱστῶμεν]
	2	διδῶτε	[τιθῆτε]	ἱστῆτε
	3	διδῶσι(ν)	τιθῶσι(ν)	ἱστῶσι(ν)
Present imperative				
s.	*2*	δίδου	τίθει	[ἵστη]
	3	διδότω	τιθέτω	[ἱστάτω]
pl.	*2*	δίδοτε	[τίθετε]	[ἵστατε]
	3	[διδότωσαν]	[τιθέτωσαν]	[ἱστάτωσαν]
Present infinitive				
		διδόναι	τιθέναι	ἱστάναι
Present participle				
		διδούς	τιθείς	ἱστάς
		διδοῦσα	τιθεῖσα	ἱστᾶσα
		διδόν	τιθέν	ἱστάν
Imperfect indicative				
s.	*1*	[ἐδίδουν]	[ἐτίθην]	[ἵστην]
	2	[ἐδίδους]	[ἐτίθεις]	[ἵστης]
	3	ἐδίδου	ἐτίθει	[ἵστη]
pl.	*1*	[ἐδίδομεν]	[ἐτίθεμεν]	[ἵσταμεν]
	2	[ἐδίδοτε]	[ἐτίθετε]	[ἵστατε]
	3	[ἐδίδοσαν]	ἐτίθεσαν	[ἵστασαν]
Future indicative				
s.	*1*	δώσω etc.	θήσω etc.	στήσω etc.

Aorist indicative

				Transitive	*Intransitive*
s.	1	ἔδωκα	ἔθηκα	[ἔστησα]	ἔστην
	2	ἔδωκας	ἔθηκας	[ἔστησας]	[ἔστης]
	3	ἔδωκε(ν)	ἔθηκε(ν)	ἔστησε(ν)	ἔστη
pl.	1	ἐδώκαμεν	[ἐθήκαμεν]	[ἐστήσαμεν]	ἔστημεν
	2	ἐδώκατε	[ἐθήκατε]	ἐστήσατε	ἔστητε
	3	ἔδωκαν	ἔθηκαν	ἔστησαν	ἔστησαν

An alternative form for ἐδώκαμεν occurs at Lk 1.2 (παρέδοσαν).

Aorist subjunctive

s.	1	δῶ	θῶ	στήσω	[στῶ]
	2	δῷς	θῇς	στήσῃς	[στῇς]
	3	δῷ	θῇ	στήσῃ	στῇ
pl.	1	δῶμεν	θῶμεν	στήσωμεν	[στῶμεν]
	2	δῶτε	[θῆτε]	στήσητε	στῆτε
	3	δῶσι(ν)	θῶσι(ν)	[στήσωσι]	[στῶσι(ν)]

Aorist imperative

s.	2	δός	θές	[στῆσον]	στῆθι
	3	δότω	θέτω	[στησάτω]	στήτω
pl.	2	δότε	θέτε	στήσατε	στῆτε
	3	[δότωσαν]	[θέτωσαν]	[στησάτωσαν]	[στήτωσαν]

Aorist infinitive

	δοῦναι	θεῖναι	στῆσαι	στῆναι

Aorist participle

	δούς	θείς	στήσας	στάς
	δοῦσα	θεῖσα	[στήσασα]	στᾶσα
	δόν	θέν	στῆσαν	στάν

Perfect and pluperfect

The perfect and pluperfect active of δίδωμι, τίθημι are formed regularly from the stems δεδωκ-, τεθεικ-.

The perfect and pluperfect active of ἵστημι (which are intransitive – see 19.1/2) are conjugated as follows:

		Perfect Indicative	Pluperfect
s.	1	ἕστηκα	[εἱστήκειν]
	2	ἕστηκας	[εἱστήκεῖς]
	3	ἕστηκε(ν)	εἱστήκει
pl.	1	ἑστήκαμεν	[εἱστήκειμεν]
	2	ἑστήκατε	[εἱστήκειτε]
	3	ἑστήκασι(ν)	εἱστήκεισαν

Infinitive ἑστάναι
Participle ἑστώς, ἑστῶσα, ἑστός or ἑστηκώς, [ἑστηκυῖα], ἑστηκός

MIDDLE

The following middle forms occur in the NT:

Present indicative: δίδοται, διδόμεθα; τίθεμαι, τίθεσθε; ἵσταται, ἵστανται
Present subjunctive: none
Present imperative: τιθέσθων; ἵστασο

Present infinitive: δίδοσθαι; τίθεσθαι; ἵστασθαι
Present participle: διδόμεν-ος, -η, -ον; τιθέμεν-ος, -η, -ον, ἱστάμεν-ος, -η, -ον
Imperfect indicative: ἐτίθετο, ἐτίθεντο; ἵστατο
Future indicative: formed regularly with the stems δωσ-, θησ-, στησ-.
Aorist indicative: ἔδοτο, ἔδοσθε, ἔδοντο; ἐθέμην, ἔθου, ἔθετο, ἔθεσθε, ἔθεντο
Aorist subjunctive: θώμεθα
Aorist imperative: θέσθε
Aorist infinitive: θέσθαι
Aorist participle: θέμεν-ος, -η, -ον

The **perfect** and **pluperfect** middle of δίδωμι and τίθημι are formed regularly from the stems δεδο- and τεθει- (e.g. δέδοται, τέθειται etc.) but on the perfect passive of the latter see 18.1/2 note 4. The perfect middle/passive forms of ἵστημι do not occur.

PASSIVE

The present, imperfect and perfect passive of these verbs have the same forms as the middle. The future and aorist passive, which occur a number of times in the NT, follow λύω (see **Appendix 1**):

Future Indicative: δοθήσομαι; τεθήσομαι; σταθήσομαι
Aorist indicative: ἐδόθην; ἐτέθην; ἐστάθην

Appendix 6

Numerals (7.1/5)

Numerals within the range given below which do not occur in the NT are either included in square brackets or omitted. The elements of compound numerals such as *twenty-five* are written separately, e.g. εἴκοσι πέντε.

Cardinals

For the declension of εἷς, δύο, τρεῖς, τέσσαρες see 7.1/5(a). διακόσιοι, τριακόσιοι etc. follow the plural of καλός (3.1/3).

1	εἷς	20	εἴκοσι(ν)
2	δύο	30	τριάκοντα
3	τρεῖς	40	τεσσαράκοντα
4	τέσσαρες	50	πεντήκοντα
5	πέντε	60	ἑξήκοντα
6	ἕξ	70	ἑβδομήκοντα
7	ἑπτά	80	ὀγδοήκοντα
8	ὀκτώ	90	ἐνενήκοντα
9	ἐννέα	100	ἑκατόν
10	δέκα	200	διακόσιοι
11	ἕνδεκα	300	τριακόσιοι
12	δώδεκα	400	τετρακόσιοι
13	[δεκατρεῖς]	500	πεντακόσιοι
14	δεκατέσσαρες	600	ἑξακόσιοι
15	δεκαπέντε	700	[ἑπτακόσιοι]
16	[δεκαέξ]	800	[ὀκτακόσιοι]
17	[δεκαεπτά]	900	[ἐνακόσιοι]
18	δεκαοκτώ	1,000	χίλιοι
19	[δεκαεννέα (?)]	10,000	μύριοι

The cardinals *two thousand, three thousand* etc. are compounds of the appropriate numeral adverbs and χίλιοι, e.g. δισχίλιοι, τρισχίλιοι etc. (for alternative forms and for μυριάς *(group of) ten thousand* see 7.1/5(a)).

Ordinals	Adverbs
πρῶτος *first*	ἅπαξ *once*
δεύτερος *second*	δίς *twice*
τρίτος *third*	τρίς *three times*
τέταρτος	τετράκις
πέμπτος	πεντάκις
ἕκτος	
ἕβδομος	ἑπτάκις
ὄγδοος	
ἔνατος	
δέκατος	

The ordinals are normal first and second declension adjectives (3.1/3), except that the feminine of ὄγδοος is ὀγδόη (not -α).

Appendix 7

Accentuation

As noted on p. 4 the pitch accent of the classical language had changed to one of stress by the time that the NT was written. However, in written Greek the old system of accentuation was retained, and this can only be understood with reference to the earlier manner of pronunciation.

Accent in classical Greek was one of **pitch**, not of stress as in English. An English-speaker, when told that ἄνθρωπος *human being* is accented on its first syllable, would naturally pronounce that syllable with a heavier emphasis. A Greek of the classical period, however, instead of emphasizing the α, would have pronounced it at a higher pitch and so given the word what we should consider a somewhat sing-song effect. We do, of course, use pitch in spoken English, but in a totally different way. In the question *you're going to Egypt?* the last word has a rising pitch, but in the statement *you're going to Egypt* it has a falling pitch.

Classical Greek has three accents:

   ´ **acute**, indicating rising pitch
   ` **grave**, indicating falling pitch
   ^ **circumflex**, indicating a combined rising and falling pitch (the sign, originally ^, is a combination of an acute and a grave). Because the time taken by this operation was necessarily longer than that indicated by an acute or a grave,

it can occur only with long vowels and diphthongs, and only on these do we find a circumflex.

These accents continued to be used in written Greek in the first century AD although by then they all indicated the same thing as far as the spoken language was concerned, viz where a word was stressed. This stress accent (as distinct from the earlier pitch accent) appears to have been much the same as the stress accent we have in English.

The basic features of Greek accentuation are:

- nearly every word has an accent, which can be on the final syllable (ποταμός *river*), or the second syllable from the end (ἵππος *horse*), or on the third syllable from the end (ἄνεμος *wind*). In forms of verbs the position of the accent is nearly always determined by the length of the final syllable; with other words whose form can change the accent is generally fixed.
- an acute or grave accent can stand on a diphthong or long or short vowel, but a circumflex only on a long vowel or diphthong.
- an acute can stand on the end syllable of a word (μαθητής *disciple*), on the second from the end (εὐλογία *flattery*), or on the third from the end (ἐπίγνωσις *knowledge*).
- a grave can stand only on a final syllable, where it automatically replaces an acute when another word follows (ὁ ὑποκριτὴς ἐκεῖνος *that hypocrite*). A final acute is retained, however, before a mark of punctuation (ὑποκριτά, ἔκβαλε πρῶτον τὴν δοκὸν ἐκ τοῦ ὀφθαλμοῦ σου (Lk 6.42) *hypocrite, first cast out the beam from your eye*) or when a word so accented is quoted.
- a circumflex can stand on a final syllable (τῶν ποταμῶν *of the rivers*) and, within certain limitations, on the second from the end (δῶρον *gift*).
- a group of monosyllabic and disyllabic words called enclitics can affect the accentuation of the previous word and, under certain circumstances, give it a second accent, e.g. ἄνθρωπός τις *a certain man*. They may, as in this example, have no accent themselves.

The following terms are used to describe words according to their accent:

Oxytone – a word with an acute on its final syllable, e.g. ποταμός.

Paroxytone – a word with an acute on its penultimate (i.e. last syllable but one), e.g. λόγος.

Proparoxytone – a word with an acute on its last syllable but two, e.g. ἄνθρωπος.

Perispomenon – a word with a circumflex on its final syllable, e.g. ποταμοῦ.

Properispomenon – a word with a circumflex on its penultimate, e.g. δῶρον.

Barytone – a word with a grave on its final syllable, e.g. ποταμὸν εἶδον *I saw a river.*

These are the only places in which each accent can occur (we cannot, for example, have an acute on the last syllable but three, or a circumflex on the last syllable but two).

For purposes of accentuation a syllable is long if it contains a long vowel or diphthong, and short if it contains a short vowel, except that **all endings in –αι and –οι** (apart from those of the optative, which is rare in the NT) **are counted as short.**

The length of the final syllable of a word and, to a lesser extent, of its penultimate is important for accentuation because:

- a word can only be proparoxytone if its final syllable is short, e.g. ἄνθρωπος.
- a word can only be properispomenon if its final syllable is short; as a circumflex must in any case stand on a long vowel or diphthong, a word so accented must end in – ˘ , or be a disyllable consisting of – ˘ (– denotes a long syllable and ˘ a short syllable), e.g. πολῖται, γλῶσσα. Conversely, if such a word is accented on its penultimate, the accent must be a circumflex, and this is why we get the change of accent from πολίτης to πολῖται (the reverse in γλῶσσα/γλώσσης).

For purposes of accentuation words are divided into five categories:

(a) *Nouns, adjectives and pronouns*

There are no overall rules about the position of the accent in the nominative singular of nouns or in the nominative masculine singular of adjectives and pronouns, and we must simply learn that ποταμός is oxytone but λόγος is paroxytone. There are some rules for certain small groups which can be learnt by observation, e.g. nouns in -ευς are always oxytone (as βασιλεύς); the accent of comparative adjectives is always as far from the end of the word as possible (σοφός but σοφώτερος).

Once, however, we know where a noun, adjective or pronoun is accented in the nominative (masculine) singular it is easy to deduce how its other forms will be accented because the accent stays on the same syllable as far as this is allowed by the rules given above for proparoxytones and perispomenons. In λόγος, for example, the accent remains unchanged (λόγε, λόγον, λόγου, λόγῳ, λόγοι, λόγους, λόγων, λόγοις), but in ἄνθρωπος the accent must become paroxytone when the ending is long: ἄνθρωπε, ἄνθρωπον, ἀνθρώπου, ἀνθρώπῳ, ἄνθρωποι, ἀνθρώπους, ἀνθρώπων, ἀνθρώποις (ἄνθρωποι because -οι does **not** count as long – see above).

In many third declension nouns the genitive singular is a syllable longer than the nominative singular, e.g. σῶμα (properispomenon, not paroxytone, because it is a disyllable of the form - ˘ ; see above): σώματος, σώματι, σώματα (the accent must change to an acute because the added short syllable makes all three forms proparoxytone), σωμάτων (the added syllable is long and therefore the accent must become paroxytone), σώμασι.

We must, however, note:

(i) Where a first or second declension word has an acute on its final syllable in the nominative singular, this becomes a circumflex in the genitive and dative (in both singular and plural, cf. 2.1/2 note 6), e.g. from ποταμός we have ποταμέ, ποταμόν, ποταμοῦ, ποταμῷ, ποταμοί, ποταμούς, ποταμῶν, ποταμοῖς. For an example of an adjective so accented see καλός (3.1/3).

(ii) All first declension nouns are perispomenon in the genitive plural (3.1/1 note 4), e.g. χωρῶν (< χώρα), νεανιῶν (< νεανίας). This does **not** apply to the gen. f. pl. of adjectives when this form would not otherwise differ from the masculine, e.g. μεγάλων is both gen. m. pl. and gen. f. pl. of μέγας. Where, however, the masculine and feminine forms differ, the rule holds, e.g. ταχύς, gen. m. pl. ταχέων, gen. f. pl. ταχειῶν (10.1/3(a)).

(iii) In the third declension, monosyllabic nouns are accented on the final syllable of the genitive and dative, in both singular and plural, e.g. σάρξ, σάρκα, σαρκός, σαρκί, σάρκες, σάρκας, σαρκῶν, σαρξί. An exception is the gen. pl. of παῖς (παίδων). Of polysyllabic nouns γυνή also follows this pattern (γυνή, γύναι (5.1/1 note 1), γυναῖκα, γυναικός, γυναικί, γυναῖκες, γυναῖκας, γυναικῶν, γυναιξί), and ἀνήρ, μήτηρ and πατήρ follow it in the gen. s. and dat. s. (6.1/1(b)). For the accentuation of πᾶς see 10.1/3(b).

(iv) The accent in the genitive (s. and pl.) of third declension nouns with stems in ι (8.1/5) is quite irregular : πόλεως, πόλεων (< πόλις).

(v) Contracted adjectives (21.1/2) follow the same rules as for contracted verbs (below (b)(i)).

(b) *Verbs*

With verbs the accent falls as far from the end of a word as possible (here too final -αι and -οι count as short[1]). In forms such as ακουετε, ακουουσι, κελευεσθαι, εκελευσαν the final short syllable shows that they must be proparoxytone: ἀκούετε, ἀκούουσι, κελεύεσθαι, ἐκέλευσαν; in disyllabic forms such as ἐλε and λυε the accent goes back to the penultimate but becomes properispomenon in λυε because of its long υ: ἕλε but λῦε (the fact that the υ of λύω is long can only be learnt by consulting dictionaries of the classical language). In κελευω, ἐλυθην, where the final syllable is long, the accent is paroxytone: κελεύω, ἐλύθην.

We must, however, note:

(i) In the forms of contracted verbs where contraction occurs, the accent follows that of the original uncontracted form according to the following rules:

• If the accent is on neither of the syllables to be contracted it remains unchanged, e.g. ἐποίει (< ἐποίε-ε).

• If the accent is on the first of the two syllables to be contracted it becomes a circumflex on the contracted syllable, e.g. ποιεῖ (< ποιέ-ει); τιμῶμεν (< τιμά-ομεν).

• If the accent is on the second of the two syllables to be contracted it stays as an acute on the contracted syllable, e.g. ἐτιμώμεθα (< ἐτιμα-όμεθα).

(ii) Certain forms of uncontracted -ω verbs and of -μι verbs are in origin contracted and for this reason the first syllable of their endings is always accented. These are:

• the aorist subjunctive passive of all verbs, e.g. λυθῶ, λυθῇς, λυθῇ, λυθῶμεν, λυθῆτε, λυθῶσι.

• the subjunctive of both present (act., mid./pass.) and aorist (act., mid.) of δίδωμι, τίθημι and their compounds, and also -ἵημι, e.g. διδῶσι, τιθῶσι, -ἰῶσι, δῶ, θῶ.

---

[1] Except in the optative endings, as noted above.

(iii) In all strong aorists the first syllable of the ending always carries the accent in the active participle (e.g. λαβών, λαβοῦσα, λαβόν), the active and middle infinitives (λαβεῖν, λαβέσθαι), and the 2nd s. imperative middle (λαβοῦ).

(iv) The first syllable of the ending also carries the accent in participles in -εις, -ους and -ως, e.g. λυθείς, λυθεῖσα, λυθέν; τιθείς, τιθεῖσα, τιθέν; διδούς, διδοῦσα, διδόν; λελυκώς, λελυκυῖα, λελυκός.

(v) In certain participles and infinitives the accent is always either paroxytone or properispomenon, depending on whether it stands on a short or long syllable. These are:

  • infinitives in -σαι (weak aorist active), e.g. λῦσαι, νικῆσαι, αἰνέσαι.
  • infinitives in -ναι (perf. act., aor. pass., root aor. act., and certain active infinitives of -μι verbs), e.g. λελυκέναι, λυθῆναι, γνῶναι, διδόναι.
  • the infinitive and participle of the perf. mid./pass., e.g. νενικῆσθαι, λελυμένος.

(vi) In compound verbs the accent cannot fall further back than the augment, e.g. ἀπῆγον (< ἀπάγω), παρέσχον (< παρέχω), or the last vowel of a prepositional prefix, e.g. παράδος (< παραδίδωμι).

(c) *Adverbs, conjunctions, interjections, particles, prepositions*
These have only one form and therefore their accent does not vary, e.g. σοφῶς *wisely,* ὅταν *whenever,* εὖ *well,* except for oxytones becoming barytones (as ἤ). A few words which would otherwise be included here are enclitic or atonic and so come under categories (d) or (e).

(d) *Enclitics*
An enclitic combines with the preceding word for pronunciation, and can affect its accentuation. When quoted by themselves (in paradigms, dictionaries, etc.) monosyllabic enclitics are written with no accent (e.g. γε), disyllabics as oxytone (e.g. ποτέ), except for τινῶν.

The total number of enclitics is small and consists of:

  (i) The present indicative of εἰμί *I am* (with the exception of the 2nd s. εἶ), and the present indicative forms of φημί that occur in the NT (φημί, φησί, φασί, see 7.1/3)
  (ii) The unemphatic forms of the personal pronouns, viz με, μου, μοι; σε, σου, σοι.

(iii) All forms of the indefinite τις (10.1/1).
(iv) The indefinite adverbs ποτέ, που, πως.
(v) The particles γε, τε.

The rules for enclitics are:

(vi) An enclitic has no accent when it follows a word accented on its final syllable, e.g. ποταμῶν τινων. If this word has a final acute (i.e. is oxytone), this accent is kept, e.g. ποταμός τις.

(vii) If the preceding word is paroxytone a monosyllabic enclitic has no accent but a disyllabic enclitic keeps the accent on its final syllable, e.g. ἵππος τις, ἵπποι τινές.

(viii) If the preceding word is proparoxytone or properispomenon, an enclitic, whether monosyllabic or disyllabic, has the effect of adding an acute to the final syllable, e.g. ἄνθρωπός τις, ἄνθρωποί τινες, δῶρόν τι, δῶρά τινα.

(ix) In groups of two or more enclitics all are accented except the last, e.g. σύνδουλός σού εἰμι (Rv 19.10) *I am your fellow slave.*

(x) ἐστί is accented on its first syllable (ἔστι) when:

- it denotes existence, e.g. τὸ μνῆμα αὐτοῦ ἔστιν ἐν ἡμῖν (Ac 2.29) *his tomb exists among us* .
- it follows ἀλλά (ἀλλ᾽ ἔστι Jn 7.28) εἰ (1 Cor 15.44), καί (Mt 21.42), οὐκ (Mt 10.24), τοῦτο (τοῦτ᾽ ἔστι Mt 27.46).
- it begins a clause (Jn 5.2).

(e) **Atonics**

Atonics are monosyllables which have no accent unless followed by an enclitic. These are:

- the nom. m. and f. (s. and pl.) of the article (ὁ, ἡ, οἱ, αἱ), εἰ, οὐ, ὡς
- the prepositions εἰς, ἐκ, ἐν.

Of these, however, οὐ is accented if it occurs as last word of a clause (Jn 1.21).

Notes

1 A few words which we would expect to be properispomenon are in fact paroxytone: οὔτε, μήτε, ὥστε and relatives whose second element is -τις (as ἥτις).

2 τίς and τί never become barytone (10.1/1).

Explanations and more literal interpretations are given in round brackets. Some (but not all) words which have no specific equivalent in the Greek original but which must be supplied in English are enclosed in square brackets. Translations are generally as literal as possible and should not be taken as reflecting the style of the original. Discrepancies with modern translations may be due to slight changes made in sentences whose reference is marked with an asterisk.

1.2

(1) Asia, Bethlehem, Beelzebub, Jerusalem, John, Job, Jonah, Joseph, Caesar, Luke, Matthew, Mary, Mark, Paul, Peter, Pilate, Rome, Simon. (*The reason for discrepancies between the Greek and English version of proper names will be found at 4.1/3*)
(2) *The meaning of the Greek words, which will be found in the vocabulary, is sometimes not the same as that of the English derivatives.*
Angel, anathema, analysis, antithesis, aroma, asbestos, automaton, bathos, genesis, diagnosis, dogma, drama, zone, ethos, echo, theatre, thermos, idea, camel, kinesis, climax, cosmos, crisis, criterion, colon, mania, metre, metropolis, miasma, orphan, pathos, paralytic, scene, stigma, trauma, hubris, fantasy, character, chasm, psyche.

2.2

(1) The time of fruits is approaching. (2) He is not casting out evil spirits. (3) He dispatches a slave to the tenant farmers.

(4) Why do you eat and drink with sinners? (5) You see the crowd. (6) Master, you speak and teach rightly and you do not show partiality. (7) I see people. (8) We find nothing wrong in the man. (9) They will send gifts. (10) Then they will fast. (11) The servant takes [his] pay and gathers up [the] harvest. (12) How does God judge the world? (13) You raise the dead, you cleanse lepers, you cast out evil spirits. (14) You know [how] to judge correctly the face of the heavens. (15) You hear and see. (16) You have an evil spirit. (17) The dead shall hear. (18) Jesus began to preach and speak. (19) Then just [men] (*or* the just) shall shine forth like the sun. (20) We are announcing Jesus Christ [as] the Lord.

Analysis of sentences 4 and 11 (according to the steps given in 2.2).

4. διὰ τί μετὰ τῶν ἁμαρτωλῶν ἐσθίετε καὶ πίνετε;

(a) διὰ τί the vocabulary tells us that this is a phrase meaning *why?* (the question mark indicates that it introduces a question). μετά preposition governing the genitive with the meaning *in the company of, with*. τῶν genitive plural (all genders) of the definite article. ἁμαρτωλῶν genitive plural of ἁμαρτωλός *sinner*. ἐσθίετε 2nd plural present indicative active of ἐσθίω *eat*. καί conjunction meaning *and*. πίνετε 2nd plural present indicative active of πίνω *drink*.

(b) There are two finite verbs, ἐσθίετε and πίνετε; therefore we have two clauses.

(c) The question mark (;) at the end of the sentence shows that we have a question as we had surmised from the introductory phrase διὰ τί *why?* There is no internal punctuation but there is a conjunction καί; as we have two finite verbs this conjunction must be used to join the clauses in which they stand. The clauses are διὰ τί μετὰ τῶν ἁμαρτωλῶν ἐσθίετε and πίνετε.

(d) As ἁμαρτωλῶν is genitive plural the preceding article (τῶν) which is in the same case must go with it; in another context these words could mean *of the sinners* but as they come after a preposition which governs the genitive (μετά) the three words must be taken together and have the meaning *with* (or *in the company of*) *the sinners*. Neither clause has a noun in the nominative and so we deduce that the subject of the verbs (*you*) is indicated by their endings.

(e) The conjunction καί *and* joins clauses of equal value; both verbs are 2nd plural and can be translated *you eat* and *you drink*; as there is no indication that the speaker is addressing a separate audience with each verb ἐσθίετε καὶ πίνετε must mean *you eat and drink.* The sentence, therefore, can be expressed in English *why do you eat and drink with the sinners?* (*in the company of* would be equally acceptable). Taken in this way the expression *the sinners* would indicate particular individuals and the Greek can be so interpreted. However, the overall context in Luke shows that we must understand τῶν ἁμαρτωλῶν as a general class (2.1/2 note 1(ii)) and our final translation should be *why do you eat and drink with sinners?*

11. ὁ δοῦλος μισθὸν λαμβάνει καὶ συνάγει καρπόν.

(a) ὁ nominative singular of the definite article. δοῦλος nominative singular of δοῦλος *slave/servant*. μισθόν accusative singular of μισθός *pay, salary*. λαμβάνει 3rd singular present indicative active of λαμβάνω *take*. καί conjunction meaning *and*. συνάγει 3rd singular present indicative active of συνάγω *gather up*. καρπόν accusative singular of καρπός *harvest*.

(b) There are two finite verbs, λαμβάνει and συνάγει; therefore we have two clauses.

(c) As in 4 above the conjunction καί is used to join the clauses. The first is ὁ δοῦλος μισθὸν λαμβάνει and the second συνάγει καρπόν.

(d) In the first clause ὁ δοῦλος is nominative and therefore must be the subject of λαμβάνει (we note that the verb agrees with ὁ δοῦλος in the way prescribed at the beginning of 2.1/4). μισθόν is accusative and as it is not preceded by a preposition it must be the object of λαμβάνει. Similarly καρπόν is the object of συνάγει (an accusative must be governed by either a verb or a preposition).

(e) Here too the conjunction καί *and* joins clauses of equal value. As the second verb is, like the first, 3rd singular but does not have a subject expressed, it must also be governed by ὁ δοῦλος, and we can translate *the servant takes pay and gathers up harvest* (as the worker is being paid the translation *servant* is the appropriate one; slaves did not normally receive any emolument). English idiom requires *his pay* (where ownership is obvious Greek does not use words such as *his, her, their*) and *the harvest* (when used without an adjective the word *harvest* is normally preceded by the definite article *the*; this does not happen with the Greek καρπός). Our final translation will be *the servant takes [his] pay and gathers up the harvest* (in the translation given in the key, words such as *his* are bracketed to indicate they have no equivalent in the Greek original; this is not done with the definite article).

3.2

(1) After much time. Concerning the kingdom of God. About [the] third hour. An eye for an eye. Through the gate. For the sake of many. In the island. Into the synagogues. (2) They do not put new wine into old wine-skins. (3) Moses writes of the righteousness from [observing] the law. (4) You are already pure on account of the word. (5) The friend of the bridegroom rejoices greatly on account of the bridegroom's voice. (6) Why does the master eat with tax-collectors and sinners? (7) We are not under [the] law. (8) He will convict the world with regard to sin and righteousness. (9) A pupil is not above the master. (10) You are the Anointed One, the Son of God. (11) Why are you timid, [you] of little faith? (12) Master, what [is] the great commandment in the law? (13) He praises God with a loud (*lit.* great) voice. (14) He is truly the prophet. (15) If you judge the law, you are not one who observes it but one who judges it (*lit.* not an observer of the law but a judge [of the law]). (16) The sabbath was made on account of man and not man on account of the sabbath. (17) The man believing in the Son has eternal life. (18) The reward [is] large in heaven. (19) Many will come from east and west. (20) The sea no longer exists (*lit.* is no longer).

Analysis of sentence 15 (according to the steps given in 2.2).

εἰ νόμον κρίνεις, οὐκ εἶ ποιητὴς νόμου ἀλλὰ κριτής.

(a) εἰ *if* conjunction. νόμον accusative singular of νόμος *law*. κρίνεις 2nd singular present indicative active of κρίνω *judge*. οὐκ *not* adverb (οὐ takes this form when used before a word beginning with a vowel which has a smooth breathing – 2.1/6(a)(i)). εἶ 2nd singular present indicative of εἰμί *be*. ποιητής nominative singular of ποιητής *doer, one who complies with*; νόμου genitive singular of νόμος *law*. ἀλλά *but* conjunction. κριτής nominative singular of κριτής *judge*.
(b) There are two finite verbs κρίνεις and εἶ; therefore, we have two clauses.
(c) The comma after κρίνεις suggests that the first three words form a clause; ἀλλά can introduce a clause but this cannot be the case here as it is not followed by a finite verb.
(d) In the first clause the fact that νόμον is not preceded by a preposition indicates that it is the object of κρίνεις. In the second clause the negative stands in front of the finite verb and therefore negates it (2.1/6(a)(i)). The verb εἰμί is followed by the nominative (3.1/6), and so the two nouns in the nominative

(ποιητής, κριτής) must combine with οὐκ εἶ to mean *you are not a ποιητής/κριτής*. As a genitive goes with a noun it stands next to, νόμου should be taken with ποιητής. As ἀλλά is not followed by a finite verb it must link two elements in the second clause and these can only be ποιητὴς νόμου and κριτής.

(e) From our analysis the first clause means *if you judge the law*, and the second *you are not a doer of the law but a judge*. When we put these together *if you judge the law, you are not a doer of the law but a judge* we have an intelligible sentence but the alternative meaning of ποιητής (*one who complies with*) gives a more idiomatic English translation, *if you judge the law, you are not one who complies with the law but a judge* (obviously, with *judge* we must mentally supply *of the law*). More idiomatic still would be: *if you judge the law you are not one who observes it but one who judges it*.

4.2

(1) In the beginning was the Word and the Word was with God and the Word was God. (2) Death, where is your sting? (3) They said to him, 'So why do you baptize if you are not the Anointed One nor Elijah nor the prophet?' (4) Similarly, just as happened in the days of Lot, they used to eat [and] drink. (5) They immediately speak to him about her. (6) And an angel of the Lord opened the doors of the prison. (7) Lord, it is good [for] us to be here. (8) You Pharisees now clean the outside of your cup but your inside [*lit*. the inside of you] is full of greed and wickedness. (9) You are no longer a slave but a son; and if [you are] a son, [you are] also an heir through [the agency of] God. (10) Therefore, brothers, we are not children of a slave girl but of the free woman. (11) Was I able to hinder God? (12) In this way we too, when we were children, were enslaved to (*lit*. under) the elemental spirits of the world. (13) For he began to teach his disciples (*lit*. the disciples of him) and speak to them. (14) And there were at Antioch prophets and teachers, both Barnabas and Symeon. (15) I have the power to release you. (16) I am the God of Abraham and the God of Isaac and the God of Jacob. (17) John kept saying to him, 'You are not allowed (*lit*. it is not permitted to you) to have her.' (18) There! Now you heard the blasphemy. (19) Behold! I send you out as sheep in the midst of wolves. (20) Both the winds and the sea obey him.

Analysis of sentence 9 (according to the steps given in 2.2).

οὐκέτι εἶ δοῦλος ἀλλὰ υἱός· εἰ δὲ υἱός, καὶ κληρονόμος διὰ θεοῦ.

(a) οὐκέτι *no longer* adverb. εἶ 2nd singular present indicative of εἰμί *be*. δοῦλος nominative singular of δοῦλος *slave/servant*. ἀλλά *but* conjunction. υἱός nominative singular of υἱός *son*. εἰ *if* conjunction. δέ *and/but* connecting particle which comes as second word in the second of the two elements it joins (4.1/4). καί is normally a conjunction meaning *and* but at 4.1/4 we learn that it can also be an adverb with the meaning *also, even, actually*. κληρονόμος nominative singular of κληρονόμος *heir*. διά preposition governing either the accusative or genitive (3.1/5) – as the noun following is in the genitive its meanings here is *through, by means of*; θεοῦ genitive of θεός *God*.

(b) and (c) We notice that there is only one finite verb (εἶ). However, the colon after υἱός suggests that we could have a second clause beginning with εἰ (and this seems confirmed both by the conjunction εἰ itself and the connecting particle δέ) – could some verb be understood? At 3.1/6 we learn that εἰμί is often omitted in clauses of the type *X is Y*. Further analysis is required but we also note that εἰ *if* cannot introduce a main clause (we cannot say as an independent statement *if you are a son*; see also the entry under *clause* in the **Glossary of grammatical and other terms**) and that the comma after υἱός could be dividing two clauses (if this is correct we shall be obliged to supply the relevant part of εἰμί twice).

(d) The words of the first clause fall easily into place *you are no longer a slave/servant but a son*. The following three words can be literally translated *and/but if a son*; if a part of εἰμί is omitted, it seems likely to be εἶ, which we have already seen in the first clause, and we would then have *and/but if [you are] a son*. καὶ κληρονόμος διὰ θεοῦ as a main clause would certainly make sense if we take καί as an adverb and supply another εἶ – the meaning would be *[you are] also/even/actually an heir through/by means of God*.

(e) When we combine our tentative interpretations we have *you are no longer a slave/servant but a son; and/but if [you are] a son; [you are] also/even/actually an heir through/by means of God*. Taking account of the overall meaning we can refine this to *you are no longer a slave but a son; and if [you are] a son; [you are] also an heir through God*. If this sentence were completely by itself, δοῦλος could mean either *slave* or *servant*; but in its context in Galatians the former is more appropriate. δέ could be rendered *and* or *but*, the latter being slightly more emphatic. We must, however, interpret καί as *also* because the person addressed is an *heir* as well as a *son*. For διά *through* seems preferable to *by means of* as the latter would normally be used of an instrument (*through* here means *through the agency of*).

5.2

(1) (i) To the other side. (ii) And on Jesus returning *or* and when Jesus returned (*a completely literal translation gives rather odd English* and in the [event of] Jesus to return). (iii) And when he spoke (*the context shows that Jesus was the speaker, hence* he). (iv) Loving your (*lit.* the) neighbour. (v) Before your asking him *or* before you ask him. (vi) The [things] of Caesar. (vii) The [things] from you. (viii) The [people] from the church. (ix) The foolish [things] (*or* the folly) of the world. (x) The hidden [things] (*or* the secrets) of the heart. (2) Jesus declared that a prophet does not have honour in his own country. (3) And because he was (*lit.* on account of [him] being) of the same trade he stayed in their house (*lit.* at the house of them). (4) They asked him, 'So what are you? Are you Elijah?' and he said, 'I am not.' (5) They were amazed at his lingering in the temple *or* that he lingered in the temple. (6) Pilate said to them, 'So what shall I do with Jesus?' (7) The lamp of the body is the eye. (8) For if you live according to [the] flesh, you are destined to die. (9) He spoke a parable on account of his being (*or* because he was) close to Jerusalem. (10) When I was a young child, I used to speak as a young child, I used to think as a young child. (11) And the high priests and all the council were seeking testimony against Jesus for killing him (*or* in order to kill him) and they were not finding [it]. (12) You are of those below, I am of those above. (13) And Jesus says to her, 'Lady, why are you weeping?' (14) So furthermore, brothers, we ask and entreat you in [the name] of the Lord Jesus. (15) Slaves must obey their earthly lords with fear and trembling in the sincerity of their hearts (i.e. with sincere hearts) [in the same way] as [they obey] Christ. (16) Jesus wept. So the Jews said, 'Behold! How he used to love him!' (17) Guards in front of the door were keeping watch over the prison. (18) You take pains to preserve the unity of the Spirit in the bond of peace. (19) And the Pharisees said, 'He is casting out the evil spirits in [the name of] the leader of the evil spirits.' (20) And he said to him, 'You shall love the Lord your God with all your heart and all your soul.'

6.2

(1) (i) We know the saviour of the people. (ii) The shepherds guarded [their] sheep. (iii) The speakers were cursing the leaders. (iv) I shall proclaim the word of God. (v) The mothers changed the names of [their] daughters. (vi) Do you know both the man and [his] daughter? (vii) He will rule the house of Jacob forever. (viii) I shall send my beloved son. (ix) The words of the witnesses revealed the deception. (x) You have words of eternal life. (2) They see my Father's face in heaven. (3) They were proclaiming the word of God in the synagogues of the Jews. (4) They were casting out many evil spirits and anointing many sick with oil and curing [them]. (5) You did not anoint my head with oil, but this woman anointed my head with perfume. (6) A husband is leader of his wife just as Christ too is leader of the (or his) church. (7) He had a daughter about twelve years old (lit. there was for him a daughter of about twelve years). (8) The anxiety of the [present] time and the deception of wealth choke the word. (9) And why do you see the speck in your brother's eye but you do not notice the beam in your eye? (10) Then he began to curse and swear, 'I do not know the man.' And immediately the cock crowed. (11) The Jews did not believe that he was blind and gained his sight. (12) You are fortunate, Simon, son of Jonah, because flesh and blood did not reveal [this] to you but my Father who is in heaven. (13) The wind abated. And those in the boat did obeisance to him, saying, 'Truly you are the Son of God.' (14) You shall not murder, you shall not commit adultery, you shall not steal, you shall not bear false witness! (15) Hypocrites, you know [how] to examine the face of the earth and the heaven. (16) I always taught in [a] synagogue and in the temple. (17) They threw themselves at (lit. to) his feet and he healed them. (18) And behold! Two men were talking with him. (19) Nations will hope in his name. (20) I baptized you with water, but he will baptize you with the Holy Ghost.

7.2

(1) The centurion ordered the army to seize Paul from their midst and bring him to the barracks. (2) So Jesus said to them, 'For a little time the light is still among you.' (3) And he took the child and his mother during the night and went away to Egypt. (4) And Herod said, 'I beheaded John.' (5) And in the fourth watch of the night he came toward them walking on the

sea. (6) And they put their hands on him and apprehended him. (7) So Pilate came outside to them and said, 'What charge do you bring against the man?' (8) After three days they found him in the temple. (9) And after eight days his disciples were again inside and Thomas with them. (10) They said, 'Master, you spoke well.' For they no longer dared to ask him anything. (11) Abraham had two sons, one from a slave girl, one from a free woman. (12) From then Jesus began to indicate to the disciples that it was necessary for him to go away to Jerusalem and to suffer much (*lit.* many [things]) from the elders. (13) I fast twice during the week. (14) If you wish, I shall make three tabernacles here, one for you and one for Moses and one for Elijah. (15) Jonah was in the belly of the sea-monster for three days and three nights. (16) And Mary said, 'My soul magnifies the Lord, and my spirit rejoiced in God my Saviour, because he looked down on the lowly station of his bondmaid. For, behold, from now all generations will call me blessed, because the mighty one did to me great things. And holy [is] his name, and from generation to generation his mercy [is] on those fearing him. He produced strength in his arm, he scattered the proud in the imagination of their hearts; he brought down rulers from their thrones and raised the humble.'

8.2

(1) Jesus Christ, Son of God, Saviour (*the symbol is the fish*, ἰχθύς *being an acronym of the phrase*). (2) And Paul said, 'I am not mad, most excellent Festus, but I speak true and rational words.' (*lit.* words of truth and rationality). (3) Why do your disciples transgress the tradition of the elders? For they do not wash their hands. (4) How do you not understand that I did not speak to you about loaves of bread? (5) Jesus said to them, 'Truly I say to you that tax-collectors and prostitutes go before you into the kingdom of God.' (6) The crowd saw that Jesus was not there. (7) He did not deny, and admitted, 'I am not the Anointed One.' (8) And darkness descended (*lit.* became) on all the earth from the sixth hour to the ninth hour. (9) And it happened [that] when he came to the Mount of Olives near Bethphage and Bethany, he dispatched two of the disciples. (10) But I tell you not to swear at all, neither by the heaven because this is God's throne, nor by the earth because this is the footstool for (*lit.* of) his feet. (11) A great fear came over (*lit.* happened on) all the church. (12) And he said to them, 'How do

they say the Anointed One is a son of David?' (13) The farmer waits for the precious harvest of the earth. (14) While he was praying the appearance of his face became different. (15) And he went out again to the sea; and all the crowd came to him and he taught them. (16) And it happened [that] when Jesus finished these words the crowds were amazed at his teaching. (17) Simon Peter said to them, 'I am going out to fish.' They said to him, 'We too are coming with you.' (18) And his disciples were hungry, and they began to pick the ears of corn and eat. (19) And it happened [that] afterwards he was journeying through city and village. (20) Then Jerusalem and all Judea and all the neighbourhood of the Jordan came out to him and they were baptized by him in the river Jordan.

9.2

(1) And he said to them, 'An enemy (*lit.* hostile man) did this.' (2) And there are also many other things which Jesus did. (3) For your Father knows the things of which (*lit.* of what things) you have need before you ask him. (4) You shall love your neighbour as yourself. (5) Your word is truth. (6) The Spirit itself testifies with our spirit that we are children of God. (7) And on the day on which (*lit.* on what day) Lot came out of Sodom, fire and sulphur rained from heaven. (8) There are eunuchs who emasculated themselves for the sake of the kingdom of heaven. (9) You are from this world, I am not from this world. (10) And I also say to you that you are Peter, and on this rock I shall build my church, and [the] gates of Hades will not gain victory over it. (11) And those tenant farmers said to themselves, 'This is the heir.' (12) But you are the same and your years will not come to an end. (13) Then you will know that it is I and [that] I do nothing from myself but just as my Father taught me these things. (14) So the Jews were seeking him at the feast and saying, 'Where is that man?' (15) So if I, your Lord and Master, washed your feet, you too (καί) should wash the feet of one another. (16) So Jesus said to them, 'My time is not yet here, but your time is always at hand.' (17) So six days before the Passover Jesus went to Bethany where Lazarus was whom he raised from the dead. (18) As intercessor before (*lit.* towards) God we have Jesus Christ [the] just, and he himself is [the] expiation concerning (*i.e.* atones for) our sins, not only our own, but [those] of all the world. (19) For the kingdom of heaven is like to a man, [the] master of the house, who went out

early in the morning to hire labourers for his vineyard. (20) I am the good shepherd, and I know my sheep and my [sheep] know me. (21) For the poor you have with you always, but me you do not have always.

10.2

(1) Even the tax-collectors do the same, don't they? (2) And Jesus said to them, 'How many loaves of bread do you have?' (3) Who is my mother and who are my brothers? (4) If anyone wishes to be first he shall be last of all and servant of all. (5) Simon and those with him searched for him and they found him and said to him, 'All are seeking you'. (6) By what power and by what name did you do this? (7) Surely a fountain does not pour forth sweet and bitter [water] from the same opening? (8) Each one started to say to him, 'Surely, Lord, it is not I?' (9) So a bishop must be irreproachable, husband of one wife, sober, prudent. (10) For how, O wife, do you know whether you will save your husband? Or, O husband, whether you will save your wife? (11) Master, we know that you are truthful and [that] you truthfully (*lit.* in truth) teach the way of God. (12) He had an only daughter of about twelve years, and she was dying. (13) Whom do they say the Son of Man to be? *or* Who do they say the Son of Man is? (14) Then Pilate said to him, 'Do you not hear how many things they testify against you?' (15) I know that cruel wolves will come to you after I depart (*lit.* after my departure).' (16) And while they were travelling he came to a village; and a woman, Martha by name, received him. (17) I was a stranger and you did not receive me, naked and you did not clothe me, sick and in prison and you did not visit me. (18) At that time Herod the king set about harming some of those from the church. (19) All this Jesus spoke in parables to the crowds, and he used to say nothing to them without parables. (20) Jesus said to them, 'Neither do I tell you on what authority I do these things.'

11.2

(1) Did you not read in the law that if the priests profane the sabbath in the temple they are [considered] innocent? (*lit.* the priests profane the sabbath in the temple and are innocent). (2) Lord, they killed your prophets, they tore down your altars, and

I alone was left and they are seeking my soul (*i.e.* life). (3) For I say to you that God can raise children for Abraham from these stones. (4) The Lord replied to him and said, 'Hypocrites, does not each of you on the sabbath untie his ox or ass from the stall?' (5) Now the Anointed One will be magnified in my body, whether through [my] life or through [my] death. (6) For who ascertained [the] mind of the Lord? Or who became his counsellor? (7) Then Jesus was led away into the wilderness by the Spirit to be tempted by the devil. (8) And the rain poured down and the rivers came and the winds blew and beat against that house and it fell, and its fall was great. (9) So I say this and implore [you] in [the name of the] Lord to walk no longer just as the Gentiles too walk in the emptiness of their minds. (10) And it happened on one day [that] he got into a boat and the disciples with him. (11) Many will say to me on that day, 'Lord, Lord, did we not prophesy in your name and cast out evil spirits in your name and perform (*lit.* do) many miracles in your name?' (12) Mary stayed with her about three months and [then] returned to her house. (13) And when the harvest time approached he sent out his slaves to the tenant farmers to take his harvests. (14) A voice was heard in Rama, weeping and much lamentation. (15) For there will be a great calamity on the land and [there will be] a judgement on this people, and they will fall by the edge of the sword and will be taken as captives into all nations. (16) And the eleven disciples went into Galilee to the mountain where Jesus ordered. (17) And his disciples replied to him, 'From where will anyone be able to feed these [people] with bread in the wilderness?' (18) And Joseph too went up from Galilee from the city of Nazareth to the city of David which is called Bethlehem because he was from [the] house and family of David. (19) I have need to be baptized by you, and you are coming to me? (20) The doctors of law and the Pharisees sat on the chair of Moses.

12.2

(1) Because I was crafty (*lit.* being crafty), I trapped you with a deceit. (2) I went up to Jerusalem to worship. (3) And the young man, having heard the message, went away grieving, for he had many possessions. (4) When I was travelling and approaching Damascus (*lit.* for me travelling and approaching D.), about midday a great light from the sky suddenly happened to flash around me, and I fell to the ground and I heard a voice saying,

'Saul, Saul, why are you persecuting me?' And I replied, 'Who are you, Lord?' and it said to me, 'I am Jesus of Nazareth, whom you are persecuting.' (5) He spoke many things to them in parables, saying, 'Behold! A sower went out to sow. And while he was sowing, some [seeds] fell by the road, and birds came (*lit.* having come) and devoured them. Other [seeds] fell on to stony [places] where they did not have much soil and sprang up immediately because they had no deep soil (*lit.* depth of soil). And when the sun rose they were scorched and they withered because they had no root. And other [seeds] fell on thorn-bushes, and the thorn-bushes came up and choked them. And other [seeds] fell on to good soil and produced a harvest.' (6) And looking up he saw the rich putting their gifts into the box for offerings; and he saw a poor widow putting [in] there two small coins, and he said, 'Truly, I tell you that this poor widow put [in] more than all; for all these [men] contributed (*lit.* put [in]) to the gifts from their ample wealth, but she in her poverty contributed all the possessions she had.' (7) And when it was decided that we sail to Italy, they handed over Paul and some other prisoners to a centurion by name Julius of the Imperial cohort; and embarking on a ship of Adramyttium [that was] going to sail to the ports on the Asian coast (*lit.* to the places in the region of Asia), we put out to sea; with us was Aristarchus, a Macedonian from Thessalonica (*lit.* Aristarchus … being with us). And on the next day we put in at Sidon, and Julius, treating Paul kindly, allowed him to journey to his friends and be looked after (*lit.* receive attention). After putting out to sea from there we sailed under the shelter of Cyprus because the winds were contrary, and having sailed across the sea by Cilicia and Pamphylia we arrived at Myra in Lycia. And there the centurion, after finding a ship of Alexandria [which was] sailing to Italy, put us on board it. Sailing slowly for many days and with difficulty getting to Cnidus, as the wind did not allow us to go further, we sailed by Salmone under the shelter of Crete, and sailing past it (Salmone) with difficulty we came to a place called Fair Harbours, which was near the city Lasaea (*lit.* to which the city Lasaea was near).

13.2

(1) What then? Are we to sin because we are not under the law but under grace? By no means (*lit.* may it not happen). (2) Heaven and earth will pass away but my words will **not** pass

away. (3) Then the Pharisees went (*lit.* having gone) [and] held counsel so that they might trap him in talk. (4) Lord, I am not worthy that you should enter under my roof. (5) For this is the will of my Father, (viz) that every [person] seeing the Son and believing in him should have eternal life. (6) Working by night and day in order not to be a burden to any one of you, we preached to you God's gospel. (7) And he said to them on that day when evening fell, 'Let us cross to the other side.' (8) For God did not send his Son into the world so that he might judge the world, but so that the world might be saved through him. (9) He told his disciples that a little boat should be ready for him on account of the crowd, so that it (the crowd) would not crush him. (10) And you, brothers, are not in darkness for the day to overtake you like a thief, for you are all sons of light and sons of day. We are not of night nor of darkness. (11) And the woman was a gentile, a Phoenician of Syria by race; and she was asking him that he cast out the evil spirit from her daughter. (12) Snakes, offspring of vipers, how are you to escape from being condemned to hell? (*lit.* the condemnation of hell) (13) Pilate said to them, 'What then shall I do (*or* what then am I to do) with Jesus, who is called the Anointed?' They all said, 'Let him be crucified!' And he said, 'Well, what wrong did he do?' And they started to shout all the more, 'Let him be crucified!' And Pilate, seeing that he was getting nowhere (*lit.* accomplishing nothing), but [that] instead a riot was starting, took water and washed [his] hands in front of the crowd, saying, 'I am innocent of (*lit.* from) this blood. It is your business!' And all the people said in reply, 'His blood [is] on us and on our children.' Then he freed Barabbas, and after flogging Jesus he handed him over to be crucified (*lit.* so that he would be crucified). (14) There was a certain man, Lazarus from Bethany, from the village of Mary and Martha, her sister. And Mary was the one who anointed the Lord with perfume and dried his feet with her hair; her brother (*lit.* whose brother) Lazarus was sick. So the sisters sent to him, saying, 'Lord, behold! [the man] whom you love is sick.' And Jesus, when he heard, said, 'This sickness will not end in death (is not [extending] up to death), but [is] for the glory of God, so that the Son of God may be praised though it.' And Jesus loved Martha and her sister and Lazarus. However, when he heard that [Lazarus] was sick, he then stayed two days in the place where he was (*lit.* in what place he was). Then, after that, he said to his disciples, 'Let us go again into Judea.' The disciples said to him, 'Master, the Jews were just now seeking to stone you, and you are going back there?'

(1) This man first finds his own brother Simon and says to him, 'We have found the Messiah.' (2) So whoever breaks the least of these commandments and teaches people [to act] thus, [will be] least in the kingdom of heaven; but whoever carries out (*lit.* does) and teaches them, this man will be called great in the kingdom of heaven. (3) And I am afraid lest perhaps, just as the serpent deceived Eve with his cunning, your minds have been corrupted. (4) But I have said these things to you so that you remember them when their time comes. (5) When I became a man I set aside the things of a child. (6) Whoever blasphemes against the Holy Ghost has no forgiveness for eternity. (7) For truly I say to you: until the heaven and the earth pass away, one iota or one stroke will not pass away from the law before everything happens. (8) And I say to you: from now I shall not drink of this fruit of the vine until that day when I drink it new in the kingdom of my Father. (9) When it became evening they started to go out of the city. (10) And whoever denies me before men, I too shall deny him before my Father. (11) And having arrested him they took him and brought him to the house of the high priest. And Peter was following at a distance. And when they lit a fire in the middle of the courtyard Peter sat in the middle of them. And a slave girl, when she saw him sitting beside the fire and looked carefully at him, said to him, 'This man too was with him.' But he denied [this], saying. 'Woman, I do not know him!' And after a short while another on seeing him said, 'You too are from them.' But Peter said, 'Fellow, I am not!' And when about an hour had passed some other insisted with the words (*lit.* saying), 'In truth, this man too was with him, for indeed he is a Galilean.' But Peter said, 'Fellow, I do not know what you mean.' And immediately, while he was still speaking, a cock crowed. And the Lord turned and (*lit.* having turned) looked at Peter, and he remembered the word of the Lord, how he had said to him, 'Before a cock crows today you will deny me three times.' And after going outside he wept bitterly. (12) So they took Jesus; and carrying his own cross (*lit.* the cross for himself) he went forth to the so-called Place of a Skull, which in Hebrew is called Golgotha, where they crucified him, and with him two others one on each side (*lit.* from this side and from this side), and Jesus in the middle. Pilate also wrote a title (*or* inscription) and put [it] on the cross; [on it] was written, JESUS OF NAZARETH THE KING OF THE JEWS. Many of the Jews read this title, because the place where Jesus was crucified was near the city, and it was written in Hebrew,

Latin [and] Greek. Accordingly, the high priests of the Jews said to Pilate, 'Do not write "The King of the Jews", but "He claimed to be the King of the Jews"' (*lit.* but that, 'he said, "I am the King ..."'). Pilate replied, 'What I have written, I have written'.

15.2

(1) For such men do not serve Christ our Lord but their own bellies. (2) Cruel wolves will come among (*lit.* into) you after I leave (*lit.* after my departure), not sparing the flock. (3) The spirit is willing but the flesh is weak. (4) If you love those who love you (lit. those loving you), what thanks do you have? For indeed sinners love those who love them. (5) After ordering the crowd to sit on the ground he took the seven loaves of bread and the fishes. (6) The one who once persecuted us now preaches the faith which he once tried to destroy. (7) And he was with them, going in and out of Jerusalem, speaking freely in the name of the Lord; and he used to talk and argue with the Jews who spoke Greek. But they were trying to do away with him. And his brethren, after discovering [this], took him down to Caesarea and sent him away to Tarsus. Meanwhile the Church enjoyed peace over the whole of Judea and Galilee and Samaria. (8) Every tree not producing a good harvest is cut down and thrown into the fire; so you will know them from their fruit. (9) His disciples came and they were surprised that he was talking with a woman. No-one, however, said, 'What are you seeking?' or 'Why are you talking with a woman?' (10) Let us possess grace, through which we may worship God in an acceptable way with reverence and awe; for indeed our God is a consuming fire. (11) For Christ died and lived for this [purpose, viz] that he should rule over the dead and the living. (12) Although I am not an apostle for others, for you at least I am. (13) And when the crowd was sent out, on entering he grasped her hand, and the girl woke. And the news went out to all that land. (14) A man was going down from Jerusalem to Jericho and fell into the hands of robbers, who, after stripping him and inflicting blows, went away, leaving [him] half-dead. And by chance a priest was going down on that road, and on seeing him went by on the opposite side. And similarly a Levite too, on coming to the place and seeing [him], went by on the opposite side. And a Samaritan, [who was] travelling, came upon him and on seeing [him] took pity; on approaching he bandaged his wounds,

pouring on oil and wine; and setting him on his own beast brought him to an inn and looked after him. And on the next day taking out two silver coins he gave [them] to the inn-keeper and said, 'Look after him, and whatever you spend in addition I shall give back to you when I return.'

16.2

(1) And it happened [that] when Jesus finished these parables he went away from there. And coming to his home town he began to teach them in their synagogue, so that they were amazed and said, 'From where does he get this wisdom and [these] powers?' (*lit.* from where [is there] for him ...) (2) God dwells in us and his love is in a state of perfection (*lit.* has been perfected) in us. (3) Nothing has been concealed which will not be revealed and [there is nothing] hidden which will not be ascertained. (4) The sabbath was created for man, and not man for the sabbath; and so the Son of Man is lord of the sabbath too. (5) After going away they began to talk to each other, saying, 'This man is doing nothing deserving death or prison (*lit.* fetters).' And Agrippa said to Festus, 'This man could have been freed (*lit.* was able to have been freed) if he had not appealed to Caesar.' (6) The rain poured down and the rivers came and the wind blew and fell upon that house, and it did not fall, for its foundations had been put on stone. (7) And when it became evening his disciples went down to the sea, and embarking on a boat they started to go across the sea to Capernaum. And it had already become dark (*lit.* darkness) and Jesus had not yet come to them, and the sea was being stirred up as a strong wind was blowing. So having rowed about twenty-five or thirty stades they saw Jesus walking on the sea and getting close to the boat, and they were afraid. (8) Blessed [are] those persecuted for the sake of righteousness because the kingdom of heaven is theirs (*lit.* of them). (9) And about midnight Paul and Silas, while praying, were singing the praise of God and the prisoners were listening to them. And suddenly a terrible earthquake occurred, with the result that the foundations of the prison were shaken and immediately all the doors were opened and everyone's fetters were unfastened. And the gaoler, on wakening (*lit.* becoming awake) and seeing the opened doors of the prison, drew a sword and (*lit.* having drawn a sword) was on the point of killing himself, thinking that the prisoners had escaped. But Paul shouted in a loud voice, saying, 'Do not do anything bad to

yourself, for we are all here.' And he (*i.e.* the gaoler), after asking for a torch, in a state of trembling (*lit.* becoming trembling) rushed in and fell in front of Paul and Silas; and taking them outside he said, 'Lords, what is it necessary for me to do in order to be saved?' And they said, 'Trust in Jesus the Lord, and you will be saved together with (*lit.* and) your family.' And they spoke the word of the Lord to him and everyone in his family. And taking them at that hour of the night he washed their wounds and straightway he himself was baptized and all his [family]; and leading them away to his house he set a table before [them], and with his whole household he rejoiced, having put his faith in God.

17.2

(1) Doctor, heal yourself. (2) He [that is] coming after me is mightier than I. (3) And you, Bethlehem, are by no means least among the leaders of Judah. (4) The least in the kingdom of God is greater than he. (5) The light has come into the world and people loved the darkness more than the light, for their actions were evil. (6) Surely you are not greater than our father Jacob? (7) No longer drink [only] water, but use a little wine on account of your stomach and your frequent illnesses. (8) After these things Jesus found him in the temple and said to him, 'Behold! You are sound; sin no longer so that something worse does not happen to you.' (9) And I have a testimony greater than John. (10) Truly I say to you, it will be easier for the land of Sodom and Gomorrah on the day of judgement than for that city. (11) The kingdom of heaven is like to a seed of mustard which a man took and sowed in his field. Mustard [seed] is smaller than all seeds (*or* is the smallest of all seeds), but when it grows it is bigger than garden plants and it becomes a tree, so that birds of the heaven come and settle on its branches. (12) And again I say to you, it is easier for a camel to go through an eye of a needle than for a wealthy man to enter (*lit.* enter into) the kingdom of God. (13) I say to you, there is no-one greater than John among those born of women. (14) When you are invited by someone to a marriage, do not recline in the place of honour lest [a person] more distinguished than you has been invited by him. (15) If someone has an ear, let him hear. (16) These were more noble-minded than those in Thessalonica. (17) We have set our hopes in the living God who is the saviour of all people, above all, of believers. (18) Our Father in heaven, let

your name be held in reverence; let your kingdom come; let your will be done on earth as well, as [it is done] in heaven; give us today our daily bread; and forgive us our sins, as we too forgave those who sinned against us; and do not bring us into temptation but rescue us from evil (or the Devil). (19) And when you see Jerusalem encircled by armies, know then that its destruction has approached. Then let those in Judea flee to the hills, and those inside it (*lit.* in the middle of her [Jerusalem]) depart, and those in the country not enter it. (20) And when an unclean spirit comes out of a man, it goes through waterless places seeking a resting place; then it says, 'I shall return to my home from where I came.' And it comes and finds it (the house) unoccupied, swept clean and decorated. Then it goes and takes along with it seven other spirits more wicked than itself, and they enter and dwell there. And the final condition of the man becomes worse than the original one.

18.2

(1) Alas for you, Chorazin; alas for you, Bethsaida; because if the miracles that occurred among you had occurred in Tyre and Sidon, they would have long ago repented in sackcloth and ashes. *(cat. 1 past)* (2) Jesus went and took the bread and gave it to them, and the fish likewise. (3) If anyone eats of this bread he will live forever (*lit.* into eternity). *(cat. 2 future)* (4) And he said, 'How are we to compare the kingdom of God or in what parable are we to present it?' (5) If we had been in the days of our fathers, we would not have been partners with (*lit.* of) them in the blood of the prophets. *(cat. 1 past)* (6) So Mary, when she went where Jesus was, on seeing him fell to his feet, saying, 'Lord, if you had been here my brother would not have died.' *(cat. 1 past)* (7) Large numbers of both men and women believing in the Lord were being added with the result that they were bringing out into the streets the sick and placing them on beds and stretchers so that, when Peter was coming, just his shadow might fall on one of them. (8) If God gave the same gift to them as [he did] to us who believe in the Lord Jesus Christ, who was I [to be] able to hinder God? *(cat. 2 past)* (9) Wicked and lazy slave, you knew that I reap where I did not sow and [that] I gather up where I did not scatter [seed]? Then you should have put my money with (*lit.* to) the bankers, and on coming I would have got what was mine with interest. (10) Am I now persuading people or God? Or am I seeking to please

people? If I were still pleasing people I would not be a servant of Christ. *(cat. 1 present)* (11) Behold! My servant whom I chose, my beloved in whom my soul rejoices. I shall put my spirit on him and he will proclaim judgement to the nations. (12) And no-one having lit a lamp covers it with a jar or places it under a bed. (13) If the relationship of a man with a woman is thus, it is not expedient to marry. *(cat. 2 present)* (14) And he said to them, 'Do not be alarmed. You are looking for Jesus the Nazarene who has been crucified. He was raised up, he is not here. Behold! The place where they put him.' (15) For Herod, after arresting John, bound him and put him in prison on account of Herodias, the wife of his brother Philip. For John said to him, 'You are not allowed to have her.' (*lit.* it is not permitted to you to have her). And he wanted to kill him but (*lit.* wanting to kill him) he was afraid of the mob because they looked upon him as a prophet. But when Herod's birthday was celebrated, Herodias's daughter danced in their midst and pleased Herod; and so Herod promised with an oath to give her whatever she asked. And she, prompted by her mother, said, 'Give me here the head of John the Baptist on a plate.' And the king [though] grieved on account of his oath and his fellow diners, ordered that it (i.e. the head) be given [to her]; and sending [an order] he had John beheaded in prison. And his head was brought on a plate and given to the girl, and she took it to her mother.

19.2

(1) And on going out at around the eleventh hour he found others standing, and he said to them, 'Why are you standing here idle for the whole day?' They said to him, 'Because no-one hired us.' (2) So who is the faithful and wise slave whom the lord appointed over his household to give them food at the proper time? (3) The Devil took him to a very high mountain and showed him all the kingdoms of the world and their glory. (4) The king was angry and sending his armies he destroyed those murderers and burnt their city. (5) On that day Jesus went out of the house and sat by the sea; and many crowds came together to him with the result that he got into a boat and sat [there], and all the crowd stood on the shore. (6) And already the axe has been put to the root of the trees. (7) What man possessing a hundred sheep and having lost one of (*lit.* from) them does not leave the ninety-nine in the wilderness and go

after the lost one until he finds it? (8) And someone from the crowd said to him, 'Master, tell my brother to share [our] inheritance with me.' And he said to him, 'Fellow, who appointed me as a judge over you?' (9) After him Judas the Galilean stood up in the days of the census and made the people revolt under (*lit.* behind) him. And that man perished and all who were his followers were scattered. (10) And I commend Phoebe, our sister, to you, who is (*lit.* being) deaconess of the church at Cenchreae, so that you may welcome her in [the name of] the Lord in a manner worthy of Christians and help her in whatever matter she has need of you. (11) And in the same district there were shepherds in the open air, guarding the watches of the night over their flock. And an angel of the Lord appeared to them and the Lord's glory shone around them, and they were extremely afraid. And the angel said to them, 'Do not be afraid, for behold! I announce to you a great joy which will be for all the people, [namely] that today a saviour was born for you in the city of David who is Christ the Lord. And this [is] the sign for you: you will find a baby wrapped in swaddling clothes and lying in a manger.' And suddenly there appeared with the angel a crowd of the heavenly army [who were] praising God and saying, 'Glory to God on high and on earth peace to those who enjoy his favour.' (12) And there was in Joppa a disciple Tabitha by name, (which being translated means Dorcas [gazelle]). She herself was full of good deeds and charitable works which she used to do. And it happened [that] in those days she fell sick and died. And they washed [her body] and placed it in an upper room. And as Lydda was near to Joppa the disciples, having heard that Peter was there (*lit.* in it [i.e. Joppa]), dispatched two men to him entreating [him], 'Do not delay to come across to us.' And Peter rose and went off with them. When he arrived, they took him up to the upper room, and all the widows stood by him weeping and showing all the tunics and cloaks which Dorcas used to make when she was with them (*lit.* being with them). And Peter, having sent everybody out, and having fallen to his knees, prayed, and turning to the body said, 'Tabitha, rise up!' And she opened her eyes and on seeing Peter sat up.

20.2

(1) (i) A jar of water (gen. of content). (ii) Your faith in (*lit.* toward) God (subjective gen.). (iii) Hear the parable of the

sower (broad use of possessive gen.). (iv) And behold! some of the doctors of law said in themselves, 'This man is blaspheming.' (partitive gen.). (v) The lord praised the unjust steward (*lit.* the steward of injustice; gen. of description). (vi) Into all the district of Galilee (gen. of explanation). (vii) For they all sinned and are without God's glory (gen. of separation). (viii) Or do you not know that your body is the temple of the Holy Spirit within you, which you have from God, and [that] you do not belong to yourselves (*lit.* are not of yourselves); for you were bought at a price (ὑμῶν possessive gen.; πνεύματος possessive gen.; οὗ see note; θεοῦ gen. after the prep. ἀπό; ἑαυτῶν possessive gen. used as a predicate; τιμῆς gen. of price). (2) The people were burned terribly (lit. burned a great burn). (3) On account of this we too, from the day we heard, have not ceased praying on your behalf and asking that you be filled with knowledge of his will. (4) Follow me (*lit.* come behind me) and I will make you fishers of men (*lit.* fishermen of people). (5) And I praise you because you remember everything about me and retain the traditions just as I handed [them] over to you. (6) I have trust in you that you think nothing else; and the person troubling you will bear judgement (i.e. will be judged), whoever he is. (7) And Jews came from Antioch and Iconium, and after persuading the crowds and stoning Paul, they dragged [him] outside the city thinking him to be dead. (8) So I have [a cause for] pride in respect of the things concerning God. (9) And he cured many suffering from various diseases, and he cast out many evil spirits, and he did not allow the evil spirits to speak because they knew him. (10) And behold they were bringing to him a cripple lying on a bed. And Jesus on seeing their faith said to the cripple, 'Take courage, [my] son; your sins are forgiven.' And behold! some of the doctors of law said within themselves, 'This man is blaspheming.' And Jesus, knowing their thoughts said to them, 'Why are you thinking evil things in your hearts? For what is the easier, to say, "Your sins are forgiven" or to say, "Arise and walk"? But so that you may know that the Son of Man has authority on earth to forgive sins — .' Then he said to the cripple, 'Rise and (*lit.* having risen) take up your bed and go to your house.' And he rose and went away to his house. (11) And when he was approaching the age of forty (lit. his fortieth year was being completed), it came to his heart to visit his brothers, the sons of Israel. And on seeing one being treated unjustly he went to help and he exacted (*lit.* did) retribution [by] striking the Egyptian. And he thought that his brothers understood that God was granting (*lit.* giving) them salvation through his hand, but they did not understand. And on the following day he came upon them fighting and tried to reconcile them and put them at peace, saying, 'Men, you are brothers; why do you wrong each other?' And the one who was wronging his neighbour pushed him aside, saying, 'Who appointed you ruler and judge over us? Do you want to kill me in the way in which you killed the Egyptian yesterday?' And because of this remark Moses fled and became an exile in the land of Midian, where he fathered two sons.

21.2

(1) (i) So if I do not know the meaning of the [speaker's] voice, I shall be a foreigner to the person speaking (i.e. I shall not understand what he is saying. τῷ λαλοῦντι dat. of reference). (ii) The person suffering in the flesh (σαρκί dat. of respect) (iii) The prophecy of Isaiah is being fulfilled for them (αὐτοῖς dat. of reference). (iv) Knowing that the same sufferings are being laid up for your brotherhood in the world (τῇ ... ἀδελφότητι dat. of disadvantage; τῷ κόσμῳ dat. after the prep. ἐν). (v) For the promise is for you and your children (ὑμῖν, τοῖς τέκνοις dat. of advantage). (vi) They were broken off because of their disbelief, you stand (i.e. hold your place) because of your faith (τῇ ἀπιστίᾳ, τῇ πίστει dat. of cause). (vii) The high priest entered the sanctuary yearly with the blood of another creature (*lit.* another's blood; ἐν αἵματι ἀλλοτρίῳ attendant circumstances). (viii) Christ is proclaimed in every way, whether in pretence or in truth (παντὶ τρόπῳ, προφάσει, ἀληθείᾳ dat. of manner). (ix) And welcome the person weak in faith (τῇ πίστει dat. of respect). (x) The race of Joseph became clear to the Pharaoh (τῷ Φαραώ dat. after the adj. φανερόν). (2) And Pharisees approached him, making trial of him and saying, 'Is it allowed to a man to divorce his wife for any reason?' (3) And he himself was in the stern sleeping on a pillow; and they woke him and said to him, 'Master, are you not concerned that we are perishing?' (4) And going through the first guard post and the second they came to the iron gate leading to the city. (5) And when the Pharisees had come together, Jesus asked them, saying, 'What do you think about the Anointed One? Whose son is he?' They said to him, '[The son] of David.' (6) If your eye is sound, all your body will be full of light (*lit.* bright). (7) For such people do not serve Christ, our Lord, but their own belly, and through their plausible talk and flattery they deceive the hearts of the

innocent. (8) The first man is earthly, [and] from the earth, the second from heaven. Earthly people are like the earthly man, heavenly people are like the heavenly man (*lit.* of what sort [is] the earthly man, of that sort also [are] earthly people, etc.). (9) The kingdom of heaven is similar to a treasure hidden in a field, which a man found and hid, and in his joy went and sold everything he had and bought that field. (10) So if you, who are evil, know [how] to give excellent gifts to your children, how much more will your father in heaven give good things to those who ask him. (11) All those who are led by the spirit of God are sons of God. (12) A man had two sons. And the younger of them said to him, 'Father, give me the share of the property due [to me].' And he (the father) divided his possessions between them. And after not many days the younger son, having gathered up all [his possessions], went away to a distant country, and there he squandered his wealth by living dissolutely. And when he had spent everything a terrible (*lit.* strong) famine occurred in that country, and he himself began to be in need. And he went and attached himself to one of the citizens of that country, and he (the citizen) sent him to his fields to feed pigs. And he (the prodigal son) wanted to eat his fill of (*lit.* from) the carob pods which the pigs were eating, and no-one gave (*lit.* was giving) [anything] to him. And coming to his senses (*lit.* coming to himself), he said, 'How many labourers of my father have bread in abundance, but I perish here from hunger. I shall rise and go to my father and I shall say to him, "Father, I sinned against heaven and against you; I am no longer worthy to be called your son. Make me as one of your labourers."' And he rose and went to his father. And when he was still far off, his father saw him and felt pity, and running up he fell on his neck and kissed him. And the son said to him, 'Father, I sinned against heaven and against you; I am no longer worthy to be called your son.' And the father said to his slaves, 'Quickly bring out the best robe and clothe him, and give [him] a ring for his hand and sandals for his feet, and bring the fattened calf; slaughter [it] and let us eat and make merry because this son of mine was dead and he came back to life; he had perished and he was found.' And they began to make merry.

principal parts of verbs

Present	Future	Aorist	Perfect	Perfect mid./pass.	Aorist passive
ἄγω *lead, bring*	ἄξω	ἤγαγον		ἦγμαι	ἤχθην
(ἐπ-) αἰνέω *praise*	ἐπαινέσω	ἐπηνεσα			
αἱρέω *take*		-εἷλον		-ᾕρημαι	-ᾑρέθην
αἴρω *lift*	ἀρῶ	ἦρα	ἦρκα	ἦρμαι	ἤρθην
ἀκούω *hear*	ἀκούσω ἀκούσομαι	ἤκουσα	ἀκήκοα		ἠκούσθην
ἁμαρτάνω *sin*	ἁμαρτήσω	ἥμαρτον (ἡμάρτησα)	ἡμάρτηκα		
ἀμύνομαι *come/go to help*		ἠμυνάμην			
ἀνοίγω *open*	ἀνοίξω	ἀνέῳξα	ἀνέῳγα	ἀνέῳγμαι	
ἀπο-θνῄσκω *die*	-θανοῦμαι	-έθανον	τέθνηκα		
ἀπο-κρίνομαι *reply*	-κριθήσομαι	-εκρινάμην			-εκρίθην
ἀπο-κτείνω ἀπο-κτέννυμι *kill*	-κτενῶ	-έκτεινα			-εκτάνθην
ἀπ-όλλυμαι *perish*	-ὀλοῦμαι	-ὠλόμην	-ὄλωλα		
ἀπ-όλλυμι *destroy, lose*	-ὀλῶ, -ὀλέσω	-ὤλεσα			
ἄρχομαι *begin*	ἄρξομαι	ἠρξάμην			
-βαίνω *go*	-βήσομαι	-ἔβην	-βέβηκα		
βάλλω *throw*	βαλῶ	ἔβαλον	βέβληκα	βέβλημαι	ἐβλήθην
βούλομαι *wish*					ἐβουλήθην

Present	Future	Aorist	Perfect	Perfect mid./pass.	Aorist passive
γαμέω *marry*		ἔγημα ἐγάμησα	γεγάμηκα		
γελάω *laugh*	γελάσω				
γίνομαι *be born, become*	γενήσομαι	ἐγενόμην	γέγονα	γεγένημαι	ἐγενήθην
γινώσκω *ascertain, know*	γνώσομαι	ἔγνων	ἔγνωκα	ἔγνωσμαι	ἐγνώσθην
γράφω *write*	γράψω	ἔγραψα	γέγραφα	γέγραμμαι	ἐγράφην
δείκνυμι δεικνύω *show* (19.1/1)	δείξω	ἔδειξα		δέδειγμαι	ἐδείχθην
δέχομαι *receive*	δέξομαι	ἐδεξάμην		δέδεγμαι	ἐδέχθην
δέω *bind*	δήσω	ἔδησα	δέδεκα	δέδεμαι	ἐδέθην
διδάσκω *teach*	διδάξω	ἐδίδαξα			ἐδιδάχθην
δίδωμι *give* (18.1/2)	δώσω	ἔδωκα	δέδωκα	δέδομαι	ἐδόθην
δοκέω *consider, seem*		ἔδοξα			
δύναμαι *be able, can*	δυνήσομαι				ἠδυνήθην ἠδυνάσθην
ἐάω *allow*	ἐάσω	εἴασα			
ἐγείρω *raise*	ἐγερῶ	ἤγειρα		ἐγήγερμαι	ἠγέρθην
ἐλαύνω *drive*		-ἤλασα	ἐλήλακα		
ἐλέγχω *convict*	ἐλέγξω	ἤλεγξα			ἠλέγχθην
ἐλπίζω *hope*	ἐλπιῶ	ἤλπισα	ἤλπικα		
ἐπι-λανθάνομαι *forget*		-ἐλαθόμην		-λέλησμαι	
ἐργάζομαι *work*		ἠργασάμην		εἴργασμαι	-εἰργάσθην
ἔρχομαι *come*	ἐλεύσομαι	ἦλθον	ἐλήλυθα		
ἐσθίω *eat*	φάγομαι	ἔφαγον			
εὑρίσκω *find*	εὑρήσω	εὗρον	εὕρηκα		εὑρέθην
ἔχω *have, possess*	ἕξω	ἔσχον	ἔσχηκα		

Present	Future	Aorist	Perfect	Perfect mid./pass.	Aorist passive
θάπτω *bury*		ἔθαψα			ἐτάφην
θέλω *wish, want*	θελήσω	ἠθέλησα			
-ἵημι *send* (20.1/1)	-ἥσω	-ἧκα		-ἕωμαι pple. -εἱμένος	-ἕθην
ἵστημι *place, make to stand* (19.1/2)	στήσω	ἔστησα (tr.) ἔστην (intr.)	ἕστηκα (intr.)		ἐστάθην
καλέω *call*	καλέσω	ἐκάλεσα	κέκληκα	κέκλημαι	ἐκλήθην
κλαίω *weep*	κλαύσω κλαύσομαι	ἔκλαυσα			
κλείω *shut*	κλείσω	-ἔκλεισα		κέκλεισμαι	-ἐκλείσθην
κομίζω *bring*	κομιοῦμαι κομίσομαι	ἐκόμισα ἐκομισάμην			
κρίνω *judge*	κρινῶ	ἔκρινα	κέκρικα	κέκριμαι	ἐκρίθην
λαμβάνω *receive*	λήμψομαι	ἔλαβον	εἴληφα	εἴλημμαι	ἐλήμφθην
λέγω *say*	ἐρῶ	εἶπον, εἶπα	εἴρηκα	εἴρημαι	ἐρρέθην
λείπω *leave*	λείψω	-ἔλιπον ἔλειψα		λέλειμμαι	ἐλείφθην
μανθάνω *learn*		ἔμαθον	μεμάθηκα		
μένω *wait*	μενῶ	ἔμεινα	μεμένηκα		
μιμνήσκομαι *remember*				μέμνημαι	ἐμνήσθην
οἶδα *know*	see 20.1/4(b)				
ὁράω *see*	ὄψομαι	εἶδον	ἑόρακα ἑώρακα		ὤφθην
πάσχω *suffer*		ἔπαθον	πέπονθα		
πείθω *persuade*	πείσω	ἔπεισα	πέποιθα (intr. *trust*)	πέπεισμαι	ἐπείσθην
πέμπω *send*	πέμψω	ἔπεμψα			-ἐπέμφθην
πίνω *drink*	πίομαι	ἔπιον	πέπωκα		ἐπόθην
πίπτω *fall*	πεσοῦμαι	ἔπεσον	πέπτωκα		
πλέω *sail*		ἔπλευσα			

Present	Future	Aorist	Perfect	Perfect mid./pass.	Aorist passive
πράσσω *do*		ἔπραξα *	πέπραχα	πέπραγμαι	
πυνθάνομαι *inquire*		ἐπυθόμην			
ῥίπτω *throw*		ἔρριψα		ἔρριμμαι	
σπείρω *sow*		ἔσπειρα		ἔσπαρμαι	ἐσπάρην
-στέλλω *send*	-στελῶ	-ἔστειλα	-ἔσταλκα	-ἔσταλμαι	-ἐστάλην
σῴζω *save*	σώσω	ἔσωσα	σέσωκα	σέσῳσμαι σέσωμαι	ἐσώθην
τελέω *complete*	τελέσω	ἐτέλεσα	τετέλεκα	τετέλεσμαι	ἐτελέσθην
τίθημι *put, place* (18.1/2)	θήσω	ἔθηκα	τέθεικα	τέθειμαι (κεῖμαι)	ἐτέθην
τίκτω *give birth to*	τέξομαι	ἔτεκον			ἐτέχθην
τρέφω *nourish*		ἔθρεψα		τέθραμμαι	-ἐτράφην
τρέχω *run*		ἔδραμον			
τυγχάνω *happen, obtain*		ἔτυχον	τέτυχα		
φέρω *bring, carry*	οἴσω	ἤνεγκα (ἐνεγκεῖν)	-ἐνήνοχα		ἠνέχθην
φεύγω *flee*	φεύξομαι	ἔφυγον	πέφευγα		
φημί *say*	see 7.1/3				
φθείρω *destroy, corrupt*	φθερῶ	ἔφθειρα		-ἔφθαρμαι	ἐφθάρην
χράομαι *use, treat*		ἐχρησάμην		κέχρημαι	

vocabulary

In using the vocabulary the following should be noted:

(a) In addition to the abbreviations explained on pp. xix–xx the following signs are used:
  † is put after a verb whose principal parts are given on pp. 249ff.
  †† is put after a compound verb whose simple form is included in the same list.

(b) The feminine and neuter forms of adjectives and the genitive of nouns are nearly always abbreviated and will **not** necessarily have the same accent as the form given in full, e.g. the genitive of ἄγγελος is ἀγγέλου, but these are listed below as ἄγγελος, -ου; in these cases the accent of the abbreviated form must be deduced from the rules for accentuation given in **Appendix 7**.

(c) The form of the article which accompanies each noun indicates its gender.

Ἀβραάμ, ὁ (indecl.) *Abraham*

ἀγαθοποιέω *do good*

ἀγαθός, -ή, -όν *good*; (neut. pl.) *good things*

ἀγαλλιάω (act. or mid.) *be glad, rejoice, exult*

ἄγαμός, -ου, ὁ/ἡ *unmarried person*

ἀγαπάω *love*

ἀγάπη, -ης, ἡ *love*

ἀγαπητός, -ή, -όν *beloved*

ἄγγελός, -ου, ὁ *messenger, angel*

ἀγέλη, -ης, ἡ *herd*

ἁγιάζω *treat as holy, reverence, sanctify*

ἅγιος, -α, -ον *sacred, holy*; (pl. m.) *God's people, Christians*; (pl. n.) *sanctuary*

ἁγιότης, -ητος, ἡ *holiness*

ἀγοράζω *buy*

ἄγρα, -ας, ἡ *catch* (of fish)

ἀγραυλέω *be in the open air*

Ἀγρίππας, -α, ὁ *Agrippa*

ἀγρός, -οῦ, ὁ *field*

ἄγω † *lead, bring; go*

ἀγών, -ῶνος, ὁ *contest*

ἀδελφή, -ῆς, ἡ *sister*

ἀδελφός, -οῦ, ὁ *brother*

ἀδελφότης, -ητος, ἡ *brotherhood*

ᾅδης, -ου, ὁ *Hades, the world of the dead; hell*

ἀδικέω *wrong, treat unjustly*

ἀδικία, -ας, ἡ *injustice, wickedness*

Ἀδραμυττηνός, -ή, -όν *of Adramyttium (sea port in Mysia)*

ἀθῷος, -ον *innocent*

αἰγιαλός, -οῦ, ὁ *shore*

Αἰγύπτιος, -ου, ὁ *Egyptian*

Αἴγυπτος, -ου, ἡ *Egypt*

Αἰθίοψ, -οπος, ὁ *Ethiopian*

αἷμα, -ατος, τό *blood*

αἰνέω † *praise*

αἱρετίζω *choose*

αἱρέω † *take*
αἴρω † *lift; take, take up*
αἰσχρός, -ά, -όν *ugly, shameful*
αἰτέω *ask (for)* (+ double acc.)
αἰτία, -ας, ἡ *cause, reason; relationship*
αἴτιον, -ου, τό *guilt*
αἰχμαλωτίζω *take as captive*
αἰών, -ῶνος, ὁ *age; eternity*
αἰώνιος, -ον *eternal*
ἀκάθαρτος, -ον *unclean*
ἄκακος, -ον *innocent*
ἄκανθα, -ης, ἡ *thorn-bush*
ἀκατακάλυπτος, -ον *uncovered*
ἀκολουθέω (+ dat.) *follow*
ἀκούω † *hear* (15.1/1(a)(iii))
ἀκριβής, -ές *strict*
ἀλείφω *anoint*
ἀλέκτωρ, -ορος, ὁ *cock*
Ἀλεξανδρῖνος, -η, -ον *of Alexandria* (city in Egypt)
ἄλευρον, -ου, τό *flour*
ἀλήθεια, -ας, ἡ *truth*
ἀληθής, -ές *true*
ἀληθῶς (adv.) *truly*
ἁλιεύς, -έως, ὁ *fisherman*
ἁλιεύω *fish*
ἀλλά *but*
ἀλλάσσω *change*
ἀλλαχοῦ (adv.) *elsewhere*
ἀλλήλους, -ας, -α (reciprocal pron.) *each other, one another* (9.1/4(b))
ἄλλος, -η, -ο *other*
ἀλλότριος, -α, -ον *belonging to another*
ἅμα (prep. + dat.) *at the same time as* ἅμα πρωΐ *early in the morning*
ἁμαρτάνω † *do wrong, sin*
ἁμαρτία, -ας, ἡ *sin*
ἁμαρτωλός, όν *sinful*
ἀμελέω (+ gen.) *neglect*
ἀμήν (adv.) *truly, verily* (15.1/2a)
ἄμπελος, -ου, ἡ *vine*
ἀμπελών, -ῶνος, ὁ *vineyard*
ἀμύνομαι † *come/go to help*
ἀμφιέννυμι *clothe*
ἄν untranslatable particle: in a main clause (+ ind. or opt.) with a potential/conditional sense (18.1/3); in a subordinate clause (+ subj.) with an indef. sense (14.1/1(b)(i), (c))
ἄν = ἐάν (18.1/3 note 3)
ἀναβαίνω †† *come/go up*

ἀναβλέπω *gain one's sight; look up*
ἀναγινώσκω †† *read*
ἀναγκάζω *force*
ἀνάγκη, -ης, ἡ *necessity; calamity*
ἀνάγω †† *bring/take up; lead away;* (pass.) *put out to sea*
ἀναζάω *come back to life*
ἀνάθεμα, -ατος, τό *object of a curse*
ἀναιρέω †† (aor. ἀνεῖλον) *kill, destroy*
ἀναίτιος, -ον *innocent*
ἀνακαθίζω *sit up*
ἀναλαμβάνω †† *take up*
ἀνάλυσις, -εως, ἡ *departure*
ἀναμιμνήσκω *remind*
ἀνάξιος, -ον *unworthy*
ἀνάπαυσις, -εως, ἡ *rest; resting place*
ἀναπεσεῖν aor. inf. of ἀναπίπτω
ἀναπίπτω †† *sit*
ἀναπληρόω *fill;* (pass.) *come true, be fulfilled*
ἀνάστασις, -εως, ἡ *resurrection*
ἀνατέλλω *rise*
ἀνατολή, -ῆς, ἡ (usually pl.) *east*
ἀναχωρέω *go away*
Ἀνδρέας, -ου, ὁ *Andrew*
ἀνέθην aor. ind. pass. of ἀνίημι
ἀνεῖλον aor. ind. act. of ἀναιρέω
ἀνεκτός, -όν *endurable, tolerable*
ἀνελεῖν aor. inf. act. of ἀναιρέω
ἄνεμος, -ου, ὁ *wind*
ἀνεπίλημπτος, -ον *irreproachable*
ἀνεῳγμένος perf. mid./pass. pple. of ἀνοίγω
ἀνήρ, ἀνδρός, ὁ *man, husband* (6.1/1(b))
ἀνήχθην aor. pass. of ἀνάγω
ἀνθρωποκτόνος, -ου, ὁ *murderer*
ἄνθρωπος, -ου, ὁ *human being, person; man*
ἀνίημι †† *loosen, unfasten; stop; desert*
ἀνίστημι †† (tr. tenses) *raise up;* (intr. tenses) *rise/stand up* (19.1/2)
Ἄννα, -ας, ἡ (note rough breathing!) *Anna*
ἀνοίγω † *open*
ἀντέχομαι (+ gen.) *hold fast to*
ἀντί (prep. + gen.) *instead of, in place of*
ἀντίθεσις, -εως, ἡ *contradiction*
ἀντίκειμι *be opposed to*
Ἀντιόχεια, -ας, ἡ *Antioch*

ἀντιπαρέρχομαι †† *go by on the opposite side* (of the road)
ἀντιπαρῆλθον aor. ind. act. of ἀντιπαρέρχομαι
ἄνυδρος, -ον *waterless*
ἄνω (adv.) *above*
ἀξίνη, -ης, ἡ *axe*
ἄξιος, -α, -ον (+ gen.) *worthy (of), deserving*
ἀξιόω *consider worthy*
ἀξίως (adv.; + gen.) *in a manner worthy of*
ἀπαγγέλλω *proclaim*
ἀπάγχω *throttle*
ἀπάγω †† *lead away*
ἅπαξ (adv.) *once*
ἀπαρνέομαι *deny, renounce*
ἅπας, ἅπασα, ἅπαν *all, every*
ἀπάτη, -ης, ἡ *deception*
ἄπειμι *be absent*
ἄπειμι *go* (20.1/4(a))
ἀπεκρίθην aor. of ἀποκρίνομαι
ἀπελθεῖν aor. inf. of ἀπέρχομαι
ἀπέναντι (prep. + gen.) *before, in front of*
ἀπέρχομαι †† *go away, go out*
ἀπέχω †† *be distant*
ἀπῆλθον aor. indic. of ἀπέρχομαι
ἀπιστία, -ας, ἡ *disbelief*
ἄπιστος, -ον *unbelieving*
ἁπλότης, -ητος, ἡ *sincerity*
ἁπλοῦς (-όος), -ῆ, -οῦν (21.1/2) *sound, healthy*
ἀπό (prep. + gen.) *from, away from*
ἀπογραφή, -ῆς, ἡ *census*
ἀπογράφω †† *register*
ἀποδημέω *go away*
ἀποδίδωμι †† *repay, give back*
ἀποδώσω fut. ind. of ἀποδίδωμι
ἀποθνῄσκω † *die*
ἀποκαλύπτω *reveal*
ἀποκεφαλίζω *behead*
ἀποκρίνομαι † *reply, answer*
ἀποκτείνω † *kill*
ἀπολαμβάνω †† *receive*
ἀπόλημαι aor. subj. mid. of ἀπόλλυμι
ἀπόλλυμι † *ruin, destroy; lose;* (mid.) *perish; be lost* (19.1/1 note 2)
ἀπολογία, -ας, ἡ *(verbal) defence*
ἀπολύω *free; divorce*
ἀπολωλώς perf. pple. of ἀπόλλυμι (19.1/1 note 2)
ἀπονίπτω *wash*

ἀποπλέω †† *set sail*
ἀποστέλλω †† *send, send out, dispatch*
ἀπόστολος, -ου, ὁ *apostle*
ἀποτίθημι †† *put away, put*
ἀποφθέγγομαι *speak*
ἅπτω *light, kindle;* (mid. + gen.) *touch*
ἀπωθέομαι (aor. ἀπωσάμην) *push aside*
ἀπώλεσα tr. aor. of ἀπόλλυμι (19.1/1 note 2)
ἀπωλόμην intr. aor. of ἀπόλλυμι (19.1/1 note 2)
ἄρα *so, then, consequently* (15.1/2(b))
ἀργός,-ή, -όν *idle, unemployed*
ἀργύριον, -ου, τό *(silver) money*
ἀργυροῦς (-εος), -ᾶ, -οῦν (21.1/2) *[made of] silver*
ἀρέσκω (+ dat.) *please*
ἀριθμός, -οῦ, ὁ *number*
Ἀρίσταρχος, -ου, ὁ *Aristarchus*
ἀρνέομαι *deny*
ἆρον aor. imp. act. of αἴρω
ἁρπαγή, -ῆς, ἡ *greed*
ἁρπάζω *seize*
ἄρρωστος, -ον *sick*
ἄρσην, -εν *male*
Ἄρτεμις, -ιδος, ἡ *Artemis*
ἄρτι (adv.) *now*
ἄρτος, -ου, ὁ *(loaf of) bread*
Ἀρχέλαος, -ου, ὁ *Archelaus*
ἀρχή, -ῆς, ἡ *beginning*
ἀρχιερεύς, -έως, ὁ *high priest*
ἄρχω *rule;* (mid.) † *begin*
ἄρχων, -οντος, ὁ *ruler*
ἄρωμα, -ατος, τό *aromatic spice*
ἄσβεστος, -ον *inextinguishable*
ἀσθένεια, -ας, ἡ *sickness*
ἀσθενέω *be sick; be weak*
ἀσθενής, -ές *sick; weak*
Ἀσία, -ας, ἡ *Asia*
ἀσκός, -οῦ, ὁ *wine-skin*
ἀσπασμός, -οῦ, ὁ *greeting*
ἀσσάριον, -ου, τό *as* (smallest unit of Roman currency)
ἀστήρ, -έρος, ὁ *star*
ἀστραπή, -ῆς, ἡ *lightning*
ἀσώτως (adv.) *dissolutely*
ἀτενίζω *look intently at*
ἄτιμος, -ον *without honour*
ἄτοπος, -ον *wrong*
αὐλή, -ῆς, ἡ *courtyard*

αὐξάνω, αὐξω   *cause to grow*; (act. &
  pass.) *grow* (intr.)
αὔριον (adv.)   *tomorrow, the next day*
αὐτόματος, -η, -ον   *by itself*
αὐτός, -ή, -ό (pron.)   *he, she, it*
  (4.1/2); *self* (9.1/3(a)); ὁ αὐτός *the
  same* (9.1/3(b))
ἀφαιρέω †† *take away*
ἀφείς aor. pple. act. of ἀφίημι
ἄφες aor. imp. act. of ἀφίημι
ἄφεσις, -εως, ἡ *pardon, forgiveness*
ἀφῆκα aor. ind. act. of ἀφίημι
ἀφίημι ††   *cancel; leave, send away*;
  (+ acc. of thing & dat. of person)
  forgive
ἄφιξις, -εως, ἡ *departure*
ἀφίστημι †† (tr. tenses)   *mislead,*
  make to revolt; (intr. tenses) *go*
  away (19.1/2)
ἄφνω (adv.)   *suddenly*
ἄφρων, -ον   *foolish*
ἄχρι (prep. + gen)   *up to*; (conj.) *until*
  (14.1/1(b)(ii))

βάθος, -ους, τό *depth*
βάλλω † *throw, cast; put*
βαπτίζω *baptize*
βαπτιστής, -οῦ, ὁ   *Baptist* (of John)
βάπτω *dip*
Βαραββᾶς, -ᾶ, ὁ *Barabbas*
βάρβαρος, -ον *non-Greek*; (as m.
  noun) *foreigner*
Βαριωνᾶς, -ᾶ, ὁ *son of Jonah*
Βαρναβᾶς, -ᾶ, ὁ   *Barnabas*
βαρύς, -εῖα, -ύ *heavy; cruel*
βασανίζω *torture*
βασιλεία, -ας, ἡ *kingdom*
βασιλεύς, -έως, ὁ   *king* (11.1/4)
βασιλεύω (+ gen. or ἐπί + acc.)   *rule,*
  be king (of)
βασιλικός, -ή, -όν *royal*
βαστάζω *carry, bear*
βεβηλόω *desecrate, profane*
βεβλημένος perf. pple. pass. of βάλλω
Βεελζεβούλ, ὁ (indecl.)   *Beelzebub*
βέλτιον (adv.) compar. of εὖ
Βηθανιά, ἡ (indecl.) and Βηθανία, -ας,
  ἡ   *Bethany* (village on Mt. of
  Olives)
Βηθλέεμ, ἡ (indecl.)   *Bethlehem*
Βηθσαϊδά, ἡ (indecl.)   *Bethsaida*
  (town on the north of the Sea of
  Galilee)

Βηθφαγή, ἡ (indecl.)   *Bethphage*
  (place on Mt. of Olives)
βία, -ας, ἡ *force, violence*
βιβλίον, -ου, τό *book*
βίος, -ου, ὁ *life; livelihood;*
  possessions
βλασφημέω *blaspheme*
βλασφημία, -ας, ἡ *blasphemy*
βλέπω *see; take precautions*
Βόες, ὁ (indecl.)   *Boaz*
βοηθέω (+ dat.)   *help, assist*
βόσκω *feed*
βουλεύω *deliberate*
βούλημα, -ατος, τό *intention*
βούλομαι † *wish*
βοῦς, βοός, ὁ/ἡ   *ox, cow*
βραδυπλοέω *sail slowly*
βραχίων, -ονος, ὁ *arm*
βραχύς, -εῖα, -ύ *short, little*
βρέφος, -ους, τό *baby*
βρέχω *rain*
βροχή, -ῆς, ἡ *rain*
βρύω *pour forth*

Γαβριήλ, ὁ (indecl.)   *Gabriel*
γαζοφυλάκιον, -ου, τό *box for*
  offerings
Γαλατικός, -ή, -όν   *Galatian*
Γαλιλαία, -ας, ἡ   *Galilee*
Γαλιλαῖος, -α, -ον   *Galilean*
γαμέω † *marry*
γαμίζω *give in marriage*
γάμος, -ου, ὁ *marriage*
γάρ# (connecting particle)   *for, as*
γαστήρ, -τρός, ἡ *stomach*
γε# *at least, at any rate; certainly,*
  indeed (15.1/2(a))
γέγονα perf. ind. of γίνομαι
γέεννα, -ης, ἡ   *Gehenna; hell*
Γεθσημανί (indecl.)   *Gethsemane*
γελάω † *laugh*
γέμω (+ gen.)   *be full (of)*
γενεά, -ᾶς, ἡ *generation*
γενέσια, -ων, τά *birthday celebration*
γένεσις, -εως, ἡ *birth*
γένημα, -ατος, τό *product, fruit*
γεννάω *beget, father*; (pass.) *be born*
γέννημα, -ατος, τό *offspring*
γεννητός, -ή, -όν *begotten, born*
γένοιτο 3 s. aor. opt. of γίνομαι
  (13.1/4)
γένος, -ους, τό *race, clan*
γεωργός, -οῦ, ὁ *(tenant) farmer*

γῆ, γῆς, ἡ *earth; soil; ground; land, country*

γίνομαι † *be born, be created, be done; become; happen* (8.1/2); (with κατά) *get to*

γινώσκω † *ascertain, know*

γλυκύς, -εῖα, -ύ *sweet*

γλῶσσα, -ης, ἡ *tongue*

γναφεύς, -έως, ὁ *fuller*

Γολγοθᾶ, ἡ *Golgotha*

Γόμορρα, -ων, τά *Gomorrah*

γονεύς, -έως, ὁ *parent*

γόνυ, γόνατος, τό *knee*

γραμματεύς, -έως, ὁ *doctor of law*

γραφή, -ῆς, ἡ *scripture, sacred writing*

γράφω † *write, write of*

γυμνός, -ή, -όν *naked*

γυνή, γυναικός, ἡ *woman, wife*

δαιμονίζομαι *be possessed of evil spirits*

δαιμόνιον, -ου, τό *evil spirit*

δάκρυ (or δάκρυον), -ύου, τό *tear*

δακρύω *weep*

δακτύλιος, -ου, ὁ *ring*

Δαμασκός, -οῦ, ἡ *Damascus*

δαπανάω *spend*

Δαυίδ, ὁ (indecl.) *David*

δέ# (connecting particle) *and, but*

δεῖ (impers.) *it is necessary*

δειγματίζω *expose*

δείκνυμι/δεικνύω † *show; indicate to* (19.1/1)

δειλός, -ή, -όν *timid*

δεισιδαίμων, -ον *religious; superstitious*

δένδρον, -ου, τό *tree*

δεξιός, -ά, -όν *right* (as opposed to left)

δέος, -ους, τό *fear, awe*

δέσμιος, -ου, ὁ *prisoner*

δεσμός, -οῦ, ὁ (pl. δεσμοί or δεσμά) *bond, fetter*

δεσμοφύλαξ, -ακος, ὁ *gaoler*

δεσμωτήριον, -ου, τό *prison*

δεσμώτης, -ου, ὁ *prisoner*

δεῦτε (adverbial formation serving as a pl. imp.) *come!*

δεύτερος, -α, -ον *second*

δέχομαι † *receive*

δέω † *bind*

δηλόω *make clear, show*

δηνάριον, -ου, τό *denarius* (Roman silver coin)

διά (prep. + acc.) *because of, on account of;* (+ gen.) *through, across; during; by means of*

διὰ τί; *on account of what? why?*

διάβολος, -ου, ὁ *the Devil*

διάγνωσις, -εως, ἡ *decision*

διαιρέω †† (aor. διεῖλον) *divide, apportion*

διακονέω *serve*

διάκονος, -ου, ὁ *servant; deacon,* (f.) *deaconess*

διακόσιοι, -αι, -α, *two hundred*

διακρίνω †† *judge correctly;* (mid.) *hesitate, waver*

διαλογίζομαι *wonder*

διάνοια, -ας, ἡ *thought, imagination*

διαπλέω †† *sail across*

διαπορεύομαι *go through*

διασκορπίζω *scatter; squander, waste*

διασπάω *tear apart*

διαστᾶσα f. pple. of intr. aor. of διΐστημι

διασῴζω †† *cure*

διαταράσσομαι *be perplexed, troubled*

διαφέρω †† (+ gen.) *be different from*

διδάσκαλος, -ου, ὁ *teacher, master*

διδάσκω † *teach*

διδαχή, -ῆς, ἡ *teaching*

δίδωμι † (18.1/1) *give*

διεγείρω †† *arouse, stir up*

διεῖλον aor. act. of διαιρέω

διερμηνεύω *interpret, translate*

διέρχομαι †† *cross over; go through; come across*

διῆλθον aor. indic. of διέρχομαι

διΐστημι *pass*

διϊσχυρίζομαι *insist*

δίκαιος, -α, -ον *just, upright*

δικαιοσύνη, -ης, ἡ *justice, righteousness*

δικαίως (adv.) *justly*

δικαστής, -οῦ, ὁ *judge*

δίκτυον, -ου, τό *net*

διό (connecting particle) *therefore*

διοδεύω *journey, travel*

διορύσσω *dig through*

διπλοῦς (-όος), -ῆ, -οῦν (21.1/2) *double, twofold*

δίς (adv.) *twice*

δισχίλιοι, -αι, -α *two thousand*

διώκω *pursue, persecute*
δόγμα, -ατος, τό *rule*
δοκέω † *consider; seem*
 δοκεῖ (impers. 21.1/1(a)(iii)) *it seems good*
δοκιμάζω *examine*
δοκός, -οῦ, ἡ *beam*
δόλος, -ου, ὁ *deceit*
δόμα, -ατος, τό *gift*
δόξα, -ης, ἡ *glory*
δοξάζω *praise*
Δορκάς, -άδος, ἡ *Dorcas* (as common noun *gazelle*)
δουλεύω (+ dat.) *serve* (as a slave)
δούλη, -ης, ἡ *female slave, female servant*
δοῦλος, -ου, ὁ *slave, servant*
δουλόω *enslave*
δοῦναι aor. inf. act. of δίδωμι (18.1/2)
δρᾶμα, -ατος, τό *deed, act*
δραμών aor. pple. of τρέχω
δύναμαι † *be able, can* (19.1/3)
δύναμις, -εως, ἡ *power, might; meaning; miracle*
δυνάστης, -ου, ὁ *ruler*
δυνατός, -ή, -όν *able; mighty*
δύο *two* (7.1/5)
δυσκόλως (adv.) *with difficulty*
δυσμή, -ῆς, ἡ (usually pl.) *west*
δώδεκα (indecl.) *twelve*
δωρεά, -ᾶς, ἡ *gift, bounty of God*
δῶρον, -ου, τό *gift*

ἐάν *if* (18.1/3 note 2)
ἐάν = ἄν in indefinite clauses (14.1/1 note 1)
ἑαυτόν, -ήν, -ό (refl. pron.) *himself, herself, itself;* in pl. *ourselves, yourselves, themselves* (9.1/4(a))
ἐάω † *allow*
ἑβδομηκοντάκις (adv.) *seventy times*
Ἑβραϊστί (adv.) *in Hebrew*
ἐγγίζω (+ dat.) *approach, come near*
ἐγγράφω †† *write in, enrol*
ἐγγύς (adv.) *near,* (prep. + dat.) *near, close to*
ἐγείρω † *raise, raise up; wake* (tr.); (imp.) ἔγειρε (intr.) *get up!;* (pass.) *rise*
ἐγένετο aor. of γίνομαι (8.1/2)
ἔγνων aor. ind. act. of γινώσκω
ἐγώ *I* (4.1/2)
ἔδαφος, -ους, τό *ground*

ἔδει impf. of δεῖ (18.1/4(b))
ἔδραμον aor. of τρέχω
ἔθηκαν aor. ind. act. of τίθημι
ἐθνικός, -ή, -όν *pagan, gentile*
ἔθνος, -ους, τό *nation, people;* (pl.) *heathen, Gentiles*
ἔθρεψαν aor. ind. act. of τρέφω
εἰ *if*
εἶδον aor. ind. act. of ὁράω
εἶδος, -ους, τό *appearance*
εἰδώς pple. of οἶδα (20.1/4(b))
εἴκοσι (indecl.) *twenty*
εἰμί *be* (3.1/6)
εἶναι inf. of εἰμί
εἶπον, εἶπα aor. ind. act. of λέγω
εἰρήνη, -ης, ἡ *peace*
εἰρηνοποιός, -οῦ, ὁ *peacemaker*
εἷς, μία, ἕν *one* (7.1/5(a))
εἰς (prep. + acc.) *to, into, on to; with regard to, in relation to*
εἰσάγω †† *bring to*
εἴσειμι *enter* (20.1/4(a))
εἰσελεύσομαι fut. of εἰσέρχομαι
εἰσέρχομαι †† *enter*
εἰσήγαγον aor. act. of εἰσάγω
εἰσῆλθον aor. of εἰσέρχομαι
εἰσήνεγκα aor. ind. act. of εἰσφέρω
εἰσπηδάω *rush in*
εἰσπορεύομαι *come/go in, enter*
εἰσφέρω †† *bring into, lead into*
εἴτε ... εἴτε *whether ... or*
εἶχον impf. of ἔχω
ἐκ (ἐξ before vowels and diphthongs; prep. + gen.) *out of, from*
 ἐκ μέσου *from the midst (of)*
ἕκαστος, -η, -ον *each, every*
ἑκατόν (indecl.) *hundred*
ἑκατοντάρχης (and ἑκατόνταρχος), -ου, ὁ *centurion* (officer in Roman army)
ἐκβάλλω †† *expel, cast out; send out; take out*
ἐκδέχομαι †† *wait for*
ἐκδίκησις, -εως, ἡ *retribution*
ἐκδύω *strip; take off (clothes)*
ἐκεῖ (adv.) *there, in that place*
ἐκεῖθεν (adv.) *from there*
ἐκεῖνος, -η, -ο (pron. and adj. 9.1/1) *that*
ἐκεῖσε (adv.) *there*
ἐκθαμβέομαι *be alarmed*
ἐκκλάω (aor. pass. ἐξεκλάσθην) *break off*

ἐκκλησία, -ας, ἡ   *church*
ἐκκόπτω   *cut down*
ἐκλάμπω   *shine forth*
ἔκλαυσα aor. ind. act. of κλαίω
ἐκλέγομαι   *choose*
ἐκλείπω †† *fail, come to an end*
ἐκλήθην aor. ind. pass. of καλέω
ἐκμάσσω   *wipe, dry*
ἐκπλήσσω   *amaze, astound*
ἐκπορεύομαι   *come/go out*
ἔκστασις, -εως, ἡ   *amazement*
ἔκτος, -η, -ον   *sixth*
ἐκφέρω ††   *bring out*
ἐκφεύγω ††   *escape*
ἐκχέω (perf. pass. ἐκκέχυμαι)   *pour out*
ἐκχωρέω   *go away, depart*
ἔλαβον aor. ind. act. of λαμβάνω
ἐλαία, -ας, ἡ   *olive tree*
ἔλαιον, -ου, τό   *(olive) oil*
ἐλάσσων, -ον (compar. of μικρός 17.1/2(b))   *younger, inferior*
ἐλαύνω †   *drive; advance; row*
ἐλάχιστος, -η, -ον   *smallest, least*
ἔλεγχος, -ου, ὁ   *proof*
ἐλέγχω †   *convict; expose*
ἐλεέω   *show mercy to*
ἐλεημοσύνη, -ης, ἡ   *alms, charitable works*
ἔλεος, -ους, τό   *mercy*
ἐλεύθερος, -α, -ον   *free*
ἐληλακώς perf. act. pple. of ἐλαύνω
ἐλήλυθα perf. ind. of ἔρχομαι
ἔλθω aor. subj. of ἔρχομαι
Ἑλληνίς, -ίδος, ἡ   *gentile woman*
Ἑλληνιστής, -οῦ, ὁ   *Greek-speaking Jew*
Ἑλληνιστί (adv.)   *in Greek*
ἐλπίζω †   *hope, hope for*
ἐλπίς, -ίδος, ἡ   *hope*
ἐμαυτόν   *myself* (refl. 9.1/4(a))
ἐμβαίνω ††   *embark*
ἐμβιβάζω   *put on board*
ἐμβλέπω (+ dat.)   *look at*
ἐμός, -ή, -όν (poss. adj.)   *my*
ἐμπίμπρημι (aor. ἐνέπρησα)   *set fire to, burn*
ἔμπροσθεν (prep. + gen.)   *in front of, before*
ἐν (prep. + dat.)   *in, on; among; with* (of an instrument; 11.1/2)
  ἐν τῷ καθεξῆς   *in the next in order*
    i.e. *afterwards*

ἕν see εἷς
ἐναντίος, -α, -ον (+ dat.)   *opposed to, opposite; contrary* (of winds)
ἔνατος, -η, -ον   *ninth*
ἕνδεκα (indecl.)   *eleven*
ἑνδέκατος, -η, -ον   *eleventh*
ἔνδοξος, -ον   *famous*
ἔνδυμα, -ατος, τό   *clothing*
ἐνδυναμόω   *strengthen*
ἐνδύω   *clothe, dress;* (mid. + acc.) *clothe oneself with, put on*
ἐνέβην aor. ind. of ἐμβαίνω
ἐνεβίβασα aor. ind. act. of ἐμβιβάζω
ἕνεκεν (prep. + gen.)   *for the sake of, on account of*
ἐνενήκοντα (indecl.)   *ninety*
ἐνέπρησα aor. ind. act. of ἐμπίπρημι
ἐνθάδε (adv.)   *here*
ἐνθυμέομαι   *think*
ἐνθύμησις, -εως, ἡ   *thought*
ἐνιαυτός, -οῦ, ὁ   *year*
  κατ᾽ ἐνιαυτόν, *yearly*
ἐννέα (indecl.)   *nine*
ἐνοικέω   *live in*
ἑνότης, -ητος, ἡ   *unity*
ἔνοχος, -ον (+ gen.)   *guilty (of), deserving*
ἐντεῦθεν (adv.)   *from here/there*
ἔντιμος, -ον   *honoured, distinguished*
ἐντολή, -ῆς, ἡ   *commandment*
ἔντρομος, -ον   *trembling*
ἐντυγχάνω (+ dat.)   *fall in with*
ἐνώπιον (prep. + gen.)   *before, in the presence of*
ἕξ (indecl.)   *six*
ἐξ see ἐκ
ἐξάγω ††   *lead out*
ἐξαιρέω ††   *take out*
ἐξαίφνης (adv.)   *suddenly*
ἐξανατέλλω   *spring up*
ἐξαπατάω   *deceive*
ἐξαποστέλλω ††   *send, send away*
ἐξεβλήθην aor. indic. pass. of ἐκβάλλω
ἔξειμι   *depart, leave* (20.1/4)
ἐξελέξατο aor. ind. of ἐκλέγομαι
ἐξέρχομαι ††   *come/go out*
ἔξεστί(ν) (impers. + dat. and inf.; 21.1/1(a)(iii))   *it is permitted/allowed*
ἐξήκοντα   *sixty*
ἐξῆλθον aor. ind. of ἐξέρχομαι
ἐξίστημι †† (tr. tenses)   *confuse, amaze;* (intr. tenses) *lose one's*

senses; *be amazed* (19.1/2)
ἐξουσία, -ας, ἡ *authority, power; right*
ἔξυπνος, -ον *awake*
ἔξω (adv.; prep. + gen.) *outside*
ἔξωθεν (adv.) *outside*
ἑορτή, -ῆς, ἡ *feast*
ἐπαγγελία, -ας, ἡ *promise*
ἐπαγγέλλομαι *promise*
ἐπάγγελμα, -ατος, τό *promise*
ἔπαθον aor. ind. of πάσχω
ἐπαινέω † *praise*
ἐπακροάομαι *listen to*
ἐπανέρχομαι †† *return*
ἔπειμι *be next* (20.1/4)
ἔπειτα (adv.) *then, next*
ἐπέρχομαι †† *come*
ἐπερωτάω *ask* (someone a question)
ἔπεσον aor. of πίπτω
ἐπέστην intr. aor. of ἐφίστημι
ἐπί (prep.) (+ acc.) *on, in; to, towards; over; for;* (+ gen.) *on, upon;* (+ dat.) *in, on; because of; by*
ἐπιβαίνω †† (+ dat.) *embark on*
ἐπιβάλλω †† *put* (acc.) ... *on* (dat.); *be due to* (by inheritance)
ἐπιβαρέω *be a burden to*
ἐπιβιβάζω *set/place on*
ἐπιβλέπω *look upon*
ἐπιγινώσκω †† *know; discover*
ἐπιγνούς aor. pple. of ἐπιγινώσκω
ἐπίγνωσις, -εως, ἡ *knowledge*
ἐπιδείκνυμι †† *show*
ἐπιθείς aor. pple. act. of ἐπιτίθημι
ἐπιθυμέω *desire*
ἐπικαλέω †† *name;* (mid.) *appeal to*
ἐπίκειμαι *press on, threaten*
ἐπιλανθάνομαι † *forget*
ἐπιμέλεια, -ας, ἡ *care, attention*
ἐπιμελέομαι (+ gen.) *look after, take care of*
ἐπιούσιος, -ον *for today*
ἐπιπίπτω †† *fall on*
ἐπισκέπτομαι *visit*
ἐπισκιάζω (+ dat.) *overshadow, cast a shadow on*
ἐπίσκοπος, -ου, ὁ *bishop*
ἐπίσταμαι *know* (19.1/3)
ἐπιστηρίζω *strengthen*
ἐπιστολή, -ῆς, ἡ *letter*
ἐπιστρέφω *return*
ἐπιτάσσω (+ dat.) *command*
ἐπιτελέω †† (+ dat.) *lay upon*

ἐπιτίθημι †† *inflict, lay on*
ἐπιτιμάω (+ dat.) *rebuke, censure*
ἐπιτρέπω (+ dat.) *allow, permit*
ἐπιχειρέω *attempt, try*
ἐπιχέω *pour on*
ἐπλήσθην aor. ind. pass. of πίμπλημι
ἐπονομάζω *call, name*
ἐπουράνιος, -ον *heavenly*
ἑπτά (indecl.) *seven*
ἑπτάκις (adv.) *seven times*
ἐργάζομαι † *work*
ἐργάτης, -ου, ὁ *labourer*
ἔργον, -ου, τό *deed, action; work*
ἐρέω fut. of λέγω
ἐρημία, -ας, ἡ *wilderness, desert*
ἔρημος, -ον *empty, desolate*
   ἡ ἔρημος *desert, wilderness*
ἐρήμωσις, -εως, ἡ *destruction*
ἔρις, ἔριδος, ἡ *strife*
ἔρχομαι † *come* (8.1/2 note)
ἐρωτάω *ask* (someone a question)
ἐσθής, -ῆτος, ἡ *garment*
ἐσθίω † *eat*
ἐσμέν 1 pl. pres. of εἰμί
ἔσοπτρον, -ου τό *mirror*
ἔσται 3 s. fut. of εἰμί
ἕστηκα perf. ind. of ἵστημι (19.1/2)
ἑστώς perf. pple. of ἵστημι (19.1/2)
ἔσχατος, -η, -ον *last, final*
ἔσω (adv.) *inside, within*
ἔσωθεν (adv.) *inside*
ἔτεκον aor. ind. act. of τίκτω
ἕτερος, -α, -ον *different; other; another*
   τῇ ἑτέρᾳ *on the next day*
ἐτέχθην aor. ind. pass. of τίκτω
ἔτι (adv.) *still*
ἑτοιμάζω *prepare, make ready*
ἕτοιμος, -η, -ον *ready*
ἔτος, -ους, τό *year*
εὖ (adv.) *well*
Εὕα, -ας, ἡ (note rough breathing!) *Eve*
εὐαγγελίζω *announce good news;* (mid.) *preach, announce*
εὐαγγέλιον, -ου, τό *gospel*
εὐαρέστως (adv.) *in an acceptable way*
εὐγενής, -ές *high-minded, noble*
εὐδοκέω (+ acc.) *take delight in, rejoice in*
εὐδοκία, -ας, ἡ *good will, favour*
εὐθέως (adv.) *immediately*

εὐθυμέω   *take courage*
εὐθύς (adv.)   *immediately, straightway*
εὐκαιρέω   *spend time*
εὐκοπώτερον (adv.)   *easier*
εὐλάβεια, -ας, ἡ   *reverence*
εὐλογία, -ας, ἡ   *flattery*
εὐνουχίζω   *emasculate*
εὐνοῦχος, -ου, ὁ   *eunuch*
εὐοδόομαι   *prosper*
εὑρίσκω   *find*
εὐφραίνομαι   *rejoice, make merry*
εὔχομαι   *pray*
ἐφ᾽ = ἐπί
ἔφαγον aor. of ἐσθίω
Ἐφέσιος, -α, -ον   *Ephesian*
ἐχθές (adv.)   *yesterday*
ἐχθρός, -ά, -όν   *hostile*; (as m. noun) *enemy*
ἔχιδνα, -ης, ἡ   *viper*
ἐχόμενος (pres. pple. mid. of ἔχω) *neighbouring*
ἔχω †   *have, possess; look upon, regard*
ἕως (prep. + gen.)   *up to, to; until*; (conj.) *until* (14.1/1(b)(ii))

ζάω   *live, be alive*
Ζεβεδαῖος, -ου, ὁ   *Zebedee*
ζητέω   *seek, look for*
ζωγρέω   *capture alive*
ζωή, -ῆς, ἡ   *life*
ζώνη, -ης, ἡ   *belt*

ἤ   *or; than*
ἤγαγον aor. act. of ἄγω
ἤγγικα perf. ind. act. of ἐγγίζω
ἡγεμών, -όνος, ὁ   *governor, leader*
ἡγέομαι   *lead*
ἠγέρθην aor. indic. pass. of ἐγείρω
ἠγοράσθην aor. ind. pass. of ἀγοράζω
ᾔδειν plpf. (= aor.) of οἶδα (20.1/4(b))
ἡδέως (adv.)   *pleasantly*
ἤδη (adv.)   *already*
ἥδιστα (adv.)   *most gladly*
ἦθος, -ους, τό   *habit*
ἥκω (may have either a present or a perfect sense)   *come, have come*
ἦλθον aor. of ἔρχομαι
Ἠλίας, -ου, ὁ   *Elijah*
ἥλιος, -ου, ὁ   *sun*
ἤλπικα perf. ind. act. of ἐλπίζω
ἥμαρτον aor. ind. act. of ἁμαρτάνω

ἡμεῖς   *we* (4.1/2)
ἤμελλον impf. of μέλλω
ἡμέρα, -ας, ἡ   *day*
ἡμέτερος, -α, -ον (poss. adj.)   *our*
ἤμην impf. of εἰμί
ἡμιθανής, -ές   *half-dead*
ἦν impf. of εἰμί
ἤνεγκα aor. ind. act. of φέρω
ἠνέχθην aor. ind. pass. of φέρω
ἠνεῴχθην aor. ind. pass. of ἀνοίγω
ἤρεσα aor. ind. act. of ἀρέσκω
ἠρχόμην impf. of ἄρχομαι or ἔρχομαι
Ἡρῴδης, -ου, ὁ   *Herod*
Ἡρῳδιάς, -άδος, ἡ   *Heriodas*
Ἠσαΐας, -ου, ὁ   *Isaiah*
ἥσσων, -ον (compar. of κακός   17.1/2(b))   *lesser, inferior*
ἥτις see ὅστις
ἥφιεν 3rd s. impf. act. of ἀφίημι   (20.1/1 note)
ἠχώ, -οῦς, ἡ   *sound, echo*

θάλασσα, -ης, ἡ   *sea*
θάμβος, -ους, τό   *amazement*
θάνατος, -ου, ὁ   *death*
θανατόω   *kill*
θάπτω †   *bury*
θαρσέω   *take courage*
θαυμάζω   *marvel, be surprised, be amazed*
θεάομαι   *see*
θέατρον, -ου, τό   *theatre*
θεῖον, -ου, τό   *sulphur*
θέλημα, -ατος, τό   *will; wish*
θέλω †   *wish, want, desire to*
θεμέλιον, -ου, τό   *foundation*
θεμελιόω   *lay the foundation of, found*
θεός, -οῦ, ὁ   *God*
θεραπεύω   *heal*
θερίζω   *reap, harvest*
θερισμός, -οῦ, ὁ   *harvest*
θεριστής, -οῦ, ὁ   *reaper*
θερμός, -ή, -όν   *hot*
Θεσσαλονικεύς, -έως, ὁ   *inhabitant of Thessalonica*
Θεσσαλονίκη, -ης, ἡ   *Thessalonica (city in northern Greece)*
Θευδᾶς, -ᾶ, ὁ   *Theudas*
θεωρέω   *see, watch*
θησαυρίζω   *store up*
θησαυρός, -οῦ, ὁ   *treasure*
θήσω fut. act. of τίθημι

θλίβω *crush*
θλῖψις, -εως, ἡ *affliction, distress*
θόρυβος, -ου, ὁ *riot*
θρίξ, τριχός, ἡ (dat. pl. θριξί) *hair*
θρόνος, -ου, ὁ *throne*
θυγάτηρ, θυγατρός, ἡ *daughter* (6.1/1(b))
θύρα, -ας, ἡ *door*
θυσία, -ας, ἡ *sacrifice*
θυσιαστήριον, -ου, τό *altar*
θύω *sacrifice; slaughter*
Θωμᾶς, -ᾶ, ὁ *Thomas*

Ἰακώβ, ὁ (indecl.) *Jacob*
Ἰάκωβος, -ου, ὁ *James*
ἰάομαι *heal*
ἰατρός, -οῦ, ὁ *doctor*
ἴδε (exclamation) *there (you are!); behold!*
ἰδέα, -ας, ἡ *appearance*
ἴδιος, -α, -ον *one's own*
ἰδού (exclamation) *behold!*
ἰδών aor. act. pple. of ὁράω
ἱερεύς , -έως, ὁ *priest*
Ἰεριχώ, ἡ (indecl.) *Jericho*
ἱερόν, -οῦ, τό *temple*
Ἱεροσόλυμα, -ων, τά and Ἰερουσαλήμ, ἡ (indecl.) *Jerusalem* (4.1/3)
Ἰησοῦς, -οῦ, ὁ *Jesus*
ἱκανός, -ή, -όν *worthy; large, great;* pl. *many*
Ἰκόνιον, -ου, τό *Iconium* (city in Asia Minor)
ἱλασμός, -οῦ, ὁ *expiation, remedy*
ἱμάς, -άντος, ὁ *strap*
ἱμάτιον, -ου, τό *garment, cloak*
ἵνα (conj.) *in order that* (expressing purpose, 13.1/3(b)(i)); *so that* (expressing result, 13.1/3(b)(ii)); *that* (with verbs of wishing, requesting, etc., 13.1/3(b(ii))
ἱνατί (interrog.) *why?*
Ἰόππη, -ης, ἡ *Joppa* (sea port on coast of Judea)
Ἰορδάνης, -ου, ὁ *Jordan* (largest river in Palestine)
Ἰουδαία, -ας, ἡ *Judea*
Ἰουδαῖος, -ου, ὁ *Jew*
Ἰούδας, -α, ὁ *Judas; Judah* (country of the tribe of Judah)
Ἰούλιος, -ου, ὁ *Julius*
ἵππος, -ου, ὁ *horse*
Ἰσαάκ, ὁ (indecl.) *Isaac*

ἴσος, -η, -ον *equal, same*
Ἰσραήλ, ὁ (indecl.) *Israel*
ἵστημι † (tr. tenses) *make to stand, set up place;* (intr. tenses) *be standing, stand* (19.1/2)
ἰσχυρός, -ά, -όν *strong, mighty*
ἰσχύς, -ύος, ἡ *strength*
ἰσχύω *be able*
Ἰταλία, -ας, ἡ *Italy*
ἰχθύς, -ύος, ὁ *fish* (8.1/5)
Ἰωάννης, -ου, ὁ *John*
Ἰώβ, ὁ (indecl.) *Job*
Ἰωνᾶς, -ᾶ, ὁ *Jonah*
Ἰωσήφ, ὁ (indecl.) *Joseph*
ἰῶτα, τό (indecl.) *iota* (smallest letter in Greek alphabet)

καθαιρέω †† *take down, destroy*
καθαρίζω *cleanse*
καθαρός, -ά, -όν *pure*
καθέδρα, -ας, ἡ *chair*
καθεξῆς (adv.) *next in order; successively*
καθεύδω *sleep*
κάθημαι *be seated, sit* (intr. 19.1/3)
καθίζω *sit*
καθίημι †† *lower*
καθίστημι †† *ordain, appoint*
καθώς (adv.) *just as*
καί (conj.) *and;* (adv.) *also; even; actually, in fact*
καὶ ... καί *both ... and*
τε# ... καί *both ... and*
καὶ γάρ *for even, for indeed* (15.1/2(b))
καινός, -ή, -όν *new*
καίπερ (adv.) *although*
καιρός, -οῦ, ὁ *time; right time*
Καῖσαρ, -αρος, ὁ *Caesar*
Καισάρεια, -ας, ἡ *Caesarea* (coastal city in Palestine, seat of the Roman governor)
κακοποιέω *do evil*
κακός, -ή, -όν *bad, evil*
κακόω *harm*
κακῶς (adv.) *badly*
καλέω † *call; name; summon, invite*
κάλλιον (adv.) compar. of καλῶς
καλός, -ή, -όν (3.1/3)
καλύπτω *cover*
καλῶς (adv.) *well, rightly*
κάμηλος, -ου, ὁ *camel*
κἄν (adv.) *even, at least;* (conj.) *and*

if, even if

Καππαδοκία, -ας, ἡ *Cappadocia*

καρδία, -ας, ἡ *heart*

καρπός, -οῦ, ὁ *harvest, fruit*

Κάρπος, -ου, ὁ *Carpus*

κάρφος, -ους, τό *speck*

κατά (prep.) (+ acc.) *according to; concerning; by reason of, for; (of space) through, to; in the region of, by, in; (of time) about*; κατά πάντα *in every way*; (+ gen.) *against*

καταβαίνω †† *come/go down*

καταγγέλλω *proclaim*

καταγελάω †† *ridicule*

καταγινώσκω †† *condemn*

κατάγω †† *bring/take down; (pass., of a ship) put in at*

καταδέω †† *bandage*

καταδιώκω *search for*

καταθεματίζω *curse*

κατακλίνομαι (pass.) *recline at table*

καταλαμβάνω †† *come upon, overtake*

καταλείπω †† *leave*

καταμαρτυρέω *testify against*

καταναλίσκω *consume, devour*

κατανοέω *notice*

καταπονέω *mistreat*

καταργέω *set aside*

καταρτίζω *mend, restore*

κατασκάπτω *tear down*

κατασκηνόω *settle*

καταφιλέω *kiss*

κατέρχομαι †† *arrive at, land*

κατεσθίω †† *eat up, devour*

κατευθύνω *direct*

κατέφαγον aor. act. ind. of κατεσθίω

κατέχω †† *hold fast, retain*

κατηγορέω *accuse*

κατηγορία, -ας, ἡ *charge*

κατῆλθον aor. of κατέρχομαι

κατήργηκα perf. ind. act. of καταργέω

κατήχθην aor. pass. ind. of κατάγω

κατισχύω (+ gen.) *win a victory over, prevail over*

κατοικέω *settle, dwell*

κάτω (adv.) *below*

καῦμα, -ατος, τό *heat; burn*

καυματίζω *scorch, burn*

καύχησις, -εως, ἡ *pride*

Καφαρναούμ, ἡ (indecl.) *Capernaum* (city by the Sea of Galilee)

Κεγχρεαί, -ῶν, αἱ *Cenchreae* (sea port of Corinth in Greece)

κεῖμαι *lie, be laid down; (used as the equivalent of the perf. pass. of* τίθημι 19.1/3 note 2) *to have been placed/set up*

κειρία, -ας, ἡ *bandage*

κελεύω *order*

κέντρον, -ου, τό *sting*

κεραία, -ας, ἡ *decorative stroke of a letter of the alphabet*

κεραμεύς, -έως, ὁ *potter*

κεράμιον, -ου, τό *jar*

κεράτιον, -ου, τό *pod (of the carob tree)*

κερδαίνω *win, gain*

κεφαλή, -ῆς, ἡ *head*

κῆνσος, -ου, ὁ *tax, tribute*

κηρύσσω *make known, announce, proclaim, preach*

κῆτος, -ους, τό *sea monster*

Κιλικία, -ας, ἡ *Cilicia* (area in the south-east of modern Turkey)

κινδυνεύω *be in danger*

κίνησις, -εως, ἡ *movement*

κλάδος, -ου, ὁ *branch*

κλαίω † *weep*

κλαυθμός, -οῦ, ὁ *weeping*

κλείω † *shut*

κλέπτης, -ου, ὁ *thief*

κλέπτω *steal*

κληθήσομαι fut. pass. of καλέω

κληθῶ aor. subj. pass. of καλέω

κληρονομία, -ας, ἡ *inheritance*

κληρονόμος, -ου, ὁ *heir*

κλῖμαξ, -ακος, ἡ *ladder*

κλινάριον, -ου, τό *bed*

κλίνη, -ης, ἡ *bed*

κλοπή, -ῆς, ἡ *damage*

Κλωπᾶς, -ᾶ, ὁ *Clopas*

Κνίδος, -ου, ἡ *Cnidus* (island off SW coast of modern Turkey)

κοιλία, -ας, ἡ *belly; womb*

κοιμάομαι *sleep*

κοινωνία, -ας, ἡ *fellowship*

κοινωνός, -οῦ, ὁ/ἡ *partner, sharer*

κόκκος, -ου, ὁ *seed, grain*

κολλάομαι *attach oneself to*

κομίζω † *bring; (mid.) get, receive, recover*

κοπάζω *abate*

κοπιάω *work hard*

κόπτω *strike; (mid.) mourn for*

κοράσιον, -ου, τό *girl*

Κόρινθος, -ου, ἡ   Corinth
κοσμέω   adorn, decorate
κόσμος, -ου, ὁ   world
κράβαττος, -ου, ὁ   stretcher
κράζω   shout, cry out
κρανίον, -ου, τό   skull
κρατέω   apprehend, arrest; take,
   grasp
κράτιστος, -η, -ον (supl. of ἀγαθός
   17.1/2(b))   most excellent
κράτος, -ους, τό   power, strength
κρείττων, -ον (compar. of ἀγαθός
   17.1/2(b))   better
κρέμαμαι   hang (intr.)
Κρήτη, -ης, ἡ   Crete
κρίμα, -ατος, τό   judgement; lawsuit;
   condemnation, sentence
κρίνω †   judge; decide
κρίσις, -εως, ἡ   judgement,
   condemnation
κριτήριον, -ου, τό   court of law
κριτής, -οῦ, ὁ   judge
κρυπτός, -ή, -όν   hidden, secret
κρύπτω   hide
κτάομαι   procure for oneself, acquire
κτῆμα, -ατος, τό   possession
κτῆνος, -ους, τό   beast of burden
κυκλόω   encircle
κῦμα, -ατος, τό   wave
Κύπρος, -ου, ἡ   Cyprus
Κυρηναῖος, -ου, ὁ   man from Cyrene,
   Cyrenian
κυριεύω (+ gen.)   rule over
κύριος, -ου, ὁ   the Lord; lord, master
κύων, κυνός, ὁ/ἡ   dog
κῶλον, -ου, τό   dead body
κωλύω   hinder, prevent
κώμη, -ης, ἡ   village
κωμόπολις, -εως, ἡ   town

λαβών aor. pple. of λαμβάνω
Λάζαρος, -ου, ὁ   Lazarus
λαλέω   say, speak, talk
λαμβάνω †   receive, take; trap, take
   advantage of
λαός, -οῦ, ὁ   people
Λασαία, -ας, ἡ   Lasaea (city on south
   coast of Crete)
λατρεύω (+ dat.)   serve, worship
λάχανον, -ου, τό   garden plant
λέγω †   say, speak
λείπω †   leave
λειτουργία, -ας, ἡ   service

λεπρός, -οῦ, ὁ   leper
λεπτόν, -οῦ, τό   small coin
Λευίτης, -ου, ὁ   Levite
λευκαίνω   whiten
λευκός, -ή, -όν   white
λήμψομαι fut. of λαμβάνω
λῃστής, -οῦ, ὁ   robber
λίαν (adv.)   exceedingly, very
λιθάζω   stone
λίθος, -ου, ὁ   stone
λιμήν, -ένος, ὁ   harbour
   Καλοὶ Λιμένες   Fair Havens (bay
   on south coast of Crete)
λιμός, -οῦ, ἡ   famine; hunger
λογίζομαι   consider
λόγος, -ου, ὁ   something said (word,
   message, talk etc.)
λοιπόν (adv.)   furthermore
λοιπός, -ή, -όν   rest, remaining
Λουκᾶς, -ᾶ, ὁ   Luke
λούω   wash
Λύδδα, -ας, ἡ   Lydda (town inland
   from Joppa)
Λυκία, -ας, ἡ   Lycia (area in the SW
   of modern Turkey)
λύκος, -ου, ὁ   wolf
λυπέω   distress, injure; (pass.) be sad,
   grieve
λύχνος, -ου, ὁ   lamp
λύω   loosen, set free; break (the law);
   destroy
Λώτ, ὁ (indecl.)   Lot

Μαδιάμ, ὁ (indecl.)   Midian (country
   in Arabia)
μαθητής, -οῦ, ὁ   pupil, disciple
μαθήτρια, -ας, ἡ   female disciple
Μαθθαῖος (Ματθαῖος), -ου, ὁ   Matthew
μαίνομαι   be mad
μακαρίζω   call blessed
μακάριος, -α, -ον   fortunate; blessed
Μακεδών, -όνος, ὁ   a Macedonian
μακρόθεν (adv.)   at a distance
μακρός, -ά, όν   distant; μακράν (adv.)
   far off
μάλιστα (adv.)   most of all, above all
μᾶλλον (adv.)   to a greater degree,
   more; rather; instead
μανθάνω †   learn
μανία, -ας, ἡ   madness
Μάρθα, -ας, ἡ   Martha
Μαριάμ, ἡ (indecl.) or Μαρία, -ας, ἡ
   Mary

Μᾶρκος, -ου, ὁ   *Mark*
μαρτυρέω   *declare; witness; approve*
μαρτυρία, -ας, ἡ   *testimony*
μαρτύρομαι   *implore*
μάρτυς, -υρος, ὁ   *witness*
μαστός, -οῦ, ὁ   *breast; chest*
ματαιότης, -ητος, ἡ   *emptiness, futility*
μάχαιρα, -ης, ἡ   *sword*
μάχομαι   *fight*
μεγαλύνω   *magnify*
μέγας, μεγάλη, μέγα (stem μεγαλ-
   3.1/3)   *great, big*
μέγιστος, -η, -ον (supl. of μέγας
   17.1/2(b))   *very great, greatest*
μεθ᾽ = μετά
μείζων, -ον (compar. of μέγας
   17.1/2(b))   *greater*
μέλας, -αινα, -αν   *black*
μέλει (impers. 21.1/1(a)(iii))   *it is of
   concern*
μέλλω (+ inf.)   *be going to, be on the
   point of; be destined to*
μέμνημαι (perf. [=pres.] of
   μιμνήσκομαι, 20.1/4(b))   *remember*
μὲν#... δέ#   *on the one hand...
   and/but on the other hand* (15.1/2(b))
μὲν# οὖν   *so, and so* (15.1/2(b))
μενοῦν, μενοῦνγε   *rather, on the
   contrary*
μέντοι#   *however* (15.1/2(a))
μένω †   *wait, stay; dwell*
μερίζομαι   *share*
μέριμνα, -ης, ἡ   *anxiety, care*
μεριμνάω   *care about*
μέρος, -ους, τό   *share, portion*
μεσημβρία, -ας, ἡ   *midday, noon*
μεσονύκτιον, -ου, τό   *midnight*
Μεσοποταμία, -ας, ἡ   *Mesopotamia*
μέσος, -η, -ον   *middle; (as neut. noun)
   midst*
Μεσσίας, -ου, ὁ   *the Messiah*
μετ᾽ = μετά
μετά (prep.) (+ acc.)   *after; (+ gen.)
   with, in the company of*
μεταβαίνω ††   *go*
μεταίρω †† (aor. μετῆρα)   *go away*
μεταλαμβάνω †† (+ gen.)   *share*
μετανοέω   *repent*
μεταστρέφω (fut. pass.
   μεταστραφήσομαι)   *change* (tr.)
μετέχω †† (+ gen.)   *share*
μέτρον, -ου, τό   *measure*
μέχρι (prep. + gen)   *up to;* (conj.)

until (14.1/1(b)(ii))
μή (+ subj.)   *lest, that not*
   (13.1/3(b)(i), 14.1/1a); *not* (with
   opt. 13.1/4; with participles,
   infinitives 8.1/3; in questions
   expecting a negative reply 10.1/2(a))
οὐ μή   *not* (in strong negation
   13.1/3(a)(iii))
μηδέ (conj.)   *and not, nor;* (adv.) *not
   even*
μηδείς, μηδεμία, μηδέν   *no, no-one,
   nothing*
μηκέτι (adv.)   *no longer*
μήν, μηνός, ὁ   *month*
μήποτε (+ subj.)   *lest* (= μή
   13.1/3(b)(i))
μήτε ... μήτε   *neither... nor*
μήτηρ, -τρός, ἡ   *mother* (6.1/1(b))
μήτι interrogative particle in hesitant
   questions or questions that expect a
   negative answer (10.1/2(a))
μητρόπολις, -εως, ἡ   *capital city*
μία see εἷς
μιαίνω   *stain*
μίασμα, -ατος, τό   *corruption*
μικρόν (adv.)   *for a short while*
μικρός, -ά, -όν   *small, little; young*
μιμνήσκομαι †   *remember*
μισέω   *hate*
μίσθιος, -ου, ὁ   *hired man, labourer*
μισθόομαι   *hire*
μισθός, -οῦ, ὁ   *pay, salary*
μισθωτός, -οῦ, ὁ   *hired labourer*
μνημεῖον, -ου, τό   *tomb*
μνημονεύω (+ gen.)   *remember*
μνηστεύω   *betroth*
μοιχάομαι   *commit adultery*
μοιχεύω   *commit adultery*
μοιχός, -οῦ, ὁ   *adulterer*
μόλις (adv.)   *scarcely, with difficulty*
μονή, -ῆς, ἡ   *dwelling place*
μονογενής, -ές   *only, sole* (of children)
μόνος, -η, -ον   *only, alone*
μόσχος, -ου, ὁ   *calf*
Μύρα, -ων, τά   *Myra* (town in Lycia)
μυριάς, -άδος ἡ   *ten thousand, myriad*
   (7.1/5(a))
μύριοι, -αι, -α   *ten thousand*
μύρον, -ου, τό   *perfume*
Μυσία, -ας, ἡ   *Mysia* (area in north-
   west of modern Turkey)
μωρός, -ά, -όν   *foolish*
Μωϋσῆς, -έως, ὁ   *Moses* (11.1/4)

Ναζαρέθ, ἡ (indecl.) *Nazareth*

Ναζαρηνός, -οῦ, ὁ *inhabitant of Nazareth, Nazarene*

Ναζωραῖος, -ου, ὁ *inhabitant of Nazareth, Nazarene*

ναός, -οῦ, ὁ *temple*

ναύτης, -ου, ὁ *sailor*

νεανίας, -ου, ὁ *young man*

νεανίσκος, -ου, ὁ *young man*

νεκρός, -ά, -όν *dead*; (as masc. noun) *dead (person), corpse*

νέος, -α, -ον *new; young*

νεότης, -ητος, ἡ *youth*

νεωκόρος, -ου, ὁ *guardian*

νήπιος, -α, -ον *very young*, (as noun) *young child*

νῆσος, -ου, ἡ *island*

νηστεύω *fast*

νηφάλιος, -α, -ον *sober*

Νικόδημος, -ου, ὁ *Nicodemus*

νίπτω *wash*

νοέω *understand*

νόημα, -ατος, τό *thought, mind*

νομίζω *think, consider*

νόμος, -ου, ὁ *law*

νόσος, -ου, ἡ *sickness*

νοῦς, νοός, ὁ *mind*

νυμφίος, -ου, ὁ *bridegroom*

νῦν (adv.) *now; just now*

νύξ, νυκτός, ἡ *night*

νυστάζω *grow sleepy*

ξένος, -η, -ον *strange, foreign*; (as noun) *stranger*

ξηραίνω *dry up*; pass. *wither*

ὄγδοος, -η, -ον *eighth*

ὁδεύω *travel*

ὁδός, -οῦ, ἡ *road; journey*

ὀδούς, ὀδόντος, ὁ *tooth*

ὀδυρμός, -οῦ, ὁ *lamentation*

ὅθεν (rel. adv.) *from where, whence; for which reason, and so*

ὀθόνιον, -ου, τό *linen cloth*

οἶδα † *I know* (6.1/2 & 20.1/4(b))

οἰκετεία, -ας, ἡ *household*

οἰκία, -ας, ἡ *house; family, household*

οἰκοδεσπότης, -ου, ὁ *master of the house*

οἰκοδομέω *build*

οἰκονόμος, -ου, ὁ *steward*

οἶκος, -ου, ὁ *house; family, household*

οἶνος, -ου, ὁ *wine*

οἷος -α, -ον *of what sort*

ὀκνέω *delay*

ὀκνηρός, -ά, -όν *idle, lazy*

ὀκτώ (indecl.) *eight*

ὀλιγόπιστος, -ον *possessing little faith*

ὀλίγος, -η, -ον *little, small*; (pl.) *few*

ὅλος, -η, -ον *whole, entire, all*

ὅλως (adv.) *at all*

ὀμνύω (aor. inf. ὀμόσαι) *swear, vow*

ὅμοιος, -α, -ον (+ dat.) *like, similar, resembling*

ὁμοιόω *make like; compare*; (pass. + dat.) *be like*

ὁμοίως *similarly*

ὁμολογέω *admit; promise*

ὁμότεχνος, -ον *practising the same trade* (τέχνη)

ὀνειδίζω *abuse*

ὀνίναμαι *benefit, have joy*

ὄνομα, -ατος, τό *name*

ὀνομάζω *name, call*

ὄνος, -ου, ὁ/ἡ *ass, donkey*

ὀπή, -ῆς, ἡ *opening*

ὀπίσω (prep. + gen.) *behind, after*

ὅπου (relative adv.) *where*

ὅπως *that, in order that* (13.1/3(b)(i))

ὁράω † *see*; (pass. + dat) *appear to*

ὀργή, -ῆς, ἡ *anger; judgement*

ὀργίζομαι *be angry*

ὀρθῶς (adv.) *rightly*

ὅρκος, -ου, ὁ *oath*

ὄρος, -ους, τό *mountain*

ὀρφανός, -ή, -όν *orphaned*

ὀρχέομαι *dance*

ὅς, ἥ, ὅ (rel. pron., 9.1/2) *who, which*

ὅσος, -η, -ον *as much/many as, how much/many* (21.1/3)

ὅστις, ἥτις, ὅ τι (relative pron.) *who, which, that* (9.1/2 note 1); *whoever, whichever* (14.1/1(c))

ὀσφῦς, -ύος, ἡ *loins*

ὅταν (conj.+ subj./ind.) *whenever* (14.1/1(b)), *when*

ὅτε (conj.) *when*

ὅτι (A) *because*

ὅτι (B) *that* (introducing an indirect statement 8.1/4(a))

οὐ, οὐκ, οὐχ *no(t)*

οὐ ... ἔτι *no longer*

οὗ (adverbial conj. of place) *where*

οὐαί (interjection) *woe!, alas!*

οὐδαμῶς (adv.)   *by no means*
οὐδέ (conj.)   *and not, nor*; (adv.) *not even*
οὐδείς, οὐδεμία, οὐδέν   *no, no-one, nothing*
οὐδέν (adverbial acc.)   *in no respect, in no way, not at all*
οὐδέπω (adv.)   *not yet*
οὐθέν = οὐδέν
οὐκ = οὐ
οὐκέτι (adv.)   *no longer*
οὖν# (particle)   *therefore, so, then; however*
οὔπω (adv.)   *not yet*
οὐράνιος, -ον   *heavenly*
οὐρανός, -οῦ, ὁ   *sky, heavens*; (s. or pl.) *the Christian heaven*
οὖς, ὠτός, τό   *ear*
οὐσία, -ας, ἡ   *property, wealth*
οὖσα fem. pple. of εἰμί
οὗτος, αὕτη, τοῦτο (pron. and adj., 9.1/1)   *this*
οὕτως (adv.)   *thus, in this way*
οὐχ = οὐ
οὐχί strengthened form of οὐ; interrogative particle in questions expecting an affirmative answer 10.1/2(a)
ὀφειλέτης, -ου, ὁ   *one who is culpable,* (+ gen.) *guilty of sin against*
ὀφείλημα, -ατος, τό   *debt; sin*
ὀφείλω   *owe; be obligated, must, ought*
ὀφθαλμός, -οῦ, ὁ   *eye*
ὄφις, -εως, ὁ   *snake, serpent*
ὄχλος, -ου, ὁ   *crowd, mob*
ὀψάριον, -ου, τό   *fish*
ὀψέ (adv.)   *late, in the evening*
ὀψία, -ας, ἡ   *evening*
ὄψομαι fut. of ὁράω

παγιδεύω   *trap*
πάθημα, -ατος, τό   *suffering*
πάθος, -ους, τό   *passion*
παιδίον, -ου, τό   *child*
παιδίσκη, -ης, ἡ   *slave girl*
παῖς, παιδός, ὁ/ἡ   *child; slave, servant*
πάλαι (adv.)   *formerly, long ago*
παλαιός, -ά, -όν   *old*
πάλιν (adv.)   *again*
Παμφυλία, -ας, ἡ   *Pamphylia* (area in the middle south of modern Turkey)

πανδοχεῖον, -ου, τό   *inn*
πανδοχεύς, -έως, ὁ   *inn-keeper*
πανοικεί (adv.)   *with one's whole household*
πανουργία, -ας, ἡ   *cunning*
πανοῦργος, -ον   *crafty, sly*
πάντοτε (adv.)   *always*
παρ᾿ = παρά
παρά (prep.) (+ acc.)   *to, towards; along, beside;* (+ gen.) *from;* (+ dat.) *at, beside; at the house of, in the presence of*
παραβαίνω ††   *transgress*
παραβολή, -ῆς, ἡ   *parable*
παραγγέλλω (+ dat.)   *command, order*
παραγίνομαι ††   *arrive*
παραδίδωμι ††   *hand over, entrust*
παράδοσις, -εως, ἡ   *tradition*
παραινέω   *advise*
παρακαλέω ††   *entreat*
παράκλητος, -ου, ὁ   *mediator, intercessor*
παρακύπτω   *stoop*
παραλαμβάνω ††   *take; take along with*
παραλέγομαι   *sail past*
παραλυτικός, -οῦ, ὁ   *cripple*
παρατίθημι ††   *set before*
παραχρῆμα (adv.)   *immediately*
παρέθηκα aor. ind. act. of παρατίθημι
πάρειμι   *be present*
παρελεύσομαι fut. of παρέρχομαι
παρέλθω aor. subj. of παρέρχομαι
παρεμβολή, -ῆς, ἡ   *barracks*
παρέρχομαι ††   *pass by/through; pass away, disappear*
παρέχω ††   *provide*
παρθένος, -ου, ἡ   *girl*
παρίημι ††   *neglect*
παρίστημι †† (tr. tenses)   *present;* (intr. tenses) *stand by, help* (19.1/2)
πάροικος, -ου, ὁ   *stranger, alien*
παρρησιάζομαι   *speak freely*
πᾶς, πᾶσα, πᾶν (10.1/3(b))   *all, every; any*
πάσχα, τό (indecl.)   *Passover*
πάσχω †   *suffer*
πατάσσω   *hit*
πατήρ, πατρός, ὁ   *father* (6.1/1(b))
πατριά, -ᾶς, ἡ   *family, clan*
πατρίς, -ίδος, ἡ   *homeland, [one's own] country*

Παῦλος, -ου, ὁ   *Paul*
παύομαι   *cease from, stop* (intr.)
πειθαρχέω (+ dat.)   *obey, listen to*
πείθω †   *persuade*; (intr. perf.
   [πέποιθα] + dat.) *trust*; (pass. + dat.)
   obey, be a follower of
πεινάω   *be hungry*
πειράζω   *make trial of, tempt*
πειρασμός, -οῦ, ὁ   *temptation*
πέλαγος, -ους, τό   *sea*
πέμπω †   *send*
πενιχρός, -ά, -όν   *poor*
πεντάκις (adv.)   *five times*
πεντακισχίλιοι, -αι, -α   *five thousand*
πέντε (indecl.)   *five*
πέποιθα intr. perf. of πείθω
πέραν (adv.)   *on the other side*; (prep.
   + gen.) *to the other side of*
περί (prep.) (+ acc.)   *about, around*;
   (+ gen.) *about, concerning*
περιάγω ††   *lead round*
περιάπτω   *kindle*
περιαστράπτω   *flash around*
περιβάλλω ††   *clothe*
περιέπεσον aor. ind. of περιπίπτω
περιέχω ††   *contain; seize*
περιΐστημι   *stand around*; (mid.)
   avoid
περιλάμπω   *shine around*
περιπατέω   *walk*; (used
   metaphorically) *live*
περιπίπτω †† (+ dat.)   *fall into the
   hands of*
περισσεύω   *be in abundance*; (mid.
   + gen.) *have in abundance*
   τὸ περισσεῦον *ample wealth*
περισσότερος, -α, -ον   *greater, more*
περισσῶς (adv.)   *all the more*
περιτέμνω   *circumcise*
περιτομή, -ῆς, ἡ   *circumcision*
περίχωρος, -ον   *neighbouring*; (as f.
   noun, *sc.* γῇ) *neighbourhood*
πετεινόν, -οῦ, τό   *bird*
πέτρα, -ας, ἡ   *rock*
Πέτρος, -ου, ὁ   *Peter*
πετρώδης, -ες   *stoney*
πηγή, -ῆς, ἡ   *fountain*
πῆχυς, [-έως], ὁ   *cubit* (8.1/5 note 2)
πικρός, -ά, -όν   *bitter*
πικρῶς (adv.)   *bitterly*
Πιλᾶτος, -ου, ὁ   *Pilate*
πίμπλημι   *fill, complete*
πίμπρημι   *burn* (tr.)

πίναξ, -ακος, ἡ   *plate, dish*
πίνω †   *drink*
πίπτω †   *fall*
πιστεύω (+ dat. or ἐπί/εἰς)   *believe,
   trust; believe in*
πίστις, -εως, ἡ   *faith*
πιστός, -ή, όν   *faithful, trustworthy,
   believing*; (as m. noun) *believer*
πλανάω   *lead astray*
πλατεῖα, -ας, ἡ   *street*
πλεῖστος, -η, -ον (supl. of πολύς
   17.1/2(b))   *greatest* (of quantity)
πλείων, πλεῖον (πλέον)   *more*
   (compar. of πολύς 17.1/2(b))
πλέκω   *plait*
πλεονάζω   *increase, grow*
πλέω †   *sail*
πληγή, -ῆς, ἡ   *blow*
πλῆθος, -ους, τό   *large number,
   multitude, crowd*
πληθύνω   *increase, multiply*
πλήρης, -ες   *full*
πληρόω   *make full, fill; fulfill, complete*
πλήρωμα, -ατος, τό   *contents*
πλησίον (adv.)   *near*
   ὁ πλησίον (indecl. noun)
   neighbour
πλοιάριον, -ου, τό   *small boat*
πλοῖον, -ου, τό   *boat*
πλοῦς, πλοός, ὁ   *voyage* (11.1/4)
πλούσιος, -α, -ον   *wealthy*
πλοῦτος, -ου, ὁ   *wealth*
πνεῦμα, -ατος, τό   *spirit*
   τὸ ἅγιον πνεῦμα   *the Holy Ghost*
πνέω   *breathe, blow*
πνίγω   *choke*
πόθεν; (interrog. adv.)   *from where?,
   whence?*
ποιέω   *make; do; do with*
ποιητής, -οῦ, ὁ   *doer, one who
   complies with*
ποικίλος, -η, -ον   *various*
ποιμήν, -ένος, ὁ   *shepherd*
ποίμνη, -ης, ἡ   *flock*
ποίμνιον, -ου, τό   *flock*
ποῖος, -α, -ον   *of what sort?; who?,
   what?* (21.1/3)
πόλις, -εως, ἡ   *city* (8.1/5)
πολίτης, -ου, ὁ   *citizen*
πολλάκις (adv.)   *often*
πολύ (adv.)   *much, greatly*
πολύς, πολλή, πολύ (stem πολλ- 3.1/3)
   much (pl. *many*); *long*

πονηρία, -ας, ἡ   wickedness
πονηρός, -ά, -όν   wicked, evil; (as m. noun) the Devil
πορεύομαι   go, travel
πορθέω   destroy
πόρνη, -ης, ἡ   prostitute
πόρνος, -ου, ὁ   fornicator
πόσος, -η, -ον   how much? how many? (21.1/3)
ποταμός, -οῦ, ὁ   river
ποταπός, -ή, -όν   of what kind?(10.1/2a)
πότε (interrog. adv.)   when?
ποτέ#   once, formerly, ever (15.1/2(a))
ποτήριον, -ου, τό   cup
ποτίζω   give to drink
ποῦ (interrog. adv.)   where?
πούς, ποδός, ὁ   foot
πρᾶγμα, -ατος, τό   matter, affair
πράσσω †   do
πρεσβύτερος, -ου, ὁ   an elder
πρεσβύτης, -ου, ὁ   old man
πρίν (conj. 14.1/1(b)(iii))   before
πρό (prep. + gen.)   before
προάγω ††   go before, precede; lead foward
πρόβατον, -ου, τό   sheep
προβιβάζω   prompt, urge on
πρόθυμος, -ον   willing
προκόπτω   progress
προνοέω   have regard for
πρός (prep. + acc.)   to, towards; beside, by; pertaining to, with reference to, concerning; (with infinitive) in order to, with a view to
προσδαπανάω   spend in addition
προσδέχομαι ††   receive, welcome
προσεάω ††   allow to go further
προσέρχομαι †† (+ dat.)   come/go to, approach
προσεύχομαι   pray
προσεῶντος gen. m. s. of pres. act. pple. of προσεάω
προσῆλθον aor. indic. of προσέρχομαι
πρόσκαιρος, -ον   short-lasting
προσκαλέομαι   call, summon
προσκαρτερέω   be ready
προσκεφάλαιον, -ου, τό   pillow
προσκόπτω (+ dat.)   beat against
προσκυνέω   do obeisance, worship
προσλαμβάνομαι   welcome, accept
προσπίπτω †† (+ dat.)   fall down in front of; fall upon

προστίθημι ††   add
προσφέρω ††   bring
προσφωνέω   summon
πρόσωπον, -ου, τό   face
πρότερον (adv.)   earlier
πρόφασις, -εως, ἡ   pretense
προφητεία, -ας, ἡ   prophecy
προφητεύω   prophesy
προφήτης, -ου, ὁ   prophet
πρύμνα, -ης, ἡ   stern (of a ship)
πρωΐ (adv.)   early
πρωτοκαθεδρία, -ας, ἡ   seat of honour
πρωτοκλισία, -ας, ἡ   place of honour
πρῶτος, -η, -ον   first
πτῶσις, -εως, ἡ   fall
πτωχός, -ή, -όν   poor
πυκνός, -ή, -όν   frequent
πύλη, -ης, ἡ   door, gate
πυνθάνομαι †   inquire, ask
πῦρ, πυρός, τό   fire
πωλέω   sell
πῶς   how?, how ...!
πως#   somehow, perhaps

Ῥαββί (indecl.)   master (form of address)
ῥάβδος, -ου, ἡ   staff
Ῥαμά, (indecl.) ἡ   Rama (town to the north of Jerusalem)
ῥαφίς, -ίδος, ἡ   needle
Ῥαχάβ, ἡ (indecl.)   Rahab
ῥέω   flow
ῥῆμα, -ατος, τό   word
ῥήτωρ, -ορος, ὁ   speaker
ῥίζα, -ης, ἡ   root
ῥίπτω †   throw
ῥύομαι   rescue, save
Ῥωμαϊστί (adv.)   in Latin
Ῥώμη, -ης, ἡ   Rome

σάββατον, -ου, τό   sabbath; week
Σαδδουκαῖος, -ου, ὁ   Sadducee
σάκκος, -ου, ὁ   sackcloth
σαλεύω   shake (tr.)
Σαλμών, ὁ (indecl.)   Salmon
Σαλμώνη, -ης, ἡ   Salmone (promontory in east Crete)
σάλπιγξ, -ιγγος, ἡ   trumpet
Σαμάρεια, -ας, ἡ   Samaria (region to the north of Jerusalem)
Σαμαρίτης, -ου, ὁ   Samaritan
σανδάλιον, -ου, τό   sandal
Σαούλ, ὁ (indecl.)   Saul

σάρξ, σαρκός, ἡ flesh
σαρόω sweep clean
Σατανᾶς, -ᾶ, ὁ Satan
σάτον, -ου, τό dry measure
σεαυτόν yourself (refl. pron. 9.1/4(a))
σεβαστός, -ή, -όν imperial
   σπεῖρα Σεβαστή see note on 12.2.7
σεισμός, -οῦ, ὁ earthquake; storm at
   sea
σελήνη, -ης, ἡ moon
σεμνότης, -ητος, ἡ dignity
σημαίνω indicate
σημεῖον, -ου, τό sign; miracle
σήμερον (adv.) today
σιδηροῦς (-εος), -ᾶ, -οῦν made of
   iron
Σιδών,-ῶνος, ἡ Sidon
Σίλας, -α, ὁ Silas (friend of Paul)
Σίμων, -ωνος, ὁ Simon
σίναπι, -εως, τό mustard
σιτευτός, -ή, όν fattened
σκανδαλίζω offend
σκεῦος, -ους, τό jar
σκηνή, -ῆς, ἡ tabernacle
σκιά, -ᾶς, ἡ shadow
σκόλοψ, -οπος, ὁ thorn
σκοτία, -ας, ἡ darkness
σκότος, -ους, τό darkness
Σόδομα, -ων, τά Sodom
Σολομών, -ῶνος, ὁ Solomon
σός, σή, σόν (poss. adj.) your (s.)
σοφία, -ας, ἡ wisdom
σοφός, -ή, -όν wise
σοφῶς (adv.) wisely
σπαργανόω wrap in swaddling
   clothes
σπάομαι draw (a sword)
σπεῖρα, -ης, ἡ cohort (unit of about
   600 men in Roman army)
σπείρω † sow
σπέρμα, -ατος, τό seed
σπερμολόγος, -ου, ὁ chatterer
σπλαγχνίζομαι (pass.) feel pity
σπόγγος, -ου, ὁ sponge
σποδός, -οῦ, ἡ ashes
σπόριμα, -ων, τά grain fields,
   standing grain
σπουδάζω be eager, take pains
σπουδή, -ῆς, ἡ haste
στάδιον, -ου, τό (pl. στάδια or στάδιοι)
   stade (c. 200 metres)
στασιαστής, -οῦ, ὁ rebel
στάσις, -εως, ἡ uprising

σταυρός, -οῦ, ὁ cross
σταυρόω crucify
σταφυλή, -ῆς, ἡ bunch of grapes
στάχυς, -υος, ὁ ear of corn/wheat
στέγη, -ης, ἡ roof
στεῖρα, -ας, ἡ woman unable to have
   children
στερεός, -ά, -όν hard
στηρίζω strengthen
στίγμα, -ατος, τό mark, scar
στίλβω shine
στοιχεῖον, -ου, τό element
στολή, -ῆς, ἡ robe
στόμα, -ατος, τό mouth; edge (of a
   sword)
στόμαχος, -ου, ὁ stomach
στράτευμα, -ατος, τό army;
   [detachment of] soldiers
στρατιά, -ᾶς, ἡ army
στρατιώτης, -ου, ὁ soldier
στρατόπεδον, -ου, τό army
στραφείς aor. pass. pple. of στρέφω
στρέφω turn (tr.); (pass.) turn (intr.)
στρουθίον, -ου, τό sparrow
σύ you (s. 4.1/2)
συγγενής, -οῦς, ὁ relative (10.1/4(a))
συγκαθίζω sit together
συγκαλύπτω conceal
συγκυρία, -ας, ἡ chance, coincidence
   κατὰ συγκυρίαν by chance
συζητέω argue; discuss
συλλαβών aor. act. pple. of
   συλλαμβάνω
συλλαλέω (+ dat.) talk (with)
συλλαμβάνω †† catch, seize; arrest
συλλέγω gather, pick
συμβαίνω †† happen
συμβουλεύω advise
συμβούλιον, -ου, τό plot, plan;
   council
   συμβούλιον λαμβάνω hold/take
   counsel
σύμβουλος, -ου, ὁ adviser, counsellor
Συμεών, ὁ (indecl.) Symeon
συμμαρτυρέω (+ dat.) testify with
συμπνίγω choke
συμπολίτης, -ου, ὁ fellow-citizen
συμφέρει (impers.) it is expedient
σύν (prep. + dat.) with, in the
   company of
συνάγω †† gather up; receive as a
   guest; (pass.) come together
συναγωγή, -ῆς, ἡ synagogue

συναλλάσσω reconcile
συνανάκειμαι recline at table with, eat with
σύνδεσμος, -ου, ὁ bond
σύνδουλος, -ου, ὁ fellow slave/servant
συνέδριον, -ου, τό council
συνεζήτει 3 s. impf. act. of συζητέω
σύνειμι come together (20.1/4)
συνέρχομαι †† assemble; (+ dat.) go off with
συνίημι †† understand
συνίστημι †† (tr. tenses) commend, prove; (intr. tenses) stand with (19.1/2)
Συροφοινίκισσα, -ης, ἡ Syrophoenician woman
σύρω drag
σύστασις, -εως, ἡ gathering
συστρέφω gather together
σφαγή, -ῆς, ἡ [act of] slaughtering
σφάζω slaughter
σφόδρα (adv.) very, very much
σφραγίς, -ῖδος, ἡ seal
σχολάζω be unoccupied
σῴζω † save, preserve
σῶμα, -ατος, τό body
σωτήρ, -ῆρος, ὁ saviour
σωτηρία, -ας, ἡ salvation
σωφροσύνη, -ης, ἡ rationality
σώφρων, -ον sensible, modest

Ταβιθά, ἡ (indecl.) Tabitha
ταπεινός, -ή, -όν lowly, humble
ταπεινοφροσύνη, -ης, ἡ humility
ταπεινόω make humble
ταπείνωσις, -εως, ἡ lowly station
ταράσσω disturb, trouble
Ταρσός, -οῦ, ἡ Tarsus (city in SE of what is now Turkey)
τάσσω (act. or mid.) order, fix; appoint
ταῦτα n. pl. nom./acc. of οὗτος (9.1/1)
ταφή, -ῆς, ἡ burial place
τάχιον (adv.) compar. of ταχύ
ταχύ (adv.) quickly
ταχύς, -εῖα, -ύ swift
τε# ... καί both... and
τέθνηκα perf. ind. of ἀποθνήσκω (20.1/4(b))
τέκνον, -ου, τό child
τελείοω bring to perfection, perfect
τελευτή, -ῆς, ἡ death
τελέω † complete, finish

τελώνης, -ου, ὁ tax-collector
τεσσαράκοντα (indecl.) forty
τεσσαρακονταετής, -ές of forty years
τέσσαρες, τέσσερα four (7.1/5(a))
τέταρτος, -η, -ον fourth
τετράκις (adv.) four times
τετραπλοῦς (-όος), -ῆ, -οῦν (21.1/2) fourfold
τηρέω keep watch over, guard; preserve; observe
τί; why?
τί οὖν; why then? what then?
τίθημι † (18.1/2) put, place; present
τίκτω † bear, give birth to
τίλλω pick
τιμάω honour
τιμή, -ῆς, ἡ honour, reverence; price
τίμιος, -α, -ον honourable; precious
τίς; τί; (interrog. pron.) who? which? what? (10.1/1)
τις, τι# (indef. pron.) a certain, someone, something (10.1/1)
τίτλος, -ου, ὁ title, inscription
τοιοῦτος, -αύτη, -οῦτο(ν) such, of such a sort, similar (21.1/3)
τόκος, -ου, ὁ interest
τολμάω dare
τόπος, -ου, ὁ place
τοσοῦτος, -αύτη, -οῦτο(ν) so much/many (21.1/3)
τότε (adv.) then
τοῦτο see οὗτος
τράπεζα, -ης, ἡ table
τραπεζίτης, -ου, ὁ banker
τραῦμα, -ατος, τό wound
τράχηλος, -ου, ὁ neck
τρεῖς, τρία three (7.1/5(a))
τρέφω † feed, nourish
τρέχω † run
τριάκοντα (indecl.) thirty
τρίς (adv.) three times
τρισχίλιοι, -αι, -α three thousand
τρίτον (adv.) the third time
τρίτος, -η, -ον third
τρόμος, -ου, ὁ trembling
τρόπος, -ου, ὁ way, manner
τροφή, -ῆς, ἡ food, nourishment, sustenance
τρύπημα, -ατος, τό hole, eye (of a needle)
τυγχάνω † happen; (+ gen.) receive, obtain
Τύρος, -ου, ἡ Tyre

τυφλός, -ή, όν *blind*
τυχεῖν aor. inf. of τυγχάνω

ὕβρις, -εως, ἡ *insult*
ὑγιαίνω *be in good health*
ὑγιής, -ές *healthy, sound*
ὑδροποτέω *drink water*
ὕδωρ, ὕδατος, τό *water*
υἱός, -οῦ, ὁ *son*
ὑμεῖς (pron.) *you* (pl. 4.1/2)
ὑμέτερος, -α, -ον (poss. adj.) *your*
  (pl.)
ὑμνέω *sing the praise of*
ὑπάγω †† *go, go out*
ὑπακούω †† (+ dat.) *obey*
ὑπαντάω *meet*
ὑπάρχω *exist, be*
ὑπεμνήσθην aor. indic. pass. of
  ὑπομιμνήσκω
ὑπέρ (prep. + gen.) *on behalf of*
ὑπερήφανος, -ον *proud, haughty*
ὑπερῷον, -ου, τό *upstairs room*
ὑπό (prep.) (+ acc.) *under*; (+ gen.)
  by (of an agent, 11.1/2)
ὑποδέομαι *put on* (sandals)
ὑποδέχομαι †† *receive*
ὑπόδημα, -ατος, τό *sandal*
ὑποκάτω (prep. + gen.) *under*
ὑποκριτής, -οῦ, ὁ *hypocrite*
ὑπολείπω †† *leave remaining* (tr.)
ὑπομιμνήσκω *remind*; (pass.+ gen.)
  remember
ὑποπλέω †† *sail under the shelter of*
ὑποπόδιον, -ου, τό *footstool*
ὑποστρέφω *return*
ὑστερέω (act. or mid.) *lack, be in
  need*
ὑστέρημα, -ατος, τό *need, poverty*
ὕστερον (adv.) *later, afterward*
ὕστερος, -α, -ον *later*
ὑψηλός, -ή, -όν *high*
ὕψιστος, -η, -ον *highest*; ἐν ὑψίστοις
  on high
ὕψος, -ους, τό *height*
ὑψόω *raise, exalt*

φανερός, -ά, -όν *clear, evident*
φανερόω *reveal, make known*
φαντασία, -ας, ἡ *outward display*
Φαραώ, ὁ (indecl.) *Pharaoh*
Φαρισαῖος, -ου, ὁ *Pharisee*
φάσκω *allege, claim*
φάτνη, -ης, ἡ *manger, stall*

φαῦλος, -η, -ον *evil, base*
φείδομαι (+ gen.) *spare*
φέρω † *carry; bring; take*; (of a road)
  lead
φεύγω † *flee, escape*
φήμη, -ης, ἡ *report, news*
φημι † *say* (7.1/3)
Φῆστος, -ου, ὁ *Festus* (Roman
  procurator of Palestine)
φθαρῶ aor. subj. pass. of φθείρω
φθείρω † *destroy; corrupt*
φιλανθρώπως (adv.) *kindly*
φιλέω *love*
Φίλιππος, -ου, ὁ *Philip*
φίλος, -ου, ὁ *friend*
φλόξ, φλογός, ἡ *flame*
φοβέομαι *fear*
φόβος, -ου, ὁ *fear*
Φοίβη, -ης, ἡ *Phoebe*
φονεύς, -έως, ὁ *murderer*
φονεύω *murder, kill*
φόνος, -ου, ὁ *murder*
φραγελλόω *flog*
φράζω *tell*
φρονέω *think, have an opinion*
φρόνιμος, -ον *wise, sensible*
Φρυγία, -ας, ἡ *Phrygia*
φυλακή, -ῆς, ἡ *act of guarding; watch*
  (of the night); *guard post; prison*
φύλαξ, -ακος, ὁ *guard*
φυλάσσω *guard*
φύσις, -εως, ἡ *nature*
φυτεύω *plant*
φωνέω *make a sound; shout; crow*
φωνή, -ῆς, ἡ *voice*
φῶς, φωτός, τό *light; torch*
φωτεινός, -ή, -όν *bright*

χαίρω *rejoice*
χαλεπός, -ή, -όν *difficult, violent*
χαρά, -ᾶς, ἡ *joy*
χαρακτήρ, -ῆρος, ὁ *exact likeness*
χάρις, -ιτος, ἡ (acc. χάριν) *favour,
  grace, mercy; thanks, gratitude*
χάσμα, -ατος, τό *chasm*
χείρ, χειρός, ἡ *hand*
χείρων, -ον (compar. of κακός) *worse*
χήρα, -ας, ἡ *widow*
χιλίαρχος, -ου, ὁ *captain*
χιλιάς, -άδος ἡ *a thousand* (7.1/5(a))
χίλιοι, -αι, -α *thousand*
χιτών, -ῶνος, ὁ *tunic*
χοϊκός, -ή, -όν *made of earth, earthly*

χοῖρος, -ου, ὁ *pig*
Χοραζίν, ἡ (indecl.) *Chorazin* (town in Galilee)
χορτάζω *feed* (tr., in 11.2.17 with acc. of person and gen. of food); (pass.) *eat one's fill* [in 11.2.17 has acc. and gen.]
χοῦς, χοός, ὁ *dust* (11.1/4)
χράομαι † (+ dat.) *use* (of things); *treat, behave towards*
χρεία, -ας, ἡ *need*
χρῄζω (+ gen.) *have need of*
χρηστολογία, -ας, ἡ *plausible talk*
χρηστός, -ή, -όν *kind, loving*
Χριστός, -οῦ, ὁ *Christ, Anointed One*
χρονίζω *linger; delay, fail to come*
χρόνος, -ου, ὁ *time; year*
χρυσοῦς (-εος), -ῆ, -οῦν (21.1/2) *golden*
χώρα, -ας, ἡ *country; district*
χωρίζω *separate;* (pass.) *leave, depart from*
χωρίον, -ου, τό *place*

χωρίς (prep. + gen.) *without, apart, separately* (from)

ψευδομαρτυρέω *bear false witness*
ψηλαφάω *touch*
ψυχή, -ῆς, ἡ *soul*
ψυχικός, -ή, -όν *worldly*

ὦ (preceding a vocative) O
ὧδε (adv.) *here*
ὠδίν, ὠδῖνος, ἡ *pain of childbirth*
ὤν masc. pple. of εἰμί
ὥρα, -ας, ἡ *hour*
ὡς (adv.) *like, just as;* (with numerals) *about;* (conj.) *when* (14.1/1(b)(i)); *how, that* (14.2.11)
ὡσεί (adv.) *about*
ὥστε (conj. 16.1/1) *so that, in order that; with the result that; consequently*
ὠφελέω *help, benefit; accomplish*
ὤφθην aor. ind. pass. of ὁράω

index

ancient greek

gavin betts & alan henry

- Are you a beginner looking for an introduction to Ancient Greek?
- Do you have some previous knowledge of the language?
- Do you want to read and enjoy original Greek texts?

Ancient Greek is equally suited to complete beginners or those with some knowledge of the language. Each unit introduces new grammar, followed by Greek sentences and passages. Original texts are studied at an early stage and enable the reader to form an idea of the wealth and extent of ancient Greek literature. A glossary of grammatical terms, revision exercises, further reading and other material are available on a free website.

latin
gavin betts

- Are you looking for a comprehensive introduction to Latin?
- Do you have some previous knowledge of the language?
- Do you want to read and enjoy original Latin texts?

Latin is a comprehensive introduction equally suited to complete beginners or those with some knowledge of the language. Each unit introduces new grammar followed by Latin sentences and passages. The clearly structured course introduces original Latin at an early level and, where appropriate, topics of interest for Latin studies. Review exercises and further reading (including examples of medieval Latin) are available on a free website.

teach® yourself

Afrikaans
Arabic
Arabic Script, Beginner's
Bengali
Brazilian Portuguese
Bulgarian
Cantonese
Catalan
Chinese
Chinese, Beginner's
Chinese Script, Beginner's
Croatian
Czech
Danish
Dutch
Dutch, Beginner's
Dutch Dictionary
Dutch Grammar
English, American (EFL)
English as a Foreign Language
English, Correct
English Grammar
English Grammar (EFL)
English for International Business
English Vocabulary
Finnish
French
French, Beginner's
French Grammar
French Grammar, Quick Fix
French, Instant
French, Improve your
French, One-Day
French Starter Kit
French Verbs
French Vocabulary
Gaelic
Gaelic Dictionary
German
German, Beginner's
German Grammar
German Grammar, Quick Fix

German, Instant
German, Improve your
German Verbs
German Vocabulary
Greek
Greek, Ancient
Greek, Beginner's
Greek, Instant
Greek, New Testament
Greek Script, Beginner's
Gulf Arabic
Hebrew, Biblical
Hindi
Hindi, Beginner's
Hindi Dictionary
Hindi Script, Beginner's
Hungarian
Icelandic
Indonesian
Irish
Italian
Italian, Beginner's
Italian Grammar
Italian Grammar, Quick Fix
Italian, Instant
Italian, Improve your
Italian, One-Day
Italian Verbs
Italian Vocabulary
Japanese
Japanese, Beginner's
Japanese, Instant
Japanese Script, Beginner's
Korean
Latin
Latin American Spanish
Latin, Beginner's
Latin Dictionary
Latin Grammar
Nepali
Norwegian
Panjabi

Persian, Modern
Polish
Portuguese
Portuguese, Beginner's
Portuguese Grammar
Portuguese, Instant
Romanian
Russian
Russian, Beginner's
Russian Grammar
Russian, Instant
Russian Script, Beginner's
Sanskrit
Serbian
Spanish
Spanish, Beginner's
Spanish Grammar
Spanish Grammar, Quick Fix
Spanish, Instant
Spanish, Improve your
Spanish, One-Day
Spanish Starter Kit
Spanish Verbs
Spanish Vocabulary
Swahili
Swahili Dictionary
Swedish
Tagalog
Teaching English as a Foreign Language
Teaching English One to One
Thai
Turkish
Turkish, Beginner's
Ukrainian
Urdu
Urdu Script, Beginner's
Vietnamese
Welsh
Welsh Dictionary
World Cultures:
    China
    England
    France
    Germany
    Italy
    Japan
    Portugal
    Russia
    Spain
    Wales
Xhosa
Zulu

the A-Z of teach yourself language titles

available from bookshops and on-line retailers